The Guild Sourcebook of Art

24

The Guild
24

Sourcebook of Art

The Resource for Finding and Commissioning Artists

Guild Sourcebooks
Madison, Wisconsin, USA

The Guild Sourcebook of Art

24

Guild Sourcebooks
An imprint of The Guild, Inc.
931 E. Main Street
Madison, Wisconsin 53703
TEL 800-930-1856
EMAIL tradeinfo@guild.com
Lisa Bayne, CEO
Terry Nelson, VP, Marketing

Sales, Marketing, & Administration
Toni Sikes, Guild Founder
Michael Baum, COO
Annik DuPaty, Director of Sourcebooks
Jenna Brandt, Sourcebook Coordinator
Deb Furlong, Administrative Assistant
Catherine Stanley, Administrative Assistant

Design, Production & Editorial
Jill Schaefer, Editorial Manager
Georgene Pomplun, Designer & Print Production Manager
Barbara Hatley, Production Coordinator & Image Specialist

Artist Marketing Consultants
Nicole Carroll, Laura Marth
Amy Lambright Murphy, Paul Murphy

©2009 The Guild, Inc.
ISBN-13: 978-1-880140-68-0

Special thanks to our 2008-2009 Review Committee:
Catherine Davidson, Owner, CR Davidson Art
Sharon Devenish, President, Devenish Associates, Inc.
Steve Larson, Founding Partner, Architectural Building Arts, Inc.
Tom McHugh, AIA
Sean Sennott, Gallery Director, Gallery 323 at Rubin's
Karin Wolf, Arts Program Administrator, City of Madison, WI

Visit Guild Sourcebooks online: **www.guildsourcebooks.com**

Page 2: *Prairie Woman*
by Stephan Cox, see page 284.
Photograph: Jan Wilson.

Opposite: *Hanging by a Thread*
by Al Lachman, see page 203.
Photograph: Profiles, Philadelphia, PA.

Contents

For more information about Guild Sourcebooks,
our artists, and our services, please visit us
online at **www.guildsourcebooks.com**

Opposite: *Joseph's Coat*
by Murphy Kuhn Fine Art
Photography, see page 87.

Left: Residential Installation
by Bonnie Hinz, see page 386.

A New Resource for Challenging Times

It is with great pleasure that I welcome you to *The Guild Sourcebook of Art 24.* This book represents the combining of our two previous stand-alone publications, *The Guild Sourcebook of Architectural & Interior Art* and *The Guild Sourcebook of Residential Art.* Now in our twenty-fourth year, we've developed *The Guild Sourcebook of Art* to be *the* comprehensive resource for finding the nation's finest commissionable artists and their work, for residential, corporate, public, liturgical, healthcare, and hospitality projects. Over 300 artists are represented within these pages, with expertise in every major medium.

In turbulent economic times, one might wonder whether art matters. After all, it neither feeds the body nor provides shelter. What is does do, though, is nourish the soul in a way that nothing else does. An encounter with art can entirely change an experience—whether that experience is the announcement of medical news, a delayed airplane, or the arrival of guests. Now, more than ever, art does matter, with its ability to transform an environment and transport the viewer.

Commissioning art directly from an artist, in particular, allows you to work with your client to create exactly the intended environment, to express the soul of the artist as well as the soul of the owner. An artist's participation in your project can help you realize the full promise of your design.

You will notice as you go through these pages that we have designed the book to make navigation simple and logical. This should allow you to more quickly find the artists or the medium for which you are looking. In addition, you can now also visit our new corresponding website, **www.guildsourcebooks.com,** to learn more about these artists and their work, email an artist directly, register in our design professional program, or post a call for artwork for your specific projects.

As always, this book is simply a gateway to the exceptional contemporary artists presented. To learn more about them, to see a larger body of their work, or to arrange a commission, please contact them directly using the information provided on their pages.

Thank you for continuing to consider the placement of original works of art in your design projects. Our public and private spaces—as well as our spirits—are better for their inclusion in our environment.

Lisa Bayne
CEO
The Guild, Inc.

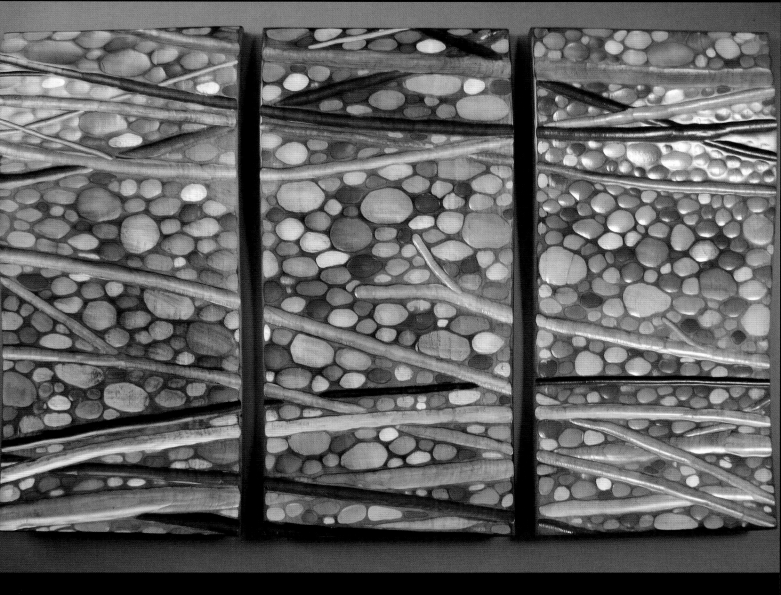

Sticks and Stones
by Michael Bauermeister,
see pages 279 and 407.

How to Use

The Guild Sourcebook of Art is the latest comprehensive directory of top North American artists accepting commission projects from design professionals.

For many in the trade, Guild Sourcebooks are an indispensable tool for generating ideas, guiding clients, and locating artists. Each artist's page contains complete contact information so you can directly reach artists whose work would enrich your projects.

The more you use *The Guild Sourcebook of Art,* the more you benefit. Use it to:

Generate ideas. Leisurely browsing through the vast array of work presented here provides wonderful raw material for your creative mind—a shape, a form, a concept, an exotic use of materials or media.

Create portfolios. Every time you think "that might work!"—flag the page, or use our online resources (see page 11) to capture images for reference or presentations.

Inspire clients. Guild Sourcebooks are tailor-made for client meetings. Showing a wealth of completed art pieces and commissions, the books are known to create client excitement and creativity.

Contact artists. The book provides full address, phone, and email addresses so you can directly reach candidates for commissions, to ascertain costs, discuss time frames, and solicit other ideas. There is no obligation or extra cost for such contact.

Juried by experts

Leading industry experts have juried every artist in these pages prior to acceptance for publication in *The Guild Sourcebook of Art.* The integrity of Guild Sourcebooks is one of the key reasons these directories have been the industry standard since 1986. All artists included meet strict criteria for experience, quality of work, professionalism of images, and a strong desire to participate in projects like yours.

Organized for your convenience

Use the section identifier on the bottom of every page to quickly find each book section. These sections, as well as the artist pages within them, are alphabetized for easy use. At the back of the book, you will find indices for finding artists by name or location.

Supplemented with practical information

In addition to the artist pages that are the heart of this book, we have included many extra features to educate you about working directly with artists and to help you identify the right artist for your project. In the pages ahead, you will find a detailed explanation of the process of commissioning artwork—everything from finding artists to establishing expectations and creating contracts. You'll also find articles scattered throughout that describe various disciplines, as well as stories of successful commissions. At the back of the book, you will find brief artist statements, where you can learn more about each artist's inspiration, techniques, and credentials.

Above: *Ad Infinitum*
by Ralfonso.com LLC,
see page 264.

Opposite: *Loft Display Case*
by Boykin Pearce Associates,
see page 97. Photograph:

This Sourcebook

Our New Website: www.GuildSourcebooks.com

The new Guild Sourcebooks website maintains a full library of artwork and resources online. To access our site, go to www.guildsourcebooks.com. From here you may:

Click on "Find Artists & Artwork" to navigate through artworks and commissions by artist name, medium/discipline, or artist location.

Order additional copies of the current Sourcebook or past Sourcebooks for your resource library and staff members.

Read feature articles and stories documenting successful collaborations between artists and design professionals.

Register in our design professional program to

- receive annual copies of *The Guild Sourcebook of Art*

- email artists directly from their Guild Sourcebooks web page

- broadcast your commission projects directly to our artist community. (Click on "Post a Project" under the "for Design Professionals" menu, and complete the online form to put your project specifications out for proposals.)

- receive a 15% discount on purchases made from our sister company, Artful Home.

The Commission

The more than 300 artists featured in *The Guild Sourcebook of Art* represent a remarkable spectrum of artistic talent and vision. Whether you're looking for a large-scale public sculpture or a residential accessory, this book can put you directly in touch with highly qualified artists throughout North America. Any one of these artists can be commissioned to create a unique work of art—but with so many exceptional artists to choose from, finding the right one for your specific project can be a challenge. Once the artist has been selected, careful planning and communication can help ensure a great outcome.

Having watched art commissions unfold since the first Guild Sourcebook was published in 1986, we can suggest steps to ensure successful partnerships between artists and trade professionals. We especially want to reassure those who have been reluctant to try such a collaboration because of questions about how the process works. This article is a how-to guide to the art commissioning process. It suggests strategies to help selection and hiring go smoothly. It also describes steps that can help establish shared (and realistic) expectations on the part of artists and clients, and explains the advantages of including the artist in the design team early in the planning process.

Finding the Artist

By far the most important step in a successful commission is choosing the right artist for your particular project and budget. This choice is the decision from which all others will flow, so it's worth investing time and energy in the selection process and seasoning the search with both wild artistic hopes and hard-nosed realism. The right choices at this early stage will make things go more smoothly later on.

Some clients will want to help select and work with the artist. Others will want only minimal involvement, leaving most of the decision-making to the design team. No matter who makes the decisions, there are several ways to find the right artist. Obviously, we recommend browsing through *The Guild Sourcebook of Art*. Every artist featured on these pages is actively seeking commission projects—that's why they're included in the book. Many of these artists have already established strong track records working with designers, architects, and art consultants; you will gain from their professionalism and experience. Others are newer in their field; their determination to prove themselves can fuel an exciting and successful collaboration.

12

The Jewel by Bill Jacobs, see page 102. Photograph: Kit Lee Photography.

Process

Narrowing the Field

Once your A-list is narrowed down to two or three names, it's time to schedule meetings, either face-to-face or by phone. As you talk, try to determine the artist's interest in your project, and pay attention to your own comfort level with the artist. Try to find out if the chemistry is right—whether you have the basis to build a working relationship. This is also the time to confirm that the artist has the necessary skills to undertake your project. Be thorough and specific when asking questions. Is the artist excited about the project? What does he or she see as the most important issues or considerations? Will your needs be a major or minor concern? Evaluate the artist's style, approach, and personality.

If it feels like you might have trouble working together, take heed. But if all goes well and it feels like a good fit, ask for a list of references. These are important calls; don't neglect to make them! Ask about the artist's work habits, communication style, and, of course, the success of the artwork. You should also ask whether the project was delivered on time and within budget. If you like what you hear, you'll be one important step closer to hiring your artist.

Expect Professionalism

If this is an expensive or complicated project, you may want to request preliminary designs. Since most artists charge a design fee whether or not they're ultimately hired for the project, start by asking for sketches from your top candidate. If you're unhappy with the designs submitted, you can go to your second choice. But if the design is what you'd hoped for, it's time to finalize your working agreement with this artist.

As you discuss contract details, be resolved that silence is not golden and ignorance is not bliss! Be frank. Discuss the budget and timetable, and tell the artist what you expect. Now is the time for possible misunderstandings to be brought up and resolved—not later, when the work is half done and deadlines loom.

Man and Star by Aaron T. Brown, see pages 234 and 275.

The Artist as Designer

Not every artist charges a design fee; some consider preliminary sketches a part of their marketing effort. However, it's more common for an artist to require a design fee of 5% to 10% of the final project budget. In some cases, especially when the artist has a strong reputation in a specialized area, the design fee may be as high as 25% of the budget. This is most common when an artist is asked to provide solutions to complicated architectural problems.

A few points about design are worth highlighting here:

1. Design Ideas Are the Artist's Property

It should go without saying that it is highly unethical, as well as possibly illegal, to take an artist's designs—even very preliminary or non-site-specific sketches—and use them without the artist's permission. Some artists may include specific language about ownership of ideas, models, sketches, etc., in their contracts or letters of agreement. Even if an artist does not use a written agreement, be sure you are clear at the outset about what you are paying for and what rights the artist retains.

2. Respect the Artist's Ideas and Vision

When you hire a doctor, you want a thoughtful, intelligent diagnosis, not just a course of treatment. The same should be true when you hire an artist to work with a design team. Most Guild artists have become successful through many years of experience and because of their excellence in both technique and aesthetic imagination. Take advantage of that expertise by bringing the artist into the project early, and by asking him or her for ideas.

3. Consider a Separate Design Budget for Your Project

A design budget is particularly helpful when you:
- want to get lots of ideas from an artist;
- need site-specific ideas that involve significant research;
- require a formal presentation with finished drawings, blueprints, or maquettes.

To evaluate designs for a project from several artists, consider having a competition with a small design fee for each artist.

4. Keep the Artist Informed of Changes

Tell the artist about changes—even seemingly minor details—that may have a significant impact on the project design. If the artist is working as a member of the design team, it's easier to include him or her in the ongoing dialog about the overall project. This is an issue of professionalism. Artists have the technical skills to do wonderful and amazing things with simple materials. But they also have sophisticated conceptual and design talents. By paying for these talents, trade professionals add vision and variety to their creative products. In such a partnership, both parties gain, and the ultimate result is a client who is delighted by the outcome of the collaboration.

Above: *Symphony in Color* (detail), by Pinter Studios, Inc., see page 137. Photograph: Ilene Brenner.

Right: *Dream Bubbles* (shown left) and *Atmospheric Momentum* (shown right) by Chin Yuen, see page 232. Photograph: Fabian Wolk.

Opposite: *Machine* by Mary Scrimgeour, see page 237. Photograph: Ken Sanville.

Working With an Art Consultant

As your project gains definition, you'll need to pay attention to its technical aspects, including building codes, lighting specifications, and details related to zoning and installation. Most designers find the artist's knowledge and understanding of materials, code, safety, and engineering complete and reassuring. However, complex projects may warrant hiring an art consultant to help with these details, as well as the initial selection of art and artists. Just as you would when hiring any other professional, call references to be sure the consultant you hire is sophisticated and experienced enough to provide real guidance with your project. He or she should be able to help negotiate the technical aspects of a very specific contract, including issues like installation, insurance, storage, transportation, and engineering costs.

Putting It In Writing

It is a truism in any kind of business that it is much cheaper to get the lawyers involved at the beginning of a process rather than after something goes wrong. A signed contract or letter of agreement commits the artist to completing his or her work on time and to specifications. It also assures the artist that he or she will get paid the right amount at the right time.

Contracts should be specific to the job. Customarily, artists are responsible for design, production, shipping, and installation. If someone else will install the artwork, be sure you specify who will coordinate and pay for the installation; if not the artist, it's usually the client. With a large project, it's helpful to identify the tasks that, if delayed for any reason, would set back completion of the project. These should be discussed up front to ensure that both parties agree on requirements and expectations.

Most trade professionals recognize that adequately compensating artists ensures the level of service needed to fulfill the client's expectations. The more complex the project, the more you should budget for the artist's work and services.

Payment schedule

Payments are usually tied to specific milestones in the process. These serve as checkpoints and confirm that work is progressing in a satisfactory manner, on time, and on budget. Payment is customarily made in three stages, although this will certainly depend on the circumstances, scope, and complexity of the project. The first payment is usually made when the contract is signed. It covers the artist's time and creativity in developing a detailed design specific to your needs. You can expect to go through several rounds of trial and error in the design process, but at the end of this stage you will have detailed drawings (and, for three-dimensional work, a maquette, or model) that everyone agrees upon. The cost of the maquette and the design time are usually factored into the artist's fee.

The second payment is generally set for a point midway through the project and is for work completed to date. If the materials are expensive, the client may be asked to advance money at this stage to cover costs. If the commission is canceled during this period, the artist keeps the money already paid for work performed.

Final payment is usually due when the work is installed. If the piece is finished on time but the building or project is delayed, the artist is customarily paid on delivery, but still has the obligation to oversee installation.

You will find that most artists keep tabs on the project budget. Be sure that the project scope does not deviate from what was agreed upon at the outset. If the scope changes, amend the agreement to reflect the changes.

KC Entryway (detail)
by Brian A. Hubel, see page 101.
Photograph: Don Jones.

A Brief Look at Commission Contracts for Artists
by Milon Townsend

A contract exists to remind us of what we were going to do, when we were going to do it, and what we were going to receive in exchange. A contract contains a simple, clear set of facts that are unambiguous and make sense. The larger and more complex the project, the more important it becomes to translate the responsibilities involved into a formal agreement.

Contracts are a brief, binding business plan. If all the parties to the agreement fulfill their various responsibilities and commitments, there is a very high likelihood of a successful outcome. In my own experience, there is a great deal more misunderstanding and miscommunication than there is malice. If malice raises its ugly head, a contract will give us recourse to whatever compensation would be appropriate to the problem that has arisen.

You don't want to get to the point where you need to enforce a contract through legal action. The attendant costs will almost certainly rob you of any net you might have created through doing the work, and the ill will that is the natural fruit of adversarial litigation will poison the atmosphere of the working relationship. Clarity and communication are the most effective preventative measures you can take against a possible negative outcome.

It might be good to begin by doing larger commissions with locally based partners. This will allow your clients to stay in touch with your own progress on the work, and give you the benefit of a common geographic legal footing. If you contract to do a project out of state, you lose a great deal of legal leverage.

These are some of the more typical concerns that need to be included in a contract for a commissioned project:

- Specific size, shape, color, design
- Standards of satisfaction
- Approval benchmarks: sketches, models, or maquettes; progress reports; updates with images; possible visit to artist's studio during fabrication process
- Preliminary design fee
- Payment schedule
- Additional costs incurred arising from changes in specifications, after work has begun
- Terms that come into play if the project needs to be postponed or canceled by either party
- Specifics regarding responsibility for delivery; installation; structural and support components; electrical work; architectural issues; required permits; insurance and liability
- Delivery/installation deadline
- Artist's right to use images of work, as well as client's name
- Repair and maintenance of the work
- Issues regarding alteration of the work after it has been installed
- Ownership of the copyright of the work

If you find something that's out of line with what you had agreed to in an early draft of the contract, contact the client about changing it. If they will not change the wording to more accurately reflect your understanding, reconsider doing the project. Review any binding legal document with your own attorney before signing it!

Milon Townsend has been working in sculptural glass for nearly forty years. He has written seven books and hundreds of articles on glass technique, art marketing, and creativity. See his work on page 347 and at www.milontownsend.com.

Koi Pond by Milon Townsend, see page 347.

A Collaborative Atmosphere

With most commission projects, it's best to bring the artist into the process at about the same time you hire a general contractor. By involving the artist at this early stage, the space will be designed with the art in mind, and the art will be designed to enhance the space. As a result, there will be no unpleasant surprises about size or suitability of artwork. Furthermore, when art is planned for early on and included as a line item in the budget, it's far less likely to be cut at the end of the project, when money is running low.

Early inclusion of the artist also helps ensure that the collaborative effort will flow smoothly throughout all phases of the project. If the artist is respected as part of the team, his or her work can benefit the project's overall design.

Naturally, the scope of the project will determine the number of players to be involved with the artist. How will decisions be made? Who is the artist's primary liaison? Will a single person sign off on designs and recommendations? Are committees necessary? It's important that all individuals understand both their own responsibilities and the responsibilities of their collaborators.

18

Above: *Ner Tamid* by Claude Riedel, see page 126. Photograph: Ted Wentink.

Right: *Bay View* by Shelby Keefe, see page 200.

Seek Two-Way Understanding

Be sure the artist understands the technical requirements of the job, including traffic flow, intended use of space, building structure, maintenance, lighting, and environmental concerns. By fully explaining these details, you'll ensure that the artist's knowledge, experience, and skills inform the project.

Keep the artist apprised of any changes that will affect the work in progress. Did you find a specified material unavailable and replace it with something else? Did the available space become bigger or smaller? These changes could have a profound impact on an artist's planning.

At the same time, the artist should let you know of any special requirements that his or her work will place on the space. Is it especially heavy? Does it need to be mounted in a specific way? Must it be protected from theft or vandalism? What kind of lighting is best? You may need to budget funds for these kinds of installation or maintenance expenses.

Most artists experienced with commissioned projects factor the expense of a continuing design dialog into their fee. There is an unfortunate belief harbored by some trade professionals (and yes, artists too) that a willingness to develop and adapt a design based on discussions with the client or design team somehow indicates a lack of commitment or creativity. On the contrary. The ability to modify design or execution without compromising artistic quality is a mark of professionalism. We recommend looking for this quality in the artist you choose, and then respecting it by treating the artist as a partner in any decisions that will affect his or her work.

Of course, part of working together is making clear who is responsible for what. Since few designers and architects (and even fewer contractors) are accustomed to working with artists, the relationship is ripe for misunderstanding. Without constant communication, things can easily fall through the cracks.

Forging a Partnership

The partnership between artists and trade professionals is an old and honorable one. Many venerable blueprints indicate, for example, an architect's detail for a ceiling with the scrawled note: "Finish ceiling in this manner." The assumption, of course, is that the artisan working on the ceiling has both the technical mastery and the aesthetic skill to create a whole expanse of space based on a detail sketched by the architect's pen.

The artists whose work fills these pages—and with whom we work every day at The Guild—are capable of interactive relationships like those described here. We're delighted to see increasing numbers of trade professionals include artists on their design teams. After seeing the arts separated from architectural and interior design for too many years, we're happy to be part of a renewed interest in collaboration.

The Apollo of Dogs by Louise Peterson, see page 341. Photograph: Jafe Parsons.

19

Commission Guidelines

- Bring the artist into the project as early as possible.

- Be as specific as possible about the scope and range of the project, even in early meetings before the artist is selected.

- Be honest and realistic when discussing deadlines, responsibilities, and specific project requirements—and expect the same from the artist. Don't avoid discussing areas where there seem to be questions.

- For larger projects, use specific milestones to assure continuing consensus on project scope and budget. It may also be necessary to make adjustments at these points.

- Choose an artist based on a solid portfolio of previous work and excellent references. It's less risky to use an artist who has worked on projects of similar size and scope, who can handle the demands of your specific job.

- Consider hiring an art consultant if the commission is particularly large or complex. The consultant should help with complicated contract arrangements and make certain that communication between artists and support staff (including subcontractors and engineers) is thoroughly understood.

- Trust your instincts when choosing an artist. Like selecting an advertising agency or an architect, choosing an artist is based partly on chemistry. You need to like the work and respect the artist, and you also need to be able to work together comfortably.

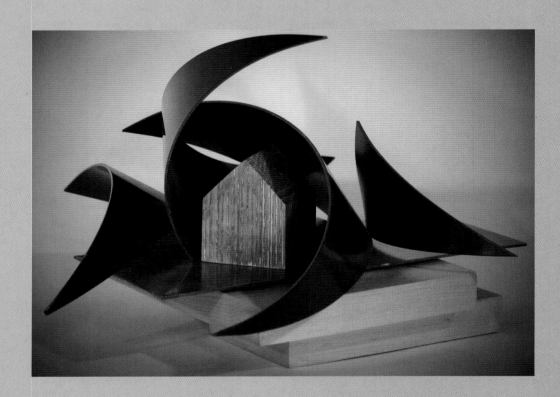

Above: *California Poppy Vase* by Carl Radke, see page 171. Photograph: Don Mayer Photography.

Right: *Infer* by Craig Robb, see page 421.

The Art of Being Green

The phrase "going green" is on everyone's lips. The green building movement has taken root across the country. Architects and designers are thinking differently about their projects from the ground up. Clients from hospital administrators to church groups are demanding spaces made with environmentally sound materials that will be sustainable to operate and maintain for years to come.

The artists featured in *The Guild Sourcebook of Art* are poised to play an important role in the green building revolution. Many, out of necessity or personal interest, have decades of experience finding ways to reuse and recycle materials in order to make works of art that will have an enduring impact on their surroundings without having a undue impact on the environment. We at The Guild believe that in years to come growing numbers of design professionals will make selecting green artwork a priority for their projects.

The Guild Sourcebook of Art is filled with remarkable artists—all top-notch professionals, juried for their experience in site-specific, architectural installations. Many are already moving toward green in exciting ways. (Read about just a few of their projects on the next two pages.) Every single artist would be delighted to bring his or her imagination and technical skill to a wide range of commission projects—green or not. All you need to do is pick up the phone and ask!

21

Heartwebs by Jeanine Briggs, article follows on next page, and see page 320. Photograph: Darius Milne.

Jeanine Briggs creates sculpture and wall pieces from found objects, finding artistic meaning in others' detritus. Her *Heartwebs* sculpture (see page 21) was initially created to benefit the San Francisco General Hospital Foundation. Made from fiberglass, acrylic paints, discarded fireplace curtains and wire, it will move to its permanent installation site at Visa after it leaves its temporary public installation site at Huntington Park in San Francisco, shown here. Briggs notes that the found materials often determine the medium, style, and subject matter of her work. In her constructive and finishing processes, she seeks out products and techniques with the least negative impact on the environment.

David Stine lives and works a green lifestyle. All of the lumber he uses in his work is native to his region of Illinois. Most of the lumber he harvests himself from family forests he personally stewards to ensure responsible sustainability. He culls only dead and dying trees for his work, which ensures proper growth of younger trees. He also works with local arborists to use timber they have cut and are looking to get rid of. He does not use exotic species or any wood that is not local, and he mills all his own boards at his shop.

In his shop Stine only uses natural, environmentally friendly finishes. He heats his shop and home with wood scraps from his work and with trees he has culled and sawed that are not suitable for furniture. He also runs his vehicles on used vegetable oil that he gets from local restaurants and then triple filters. He even takes barrels of filtered vegetable oil with him when he goes to shows and makes deliveries!

Archie Held installed this sculptural rainwater collection tank at the new Life Sciences Building at Mills College in Oakland, California. The Life Science Building is set to receive a LEED Silver Rating. As part of their sustainable design, the architects worked with Held to design a the rainwater collection tank for treatment and re-use of rainwater within the building. Held found the tank—an old mayonnaise vat—at a used equipment dealer in the Midwest and repurposed it to create a functional, green work of art. Held and crew added the cast bronze basins, which create the dramatic cascading water feature.

Julie Conway is the founder of BioGlass, whose mission is to encourage the research, development, and utilization of renewable fuels and community resources in a worldwide effort to create a new perspective in the art glass studio, to help glass artists make more profit, and to use energy efficiently, therefore helping to protect the environment and the future existence of glass arts. BioGlass offers studies and reports on studios that are taking initiatives to reduce greenhouse gases and simultaneously cut overhead costs. Through their website artists are invited to share how they use current resources efficiently and introduce alternative renewable heating technologies for glass melting needs.

23

Elizabeth Embler has created a series of green paintings in which she uses only "green" materials. She wraps her wood frames in old linen to make her canvases, then primes them with low- or no-VOC paint. She then incorporates found or recycled objects into her pieces, and finishes the painting using water-soluble oils. "Because paintings become a part of a home or building and share space with its occupants, I believe it is important that the materials I use be as non-toxic as possible and sourced in a sustainable way," says Embler. "My goal is to comply with NAHB Green or LEED Standards for Green Buildings and reduce the impact my work has on the environment."

Bottom left: *Lowder Table*
by David Stine, see page 110.
Photograph: Tory Rae.

Center left: *The Mills College
Rainwater Collection Tank*
by Archie Held, see pages 248-249.

Above: *Nest* by Illuminata,
see page 121. Photograph:
Jon Hustead.

Right: *Peaceful* by Elizabeth Embler,
see page 234. Photograph:
Andre Photography.

Putting the Pieces Together
A Mosaics Q&A with Rhonda Heisler

Beginning with this edition of *The Guild Sourcebook of Art,* mosaic artists are now featured in a stand-alone section in recognition of their growing prominence in American art. (The mosaics section begins on page 128.) The Guild asked New Jersey mosaicist Rhonda Heisler, an officer in the Society of American Mosaic Artists, to comment on current trends in this compelling art form.

Why the recent fascination with mosaic art?

Mosaics are experiencing a renaissance in the U.S. and abroad. You see evidence in both the quantity and quality of mosaic art being produced and the degree to which architects and designers are incorporating commercially designed mosaics into homes and public spaces as expressive focal points or sophisticated background texture. The growth of mosaic fine art is an important aspect of this trend, as contemporary artists are drawn to mosaics by way of its rich traditions, creative possibilities, and technical challenges.

In addition to the proliferation of new talent, new materials, and new design options, there is an increasingly sophisticated clientele who've learned to appreciate mosaics though travel to ancient sites and important ecclesiastical centers. Often they're looking for art for their home or place of business that is unique, dynamic, and lasting. Contemporary mosaics are the perfect combination of old-world craftsmanship and cutting-edge sensibility.

What makes mosaic unique among the art media?

Few media provide such powerful and direct testimony to the process of artistic creation as mosaics. The finished piece is the product of literally thousands of interrelated decisions, the mosaicist selecting from a broad array of exquisitely tactile materials, then cutting, manipulating, or editing each piece (called a tessera, plural form tesserae) and positioning it just so, for maximum visual and expressive impact within the design. The process is very labor-intensive, to be sure. But as the artist will tell you, making a mosaic can be meditative, highly intuitive, and a labor of love.

It's common for a viewer of mosaic to move in as close as possible to focus on a small area or to admire the intricate patterning and surface detail, then step back to take in the interplay of the various elements and the composition as a whole. It's this duality of focus, this tension, that makes owning mosaic art an endlessly fascinating process of discovery. Not only that, mosaic art is eminently collectible and well-priced.

Tell us more about the materials and techniques being used in contemporary mosaics.

Today's mosaicist can select from a variety of luscious materials that, until quite recently, simply were not widely available in this country. In addition to traditional materials like marble and stone, glass (stained, mirrored, and vitreous), and ceramic tile, artists are working in Italian and Mexican smalti (enameled glass with a unique depth of color and surface texture), tempered and fused glass, and found objects. Organic materials and fossils are finding their way into mosaics, along with beads, polymer clay, concrete and asphalt, metal, and handmade ceramic.

We see mosaicists mixing conventional and unconventional materials in surprising combinations and new formats. Others are using new industrial materials to depict traditional themes and narratives. *Andamento,* the placement of tesserae in a flowing pattern to suggest movement and rhythm, is a hallmark of fine mosaics and can be a signature feature of an individual artist's style. Mosaicists are working in both two- and three-dimensional formats, from small-scale work to large murals and public art projects. Some are experimenting with bas-relief and trompe l'oeil effects. It's an exciting medium, ripe with creativity and innovation.

In addition to serving as vice president of the Society of American Mosaic Artists, Rhonda Heisler has been creating custom and one-of-a-kind mosaic art since 1999. View more of her work on page 134 and at www.rhondaheislermosaicart.com.

What do mosaics lend to their environment? Why are they a good solution for public art projects?

The work has a strong physicality and an often shimmering presence that simply does not transmit in a photograph but looks great on the wall, where the field of tesserae creates stunning color and textural effects that modulate with the changing light. Mosaic is well-suited to large-format work, durable, and colorful. This makes it a versatile selection for interior or exterior wall-oriented or sculptural work. The mosaicist working on a public art commission often can incorporate materials and themes that give the piece a strong geographic or historical identity. Sometimes such mosaics are community-built, promoting local pride and signaling an investment in the community where the piece is situated.

How do I commission a mosaic?

Most professional mosaicists welcome site-specific commissions, either for portable panels, installation pieces, or sculptures. Mosaics can be custom-designed, custom-colored, and custom-sized to fit client requirements. Many of the best mosaicists are trained in fine arts and welcome the opportunity for hands-on involvement in all phases of the project: design, production, and installation. This is preferable to picking a pattern from a book or asking a painter to provide a color rendering for mosaic fabrication, since only someone who speaks the special language of mosaic can take full advantage of the unique properties of the material.

Most mosaicists charge a design fee that can be applied to a project once a contract is signed. Keep in mind that mosaic production can be slow, so allow ample lead time. Note, however, that a mosaic artist often has a selection of ready-to-hang work that may suit your requirements.

Tell us about SAMA, the Society of American Mosaic Artists.

This non-profit organization, founded in 1999, is at the center of mosaic art activity in the United States. Its members are artists, instructors and scholars, mosaic enthusiasts, and industry partners, all dedicated to educating, inspiring, and promoting excellence in fine mosaic art. Major programs include a yearly conference with an impressive array of workshops and presentations, annual juried (Mosaic Arts International) and non-juried (Mosaic Art Salon) exhibition opportunities, a quarterly newsletter, and a scholarship fund. A visit to the SAMA website, www.americanmosaics.org, is the perfect place to start your exploration of contemporary mosaics. You'll find a Members' Gallery and links to member websites, as well as information about conferences, exhibitions, and classes. Catalogs of past exhibitions and other publications are available in the online SAMA store.

Progression III ©2006 by Rhonda Heisler Mosaic Art, see page 134. Photograph: Ross Stout.

Waxing Eloquent
Fanne Fernow Explains the Fine Art of Encaustic

Though created using centuries-old techniques, encaustic painting is a largely unfamiliar art form that combines the skills of colorist, painter, and sculptor within a single work of art. Here, encaustic painter and International Encaustic Artists officer Fanne Fernow responds to The Guild's inquiries about this unique art form—and why it's a good choice for commission work.

How are encaustic works made?

Encaustic painting is a process of painting with molten wax and fusing the layers together with either a propane or butane torch or electric heat from an iron or a heat gun, which is like an industrial-strength hair dryer. Damar resin (a straw-colored resin gathered from trees) is melted into beeswax resulting in a harder, more luminous wax. Fusing layer to layer to layer further strengthens these paintings. In the end, encaustic works are stronger than one might imagine.

Encaustic is not a new medium—there are examples of encaustic paintings dating back to the sixth century. The word "encaustic" comes from the Greek word *encaustikos,* which means "to burn in." The fusing of the layers of paint is as important to the creation of an encaustic work as the actual painting.

Are there new materials being used in encaustic work?

In its truest form, encaustic materials are beeswax, damar resin (not varnish), and pigment painted on a wooden support. Today, however, encaustic can go as far as the human mind can take it. There are many artists, myself included, who make wax-based mixed-media pieces. There are others out there doing fabulous monoprints on paper, painting on Plexiglas, and dunking or painting on anything they can think of. Heather Hutchinson works with Plexiglas. Wendy Aikin and Judy Stabile have recently "encausticated" household items including tea cups, sugar cubes, glasses, books, keys, cell phones, and a chair. Paper loves wax, so many book artists, collagists, and assemblage artists use wax as well.

It seems that working with wax must be very difficult. What is it that makes encaustic work so appealing?

Encaustic painting is very organic. Beeswax comes from bees, damar resin is stuff that drips out of pine trees, most pigments are organic, and it is best to use natural wood substrates. I like it that we use things that come from the earth. It smells good, though it is best to work in a well-ventilated room.

With encaustic paint, I find that it is very easy to make my own paint from scratch, which is very empowering and fun. I make my own medium, which is a mixture of the wax and the damar, and then introduce dry pigment. I can customize my paints and colors in ways I never thought possible. I find it very satisfying that in the end, I have "made" all the paint.

Do you find that there are certain types of artists who are drawn to encaustic work?

Encaustic is perfect for the artist who loves processes and figuring things out. It is great fun to say, "Oh, look at this wood burner. What can I do with this?" A quick exploration says that you can't really work the wax with a wood-burning tool because it burns too hot, and just leaves the wax in a puddle. But try turning down the heat and putting some absorbent paper on the wax, and then using the wood burner. Fusing the wax to the paper gives the wax a whole new dimension. Continuing to layer the wax over the paper layer will continue to enhance it. Encaustic is for the artist who wants to explore, who is brave enough to say "What will happen if I try this?"

Of course, there is also a whole school of artists out there who do very traditional work. I have seen amazing representational landscapes painted with hot wax using tiny brushes. I find those works to be mind-bogglingly perfect.

Fanne Fernow is an encaustic artist living in Santa Cruz, California. She owns Clairvoyant Encaustics, an encaustic medium company, and is the Chief Empowerment Officer of International Encaustic Artists. Visit her work on page 431 and at www.fannefernow.com.

Why are encaustics a good option for commissions?

It is hard to talk about encaustics in general terms because there are so many different paths an artist can take. One of the universal truths about encaustic is that there is an intrinsic luminosity of the wax.

I find many encaustic paintings to be very meditative, and in a way, some two-dimensional works can almost seem three dimensional because of the textures. Often decorators and architects are looking for great surfaces, and with encaustic, the possibilities are limitless. Encaustic also lends itself well to giclée prints.

What's the role of International Encaustic Artists?

About four years ago, some "waxers" from the Bay Area gathered in an informal way to see if they could promote encaustic art in San Francisco. The response was immediate, and artists from all over wanted to join in. Ultimately, they formed International Encaustic Artists as a formalized way to promote encaustic painting and encaustic artists. The official objective is to seek "to raise the level of excellence in fine art encaustic work by providing global information exchange and raising interest about encaustics in the art world and with the general public."

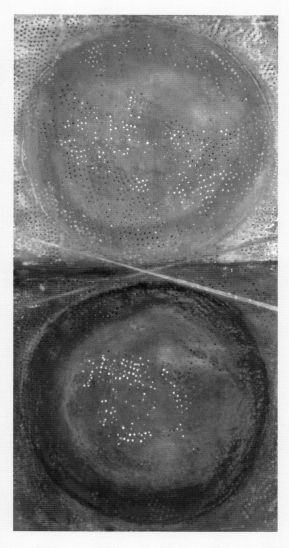

In addition, IEA has a fabulous sense of community. People love sharing their methods and techniques. Because encaustic painting is growing in popularity right now, IEA is a great place to learn new things and get answers to questions. There is a lot of mentoring and empowerment in IEA. We also sponsor shows, and our members are asked frequently to curate or help curate encaustic shows.

IEA holds a retreat in the Carmel Valley in California every year, where there is a lot of teaching in both encaustic painting and career building. For more information you can visit the IEA online at www.international-encaustic-artists.org.

Waxing Moons 2 by Fanne Fernow, see page 431. Photograph: RR Jones.

Architectural

Elements

Elizabeth Austin
Kristin DeSantis Contemporary Metal
Greg Leavitt
Marc Maiorana
Sabiha Mujtaba
Ken Roby

Elizabeth Austin

Elizabeth Austin Studio   12 Woodrow Road, Hanover, NH 03755   TEL 603.643.4148
TEL 603.728.8193   FAX 603.643.8085   EMAIL e.austin.asch@gmail.com

Top left: Music Room Study (night view), 2007, Villa Terrace Decorative Arts Museum, mixed media, 43" x 32". Top right: Music Room Study, (daytime view).
Bottom left: *Life on Hewes Brook,* 2008, Crossroads Academy, Lyme, NH, mixed media, 98" x 64". Photographs: Greg Hubbard, GBH Studios.
Bottom right: *Life on Hewes Brook* (detail).

ARCHITECTURAL ELEMENTS

Kristin DeSantis Contemporary Metal

Kristin DeSantis   PO Box 397, Allenspark, CO 80510   TEL/FAX 303.747.2077
TEL 303.875.8837   EMAIL kristin@kristindesantis.com   WEB www.kristindesantis.com

Top: *Porter Portal*, 2008, Porter residence, Albuquerque, NM, aluminum relief entry doors and sconces, doors 8' x 6' x 6".
Bottom left: *Four Graces*, 2007, RAA Radiology Associates of Albuquerque, aluminum relief, 63" x 15.5' x 3". Bottom right: *Abstract Spires*,
2007, RAA Radiology Associates of Albuquerque, curved aluminum panels, 60" x 68" x 4". Photographs: Chas McGrath.

ARCHITECTURAL ELEMENTS

Greg Leavitt

Leavitt Studios   914 Powder Mill Hollow Road   Boyertown, PA 19512-8233   TEL 610.367.8867   TEL 610.331.4016
FAX 610.473.8860   EMAIL gregoryaleavitt@yahoo.com   WEB www.gregleavitt.com

Top left: *Waterfall Bas Relief,* 2007, Allentown, PA, forged and fabricated copper, 10'H x 8'W x 2'D. Top right: *Wahl Garden Gate,* 2007, Wilmington, DE, forged and fabricated steel, 8'H x 5'W. Photograph: Tiana Leavitt. Bottom: *Atunyote Gate at Turning Stone,* 2006, Verona, NY, forged and fabricated steel and copper, gate 13'H x 18'W, gate arch 24'H x 30'W x 4'D. Photograph: Matt Falvo.

ARCHITECTURAL ELEMENTS

Marc Maiorana

Marc Maiorana and Iron Design Company   3353 Mountain Road, Cedar Bluff, VA 24609
TEL 828.712.7959   EMAIL info@irondesigncompany.com   WEB www.irondesigncompany.com

Top: *Book Sconce,* 2008, steel, 7" x 6" x 6". Photograph: Tom Mills.
Bottom: *Penland Railing,* 2006, Penland School of Crafts, Penland, North Carolina, 38" x 288" x 10".

ARCHITECTURAL ELEMENTS

Sabiha Mujtaba

Chrysalis Woodworks   1078 De Leon Drive, Clarkston, GA 30021   TEL 404.228.1010
EMAIL sabiha@chrysaliswoodworks.com   WEB www.chrysaliswoodworks.com

34

Room divider, 2008, private residence, Atlanta, GA, cherry, veneer, and glass, 81" x 72" x 4".
Inset: Room divider (detail).Photographs: Bart Kasten.

Ken Roby

Village Blacksmith Inc.   11193 Taylor May Road, Chagrin Falls, OH 44023   TEL 440.543.4977
FAX 440.543.0529   EMAIL kgroby@msn.com   WEB www.villageblacksmithinc.com

35

Top left: Railings in private residence, 2006, hand-forged iron. Top right: Railings in private residence, 2007, hand-forged iron. Bottom left: *Cattails,* 2008, hand-forged iron. Bottom right: *Lion,* 2008, hand-forged iron. Photographs: Itamar Gat, Eyes of the World Photography.

ARCHITECTURAL ELEMENTS

Architectural

Glass

Pablo Rivera

Guild Sourcebooks at Work

Case Study #1

ARTIST: Matthew Bezark
ARTWORK TITLE: *Repeated Travel*
MEDIA: Fabricated glass with inclusions
SIZE: 10' x 8' x 3"
INSTALLATION: Jacksonville International Airport, Jacksonville, FL

38

"Matt replied to a 'Call to Artists' [posted on Guild Sourcebook's Commission Opportunities list] and was selected from an international pool of 200 applicants. Working with him was wonderful! He was professional, easy going, and went out of his way to ensure things went well."

Cabeth Cornelius,
Arts Commission Program Coordinator
Jacksonville International Airport
www.jiaarts.org

"I've had the idea of using glass as an artistic "container" for some time. Everyday items placed in the space between sheets of glass create visually interesting patterns and textures by repeating colors and shapes. The airport setting of this project inspired me to use planes and globes to celebrate travel and exploration.

"This installation uses two different types of fabrication. The panels with the airplanes were created like triple-pane windows, with one frosted pane of privacy glass in the center, with airplanes and clear glass sealed to both sides of it. The globes were inserted on site into custom curtain wall sections with mirrored rear glass, which enhances the visual effect.

"The challenges of coordinating the creation for and installation in an operating airport were extremely rewarding. I built the airplane panels in Denver while the globe sections were being fabricated in Ohio. All of the pieces were shipped to Jacksonville, where I worked with a crew to complete the assembly and install the final work."

See more work by Matthew Bezark on page 42.

Art Glass Ensembles

Christie A. Wood   513 Bolivar Street, Denton, TX 76201   TEL 940.591.3002
FAX 940.591.7853   EMAIL info@artglassensembles.com   WEB www.artglassensembles.com

Willow Tree Autumn, 2008, private residence, El Dorado, CA, stained glass, 8.75'H x 6'W.

ARCHITECTURAL GLASS

Kathy Barnard

Kathy Barnard Studio   1605 Locust Street, Kansas City, MO 64108   TEL 816.472.4977
EMAIL kathy@kathybarnardstudio.com   WEB www.kathybarnardstudio.com

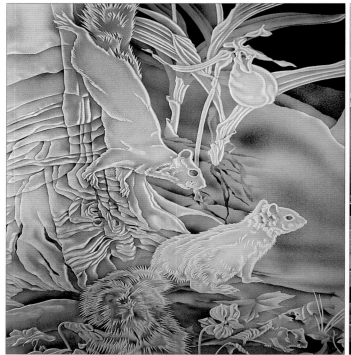
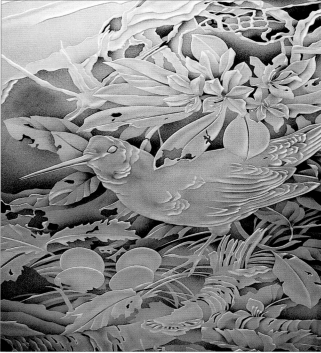

40

Beauty in the Cycle of Life (three details), 1986-2006, twelve entry doors, Grace Covenant Presbyterian Church, Overland Park, KS, carved glass, each door 8' x 3'. Photographs: Lea Murphy.

ARCHITECTURAL GLASS

Kathy Barnard

Kathy Barnard Studio   1605 Locust Street, Kansas City, MO 64108   TEL 816.472.4977
EMAIL kathy@kathybarnardstudio.com   WEB www.kathybarnardstudio.com

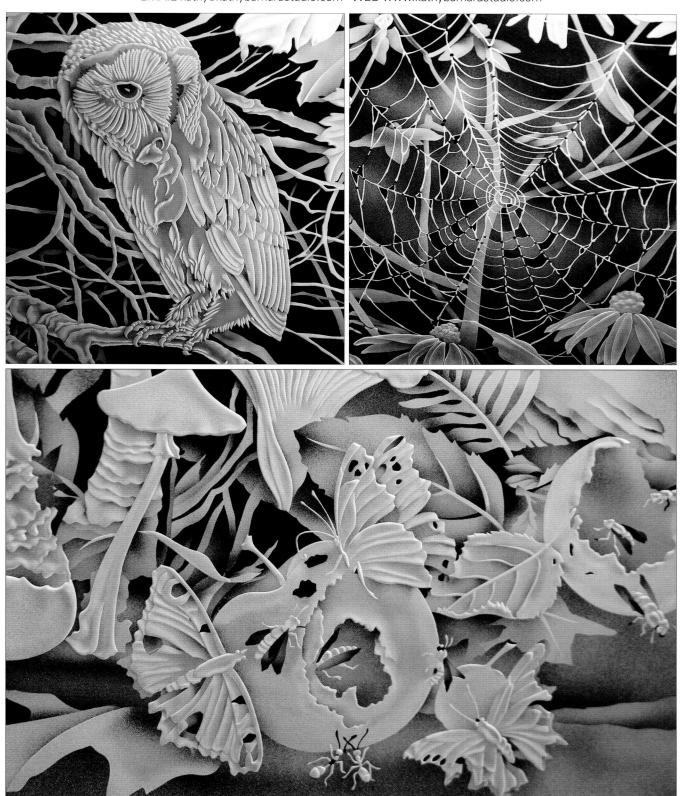

41

Beauty in the Cycle of Life (three details), 1986-2006, twelve entry doors, Grace Covenant Presbyterian Church, Overland Park, KS, carved glass, each door 8' x 3'. Photographs: Lea Murphy.

ARCHITECTURAL GLASS

Matthew Bezark

Mountain Glassworks   2777 Middle Fork Road, Boulder, CO 80302   TEL 303.434.7267
EMAIL mattbezark@mac.com   WEB www.mountainglassworks.com

Repeated Travel, 2008, Jacksonville International Airport, FL, fabricated glass with inclusions, 10'H x 8'W x 3"D. Photographs: Pablo Rivera.

ARCHITECTURAL GLASS

Kathy Bradford

North Star Art Glass, Inc.   142 Wichita, Lyons, CO 80540   TEL 303.823.6511
FAX 303.823.5350   EMAIL kathybradford@earthlink.net   WEB www.kathybradford.com

43

Top, and bottom left: *Aspens for Stennette* (details).
Bottom right: *Aspens for Stennette,* 2007, Estes Park, CO, sand-carved glass, 83" x 28".

David Wilson Design

David Wilson   202 Darby Road, South New Berlin, NY 13843-2212   TEL 607.334.3015
FAX 607.334.7065   EMAIL mail@davidwilsondesign.com   WEB www.davidwilsondesign.com

44

Top: Atrium glass art, 2007, exterior view in early morning light, Greystone Park Psychiatric Hospital, Morris Plains, NJ, over 3,000 sq. feet. A project for the New Jersey Economic Development Authority and the New Jersey State Council on the Arts. Bottom: Atrium glass art (detail), interior view in early morning light.

ARCHITECTURAL GLASS

Joline El-Hai

Bella Luz Studio   3737 NE 135th Street, Seattle, WA 98125   TEL 206.364.8053
FAX 206.364.7235   EMAIL glass@bellaluz.com   WEB www.bellaluz.com

Unfamiliar Bud, 2008, residence, Seattle, WA, glass, 34" x 26". Photographs: Ken Wagner.

ARCHITECTURAL GLASS

Franz Mayer of Munich, Inc.

607 President Street, Brooklyn, NY 11215   TEL 718.399.1817   EMAIL ebehrens@mayer-of-munich.us
Seidlstrasse 25, 80335 Munich, Germany   TEL 888.661.1694   EMAIL g.mayer@mayer-of-munich.com
WEB www.mayer-of-munich.com

Top: *Mosaic Murals (Fish and Orchard Themes)* by Ming Fay, 2004, Delancey/Essex Street Subway Station, New York, NY, MTA Arts for Transit.
Center: Architectural glass at third floor main stairway (detail) by Joachim Jung, 2001, Technical College, Jena, Germany. Photograph: Roland Dressler.
Bottom: *Caisse de Dépôt* by Genevieve Cadieux, 2005, Montréal, Canada, freestanding glass wall. Photograph: R.M. Tremblay.

ARCHITECTURAL GLASS

Franz Mayer of Munich, Inc.

607 President Street, Brooklyn, NY 11215   TEL 718.399.1817   EMAIL ebehrens@mayer-of-munich.us
Seidlstrasse 25, 80335 Munich, Germany   TEL 888.661.1694   EMAIL g.mayer@mayer-of-munich.com
WEB www.mayer-of-munich.com

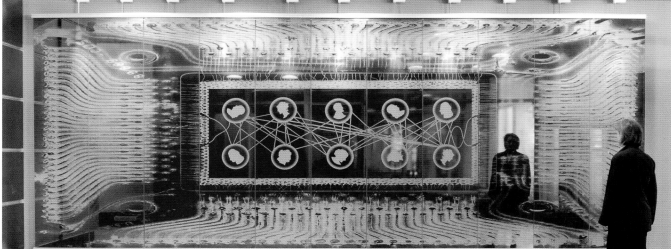

Top: *Floating Mount Evans Sky* by Reiner John, 2008, hanging art glass sculpture for lobby, 1001 17th Street, Denver, CO: Photograph: Havey Production.
Center: *Circuit Stream* by Ellen Driscoll, 2000, Gateway Village 800, Bank of America, Charlotte, NC, glass mural.
Bottom: One of seven floor mosaic medallions (different artists) by Beatrice Lebreton, 2005, Dallas Fort Worth Airport, TX, 20'DIA.

ARCHITECTURAL GLASS

Fusio Studio Inc.

Richard Parrish   6693 Lynx Lane #3, Bozeman, MT 59718   TEL 406.522.9892
EMAIL glass@fusiostudio.com   WEB www.fusiostudio.com

48

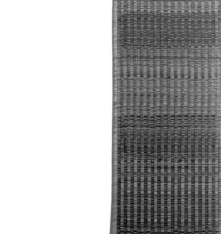

Top: Chapel windows, 2007, Children's Hospital, Aurora, CO, kiln-formed glass. Photograph: Grant Oakes. Bottom left: *Tapestry B,* 2008, kiln-formed glass, 40" x 12" x 3". Photograph: Tom Ferris. Bottom center: *Taking Measure of My Soul,* 2007, kiln-formed glass, 31" x 12" x 2". Photograph: Tom Ferris. Bottom right: *Aspen & Cedar Wall Panel,* 2008, kiln-formed glass, 54" x 16" x 4". Photograph: Tom Ferris.

ARCHITECTURAL GLASS

Josephine A. Geiger

J. A. Geiger Studio   1647 Beech Street, Saint Paul, MN 55106   TEL 612.964.6081
EMAIL jageiger.studio@comcast.net   WEB www.jageigerstudio.com

49

Gothic Aspens, 2005, private residence, Menomonie, WI, leaded stained glass, 57" x 49". Photograph: Dave Wallace.

ARCHITECTURAL GLASS

Glassic Art

Leslie Rankin   5850 South Polaris Avenue Suite 700, Las Vegas, NV 89118   TEL 702.658.7588
EMAIL glassicart@glassicart.com   WEB www.glassicart.com

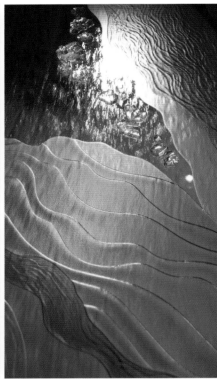

Top left: Countertop with vessels, 2007, Las Vegas, NV, glass, 12" x 24" x 84". Photograph: Curtis Fairman. Top center: *Waterwall* (detail). Photograph: Britt Pierson.
Top right: Pendant lights, 2008, 40" x 24". Photograph: Debbie Pierce. Bottom: *Waterwall*, 2007, Las Vegas, NV, glass, 9' x 14'. Photograph: Britt Pierson.

Glassic Art

Leslie Rankin   5850 South Polaris Avenue Suite 700, Las Vegas, NV 89118   TEL 702.658.7588
EMAIL glassicart@glassicart.com   WEB www.glassicart.com

Top: *Dining Divider*, 2008, Las Vegas, NV, glass, 6' x 9'.
Bottom: GRG office building, 2007. Photographs: Darius Kuzmickas.

Nancy Gong

Gong Glass Works   42 Parkview Drive, Rochester, NY 14625-1034   TEL 585.288.5520
FAX 585.288.2503   EMAIL nancy@nancygong.com   WEB www.nancygong.com

52

Top: *Gestures*, Shumway Dining Hall, National Institute for the Deaf, Rochester, NY, glass, 6'H x 18'W. Photograph: Tim Wilkes.
Bottom: *Fleeting Moments*, 1999, Elizabeth G. and Jennifer J. Hildebrandt Hospice Center, Rochester, NY, glass, lead, and steel, 3.75'H x 45'W.

ARCHITECTURAL GLASS

Lynn Goodpasture

Goodpasture Art & Design   10753 Weyburn Avenue, Los Angeles, CA 90024
TEL 310.470.2455   FAX 310.470.4256   EMAIL lynn@lynngoodpasture.com

Solar Illumination I: Evolution of Language, 2008, Pearl Avenue Library, San Jose, CA, collection of the City of San Jose Public Art, fabrication by Peters Glass Studio, four 8' x 3' art glass windows embedded with photovoltaic cells provide electricity for glass lamp, illuminated with color-changing LED lights, suspended at library entrance, 20" x 36" x 36". Photographs (top and bottom left): Lucas Fladzinski. Photograph (bottom right): Richard Johns.

ARCHITECTURAL GLASS

J. Gorsuch Collins Architectural Glass

J. Gorsuch Collins   8283 West Iliff Lane, Lakewood, CO 80227   TEL 303.985.8081
FAX 303.980.0692   EMAIL dalewcollins@juno.com   WEB www.collinsarchitecturalglass.com

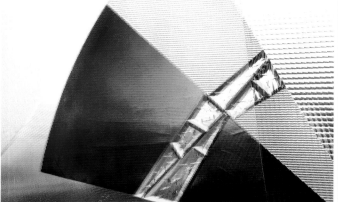
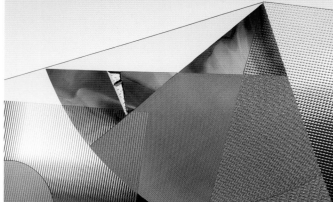

1290 Broadway, 2007, laminated glass, 4.5'H x 17'W x 2"D. Photographs: Ron Johnson.

BJ Katz

Meltdown Glass Art and Design   6810 South Clementine Court, Tempe, AZ 85283   TEL 480.633.3366
FAX 480.633.3344   EMAIL sales@meltdownglass.com   WEB www.meltdownglass.com

55

Left: *Flow of Life,* Mesa, AZ, 103"H x 181"W. Right top and bottom: *Flow of Life* (details). Photographs: Derek Nadeau.

Guy Kemper

Kemper Studio   1425 Elliston Lane, Versailles, KY 40383   TEL/FAX 859.873.3315
EMAIL guy@kemperstudio.com   WEB www.kemperstudio.com

Jet Trails, 2008, Terminal 1, O'Hare International Airport, Chicago, IL, 12' x 50'.
Fabricated by Derix Glasstudios. Photograph: James Steinkamp Photography.

ARCHITECTURAL GLASS

Kessler Studios, Inc.

Cindy Kessler   273 East Broadway Street, Loveland, OH 45140-3121   TEL 513.683.7500
FAX 513.683.7512   EMAIL info@kesslerstudios.com   WEB www.kesslerstudios.com

57

Top: *Clare & Francis* (detail), 2008, Chapel, The Clare at the Water Tower Retirement Community, Chicago, IL, stained glass, 18' x 89'.
Bottom left: *Clare & Francis* (exterior view). Bottom right: *Clare & Francis* (detail). Photographs: Bob Kessler.

Mark Eric Gulsrud Architectural Glass

Mark Eric Gulsrud   3309 Tahoma Place West, Tacoma, WA 98466   TEL 253.566.1720
EMAIL mark@markericgulsrud.com   WEB www.markericgulsrud.com

Reflection, 2007, Cherry Hills Community Church, Highlands Ranch, CO, 13' x 78',
laminated glass constructed in collaboration with Derix Glasstudios of Germany.

Pearl Glassworks Ltd.

Margery Pearl Gurnett   1237 East Main Street, Rochester, NY 14609   TEL 585.654.7551
FAX 585.385.2921   EMAIL pearlglassworks@yahoo.com   WEB www.pearlglassworks.com

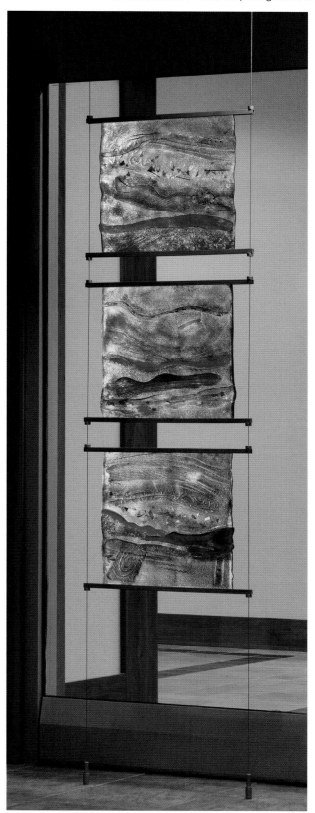

Left: *Strata,* 2008, Rochester General Hospitals, Lipson Cancer Center at Linden Oaks, Rochester, NY, kiln-cast glass, 96" x 18". Photograph: Clear Digital Photography. Right: Deco-style sidelights, 2008, private residence, Rochester, NY, sandblasted and enameled glass, 79"H x 9"W. Photograph: Bob Klein.

ARCHITECTURAL GLASS

Stanton Glass Studio, LLC

Bryant J. Stanton   318 Roger's Hill Road, Waco, TX 76705   TEL 800.619.4882   TEL 254.829.1151
FAX 254.829.2521   EMAIL info@stantonglass.com   WEB www.stantonglass.com

Top, and bottom right: *Wind, Tumbling Leaves* (detail). Bottom left: *Wind, Tumbling Leaves,* 2008, craft room door,
private residence, Chilton, TX, leaded and iridized glass with etched oak leaves, 67"H x 21".

ARCHITECTURAL GLASS

Stanton Glass Studio, LLC

Bryant J. Stanton   318 Roger's Hill Road, Waco, TX 76705   TEL 800.619.4882   TEL 254.829.1151
FAX 254.829.2521   EMAIL info@stantonglass.com   WEB www.stantonglass.com

61

Southern Cross II, 2008, Waco Chamber of Commerce, Waco, TX, stained and leaded glass and iron, 80"H x 6'DIA.

Atrium

Sculpture

Lanny Bergner

Fidalgo Studios   7064 Miller Road, Anacortes, WA 98221-8321   TEL 360.672.8408   TEL 360.299.0514
EMAIL lbergner@wavecable.com   WEB http://home.wavecable.com/~lbergner/

64

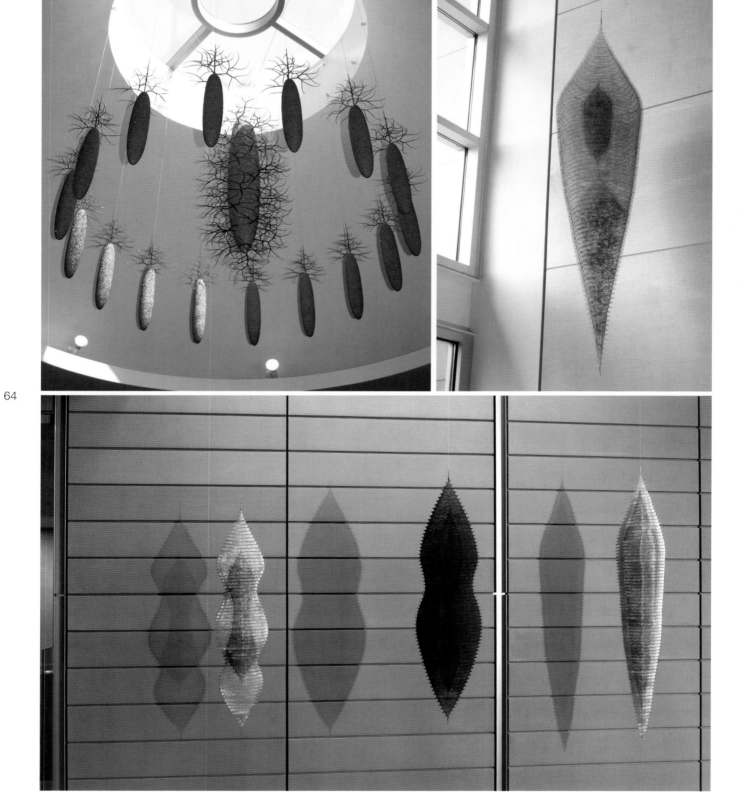

Top left: *Forest Sky,* 2005, Anacortes Public Library, Anacortes, WA, glass frit, wire, and hydrocal, 98"H x 98"W x 98"D. Top right: *Ether II,* 2008, Skagit Valley College, Mount Vernon, WA, bronze, brass, and aluminum wire mesh, 79"H x 17"W x 17"D. Bottom: *Symbiote Red, Inside and Outside, Ether Rising,* 2008, Bellevue Sculpture Exhibition, Bellevue, WA, bronze, stainless steel, brass, and aluminum wire mesh, 70"H x 130"W x 15"D.

ATRIUM SCULPTURE

Clowes Sculpture

Jonathan and Evelyn Clowes   98 March Hill Road, Walpole, NH 03608   TEL/FAX 603.756.9505
EMAIL stacey@clowessculpture.com   WEB www.clowessculpture.com

A Beatitude of Birds, St. Mary's Hospital, Navtech rod with formed and painted aluminum, 35'H x 17'W. Photograph: Cris Burkhalter.

Goldstein Kapellas Studio

Daniel Goldstein and John Kapellas   224 Guerrero Street, San Francisco, CA 94103
TEL 415.621.5761   EMAIL daniel@goldsteinkapellas.com   WEB www.goldsteinkapellas.com

Top left: *Von Leewenhoek* (from below). Photograph: Peter Lippman. Top right: *Von Leewenhoek,* 2005, California Department of Health Services, Richmond, CA, painted expanded aluminum, 25' x 25' x 25'. Photograph: Peter Lippman. Bottom: *Concentric,* 2004, Sallie Mae Corporation, Reston, VA, anodized aluminum, 13' x 13' x 10'. Photograph: Maxwell MacKenzie.

ATRIUM SCULPTURE

Goldstein Kapellas Studio

Daniel Goldstein and John Kapellas   224 Guerrero Street, San Francisco, CA 94103
TEL 415.621.5761   EMAIL daniel@goldsteinkapellas.com   WEB www.goldsteinkapellas.com

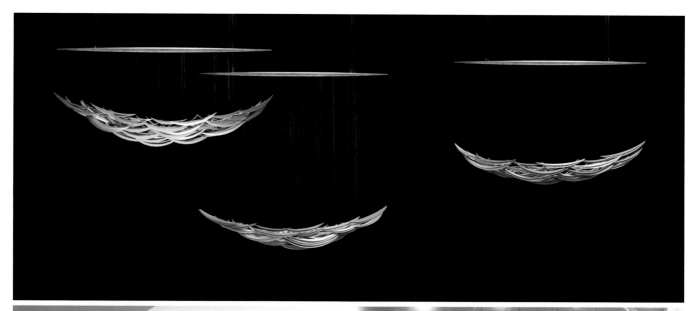

Top: *Embarking* (detail), 2008, Ritz Carlton, Shenzhen, China, stainless steel and anodized aluminum, 8' x 42' x 3'.
Bottom left: *Breath of Life*, 2007, Memorial Hospital, Modesto, CA, steel and powder-coated aluminum, 12' x 12' x 25'. Photograph: Peter Lippman.
Bottom right: *Healing Waters*, 2008, Banner Hospital, Glendale, AZ, anodized aluminum, 13' x 40' x 20'.

ATRIUM SCULPTURE

Gordon Auchincloss Designs, LLC

Gordon Auchincloss   972 West Hill Road, Hardwick, VT 05843   TEL 802.472.5803
FAX 802.472.6464   EMAIL gordon@ambientflow.com   WEB www.ambientflow.com

From Here on Out, 2008, Lindner Center for Hope, Mason, OH, 7'H x 12'W, hand-forged steel branches with verde and brushed copper leaves. Inset: *From Here on Out* (detail). Photographs: Denise Owens.

Tom Philabaum

Philabaum Glass Studio and Gallery   711 South Sixth Avenue, Tucson, AZ 85701   TEL 520.884.7404
FAX 520.884.0679   EMAIL philabaumgallery@qwestoffice.net   WEB www.philabaumglass.com

Top left and right: *Another Way to Fly* (details). Bottom: *Another Way to Fly,* 2008, Tucson International Airport,
slumped and fused glass, 7'H x 25' x 25'. Photographs: Martha Patey.

ATRIUM SCULPTURE

Rob Fisher Sculpture, LLC

Talley Fisher   228 North Allegheny Street, Bellefonte, PA 16823   TEL 814.355.1458
FAX 814.353.9060   EMAIL robfishersculpture@yahoo.com   WEB www.robfishersculpture.com

Top and bottom left: *JetStream,* 2008, New Indianapolis Airport, IN, aluminum and stainless steel, 50'H x 200'DIA.
Bottom right: *Sea Turtles,* 2008, One Ocean Resort, Atlantic Beach, FL, aluminum and stainless steel, 8'H x 4'DIA.

ATRIUM SCULPTURE

Rob Fisher Sculpture, LLC

Talley Fisher   228 North Allegheny Street, Bellefonte, PA 16823   TEL 814.355.1458
FAX 814.353.9060   EMAIL robfishersculpture@yahoo.com   WEB www.robfishersculpture.com

71

Top left and bottom left: *Alhambra Archetype,* 2008, Old Sauk Trails Office and Research Park, Madison, WI, aluminum and stainless steel, 18'H x 9'W.
Top right and bottom right: *Transformation,* 2008, Erdman Building, Old Sauk Trails Office and Research Park, Madison, WI, aluminum and stainless steel, 12'H x 10'DIA.

ATRIUM SCULPTURE

Sable Studios

Paul Sable 100 North Rodeo Gulch Drive, Suite #36, Soquel, CA 95073 TEL 831.475.4012
TEL 831.345.3540   EMAIL paul@sablestudios.com   WEB www.sablestudios.com

Top: *Kaliope Dance*, 2006, Children's Hospital, Boston, Sintra® and paint, 10'H x 152'L. Photograph: Kris Snibbe.
Bottom: *The World Within,* 2005, Children's Hospital, Boston, Waltham Campus, Varia™ resin panels, 12' x 12' x 12'.

ATRIUM SCULPTURE

Marsh Scott

2795 Laguna Canyon Road #C, Laguna Beach, CA 92651   TEL 949.494.8672
EMAIL marsh@marshscott.com   WEB www.marshscott.com

Drifting Leaves, 2007, Flowers Hospital, Dothan, AL, stainless steel.

ATRIUM SCULPTURE

Media Wright

Guild Sourcebooks at Work

Case Study #2

ARTIST: Jonathan and Evelyn Clowes
ARTWORK TITLE: *Reflections*
MEDIA: Fiberglass, blown glass, and bronze coating
SIZE: 10'H x 2'DIA.
INSTALLATION: St. Vincent Primary Care Center, Indianapolis, IN

74

"We became familiar with Jonathan a number of years ago through *The Guild Sourcebook,* and our experience [working with him] was very positive. We knew going into it that there were a number of constraints, and I worried that either Jonathan wouldn't be interested or there wouldn't be the time or resources to complete it. However, I was pleasantly surprised to find that rather than be put-off, he was intrigued by the parameters and more than willing to meet the constraints of the budget and timeline.

"Over the years we've been in business, we've found *The Guild Sourcebook* to be an excellent source of high-quality artists from a variety of disciplines. The images are beautiful and can easily be used for presentation purposes, particularly when we're trying to convince a client to commission a piece of artwork. For many clients this is a huge leap of faith and the more visual "evidence" you can show them, the more likely they will be to appreciate the concept and move forward on the project."

Soni Kercheval, Partner/Art Consultant
InSite Art Consulting Group, Inc.
www.insiteart.com

"We were contacted by Soni Kercheval [principal at InSite Art Consulting Group Inc.] about this project. She had already shared many images of our work with the client, and they had a well-developed idea of what aspects of our work appealed to them. They knew the space in the Reflection Room was limited, and they needed a tall, graceful centerpiece. The client requested that we modify an existing design to suit their environment.

"To create *Reflections* we used a combination of materials and techniques. The inner core of the piece has a steel armature with a composite material that defines the elegant gesture. The entire sculpture was then faired and sealed with a thin layer of bronze. The techniques used to develop this sculpture were a mixture of innovation and new technology, which when combined, yielded this economical and beautiful work. The central sphere is blown glass, and the pedestal is made of Indiana limestone, which was carved about thirty miles from St. Vincent's.

The entire project was a real "dream team" endeavor. This was our first project with Soni and In-Site Art Consulting; they came to us with clear directives, good vision, and a willing client who was motivated to have our artwork in their facility. We were very pleased to collaborate with capable partners. Though the project was on a very tight deadline, it was a nearly seamless process; the commissioned artwork looks terrific and reflects this good partnership.

See more work by Clowes Sculpture on page 65.

Dierk Van Keppel

Rock Cottage Glassworks, Inc.   6801 Farley, Merriam, KS 66203   TEL 913.262.1763
FAX 913.262.0430   EMAIL info@rockcottageglassworks.com   WEB www.vankeppelartglass.com

Blue Sun, 2006, H & R Block, Kansas City, MO, blown and fused glass
with aluminum armature, 17'H x 9'D overall, glass panels 42"H x 25"W.

ATRIUM SCULPTURE

Fine Art

Photography

Sally Dougan

Scanning Nature   25 McCatharn Road, Lebanon, NJ 08833   TEL 908.236.7585
EMAIL saldougan@aol.com   WEB www.scanningnature.com

78

Top left: *String Beans,* 2008, New Jersey, scanned image, various sizes. Top right: *Maple Seed Cluster,* 2008, scanned image, various sizes.
Bottom left: *Scallions,* 2008, scanned image, various sizes. Bottom right: *Carrots,* 2008, scanned image, various sizes.

Sally Dougan

Scanning Nature   25 McCatharn Road, Lebanon, NJ 08833   TEL 908.236.7585
EMAIL saldougan@aol.com   WEB www.scanningnature.com

Top left: *Hydrangea,* 2008, New Jersey, scanned image, various sizes. Top right: *Sweet Peas,* 2008, scanned image, various sizes.
Bottom left: *Magnolias,* 2008, scanned image, various sizes. Bottom right: *Buttercups,* 2008, scanned image, various sizes.

FINE ART PHOTOGRAPHY

Doris K. Hembrough

Hembrough Gallery   33 Brodhead Street, Mazomanie, WI 53560   TEL 608.575.7750
FAX 608.274.5845   EMAIL info@hembroughgallery.com   WEB www.hembroughgallery.com

80

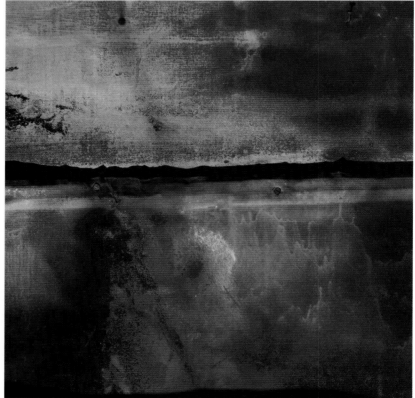

Top: *Texas,* photograph, 25" x 25". Bottom: *Birds of Paris I,* photograph, 25" x 25".

FINE ART PHOTOGRAPHY

Henry Domke Fine Art

Henry F. Domke   3914 Foxdale Road, New Bloomfield, MO 65063   TEL 573.295.6349
EMAIL henry@henrydomke.com   WEB www.henrydomke.com

Top: *Water Lily 13548*. Bottom left: *Horse Tail 5723*. Bottom right: *Sycamore 8837*, Westminster College.

FINE ART PHOTOGRAPHY

Adam Jahiel

Adam Jahiel—Photographer   PO Box 501, 90 North Piney Road, Story, WY 82842
TEL 307.683.2862   FAX 307.683.2730   EMAIL ajahiel@fiberpipe.net   WEB www.adamjahiel.com

82

Remuda, Spanish Ranch, 1995, platinum print, 14" x 14".

FINE ART PHOTOGRAPHY

Adam Jahiel

Adam Jahiel—Photographer   PO Box 501, 90 North Piney Road, Story, WY 82842
TEL 307.683.2862   FAX 307.683.2730   EMAIL ajahiel@fiberpipe.net   WEB www.adamjahiel.com

Horse Shadows, 1995, Spanish Ranch, NV, silver gelatin print, 30" x30".

FINE ART PHOTOGRAPHY

Kim Ellen Kauffman

Synecdoche Studio   712 Terminal Road, Lansing, MI 48906   TEL/FAX 517.321.2815
EMAIL kim@synecdochestudio.com   WEB www.synecdochestudio.com

84

Aura, 2008, part of the *Florilegium* series of limited-edition photo collages from multiple scans of original objects.

FINE ART PHOTOGRAPHY

Judy Mandolf

Studio One   2945 Denver Street, San Diego, CA 92117   TEL 619.276.5760   TEL 619.549.5760
FAX 619.276.5787   EMAIL judymandolf@yahoo.com   WEB www.judymandolf.com

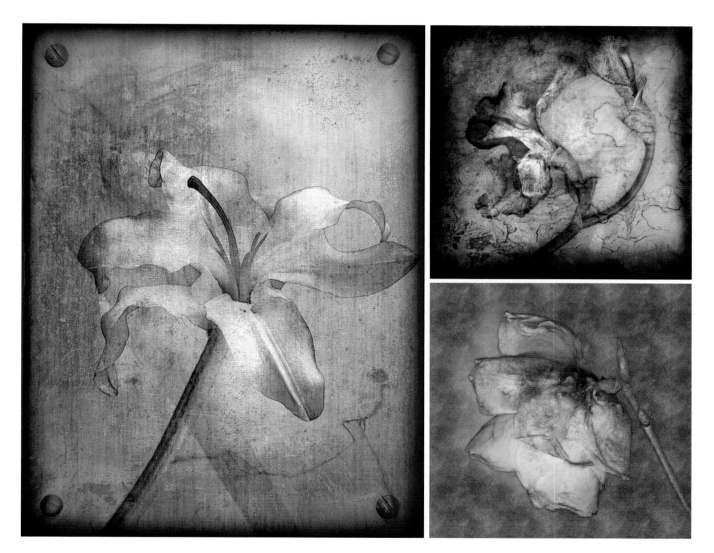

Left: *Golden Gazer,* 2007, giclée on wood panel, 30" x 24". Top right: *Iris,* 2007, 16" x 16". Bottom right: *Camellia,* 2007, 16" x 16".

FINE ART PHOTOGRAPHY

Bonnie McCann

Photography by Bonnie   47-249A Hui Iwa Street, Kaneohe, HI 96744   TEL 808.239.1661
EMAIL mccannr002@hawaii.rr.com   WEB www.photobybonnie.com

86

Top: *The Stand,* 2007.
Bottom: *Haleakala III,* 2007.

FINE ART PHOTOGRAPHY

Murphy Kuhn Fine Art Photography

Murphy Kuhn   43 Langlo Terrace, Santa Barbara, CA 93105   TEL 805.682.8252
EMAIL imagesbymurphykuhn@cox.net   WEB www.murphykuhn.com

Top left: *Manzanita,* 2008, UBS, Santa Barbara, CA, 50" x 37.5". Top right: *Date Palm,* 2008, 50.5" x 38".
Bottom: *Lone Oak,* 2008, UBS, Santa Barbara, CA, 32.5" x 50".

Xavier Nuez

Xavier Nuez Photography, Inc.   PO Box 1412, Fremont, CA 94538
TEL 510.648.6810   EMAIL x@nuez.com   WEB www.nuez.com

88

Top: *Alley No. 102, Goast Pier, 2008, San Francisco, CA, 11:30 pm,* 16" x 20" up to 44" x 55".
Bottom: *Alley No. 100, Ghost Story, 2007, Kansas City, MO, 11:45 pm,* 16" x 20" up to 44" x 55".

PJ Boylan Photography

PJ Boylan   Milwaukee, WI 53220   TEL 414.530.0326   TEL/FAX 414.231.9315
EMAIL mail@pjboylanphotography.com   WEB www.pjboylanphotography.com

Fountain, 2007, 16" x 20" and larger.
Delta Lily and Bud, 2008, 16" x 20" and larger.

FINE ART PHOTOGRAPHY

Daniel Sroka

Daniel Sroka Designs LLC   26 Blackberry Lane, Morris Township, NJ 07960
TEL/FAX 815.301.8836   EMAIL ds@danielsroka.com   WEB www.danielsroka.com

90

Horizon I: Abstract of a Fallen Leaf, 2007, pigment print, 25" x 20".

FINE ART PHOTOGRAPHY

Lee Carver

Lee Carver Photography   PO Box 2890, Vail, CO 81658   TEL 858.373.7017
EMAIL lee@leezwebgallery.com   WEB www.leezwebgallery.com

Left: *Maroon Lake, CO,* 2007, Excell Marking, Denver, CO, multi-image mural, 48" x 42".
Right: *Big Sur, CA,* 2005, City of Hope Hospital, Duarte, CA, multi-image mural, 40" x 42".

Jaimi Novak Photography

Jaimi Novak   Minneapolis, MN   TEL 612.275.0347
EMAIL jaiminovak@yahoo.com   WEB www.jnovakphotography.com

Left: *Palm Tree.* Right: *Motel Sign.*

FINE ART PHOTOGRAPHY

Julie Boehm Photography

Julie Boehm   Portland, OR   TEL 888.335.6308
EMAIL julie@julieboehm.com   WEB www.julieboehm.com

Neah Bay, 2006, giclée print, 16" x 20" or 20" x 24".

Kevin Sink Photography

1817 Grand Boulevard, Kansas City, MO 64108   TEL/FAX 816.472.0711
TEL 800.262.2749   EMAIL info@kevinsink.com   WEB www.kevinsink.com

Left: *Konza Hillsides,* color photograph, 59 x 94".
Right: *Wheat Sunset,* color photograph, 24" x 20".

Pamela Gleave Fine Art

Pamela Gleave   9642 Marshall Road, Olivet, MI 49076   TEL 269.749.9532
EMAIL gleave.pamela@gmail.com   WEB www.pamgleave.com

Left: *Warbonnet,* 2007, photomicrograph of ortho-aminobiphenyl, 20" x 16".
Right: *La Bocca,* 2007, Fireside Books, Marshall, MI, photomicrograph of ortho-aminobiphenyl, 35" x 44". Photograph: Dyan Sykora.

Karen Scally

Scally Art   TEL 925.209.7323   FAX 425.952.0587
EMAIL kjscally@earthlink.net   WEB www.karenscally.com

Windmill.

Furniture &

Floor Coverings

Scott E. Armstrong	Jeff Soderbergh
Boykin Pearce Associates	Stephen T. Anderson, Ltd.
David J. Lunin Furniture Maker	John C. Sterling
Patricia Dreher	David Stine
Constantine Fedorets	Bilhenry Walker
Brian A. Hubel	Timothy White
Bill Jacobs	William Wells Studio
Lederer Studio Furniture	Kevin Heram
Mark S. Levin	Vincent T. Leman
Bill Masterpool	Joseph Murphy
Red Iron Studio	Leslie Webb

Scott E. Armstrong

Arrowleaf Studio   150 South Jones Street, Powell, WY 82435   TEL 307.754.8019
EMAIL scott@arrowleafstudio.com   WEB www.arrowleafstudio.com

Top: *Linda and Elijha Chests*, 2006, imbuya and walnut, 60"H x 30"W x 20"D and 50"H x 42"W x 20"D. Bottom: *Linda Chest* (detail). Photographs: Elijha Cobb.

FURNITURE & FLOOR COVERINGS

Boykin Pearce Associates

Dave Boykin   1875 East 27th Avenue, Denver, CO 80205   TEL/FAX 303.294.0703
EMAIL dave@boykinpearce.com   WEB www.boykinpearce.com

Top: *Cloud Dining Set,* 2008, Longmont, CO, cherry. Photograph: Ron Ruscio. Bottom: *Curvilinear Bed,*
2005, Denver, CO, mahogany with stainless steel inlay 54" x 61" x 88". Photograph: Jim Stayton.

FURNITURE & FLOOR COVERINGS

David J. Lunin Furniture Maker

David J. Lunin   1134 Elizabeth Avenue, Lancaster, PA 17601   TEL 717.293.1504
EMAIL dave@djlfurnituremaker.com   WEB www.djlfurnituremaker.com

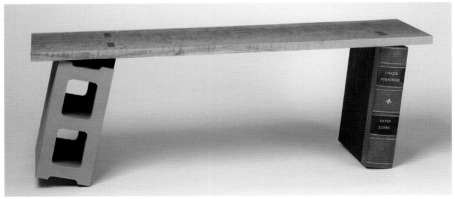

Top: *Floating Hall Table,* 2007, Chevy Chase, MD, tiger maple, 30" x 38" x 14".
Center: *Kneeling Coffee Table,* 2006, walnut, 18" x 44" x 19".
Bottom: *Falling Bench,* 2008, cherry, plywood, and leather, 14" x 48" x 17". Photographs: David Gentry.

FURNITURE & FLOOR COVERINGS

Patricia Dreher

800 Heinz Avenue #2, Berkeley, CA 94710   TEL 510.849.2036
EMAIL info@patriciadreher.com   WEB patriciadreher.com

Left: *Lattice Circle,* 2008, San Francisco, CA, painted canvas, 6'DIA.
Right: *Circles and Squares,* 2008, painted canvas, 4' x 14'. Photographs: Joe Schopplein.

FURNITURE & FLOOR COVERINGS

Constantine Fedorets

Ugol Inc. Woodworks   560 Mineral Spring Avenue, Pawtucket, RI 02860
TEL 401.378.7583   EMAIL ugolinc@gmail.com

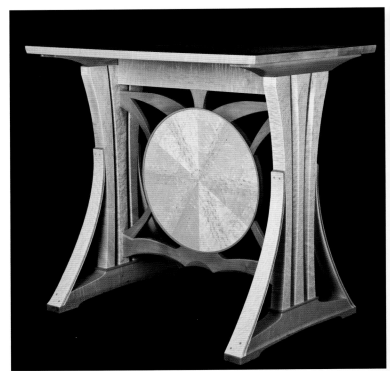

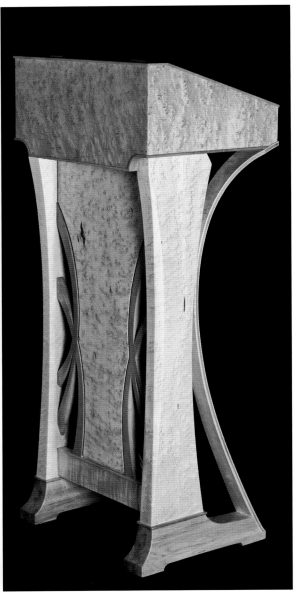

Top left: *Altar*, 2008, Chapel, Wheeling, WV, bird's-eye maple and pear. Right: *Ambo*, 2008, Wheeling, WV, bird's-eye maple and pear.
Bottom left: *Ambo* (detail). Photographs: Andrey Aloshine.

FURNITURE & FLOOR COVERINGS

Brian A. Hubel

Hubel Handcrafted Inc.   1311 North Corona Street, Colorado Springs, CO 80903
TEL 719.667.0577   EMAIL info@hubelhi.com   WEB www.hubelhi.com

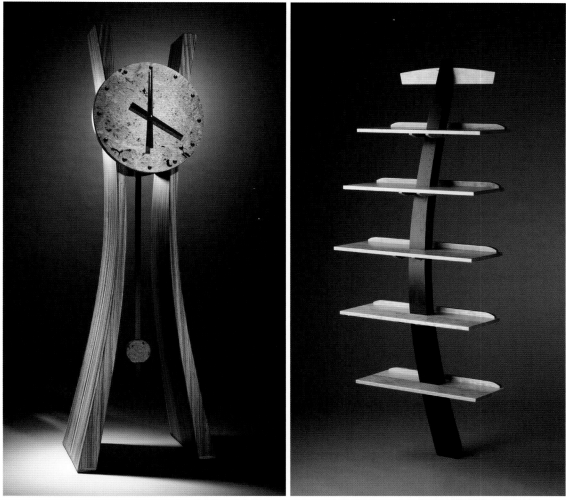

101

Top left: *Passage in Time,* 2007, Monument, CO, zebrawood, maple burl, and ebony, 70"H x 21"W x 11"D. Top right: *Recurve,* 2008, Montclair, NJ, cherry and ebonized ash, 91"H x 36"W x 19"D. Bottom: *Low Ryder,* 2008, Montclair, NJ, cherry, ebonized ash, and maple, 24"H x 72"W x 19"D. Photographs: Don Jones.

FURNITURE & FLOOR COVERINGS

Bill Jacobs

W. T. Jacobs Inc. 3300 Meridian Avenue North #206, Seattle, WA 98103 TEL 206.854.6418
TEL 206.547.4011 FAX 206.547.4020 EMAIL wtjacobs@comcast.net WEB www.wtjacobsinc.com

Top left: Pedestal sink, 2008, Seattle residence, khaya, wenge, and camphor burl, 36"H x 36"W x 16"D. Top right: Entry table, 2008, 32"H x 48"W x 11"D. Bottom: Console table, 2008, Seattle residence, 30.5"H x 48"W x 12"D. Photographs: Michael Cole.

Lederer Studio Furniture

Thomas F. Lederer   24059 West Main Street, Columbus, NJ 08022   TEL 609.324.0900
FAX 609.499.4339   EMAIL tom@ledererstudiofurniture.com   WEB www.ledererstudiofurniture.com

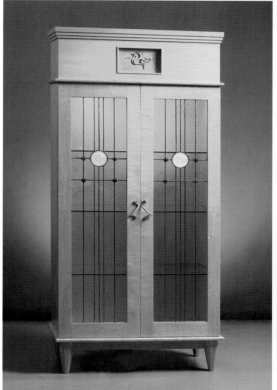

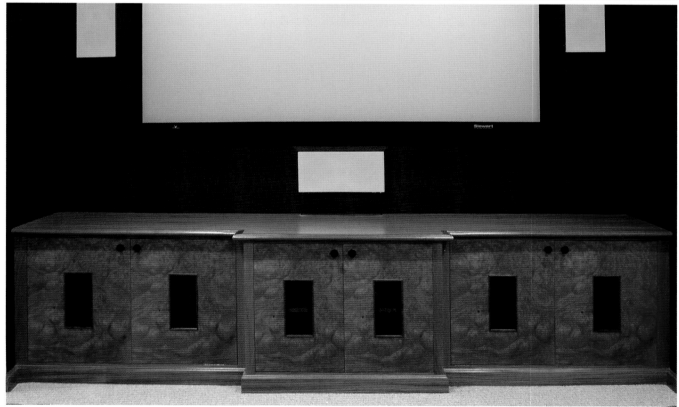

Top left: *Water Lily Cabinet,* 2006, maple, bird's-eye maple, English limewood, and leaded glass with etched rondels, 81"H x 36"W x 18"D, leaded glass by Hecter Studio/Artglass, Frenchtown, NJ. Photograph: Taylor Photographics, Inc. Top right: *Sculpted Swiss Pear Table,* 2008, Swiss pear and curly maple, 32"H x 27.5"W x 16"D. Photograph: Taylor Photographics, Inc. Bottom: *Home Theater Breakfront Credenza,* 2008, mahogany, Pelin burl, black walnut, and white maple, 25"H x 103"W x 24"D.

FURNITURE & FLOOR COVERINGS

Mark S. Levin

Levin Studio   PO Box 109, San Jose, NM 87565-0109   TEL 575.421.3207
FAX 888.672.7357   EMAIL markslevin@yahoo.com   WEB www.marklevin.com

Top: *Sun Valley Leaf Hall Table*, 2007, cherry, 31"H x 54"W x 29"D.
Bottom: *Apple Coffee Table*, 2008, cherry and cocobolo, 16"H x 48"W x 41"D. Photographs: Margot Geist.

FURNITURE & FLOOR COVERINGS

Bill Masterpool

La Bella Ferro Designs, LLC   PO Box 745, Fallon, NV 89407   TEL 775.423.7402
FAX 775.423.1905   EMAIL wmasterpool@charter.net

Top: Coffee table, 2005, forged steel and granite, 17"H x 49"W x 35"D. Bottom: *Occasionable Table,* 2007, forged steel and marble, 25"H x 28" DIA. Photographs: Jeff Ross Photography.

Red Iron Studio

Michael Route   114 Wisconsin Avenue North, Frederic, WI 54837   TEL 715.371.0034
EMAIL mike@redironstudios.com   WEB www.redironstudios.com

106

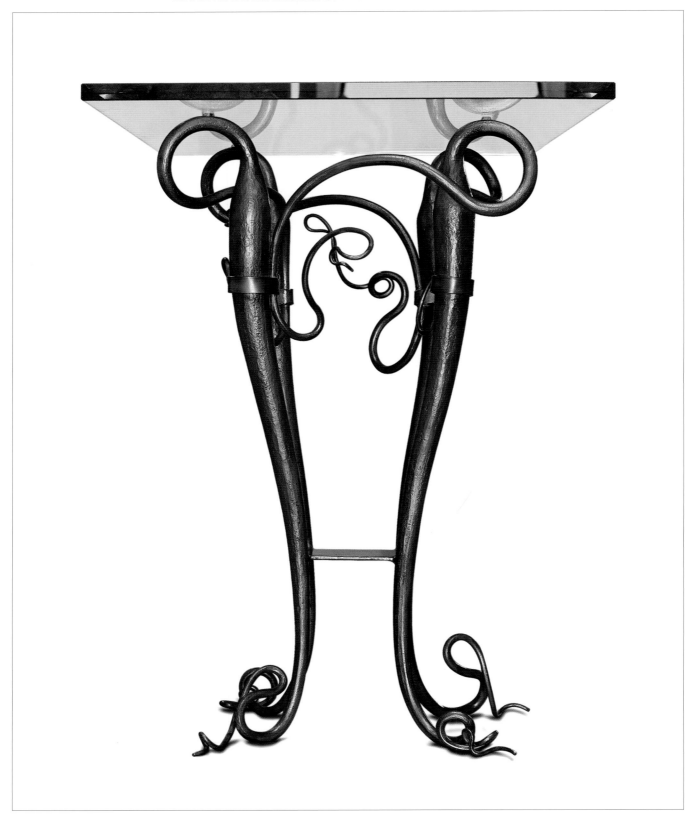

Entry table, 2008, forged steel and glass, 29" x 20" x 20".

Jeff Soderbergh

Jeff Soderbergh Furniture/Sculpture/Design   PO Box 3362, Newport, RI 02840
TEL/FAX 401.845.9087   EMAIL info@reflectart.com   WEB www.jeffsoderbergh.com

Top: *Dublin Bed,* church window *circa* 1875, Dublin, Ireland, leaded Japanese water glass, walnut and antique iron fence scrolls, king size, 66"H. Photograph: Dave Hansen. Bottom left: *Steel Tea House,* Victorian heat register *circa* 1880, Mystic, CT, Vermont cherry legs and jatoba rails, 22"H x 36"W x 32"D. Photograph: Dave Hansen. Bottom right: *Anne Black,* spruce blacksmith sign cornice *circa* 1735, Chestnut Hill, PA, Vermont maple legs, 33"H x 40"W x 21"D. Photograph: Bill Durvin.

FURNITURE & FLOOR COVERINGS

Stephen T. Anderson, Ltd.

Stephen T. Anderson   1071 First Avenue Suite 2S-2N, New York, NY 10022   TEL 212.319.0815
FAX 212.980.5453   EMAIL standerson21@earthlink.net   WEB www.stephentanderson.com

108

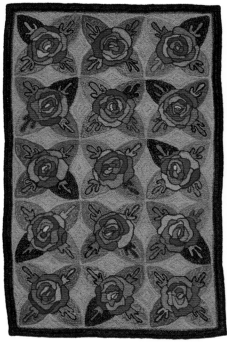

Fine Hand-Hooked Rugs Made In America
Top: *Mariposa Blue Rug,* hand-hooked rug, 35" x 82". Bottom left: *Red Roses Rug,* hand-hooked rug, 62" x 39".
Bottom center: *Faux Oriental Rug,* hand-hooked rug, 88" x 50". Bottom right: *Agate Rug,* hand-hooked rug, 75" x 48".

FURNITURE & FLOOR COVERINGS

John C. Sterling

J.C. Sterling Woodworking   3855 Creek Road, Millmont, PA 17845   TEL 570.922.1608
EMAIL jsterl@dejazzd.com   WEB www.jcsterling.com

Top: *Shibui Coffee Table*, black walnut.
Bottom: *Davis Road Sideboard*, cherry.

David Stine

David Stine Woodworking   16376 Bartlett Road, Dow, IL 62022   TEL 618.954.8636
EMAIL dave@stinewoodworking.com   WEB www.stinewoodworking.com

Top left: *Symes Table*, 2008, St. Louis, MO, black cherry and black walnut, 25"H x 24"W x 24"D. Top right: *Gallery Bench,* 2008, black walnut and white oak, 18"H x 48"W x 30"D. Bottom: *Strawn Table,* 2008, Chicago, IL, sycamore, 120"W x 48"D. Photographs: Tory Rae.

Bilhenry Walker

Bilhenry Gallery   4038 North Sixth Street, Milwaukee, WI 53212   TEL 414.332.2509
FAX 414.332.2524   EMAIL bilhenry@execpc.com   WEB www.bilhenrygallery.com

111

Top left: *Diamond Spine Armchair*, 2008, aircraft aluminum frame with carved aluminum arms, carved foam cushions, and pebble-steel vinyl, 45" x 23" x 23".
Top right: *Starship Sofa Chair*, 2008, aircraft aluminum frame with stainless ball feet, carved foam cushion, pebble-steel vinyl, and eight-way tie springs.
Bottom: *Tornado Table I*, 2008, special aluminum extrusion and stainless fasteners with ½" plate glass, 30"H x 42"-60"DIA.

FURNITURE & FLOOR COVERINGS

Timothy White

Spellbound Furniture Works   337 Buckley Drive #3, PO Box 2215, Crested Butte, CO 81224
TEL 970.349.7292   EMAIL spellboundfurniture@mindspring.com   WEB www.timothywhitefurniture.com

Libeskind, 2007, cherry, ebonized poplar and stainless steel, 30.25" x 36" x 13.75".
Burly, 2007, bigleaf maple burl and claro walnut, 32" x 36" x 16".

FURNITURE & FLOOR COVERINGS

William Wells Studio

William Wells   5531 Ellis Road, Ypsilanti, MI 48197   TEL 734.528.0405
TEL 734.646.5247   EMAIL billandjoann.wells@gmail.com   WEBwww.williamwellsfurniture.com

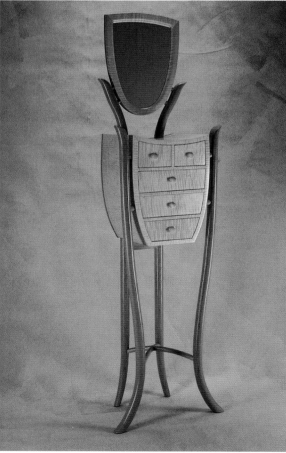

Top: Walnut/walnut burl coffee table, 2006, Chicago, 18"H x 50"W x 30"D. Bottom left: Ebonized cherry quilted maple table (detail), 2003, 32"H x 52"W x 12"D. Bottom right: Curly maple and white oak standing jewelry cabinet, 2002, 70"H x 18"W x 11"D. Photographs: JoAnn Wells.

Kevin Heram

Heram Custom Woodworking   W7840 County Road ZN, Onalaska, WI 54650   TEL 608.781.1867
FAX 608.781.5633   EMAIL kevin@heramcw.com   WEB www.heramcw.com

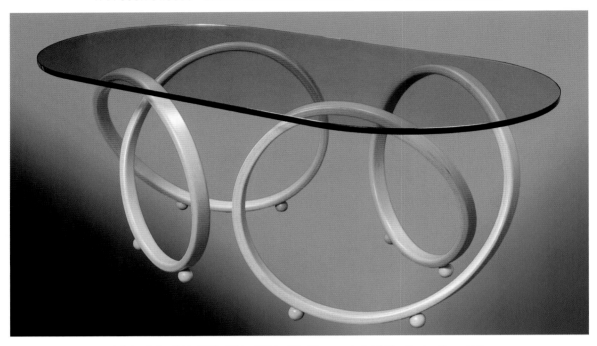

Infinity Coffee Table, 2008, 18"H x 24"W x 48"L. Photograph: Publishing Design Group LLC.

Vincent T. Leman

Dust Furniture   456 South Campbell Street Suite C, Valparaiso, IN 46385   TEL 219.464.9100   TEL 219.309.9990
FAX 866.208.2591   EMAIL vincent@vincentleman.com   WEB www.vincentleman.com

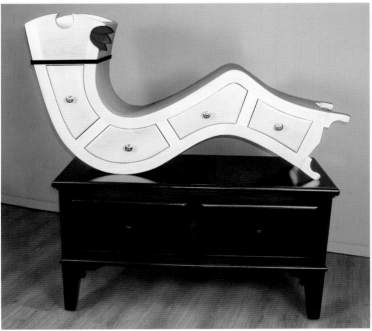

Left: *Olympia,* 2003, private collection, birch, 54"H x 56"W x 22"D.
Right: *Cabinet No. 2,* 2004, private collection, dyed and glazed oak, 80"H x 32"W x 17"D.

Joseph Murphy

Joseph Murphy Furniture Maker   1201 Chrisland Court, Annapolis, MD 21403   TEL 443.482.9240
EMAIL info@josephmurphy.net   WEB www.josephmurphy.net

Left: *Little Demon Bench,* 2007, walnut and ebony, 29"H x 36"W x 25.5"D.
Right: *A Door and Two Drawers,* 2008, curly walnut, Douglas fir, ebonized walnut, ebony, and pear, 24"H x 7"W x 5.5"D.

Leslie Webb

Leslie Webb, LLC   4732 Stenton Avenue, Philadelphia, PA 19144   TEL 215.704.2595
EMAIL leslie@lewebb.com   WEB www.lewebb.com

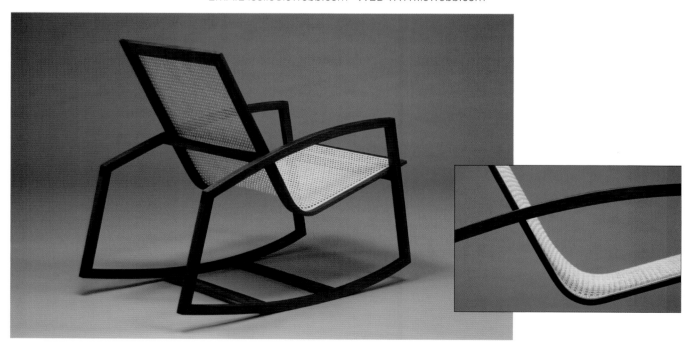

Linda Lou Rocker, 2007, black walnut and rattan, 33"H x 22.5"W x 36"D. Inset: *Linda Lou Rocker* (detail).

FURNITURE & FLOOR COVERINGS

Lighting

Beeline Studio LLC

Deborah A. Bruns-Thomas   1007 Blue School Road, Perkasie, PA 18944   TEL 215.527.5586
EMAIL deborah@beelinestudio.net   WEB www.beelinestudio.net

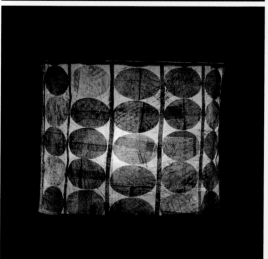

Dickinson Designs

Anne Dickinson   The Fire Works Studios, 38 Harlow Street, Worcester, MA 01605
TEL 508.451.7988   FAX 501.694.5230   EMAIL anne@dickinson-designs.com   WEB www.dickinson-designs.com

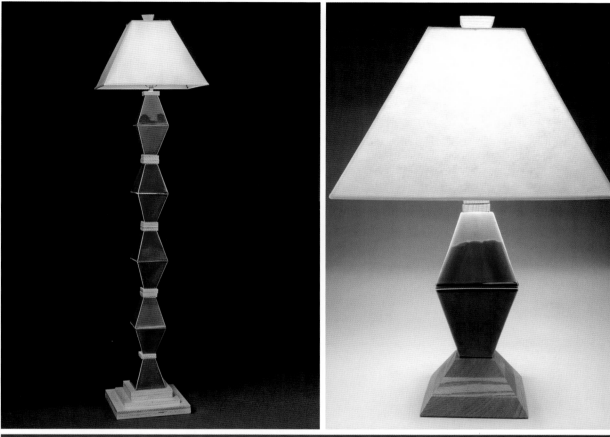

Top left: *Edgar Floor Lamp,* 2007, porcelain and wood, 65"H x 15"W x 15"D. Photograph: Bob Barrett.
Top right: *Webster Square Lamp,* 2008, porcelain and wood, 26"H x 15"W x 15"D.
Bottom: Coffee table, 2008, porcelain, wood, and glass, 16"H x 48"W x 24"D on a 26"W x 16"D base. Photograph: Steve Briggs.

Eccentric Luxuries

Crystal Brooke McCann and Brandon Fenninger   845 West Fulton Market #213, Chicago, IL 60607
TEL 608.201.0493   EMAIL crystal@artbohemian.com   WEB www.eccentricluxuries.com

Lightboxes, 2008, Merchandise Mart, Chicago, IL, handmade paper, organic materials, and custom woodworking, each 6'H x 3'W. Photograph: Larry Teckman.

LIGHTING

Illuminata

Julie Conway   TEL 402.558.1150
EMAIL info@illuminataglass.com   WEB www.illuminataglass.com

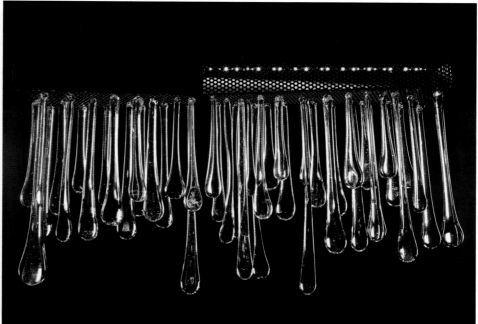

Left: *Incalmo Spirale Chandelier*, 2008, blown glass, steel, and LED lighting, 48"H x 22"W.
Right: *Pioggia (Rain)*, 2008, sculpted glass, steel, and LED lighting, 26"H x 38"W x 7"D. Photographs: Scott Drickey.

Furniture, Floor Coverings & Lighting: Common Terms and Their Meanings

Burl A dome-shaped growth on the trunk of a tree. Intricately patterened burl wood is often used by wood turners and furniture makers.

Forged A blacksmithing technique in which metal is shaped by hammering, usually while at red or white heat.

Inlay A decorating technique in which an object is incised with a design, a colorant is pressed into the incision, and the surface is then scraped to confine the colored inlay to the incisions.

Laminate A thin material such as wood or plastic that is affixed to the exterior of a cabinet or other surface.

Patina A surface coloring, usually brown or green, produced by oxidation of bronze, copper, or other metal. Patinas occur naturally and are also produced artificially for decorative effect.

Pommele A wood term used in conjunction with wood names; the term means figure, which is the pattern produced in a wood surface by annual growth rings, rays, knots, deviations from natural grain such as interlocked and wavy grain, and irregular coloration.

Quilted Wood A section of hardwood (e.g., maple, bubinga, cherry) with an elaborately figured grain.

Weft The set of strips of cloth or yarns perpendicular to the selvage; the horizontal or crosswise elements of a woven construction; also called filling, picks, and woof.

QUILTED WOOD

Ebonized cherry quilted maple table by Wiliam Wells Studio, see page 113. Photograph: JoAnn Wells.

LIGHTING

Liturgical Art

Erling Hope
Kirschling Studios, Inc.
Claude Riedel
Brigid Manning-Hamilton
Matteo Randi Mosaics

Erling Hope

Hope Liturgical Works   1455 Sag/Bridge Turnpike, Sag Harbor, NY 11963
TEL/FAX 631.725.4294   EMAIL hopelitwrk@aol.com

124

Kirschling Studios, Inc.

Kris Kirschling   850 Dousman Street, Green Bay, WI 54303   TEL 920.494.5757
FAX 920.494.4139   EMAIL kris@kirschlingstudios.com   WEB www.kirschlingstudios.com

Pentacost, 2006, Resurrection Church, Green Bay, WI, stained glass, 7.5'H x 7'W. Photograph: Image Studios.

LITURGICAL ART

Claude Riedel

5133 Bryant Avenue South, Minneapolis, MN 55419 TEL 612.805.2533
FAX 651.645.2439 EMAIL riede006@umn.edu WEB www.clauderiedelart.com

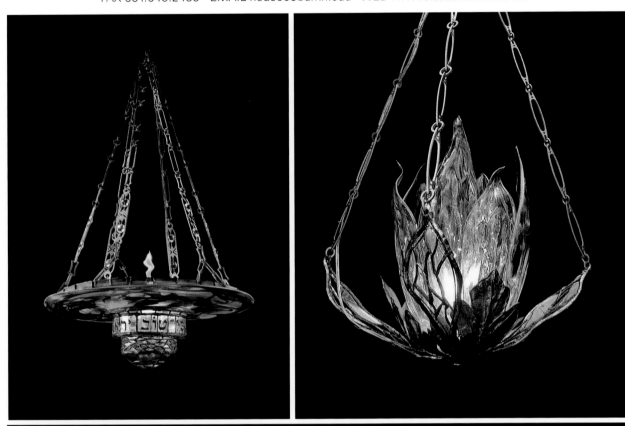

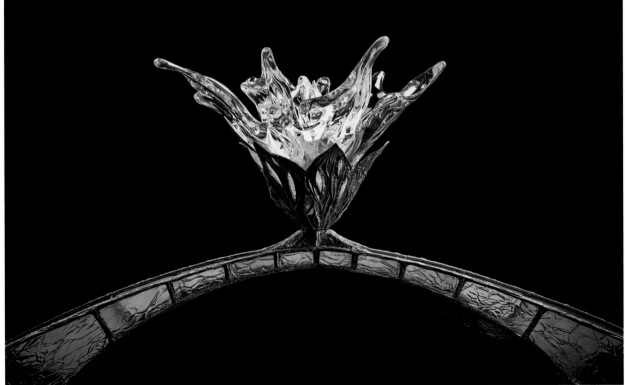

126

Top left: *Ner Tamid*, 2006, Young Israel of Lawrence of Cedarhurst, Long Island, NY, blown and leaded stained glass with copper metalwork, 30" x 18".
Top right: *Ner Tamid*, 2007, Temple Israel, Tallahassee, FL, blown and leaded stained glass with copper metalwork, 30" x 16". Photograph: Ted Wentink.
Bottom: *Ner Tamid*, 2008, Shaarei Tikvah Synagogue, Scarsdale, NY, blown and leaded stained glass with copper metalwork, 24" x 40". Photograph: Ted Wentink.

LITURGICAL ART

Brigid Manning-Hamilton

I.E. Textiles   1419 South 14th Street Suite 2, Lafayette, IN 47905   TEL 765.471.2956
TEL 317.918.1123   EMAIL ietextiles@comcast.net   WEB www.ietextiles.com

Left: *Tree of Life,* 2005, Sand Creek School, Fishers, IN, mixed textiles and copper, 57" x 17"x 6". Right: *Tree of Life* (detail).

Matteo Randi Mosaics

Matteo Randi   1901 South Ives Street, Arlington, VA 22202   TEL 703.892.4783
TEL 440.552.4737   EMAIL info@matteorandimosaics.com   WEB www.matteorandimosaics.com

Left: Baptistry, 1996, Church of Saints Peter and Paul, Ferrara, Italy, mosaic, 6' x 8'.
Right: *Star (Galla Placidia),* 2007, mosaic, 12" x 12".

Anne Oshman Mosaics

Anne Oshman   71 Stonebridge Road, Montclair, NJ 07042   TEL 973.222.6937
EMAIL studio@anneoshman.com   WEB www.anneoshman.com

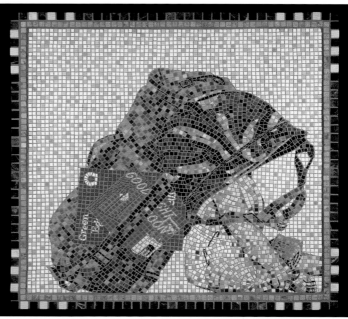

Left: *Stalagmite Series I,* 2008, stained glass mosaic, 33"–59" x 14.5"DIA. Photograph: Greg Leshe. Top right: *The Draft,* 2008, mosaic, 33" x 35". Photograph: John Fletcher. Bottom right: *Cupcake,* mosaic, 19" x 19" x 19". Photograph: Greg Leshe.

Bonnie Fitzgerald

Maverick Mosaics   145 Church Street NW, Vienna, VA 22180   TEL 703.938.1755
EMAIL contact@maverickmosaics.com   WEB www.maverickmosaics.com

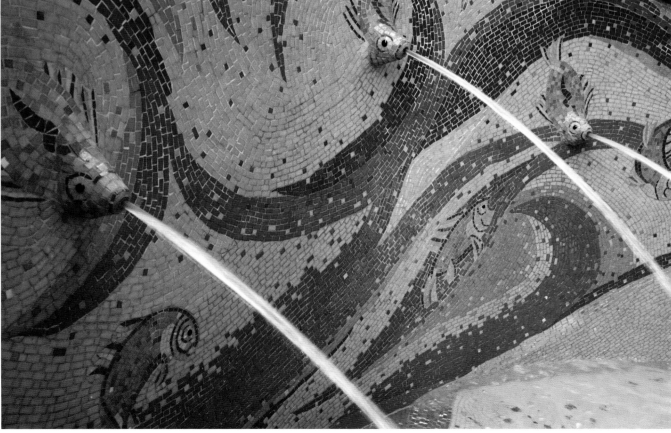

Top: *Wild Trout Stream,* 2007, Rockville Town Square, Rockville MD, mosaic, 7.5'H x 14.5' W.
Bottom: *Wild Trout Stream* (detail). Photographs: Mike Barolet.

Gasch Design

Michael Gasch   1649 Sunfield Street, Madison, WI 53704   TEL 608.469.7276
EMAIL mikeg@gaschdesign.com   WEB www.gaschdesign.com

Waterfalls, 2008, Madison, WI, stone and copper, 10' x 12'.

Suzan Germond

Major Mosaics Art Studio   1200 Lakeway Drive Suite 16, Austin, TX 78734
TEL 512.261.5767   EMAIL majormosaics@sbcglobal.net   WEB www.majormosaics.com

133

Left: *Roadside Blossom,* 2008, hubcap, safety glass, glass, beads, jewels, and found objects, 36" x 24". Photograph: Bruce McDonald.
Right: *Water the Flowers,* 2008, private collection, glass, tile, safety glass, and faucets, 36" x 24". Photograph: Thomas McConnell.

Rhonda Heisler

Rhonda Heisler Mosaic Art   8 Stone Mountain Court, Skillman, NJ 08558   TEL 609.466.2231
FAX 609.466.9043   EMAIL rhonda@rhondaheislermosaicart.com   WEB www.rhondaheislermosaicart.com

Encoded IV, 2008, stained glass mosaic, 33"H x 26"W. Photograph: Ross Stout.

Jolino Architectural Mosaics

Jolino Beserra   2121 Apex Avenue, Silver Lake, Los Angeles, CA 90039   TEL 323.660.3525   TEL 323.313.2181
FAX 323.660.1603   EMAIL jolinobyrd@roadrunner.com   WEB www.jolinoarchitecturalmosaics.com

Top: Young Adults Reading Room, 2007, Camarillo, CA, Public Library, pique-assiette mosaic, 20'H x 50'W.
Bottom: Children's Reading Room, 2008, Alhambra, CA, Public Library, pique-assiette mosaic, 10'H x 13'W x 2'D. Photographs: Don Saban.

Jonathan Mandell Designs Inc.

Jonathan Mandell   PO Box 392, Narberth, PA 19072   TEL 610.668.9909
FAX 610.668.9910   EMAIL fineartmosaics@aol.com   WEB www.jonathanmandell.com

Top: *Citizens Bank Park*, 2004, Citizens Bank Park, Philadelphia, PA, mosaic, 72"H x 96"W x 2"D.
Bottom: *Bethany Beach, DE, Scene*, 2008, mosaic, 24"H x 75"W x 3"D. Photographs: Lee Moskow.

Pinter Studio Inc.

Donna Pinter   480 Knollwoods Drive, Roswell, GA 30075   TEL 678.557.7871   TEL 770.992.4193
EMAIL donna@donnapinter.com   WEB www.pintermosaics.com   WEB www.donnapinter.com

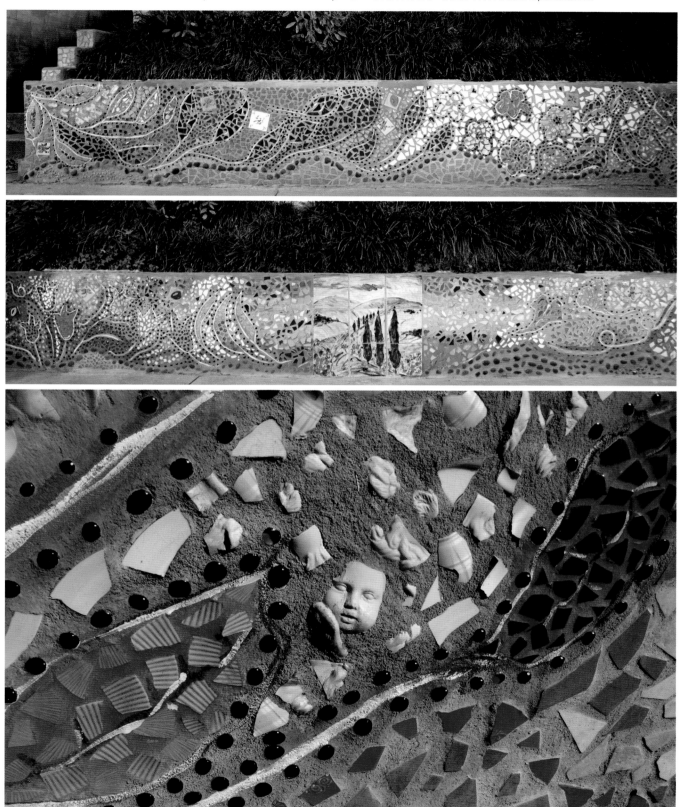

137

Top and center: *Symphony in Color,* 2008, Atlanta, GA, mosaic, 3' x 100'. Bottom: *Symphony in Color* (detail). Photographs: Dan Carmody at Studio 7.

Tesserae Mosaic Studio, Inc.

Shug Jones & Julie Dilling   1111 North Jupiter Road #108-A, Plano, TX 75074   TEL 972.578.9006   TEL 972.896.4619
FAX 972.423.6503   EMAIL info@tesseraemosaicstudio.com   WEB www.tesseraemosaicstudio.com

Top: *Turtle Grass*, stovetop backsplash, 2008, private residence, Reno, NV, glass mosaic, 30" x 50".
Bottom: *Healing Waters*, seven backlit hospital reception desk panels, 2007, each 2' x 2'.

Matteo Randi Mosaics

Matteo Randi   1901 South Ives Street, Arlington, VA 22202   TEL 703.892.4783
TEL 440.552.4737   EMAIL info@matteorandimosaics.com   WEB www.matteorandimosaics.com

Bassa Marea (Low Tide), 2008, mosaic, 16.5" x 50" . Inset: *Bassa Marea* (detail).

Showcase Mosaics

Carl and Sandra Bryant   1274 Thalen Drive, Lynden, WA 98264   TEL 360.927.5402
EMAIL info@showcasemosaics.com   WEB www.showcasemosaics.com

Sanctuary (detail), 2008, private commission, Lynden, WA, glass mosaic, 6' x 9'.

Murals, Tiles &

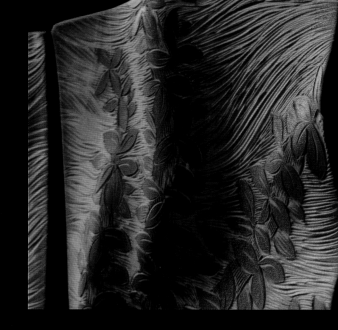

Wall Reliefs

Joy Colclough

Guild Sourcebooks at Work

Case Study #3

ARTIST: Karen Heyl
ARTWORK TITLE: *Oregon Wildlife* and *Oregon Sea Life*
MEDIA: Indiana limestone
SIZE: 52" x 52" each of twelve panels
INSTALLATION: Sacred Heart Medical Center, Eugene, OR

"I found Karen through *The Guild Sourcebook* —actually, an old one. I rely on The Guild Sourcebooks for absolutely the very highest quality work, regardless of medium. I have loved Karen's work for years and finally found a project that was perfect for her. Karen was fantastic to work with. This was an extremely complicated project requiring meticulous detail and coordination, which she provided in a seamless manner. The process could have not gone smoother!"

Kathy Hathorn, CEO and Creative Director
American Art Resources
www.americanartresources.com

"Sacred Heart Medical Center wanted artwork throughout the hospital to support a prescription for healing. Most of my projects are about nature, which is a healing force. The strength and beauty of the animals, and their ability to survive and endure, supports this message of healing.

"After researching the wildlife of Oregon, I submitted many designs, of which twelve were chosen by client, six representing sea life and six representing wildlife. Each of the twelve Indiana limestone panels was hand carved in my studio using an air hammer to power my chisels. The pieces were then finished using riffler files [for detail and smoothing].

"This commission was particularly rewarding because of its monumental size—it's one of my largest projects to date—and its high visibility at such a public venue. I was also pleased with the respect I was given as the artist, by both the client and the art consulting firm."

See more work by Karen Heyl on pages 152-153.

Susan Ahrend

Cottonwood Design   321 Saint Joseph Avenue, Long Beach, CA 90814   TEL 562.438.5230
EMAIL sue@cottonwoodtile.com   WEB www.cottonwoodtile.com

Left: *Sweet Lips,* 2008, Camp Aldersgate, Little Rock, AR, ceramic tile, 6' x 4'.
Top right: *Lily Pond,* 2008, residence, Long Beach, CA, ceramic tile, 18" x 30". Photograph: Jay Ahrend.
Bottom right: *Blue Tang,* 2008, Camp Aldersgate, Little Rock, AR, ceramic tile, 6' x 4'.

MURALS, TILES & WALL RELIEFS

Mary Lou Alberetti

Alberetti Studios   16 Possum Drive, New Fairfield, CT   TEL 203.746.1321
EMAIL mlalberetti@sbcglobal.net   WEB www.maryloualberetti.com

144

Top left: *Cuenca,* ceramic relief, 13" x 13" x 2". Top right: *Intrados,* ceramic relief, 15.5" x 14" x 2".
Bottom: *Chiarita,* ceramic relief, 18" x 25" x 2". Photographs: Bill Quinnell.

Mary Lou Alberetti

Alberetti Studios   16 Possum Drive, New Fairfield, CT   TEL 203.746.1321
EMAIL mlalberetti@sbcglobal.net   WEB www.maryloualberetti.com

Top left: *Blue Portal*, 2008, ceramic relief, 15"H x 14.5"W x 2"D. Top right: *Portal*, 2008, ceramic relief, 11.5"H x 11.5"W x 2"D.
Bottom: *Desert Wall*, 2008, ceramic relief, 16"H x 22"W x 2"D.

MURALS, TILES & WALL RELIEFS

BellFlower Design Studio

Rachel Tribble   350 NW Alice Avenue, Stuart, FL 34994   TEL 772.708.8400
EMAIL info@racheltribble.com   WEB www.racheltribble.com

Nature Fine Art Tiles, 2008, 6" x 6" and 10" x 8".

BellFlower Design Studio

Rachel Tribble   350 NW Alice Avenue, Stuart, FL 34994   TEL 772.708.8400
EMAIL info@racheltribble.com   WEB www.racheltribble.com

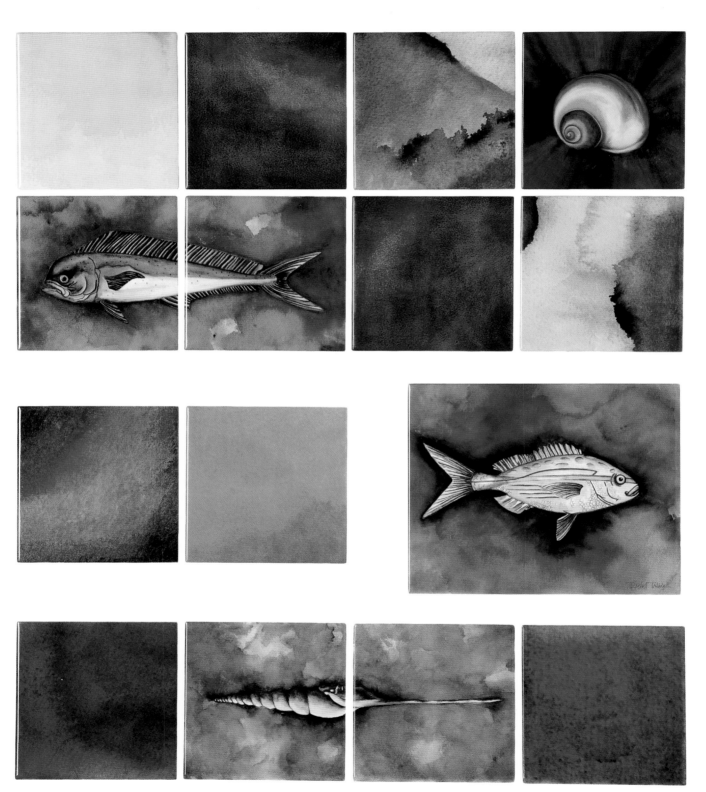

Nautical Fine Art Tiles, 2008, 6" x 6" and 10" x 8".

Bruce Middleton and Co.

Bruce Middleton   222 Tettemer Avenue, Hamilton, NJ 08610   TEL 609.585.3167
TEL 609.505.2202   EMAIL bruce@brucemiddleton.com   WEB www.brucemiddleton.com

148

Top: Empire Room deco wall, 2007, The Merion, Cinnaminson, NJ, mixed media, 15' x 26'.
Bottom: Empire Room deco bar, 2007, rosewood, aluminum, poplar, and fiberglass, 12' x 18'.

MURALS, TILES & WALL RELIEFS

ClayGal

Rafik and Naira Barseghian   10600 Sable Avenue, Sunland, CA 91040   TEL 818.353.1687
FAX 818.353.4803   EMAIL naira@claygal.com   WEB www.claygal.com

Left: *Piano*, ceramic, 50" x 40". Top right: *Path*, ceramic, 32" x 24". Bottom right: *Sunset*, ceramic, 26" x 19".

MURALS, TILES & WALL RELIEFS

Lester Coloma

303-325 James Street South, Hamilton, ON L8P 3B7, Canada   TEL 416.712.2722
FAX 905.540.4679   EMAIL info@lestercoloma.com   WEB www.lestercoloma.com

150

Interior retail mural (detail), Whole Foods, FL, acrylic on canvas, 3' x 40'. Photograph: Roy Tim.
Interior retail mural (detail), Whole Foods, Oakville, ON, acrylic on canvas, 3' x 40'. Photograph: Robert Lear.

MURALS, TILES & WALL RELIEFS

Christopher Gryder

4323 Toddsbury Drive, Vinton, VA 24179   TEL 540.797.4687
EMAIL chris@chrisgryder.com   WEB www.chrisgryder.com

Top: *Big Bang,* 2008, ceramic relief tiles, 38" x 51" x 2".
Bottom: *Tamalpais,* 2008, ceramic relief tiles, 38" x 90" x 2".

MURALS, TILES & WALL RELIEFS

Karen Heyl

1310 Pendleton Street, Cincinnati, OH 45202   907 Sonia Place, Escondido, CA   92026
TEL 513.421.9791   TEL 760.489.7106   EMAIL klheyl@aol.com   WEB www.karenheyl.com

152

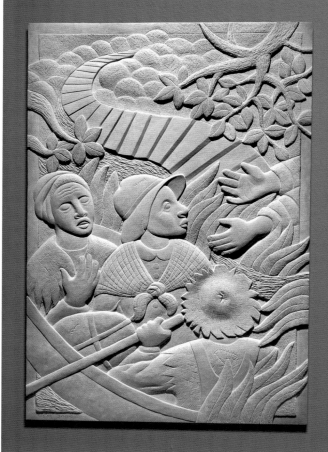 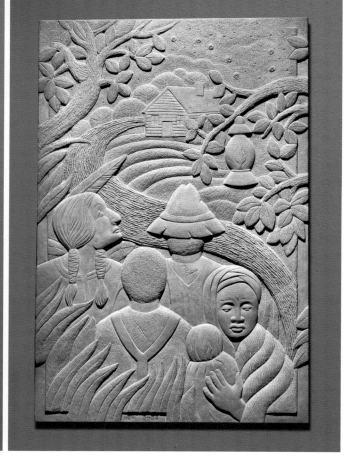

Top: *Flight to Freedom,* 2004, National Underground Railroad Freedom Center, Cincinnati, OH, Indiana limestone, six panels, 43'L.
Bottom left and right: *Flight to Freedom,* two of six panels. Photographs: Charles Behlow.

Karen Heyl

1310 Pendleton Street, Cincinnati, OH 45202   907 Sonia Place, Escondido, CA   92026
TEL 513.421.9791   TEL 760.489.7106   EMAIL klheyl@aol.com   WEB www.karenheyl.com

Top: *Family Care,* 2008, Caresource Corporate Headquarters, Dayton, OH, limestone, 36"H x 18" x 3".
Bottom: *Family Care* (details). Photographs: Charles Behlow Photography.

MURALS, TILES & WALL RELIEFS

Richard Houston

610 Experiment Station Road, Medford, OR 97501   TEL 541.245.8500
EMAIL rhousto200@earthlink.net   WEB www.richardhoustonart.com

154

Top: *A Higher Vision,* multi-layered mural with metal sculptures, 19'H. Bottom left: *Raindrops,* multi-layered mural with carved panels and sand-finish plaster castings. Bottom right: *Eternal Flame,* corner detail of a much larger multi-layered mural, 18'H.

Jensen & Marineau Ceramics

Barbara Jensen   22017 NW Beck Road, Portland, OR 97231   TEL 503.621.3487
EMAIL bjensen@jensenandmarineau.com   WEB jensenandmarineau.com

155

Top: *Undersea Bath*, 2000. Bottom: *Undersea Vanity,* 2000, residence, Portland, OR, ceramic tile and glaze, 2' x 5'.

Elizabeth MacDonald

PO Box 186, Bridgewater, CT 06752   TEL 860.354.0594
EMAIL epmacd@earthlink.net   WEB www.elizabethmacdonald.com

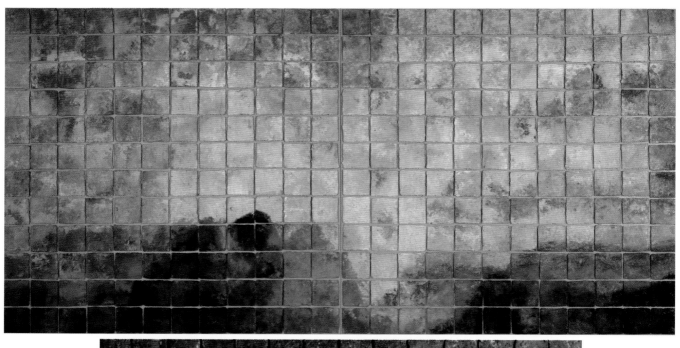

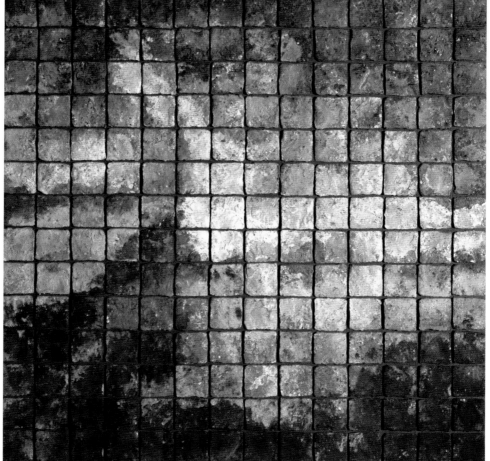

Top: *Sunset,* ceramic diptych, 42" x 84". Bottom: *After the Storm,* ceramic, 21" x 21".

Megan McKeithan

Visionary Mural Co.   923 Chattahoochee Circle, Roswell, GA 30075   TEL 404.310.9942
EMAIL megan@visionarymuralco.com   WEB www.visionarymuralco.com

Give it Time, 2006, Mindful Body Natural Healing Services, Roswell, GA, acrylic on canvas, 8' x 38'. Photograph: Dan Carmody, Studio 7.

musickstudio

Pat Musick   10 Studio Place, Colorado Springs, CO 80904   TEL 719.634.2405
EMAIL musickstudio@juno.com   WEB www.musickstudio.com

Top: *Infinite Nature* (detail); Bottom left: *Infinite Nature*, 1998, Mesa State College, Grand Junction, CO, enameling on copper, 10.25' x 23'.
Bottom right: *Canyon Lifeblood*, 2007, Grand Canyon National Park, AZ, etched and enameled copper with silver foil, 16" x 20".

MURALS, TILES & WALL RELIEFS

Natalie Blake Studios

Natalie Blake   74 Cotton Mill Hill A330, Brattleboro, VT 05301   TEL 802.254.9761
FAX 802.251.0303   EMAIL info@natalieblake.com   WEB www.natalieblake.com

Undulating Porcelain Tiles, (detail), each tile 12" x 12" or 14" x 14".
Eight possible points of hanging on a single hook. Twenty available colors. Photograph: Jeff Baird.

MURALS, TILES & WALL RELIEFS

Anthony Novak

Anthony Novak Studio   5010 Idaho Avenue, Nashville, TN 37209   TEL 615.385.4368
EMAIL info@tonynovakstudio.com   WEB www.anthonynovak.com

160

Top: *Vessel of Hope,* 2007, St. Thomas Hospital, Nashville, TN, hollow cast relief sculpture, 26" x 44".
Bottom: *The Good Samaritan,* 2005, Baptist Hospital, Nashville, TN, hollow cast relief sculpture, 27" x 44". Photographs: Jackson DeParis.

MURALS, TILES & WALL RELIEFS

T. S. Post

Sara Post   604 Barbera Place, Davis, CA 95616   TEL/FAX 530.758.9365
EMAIL tspostart@gmail.com   WEB www.tspost.com

Top left: *Lloyd's Farm,* 2008, ceramic collage, 24" x 24". Top right: *Urchin,* 2007, ceramic collage, 18" x 18".
Bottom left: *Leaves,* 2007, ceramic collage, 12" x 12". Bottom right: *Garden,* 2008, ceramic collage, 18" x 18". Photographs: Tomas Post.

Tile Surface Impressions

Randy Hopfer   6709 NE 232nd Avenue, Vancouver, WA 98682   TEL 360.944.6280
FAX 360.546.0122   EMAIL randy@surfaceimpressions.com   WEB www.surfaceimpressions.com

162

Top: *Lanikai Beach, Oahu*, 2008, private residence, Gresham, OR, photograph reproduced on glass tile, 84" x 108". Bottom left: *Koi Anyway*, 2008, watercolor painting reproduced on glass tile as moveable art, 60" x 48". Bottom right: *Tractor & Tulips*, 2008, photograph reproduced on tumbled stone tile, 30" x 42".

Sam Bates

1717 Swede Pass Road, Evans, WA 99126   TEL/FAX 509.684.8288
EMAIL sam@carvedstonebysambates.com   WEB www.carvedstonebysambates.com

Left: *Double Helix Celtic Cross* (detail), 2006, Providence Hospital, Centralia, WA, hand-carved stone, 6' x 4'.
Right: *Memory* (detail), 2008, private residence, Olympia, WA, hand-carved stone, 24" x 18".

Murals, Tiles & Wall Reliefs: Common Terms and Their Meanings

Hollow Casting   Pouring liquid clay slip into a hollow plaster mold to create a shell of a specific shape.

Pigment   Dry coloring matter used in making paint and ink. Pigments are not water soluble, but suspended in a vehicle; water-soluble colors are called dyes.

Raku   A technique of rapidly firing low-temperature ceramic ware. Raku firings were used traditionally in Japan to make bowls for tea ceremonies.

Saggar   1) Refractory container or fire-clay box in which pottery is stocked during firing for protection from direct flame; can be used routinely in wood-burning kilns. 2) A container for holding fuming materials such as metal oxides, chemical salts, and organic substances, that will act on the ware in the saggar during the fire.

Sgraffito   A decorative process. A line is scratched through a layer of slip or glaze before firing to expose the clay underneath. From the Italian meaning "to scratch."

Slip Casting   A process of forming a clay object by pouring clay slip into a hollow plaster mold.

Trompe L'oeil   Literally, "fool the eye" (French). An object or scene rendered so realistically that the viewer believes they are seeing the real thing.

Wax Resist   Wax emulsion or melted wax is used to create patterns on ceramics. The wax is painted onto unfired ceramic ware to keep those pattern areas from being covered in slip or glaze. Next, the piece is painted with slip or glaze and then fired. The firing melts the wax and reveals the unfired clay beneath it.

PIGMENT

Willows by Elizabeth MacDonald, see page 156. Photograph: Nathaniel Cardonsky.

Objects

Michael Allison
Ronald R. Franklin
Glassics
Carol Green
Jennifer C. McCurdy
Carl Radke
Ron Cook Studios
Mia Tyson

Michael Allison

Wood Turned Art   549 Gurleyville Road, Storrs, CT 06268   TEL 860.429.3490
EMAIL michael.allison@snet.net   WEB www.michaelallison.us

Top left: Hollow form ash vessel with pierced finial, 2007, turned wood, 13.5"H x 10"W. Top right: Pierced ash vase, 2008, turned wood, 10"H x 10"W. Bottom: Natural-edge ash bowl, 2006, turned wood, 7"H x 16"W.

Ronald R. Franklin

Atelier Du Lac Ltd.   5338 Orange Grove Road, Hillsborough, NC 27278
TEL/FAX 919.929.6185   EMAIL atelierdulac@hotmail.com   WEB www.atelierdulac.com

Left: *Ascension*, 2006, 17" x 6.5" x 6.5". Top right: *Lineage*, 2007, raku clay, 14" x 10.75" x 10.75".
Bottom right: *Fire Speak*, 2006, raku clay, 15.5" x 10" x 10".

Glassics

Sherry Salito-Forsen   204 Avenida Sierra, San Clemente, CA 92672   TEL 949.498.6489
EMAIL glassics1@cox.net   WEB www.glassicsart.com

Top left: *Horizon*, 2008, glass, 26" x 23"W. Top right: *Wabi Sabi*, 2008, fused glass, black walnut, and copper, 29" x 22".
Bottom: *Trinity*, 2008, fused glass with curly maple, 26" x 33". Photographs: Rick Lang.

Carol Green

Carol Green Studio   Elburn, IL   TEL 630.365.1238   FAX 630.365.1337
EMAIL carol@carolgreen.com   WEB www.carolgreen.com

169

Top left: *Candle Branch Pair,* cast bronze and patina, 3.5" x 7" x 1.5" and 3" x 6" x 3". Top right: *Gourd with Double Wandering Vine,*
wheel-thrown mica-impregnated earthenware, copper, and cast bronze with patina, 11" x 11" x 11".
Bottom: *Triple Candle Branch II,* cast bronze and patina, 3" x 13" x 11".

Jennifer C. McCurdy

PO Box 138, Vineyard Haven, MA 02568   TEL 508.627.0443
FAX 508.696.0262   EMAIL jen@jennifermccurdy.com   WEB www.jennifermccurdy.com

Contour Floor Vase, terra cotta with metallic black glaze, 23"H x 18"DIA.
Contour Eggs, porcelain, 4"H x 3"DIA. and 8"H x 6"DIA.

Carl Radke

Phoenix Studios   PO Box 1474, Templeton, CA 93465   TEL/FAX 805.462.8893
EMAIL carl@carlradke.com   WEB www.carlradke.com

Cherry Blossom Lamp, Tall Cherry Blossom Vase, and *Cherry Blossom Lidded Jar,* 2008, glass,
lamp: 20" x 11"; vase: 12" x 5.5"; jar: 8.5" x 7". Photograph: Dan Mayor.

Ron Cook Studios

Ron Cook   147 Sacramento Avenue, Santa Cruz, CA 95060   TEL 831.425.4933
EMAIL ron@roncookstudios.com   WEB www.roncookstudios.com

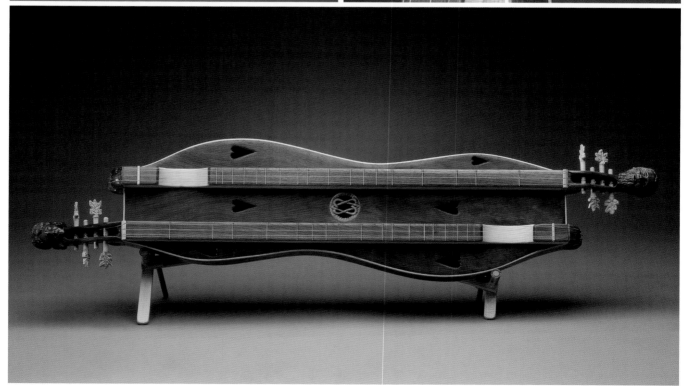

Top left: *London Bridge Pianoforte*, 2008, wood, 28" x 18" x 12". Top right: *Mountain Dulcimer: The Gryphon* (detail), 2006, wood, 34" x 6" x 3". Bottom: *Courting Dulcimer*, 2007, wood, 13" x 40" x 3". Photographs: Paul Schraub.

Mia Tyson

11002 Dogleg Trace, Tega Cay, SC 29708   TEL/FAX 803.548.4534
TEL 704.293.8183   EMAIL mia.tyson@miatyson.com   WEB www.miatyson.com

Top left: *Masks*, 2008, Hotel Palomar, Atlanta, GA, one-of-a-kind original drawings hand built with porcelain clay, each 8"H x 6"W x 2.5"D.
Top right: *Swan Dance*, 2008, Retirement Resort, Plano, TX, one-of-a-kind original drawing hand built with porcelain clay, 26"H x 18"W x 7"D.
Bottom: *Couple*, 2008, 13"H x 20"W x 6"D. Photographs: Arrow Photography.

Paintings &

Art and Soul
Carl Borgia
Ursula J. Brenner
Fran Bull
Betty Butler
Carina
Diana Zoe Coop
Jesse Corning
Barbara De Pirro
Lori Feldpausch
Cheri Freund
Deborah Garber
Katherine Greene

Carol Griffin
Mary Hatch
Yoshi Hayashi
Stephen Henning
Douglas Hyslop
Nicolette Jelen
Randy Johnson
Scott Kahn
Shelby Keefe
Ken Roth Studio
Anne Kessler
Al Lachman
Marlene Lenker

Prints

Art and Soul

Giorgio Tuscani   11947 Iredell Street, Studio City, CA 91604   TEL 818.754.1178   TEL 310.779.4297
FAX 818.754.1187   EMAIL giorgiotuscani@gmail.com   WEB www.giorgiotuscaniart.com

176

Top left: *My Soul Seeks for What My Heart Lost,* 2008, oil on canvas, 56" x 30". Top right: *Love and Only Love Can Make my Soul Take Flight,* 2008,

Carl Borgia

Carl Borgia Fine Art 5186 Brian Boulevard, Boynton Beach, FL 33472 TEL 561.738.0128
EMAIL carlborgia@gmail.com WEB www.carlborgia.com

177

Venetian Sun, giclée print of an original oil painting, custom sizes.

Ursula J. Brenner

Ursula J. Brenner Fine Art Inc.   948 Butterfly Court, Cincinnati, OH 45231-5801   TEL 513.300.9997
FAX 513.521.0584   EMAIL ujbrenner@fuse.net   WEB www.ursulabrenner.com

178

Top: *Distant Trees*, 2008, painting on canvas, 24" x 60". Bottom: *Nowhere to Go*, 2008, painting on canvas, 36" x 60". Photographs: Robin Imaging.

Fran Bull

Fran Bull Studio   PO Box 401, Brandon, VT 05733   TEL 802.558.8609
EMAIL franbull@franbull.com   WEB www.franbull.com

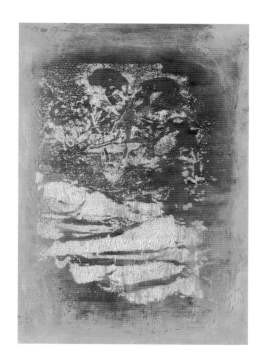

Top left: *Season of Bones: The Keys Have Bled Their Rust,* 2008. Top right: *Season of Bones: Winter,* 2008. Bottom left: *Season of Bones: Autumn,* 2008.
Bottom right: *Season of Bones: Before the Mind Drops its Curtain,* 2008. Copperplate and mixed-media etchings, each 47.75" x 31.5". Photographs: Michael Heeney.

PAINTINGS & PRINTS

Betty Butler

Chicago, IL   TEL 847.347.3144   EMAIL responsiveart@comcast.net   WEB www.responsiveart.com

Edgy Tulips, 2008, acrylic on canvas, 24" x 30".

Betty Butler

Chicago, IL   TEL 847.347.3144   EMAIL responsiveart@comcast.net   WEB www.responsiveart.com

Top: *Yellow Bud,* 2008, acrylic on canvas, 24" x 30". Bottom: *Abstract Garden,* 2008, acrylic on canvas, 30" x 40".

PAINTINGS & PRINTS

Carina

Carine Mascarelli   9314 Matterhorn Court, Reno, NV 89506   TEL 775.240.6312
EMAIL carina@carina-art.com   WEB www.carina-art.com

182

Top left: *Sundance,* 2006, oil painting, 48" x 36". Top right: *Tahoe Steps,* 2007, oil painting, 48" x 36".
Bottom: *Sol en Alma,* 2008, oil painting, 36" x 60".

Diana Zoe Coop

Island Studio   1551 Duranleau Street, Granville Island, Vancouver, BC, V6H 3S3, Canada   TEL 604.669.1551
TEL 604.671.7577   EMAIL dianazoecoop@shaw.ca   WEB www.dianazoecoop.com

183

Japanese Garden Triptych, 2008, Drs. Braverman and Walter, oral surgeons, Vancouver,
Canada, acrylic on canvas, 38" x 76". Photographs: Stephen D. Mitchell.

PAINTINGS & PRINTS

Jesse Corning

13603 Sablerun Lane, Houston, TX 77014   TEL 281.586.0870
EMAIL jessecorning@sbcglobal.net   WEB www.jessecorning.com

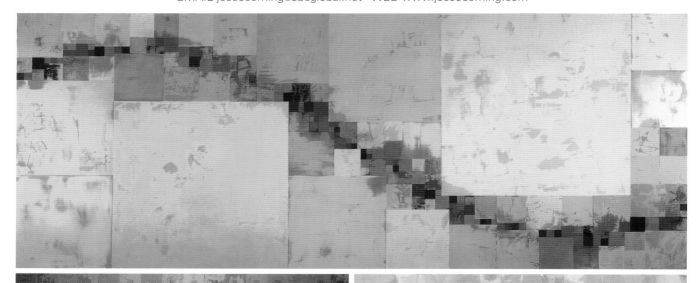

184

Top: *Square Root of the Curve,* 2005, mixed media, 38" x 96". Bottom left: *Promise,* 2005, mixed media, 48" x 32".
Bottom right: *Going with the Flow,* 2004, mixed media, 48" x 32". Print editions of select paintings available.

Barbara De Pirro

Tacoma, WA   TEL 360.426.6899   EMAIL depirro@earthlink.net   WEB www.depirro.com

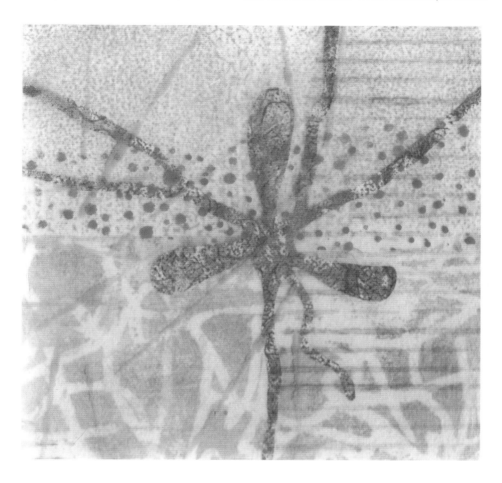

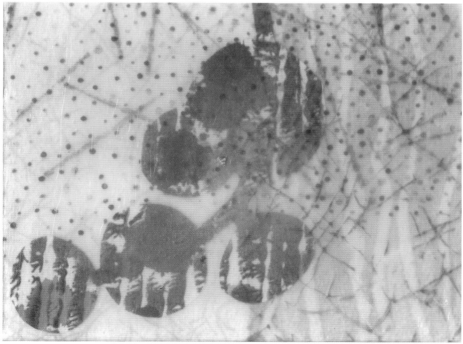

Top: *Reveal – Conceal 1*, 2008, acrylic. Bottom: *Reveal – Conceal 7*, 2008, acrylic.

Lori Feldpausch

Stuart Lake Studio   1207 Orchard Drive, Marshall, MI 49068   TEL 269.781.7794
EMAIL lori_feldpausch@mac.com   WEB www.lorifeldpausch.com

186

Top: *Ausable River*, 2008, oil on linen board, 12"x 14". Bottom left: *Autumn Aspens*, 2008, oil on linen board, 16" x 12".
Bottom right: *Moonlight Path*, 2008, oil on linen board, 16" x 12". Photographs: Conway Photography.

Cheri Freund

Pixel Artist   2207 Napa Trail, Waukesha, WI 53188-4733   TEL 206.850.0610
EMAIL cheri@pixel-artist.com   WEB www.pixel-artist.com

Top: *Tulips*, 24" x 36". Bottom left: *Autumn Branch*, 30" x 30". Bottom right: *Pink Whisper*, 30" x 30".

Deborah Garber

1105 G Street, Petaluma, CA 94952   TEL 707.769.8709
EMAIL dg@deborahgarber.com   WEB www.deborahgarber.com

188

Top: *Sun-Washed Village*, pastel, 2008, 14" x 24". Bottom: *A Different Season*, 2008, pastel, 17.5" x 24".
Many works also available as limited-edition giclée prints.

Katherine Greene

PO Box 1393, Sonoma, CA 95476 TEL 707.935.8912
EMAIL art@katherinegreene.net WEB www.katherinegreene.net

Top: *Seville,* 2008, acrylic on canvas, 30" x 48".
Bottom: *Go Between,* 2008, acrylic on canvas, 30" x 48". Photographs: Chris Berggren, Sonoma, CA.

PAINTINGS & PRINTS

Al Mida

Guild Sourcebooks at Work

Case Study #4

ARTIST: Daniel Sroka
ARTWORK TITLE: *Botanical Abstracts* series
MEDIA: Photographs
SIZE: 20" x 30" to 45" x 30"
INSTALLATION: Miraval Luxury Resort and Spa, Tucson, AZ

190

"I found Daniel in *The Guild Sourcebook*, which I've been using for the last four years. The Sourcebook is a great resource for researching artists, and the response of the artist is professional and quick. Working with Daniel has been a wonderful experience and very professional."

Kim Roseman, Art Consultant
Karin Newby Gallery & Sculpture Garden
www.NewbyGallery.com

"These photographs are from my *Botanical Abstracts* collection, where I explore the wild and unpredictable nature of the most common objects of nature: leaves, flowers, sticks, and seeds. Each photograph attempts to encourage us to see past our easy assumptions about what nature is and experience the wildness that actually exists all around us.

"Each photograph in this series is a pigment print, made on canvas, and gallery wrapped to provide a seamless image. The client had a large empty wall in the lobby of his high-end spa that he wanted to fill, so I custom sized each print to best fill the space and create an uninterrupted visual flow.

"My photography is about re-experiencing the natural world and reconnecting with things that we tend to overlook. I feel that it is perfectly suited for the contemplative and regenerative atmosphere of a resort and spa like Miraval. The client, gallery owner, and I worked together to select a series of photographs that we felt would enhance the contemplative mood of the space."

See more work by Daniel Sroka on page 90.

Carol Griffin

185 East 85th Street #17L, New York, NY 10028   TEL 917.570.6539
FAX 212.534.2293   EMAIL ggriffin2@nyc.rr.com   WEB web.mac.com/cgriffin6

Top: *Series 6, #1,* 2003, gouache on paper, 9" x 9". Bottom: *Series 6, #3,* 2003, gouache on paper, 9" x 9". Photographs: Stuart Tyson.

Mary Hatch

6917 Willson Drive, Kalamazoo, MI 49009   TEL 269.375.0376
EMAIL mary_hatch@sbcglobal.net   WEB www.maryhatch.com

Bouquet Day, oil on linen, 48" x 34". Photograph: Lacey Vogt.

Mary Hatch

6917 Willson Drive, Kalamazoo, MI 49009 TEL 269.375.0376
EMAIL mary_hatch@sbcglobal.net WEB www.maryhatch.com

193

Flower Dance, 2006, oil on linen, *48" x 34".* Photograph: Lacey Vogt.

Yoshi Hayashi

Yoshi Hayashi Studio   255 Kansas Street #330, San Francisco, CA 94103   TEL 415.924.9224
TEL/FAX 415.552.0755   EMAIL hayashi44@yahoo.com   WEB www.yoshihayashi.com

194

Top: *Spring Cloud,* 2004, gold and silver leaf with oil paint on wood panel, 42"H x 88"W.
Bottom: *Morning Moon,* 2005, Reno, NV, gold, silver, and copper leaf with oil paint on wood panel, 48"H x 72"W. Photographs: Ira D. Schrank.

Stephen Henning

22399 Oak Hill Road NW, Evansville, MN 56326   TEL 218.948.2288
FAX 218.948.2344   EMAIL henning@gctel.com   WEB www.stephenhenning.com

Top: *Afterglow,* 2008, oil pastel, 14" x 17".
Bottom: *Watershed,* 2008, acrylic on canvas, 24" x 36". Photographs: Jerry Mathiason.

PAINTINGS & PRINTS

Douglas Hyslop

2532 Gregory Street, Madison, WI 53711   TEL 608.263.6560
TEL 608.238.3186   EMAIL dbhyslop@wisc.edu

Top: *Tambourine Dance,* acrylic on canvas, 48" x 60". Bottom left: *Jester's Family,* 54" x 36". Bottom right: *Ice Cream Sunday,* 54" x 38".

Nicolette Jelen

49 Bayview Avenue, Sag Harbor, NY 11963   TEL 631.725.2385   TEL 631.793.3360
EMAIL nicolette.jelen@verizon.net   WEB www.nicolettejelen.net

Top: *Light and Time,* 2008, oil on canvas, 30" x 40". Bottom: *Afternoon Storm,* 2008, oil on canvas, 30" x 40".

Randy Johnson

Johnson ArtWorks   1029 Vista Drive, Grants Pass, OR 97527   TEL 541.660.2097
EMAIL info@johnsonartworks.com   WEB www.johnsonartworks.com

Caleo Seon—Firer Odata, 2007, acrylic/digital hybrid painting on canvas, 33" x 25".

Scott Kahn

13-2 Griswold Point Road, Old Lyme, CT 06371   TEL 860.434.1880
EMAIL scottkahnpainter@att.net   WEB www.scottkahnpainter.com

Top: *Berkshire Nightscape,* 2005, oil on linen, 36" x 40".
Bottom: *Early Spring,* 1992, oil on linen, 32" x 36". Photographs: Jeffrey Sturges.

Shelby Keefe

522 East Otjen Street, Milwaukee, WI 53207   TEL 414.486.1609
TEL 414.687.6241   EMAIL shelbykeefe@tds.net   WEB www.studioshelby.com

Top left: *Seaside Road,* 2007, oil on canvas, 20" x 30". Top right: *Downtown Wreaths,* 2004, private collection, Milwaukee, WI, oil on canvas, 24" x 18". Photograph: Sanders Visual Images. Bottom: *October 20th on Brady Street,* 2007, private collection, Milwaukee, WI, oil on canvas, 36" x 48".

PAINTINGS & PRINTS

Ken Roth Studio

Ken Roth   63551 Brahma Court, Bend, OR 97701   TEL 541.317.1727
TEL 541.420.1589   EMAIL ken@kenrothstudio.com   WEB www.kenrothstudio.com

Top: *Wonder into Wonder,* 2008, oil, 42" x 54".
Bottom: *Riverbend,* 2008, private collection, oil, 20" x 24". Photograph: Gary Alvis, Studio 7.

Anne Kessler

PO Box 147, Point Arena, CA 95468   TEL 707.882.3224
EMAIL akess@mcn.org   WEB www.annekesslerpastels.com

202

Top: *Alder Reflection,* 2007, pastel on paper, 24" x 36". Bottom: *Pudding Creek,* 2007, 36" x 24". Photographs: Ron Bolander.

Al Lachman

Lachman Gallery   Peddler's Village, Street Road, PO Box 155, Lahaska, PA 18931
TEL 267.614.1076   EMAIL lachmanstudios@msn.com   WEB www.lachmanstudios.com

Top: *Once Upon a Time*, 2008, Bucks County, PA, oil and acrylic, 52" x 78".
Bottom: *Almost Home*, 2008, acrylic and pastel, 24" x 38". Photographs: Profiles, Philadelphia, PA.

PAINTINGS & PRINTS

Marlene Lenker

Lenker Studio   13 Crosstrees Hill Road, Essex, CT 06426   TEL 860.767.2098
TEL 973.239.8671   EMAIL lenkerart@prodigy.net   WEB www.marlenelenker.com

204

Top left: *Taos Spring*, 2008, acrylic on canvas, wrapped, 30" x 30". Top right: *Western Strata II,* 2008, acrylic on canvas, wrapped, 24" x 24".
Bottom: Installation, 2006, one-person show at the Chase/Freedman Gallery, West Hartford, CT.

PAINTINGS & PRINTS

Lisette T. Lichtenstein

7933 Greenside Lane, Columbus, OH 43235 TEL 614.888.8284
EMAIL guild@lisettelichtenstein.com WEB www.lisettelichtenstein.com

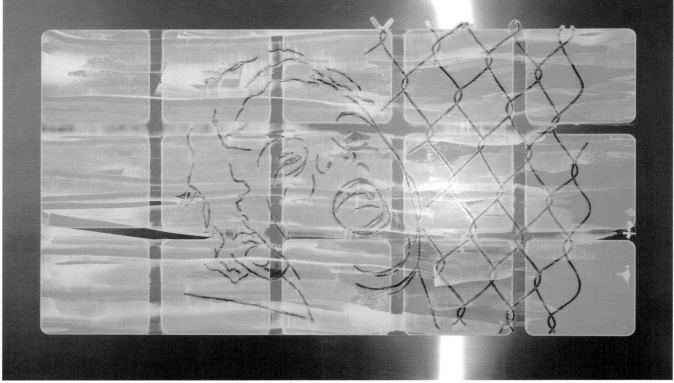

Top: *Free Radicals,* oil on metal, 18" x 48".
Bottom: *Prodigal Son,* oil on metal, 48" x 78". Photographs: Randy Weidenbush/Flashback Photography.

PAINTINGS & PRINTS

Åndria Linn

Åndria Linn Fine Art   524 Wofford Road, Durham, NC 27707   TEL 919.403.7939
EMAIL andria@andrialinn.com   WEB www.andrialinn.com

206

Top: *Amelie's Dance,* 2007, private residence, Chapel Hill, NC, acrylic on canvas, 36" x 60". Bottom left: *Inside or Out?,* 2007, private residence, Chapel Hill, NC, acrylic on canvas, 40" x 30". Bottom right: *Without You,* 2008, private residence, Durham, NC, acrylic on canvas, 40" x 30".

Lisa Kesler Studio

Lisa Kesler   1801 West Hensley Road, Champaign, IL 61822   TEL 217.531.9956
TEL 217.721.4738   EMAIL kesler.lisak@gmail.com   WEB www.lisakesler.com

Top: *Circles and Branches,* 2008, acrylic on board, 12" x 24".
Bottom: *Red Concentric 3,* 2008, acrylic on board, 16" x 16".

Fred Lisaius

15143 SE 48th Drive, Bellevue, WA 98006   TEL 425.643.3497
EMAIL fredartist@comcast.net   WEB www.fredlisaius.com

208

Top: *Anderegg's Garden,* 2008, 48" x 96".
Bottom: *Peony,* 2008, 14" x 48".

Cathy Locke

560 Trumbull Avenue, Novato, CA 94947   TEL 415.893.9292   FAX 415.893.9464
EMAIL cathy@cathylocke.com   WEB www.cathylocke.com

Texture 1, 2008, oil and cold wax, 48" x 36".

Margaret Lockwood

Woodwalk Gallery   6746 County Road G, Egg Harbor, WI 54209   TEL 920.868.2912
EMAIL info@woodwalkgallery.com   WEB www.woodwalkgallery.com

210

Top: *Clouds: Captured Light,* oil on canvas, 68" x 60". Bottom left: *Trees: Beginnings II,* oil on canvas, 60" x 68".
Bottom right: *Ripples II,* oil on canvas, 60" x 60". Photographs: Matt Norman Photography.

Bettina Madini

North 1294 Highway F, Montello, WI 53949   TEL 608.297.9593   EMAIL bettinamadini@hotmail.com
WEB www.earthangelproductions.com   WEB www.bettinamadini.com

211

Left: *Spirit of Life,* 2008, acrylic on canvas, 48"H x 24"W. Top right: *Sacred Oneness,* 2007, acrylic on canvas, 12" x 12".
Bottom right: *New Bloom,* 2007, acrylic on canvas, 12" x 12". Photographs: Opacolor, Madison, WI.

PAINTINGS & PRINTS

Barry Masteller

PO Box 397, San Juan Bautista, CA 95045 TEL 831.320.8568
EMAIL barry_masteller@live.com WEB www.barrymasteller.com

212

Top left: *The Woods 56,* 2008, oil on canvas, 50" x 40". Top right: *The Woods 57,* 2008, oil on canvas, 50" x 40".
Bottom: *The Woods 55,* 2008, oil on canvas, 36" x 66".

Nathaniel Hester Fine Arts

Nathaniel Hester   3992 Gordonton Road, Hurdle Mills, NC 27541   TEL 336.504.4921
TEL 336.599.1525   EMAIL info@nathanielhester.com   WEB www.nathanielhester.com

213

Top: *The Countdown Series* (from left) *#17, #33, #2,* 2008, oil on canvas, each 14" x 14". Photographs: Peter Geoffrion. Bottom: *The Countdown Series #14, #5, #6, #7,* 2008, Kress Building, Durham, NC, oil on canvas, largest piece 71" x 71" framed. Photograph: Jerry Blow.

PAINTINGS & PRINTS

Susan Ogilvie

Susan Ogilvie, LLC   220 Machias Loop Road, Port Ludlow, WA 98365   TEL 360.437.0416
FAX 360.437.2712   EMAIL susanogilvie@cablespeed.com   WEB www.susanogilvie.com

214

Top left: *Downstream,* 2008, pastel on panel, 36" x 24". Top right: *Old Growth,* 2008, pastel on panel, 24" x 12".
Bottom: *Valley Iris,* 2008, pastel on panel, 16" x 20". Photographs: Frank Ross Photographic.

Glenys Porter

24443 Montevista Circle, Valencia, CA 91354   TEL 661.702.9926
EMAIL inquiries@glenysporter.com   WEB www.glenysporter.com

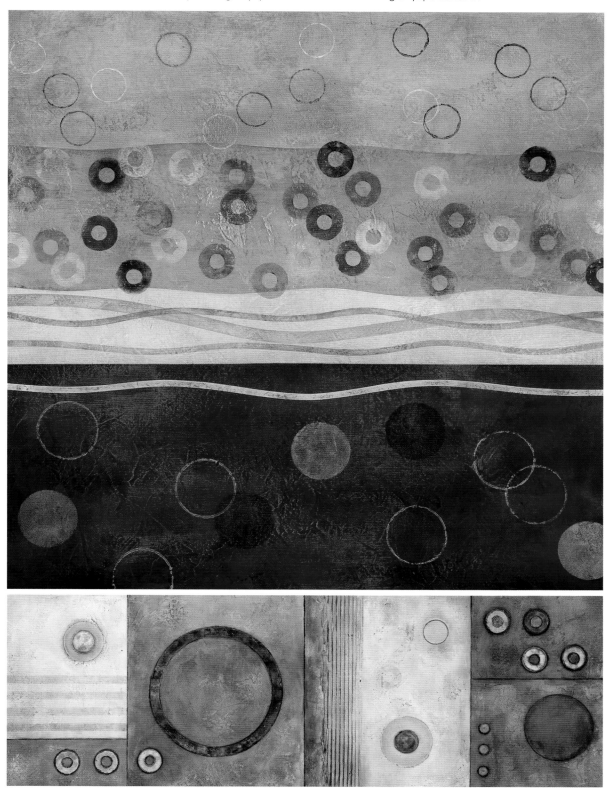

Top: *Strata,* 2008, acrylic on canvas, 24" x 24".
Bottom: *Interplay,* 2008, acrylic on canvas, 12" x 36".

Joni Purk

Purk Art Studio   2836 Olympus Drive, Charlotte, NC 28214   TEL 513.571.6095
TEL 704.394.1190   EMAIL joni@purkartstudio.com   WEB www.purkartstudio.com

Top left: *Marsh I,* 2008, oil on canvas, 16" x 20". Top right: *Morning Light on East Bay,* 2008, oil on canvas, 16" x 20".
Bottom left: *Rainbow Rising,* 2008, oil on canvas, 16" x 20". Bottom right: *Marsh II,* 2008, oil on canvas, 16" x 20".

Richard Hall Fine Art

Richard Hall   5130 East Emile Zola Avenue, Scottsdale, AZ 85254   TEL 602.819.7199
TEL 480.229.5755   EMAIL richardhallfineart@cox.net   WEB www.richardhallfineart.com

River Song, 2008, private collection, oil on canvas, 48" x 48".

Kim Rody

Fishartista®   418 SE Krueger Parkway, Stuart, FL 34996   TEL 772.223.7378
EMAIL kim@rody.com   WEB www.rody.com   WEB www.fishartista.com

218

Top: *Powder Blue Tangent Triptych,* 2008, acrylic on canvas, 20" x 50". Photograph: Brian Gillagan.
Bottom: *Bling,* 2006, acrylic on canvas, 48" x 60". Photograph: Stuart Photo.

PAINTINGS & PRINTS

Joan Skogsberg Sanders

3156 Stevely, Long Beach, CA 90808   TEL 562.421.5369
FAX 562.420.6171   EMAIL skogsberg@aol.com   WEB www.guild.com

Top: *Belmont Shore,* 2008, acrylic, 16" x 16".
Bottom: *Abu Dhabi,* 2008, acrylic, 16" x 16".

Roy Secord

Fine Arts Abstractionist   360 West 127 Street #2W, New York, NY 10027   TEL 212.662.5430
FAX 212.599.0434   EMAIL secordrw@aol.com   WEB www.roysecord.com

Left: *Manhattan Snowfall,* 2006, acrylic collage, 72" x 36". Top right: *A New Day,* 2008, acrylic on canvas, 51" x 51". Center right: *Hip(iddy) Hop,* 2008, acrylic on canvas, 48" x 48". Bottom right: *April 15th,* 2008, acrylic on canvas, 51" x 51". Photographs: Photographics Unlimited.

Yvette Sikorsky

Yvette Sikorsky Studio   PO Box 146, Mohegan Lake, NY 10547-0146   TEL 914.737.5167

Kailua, 2008, Weschester, NY, acrylic 48" x 36". Photograph: Howard Copland.

Todd Starks

Toadhouse Studios LLC   9216 North Serns Road, Milton, WI 53563
TEL 608.868.3020   EMAIL todd@toddstarks.net   WEB www.toddstarks.net

222

Top: *Laughing Like the Morning Wind*, 2005, oil on canvas, 53" x 89".
Bottom: *Donum (A Gift),* 2006, oil on canvas, 54" x 75".

Todd Starks

Toadhouse Studios LLC   9216 North Serns Road, Milton, WI 53563
TEL 608.868.3020   EMAIL todd@toddstarks.net   WEB www.toddstarks.net

Top: *Meanwhile*, 2008, oil on wood panel, 24" x 48".
Bottom: *Common Ground*, 2008, oil on wood panel, 16" x 24".

PAINTINGS & PRINTS

Joel E. Traylor III

3311 Rhode Island Avenue #218, Mount Rainier, MD 20712   TEL 202.413.5469
EMAIL joel@jetgallery.com   WEB www.jetgallery.com

224

Top: *Frequency 1,* 2008, oil on canvas, cut and reassembled, 24" x 24".
Bottom: *Frequency 2,* 2008, oil on canvas, cut and reassembled, 24" x 24".

Rachel Tribble

350 NW Alice Avenue, Stuart, FL 34994   TEL 772.708.8400
EMAIL info@racheltribble.com   WEB www.racheltribble.com

Top left: *Crescent,* 2004, watercolor, 14" x 10", giclée prints available. Top right: *Two Flowers,* 2008, oil, 48" x 36", giclée prints available.
Bottom left: *Mexico,* 2004, watercolor, 14" x 10". Bottom right: *Dragonfly,* 2004, watercolor, 14" x 10".

PAINTINGS & PRINTS

Helen Vaughn

703 Oak Park Drive, Huntsville, AL 35801   TEL 256.534.4422   TEL 256.534.4202
EMAIL vaughnart@bellsouth.net   WEB www.helenvaughn.com

226

Top: *Tomatoes and Jackson Vine*, 2008, oil on canvas, 22" x 28".
Bottom: *Life is Just...*, 2007, oil and gold leaf on canvas, 24" x 36". Photographs: Doug Brewster.

Dana Wigdor

PO Box 1483, Brattleboro, VT 05302   TEL 802.221.1199
EMAIL dana@wigdor.net   WEB www.danawigdor.com

Memories, 2005, oil on canvas, 48" x 29". Photograph: John Polak.

Donna Wojcik

9700 Main Street, Clarence, NY 14031   TEL 716.866.4044
FAX 716.759.2388   EMAIL wojcikd@roadrunner.com   WEB www.donnawojcik.com

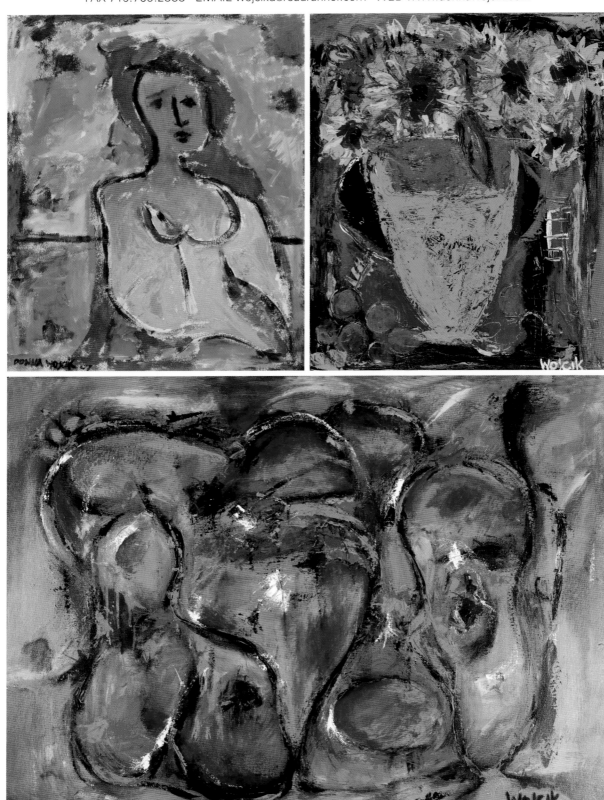

Top left: *Presence*, 2007, acrylic on paper, 20" x 16". Top right: *Blue Vase*, 2008, acrylic on canvas, 30" x 24".
Bottom: *Emergence*, 2008, acrylic on canvas, 30" x 40". Giclée prints of my work are available in various sizes. Photographs: Randy E. Zack.

PAINTINGS & PRINTS

William Wright

Light Threads   2206 Lockhaven Drive, Colorado Springs, CO 80909   TEL 719.494.4264
FAX 719.632.4643   EMAIL wm@lightthreads.com   WEB www.lightthreads.com

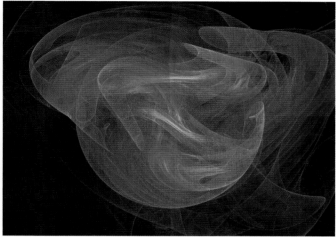

Top left: *Diaphanous*, 2008, private collection, Las Vegas, NV, pigment on canvas, 33" x 44". Top right: *Breath of Creation,* 2008, pigment on canvas, 44" x 60". Bottom: *Energized Oz,* 2007, Plummer Architecture, Indianapolis, IN, pigment on canvas, 5.5' x 16' and 5.5' x 8.5'.

PAINTINGS & PRINTS

Marlene Sanaye Yamada

Artwork by Sanaye   Manhattan Beach, CA   TEL 310.435.7878   FAX 310.376.2695
EMAIL marleneyamada@yahoo.com   WEB www.artworkbysanaye.com

230

Top: *Rise,* 2008, acrylic on canvas, 36" x 36".
Bottom: *Quiescence #6,* 2008, acrylic on canvas, triptych, each panel 36"H x 18"W, total size 36"H x 60"W.

Stephen Yates

Yates Arts   PO Box 744, Port Townsend, WA 98368   TEL 360.385.4330
EMAIL yatesart@olympus.net   WEB www.stephenyatesart.com

Top: *Wisteria, Sword Fern, and Japanese Maple*, 2008, Overlake Hospital, Bellevue, WA, acrylic on canvas, each 5' x 5'.
Bottom left: *Warm Currents*, 2005, Lincoln Square, Bellevue, WA, oil on wood panel triptych, 80" x 108".
Bottom right: *Juan de Fuca Fault II*, 2007, Kitsap Government Building, Port Orchard, WA, 6' x 12' in three panels.

PAINTINGS & PRINTS

Chin Yuen

4606 Boulderwood Drive, Victoria, BC, V8Y2V2, Canada   TEL 250.381.1688
TEL 250.881.0833   FAX 250.381.1687   EMAIL chin@chinyuenart.com   WEB www.chinyuenart.com

232

Top: *Abstract Diary October #3-07,* 2007, acrylic on canvas, 24" x 24".
Bottom: *That Bubbly Feeling,* 2007, acrylic on canvas, 24" x 24".

PAINTINGS & PRINTS

Karen Berman

177 Lindholm Lane, Bayside, CA 95524 TEL 707.825.6532
EMAIL rkberman@suddenlink.net WEB www.karenbermanartist.com

Signs of Spring, 2008, watercolor, 30" x 42". Photograph: Ron Berman.

Paintings & Prints: Common Terms and Their Meanings

Acrylic A water-soluble paint made with pigments and synthetic resin; used as a fast-drying alternative to oil paint.

Artist Proofs Prints created by a print publisher for the artist to review and work with the publisher to make any necessary adjustments to coloring, tone, darkness, etc., before the numbered-edition prints are printed. Approved artist proofs are signed, numbered, and inscribed as artist proofs (AP). Artist proofs that are not approved by the artist are destroyed. Artist proofs are considered of higher value than the proofs in the numbered edition because of their limited quantity.

Etching A printing process in which chemical agents are used to deepen lines drawn onto a printing plate.

Giclée French term meaning "to spray." A process by which an image is rendered digitally by spraying a fine stream of ink onto archival art paper or canvas.

Gouache An opaque watercolor paint, or work so produced. Gouache is applied like watercolor, but reflects light due to its chalky finish.

Museum Wrap A finishing technique for artwork mounted on stretchers. The fabric is mounted onto stretcher bars with no visible staples on the edge of the frame. Edges are painted, usually dark, and no framing is necessary.

Oil Refers to a paint medium and its associated techniques or any work so produced. Oil paint is made from ground pigments suspended in oil, usually linseed. The most flexible and luminous of all paint mediums.

Pastel A crayon of ground pigment bound with gum or oil. Pastel crayons have varying ratios of pigment to chalk and gum; the more pigment, the more intense the color.

OIL

Sintra by Carl Borgia, see page 177. Photograph: Gary Kerr.

Aaron T. Brown

154 Putnam Hill Road, Lyndeborough, NH 03082   TEL 603.654.6115
TEL 603.654.2933   EMAIL aarontbrown@tds.net   WEB www.aarontbrown.com

Order 1, 2008, hand-pulled print, 31" x 60".

Elizabeth Embler

146 Hokum Rock Road, Dennis, MA 02638   TEL 508.280.1417
EMAIL eembler@gmail.com   WEB www.elizabethembler.com

 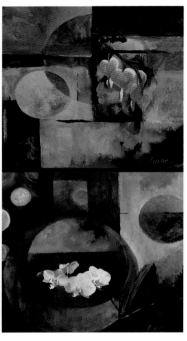

Left: *Cape Escape,* 2008, oil painting, 24" x 36".
Right: *Love* (top) and *Harmony* (bottom), 2008, oil paintings, each 16" x 16". Photographs: Andre Studio.

Bill Hueg

Peacock Studios, Inc.   12919 North Vallejo Circle, Westminster, CO 80234
TEL 720.281.5349   EMAIL billhueg@msn.com   WEB www.billhueg.com

Left: *Earth Reincarnate,* 2003, collection of Kelly Thorsen, Holdfast, Saskatchewan, oil on canvas, 40" x 27".
Right: *Celestial Splendor Illuminated by the Divine Nautilus,* 2007, oil on canvas, 54" x 36". Photographs: Chuck Renstrom.

Vitali Komarov

303 Oakleaf Drive, San Antonio, TX 78209   TEL 210.828.1362
EMAIL komarov@komarovart.com   WEB www.komarovart.com

Left: *Small Island in the Park Pond,* 2004, Lednice Castle Park, South Moravia,
oil on canvas, 15.75" sq. Right: *Springtime,* 2008, oil on canvas, 19.6" x 15.75".

Marie Martin

Marie Martin Art   17151 Newhope Street, Fountain Valley, CA 92708
TEL 714.876.8787   EMAIL martin.art@mac.com   WEB www.marie-martin.com

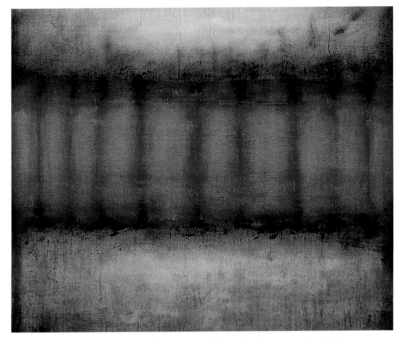

Lake District I, 2007, acrylic on canvas, 36" x 36". Photograph: Bob Smith.

Victoria Ryan

2286 Ralphs Court, Eureka, CA 95503   TEL 707.442.9160   FAX 707.443.8884
EMAIL victoria@victoriaryan.com   WEB www.victoriaryan.com

Wine Country Evening #2, 2006, private collection, San Francisco, CA,
pastel on board, 25" x 39". Photograph: Mark Lufkin.

Mary Scrimgeour

Mary Scrimgeour Studio   810 Alpine Avenue, Boulder, CO 80304
TEL 720.479.6388   EMAIL mkscrim@comcast.net   WEB www.maryscrimgeour.com

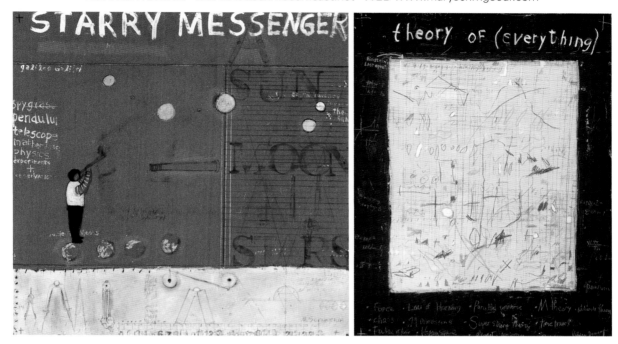

Left: *Starry Messenger*, 2008, oil and mixed media, 30" x 30".
Right: *Theory of Everything*, 2007, Barkley Advertising, Kansas City, MO, oil and mixed media, 40" x 30". Photographs: Ken Sanville.

Michael Shemchuk

1111 Kains Avenue, Albany, CA 94706   TEL 510.527.3904
FAX 510.527.2319   EMAIL shem@mshem.com   WEB www.mshem.com

Small Pleasures, triptych, 48" x 100".

Public Art

Amos Fine Art Studios
Atelier Huck Fisher
C Glass Studio
Teresa Camozzi
Douglas Olmsted Freeman
Archie Held
Eric Higgs
Jeff and Sandy Jackson
Tuck Langland
Eric David Laxman

Kathleen Lee Meehan
National Sculptors' Guild
Bruce A. Niemi
Zachary Oxman
Ulrich Pakker
Matthew Placzek
Ralfonso.com LLC
Ray Miller Studio
Barton Rubenstein
Margo Sawyer

Michael Szabo
Luis Torruella
Ellen Tykeson
Aaron P. Van de Kerckhove
James Vilona
Jamie and Jeremy Wells
Jeannine Young
Aaron T. Brown
Mike Hansel

Amos Fine Art Studios

Barbara Amos   131 Rosery Drive NW, Calgary, AB T2K IL6, Canada   TEL 403.560.4067
TEL 403.289.4284   EMAIL barbaraamos@shaw.ca   WEB www.barbaraamos.com

Top: *Celebrations* (detail) from left to right: *Audience*, 8' x2'; *LaCrosse Player*, 8' x 4'; *Basketball*, 4' x 4'; *City Abstract*, 8' x 2'.
Bottom: *Celebrations*, 2004, Cardel Place, Calgary, Alberta, Canada, acrylic on panel, 24' x 90'.

Atelier Huck Fisher

Laura Fisher and Christopher Huck   Lunenburg, Canada   TEL 902.634.7125   Scottsdale, AZ   TEL 602.490.8098
Oaxaca, Mexico   TEL 011.52.1.951.118.0847   EMAIL info@huckfisher.com   WEB www.huckfisher.com

Seasons of Vail Maypole, 2008, The Arrabelle at Vail Square, a Rock Resort, Vail, CO,
hand-forged, fabricated, and hand-painted aluminum, 32' x 9'. Photograph: Brent Bingham/photofxvail.com.

Stuart Huck, Basalt, CO

Guild Sourcebooks at Work

Case Study #5

ARTISTS: Laura Fisher and Christopher Huck
ARTWORK TITLE: *Seasons of Vail Maypole*
MEDIA: Hand-forged, fabricated, and hand-painted aluminum
SIZE: 32' x 9'
INSTALLATION: The Arrabelle at Vail Square, Vail, CO

242

"The Guild Sourcebook was the first place we went during our research to identify an artist. We appreciated the professionalism of [Laura Fisher and Christopher Huck] and enjoyed their creativity. Their sculptures represent Vail in a very colorful and meaningful way. When fulfilling an extensive demand for art, as we needed for The Arrabelle at Vail Square, the Guild Sourcebook is a tremendous resource to begin your search for the right artists."

Matt Lydens, Project Manager
The Arrabelle at Vail Square LLC
www.vailresorts.com

"The theme of a Bavarian-style maypole, which traditionally incorporates figures donated by local guilds, was determined by the designer. When approached with the basic idea, I was instantly inspired to depict the seasons of Vail because they vary so dramatically and the colors are so beautiful. The flora, fauna, and activities were really fun to research and illustrate.

"I translated my designs into vector drawings using Adobe Illustrator, and then had them cut by water jet from aluminum sheet and plate. To make each two-sided sculpture, I hammered over 500 pieces into shape and puzzled them into place, using my TIG welder and MIG aluminum welding gun. After applying the appropriate undercoating, I hand painted each piece, and finished with a clear epoxy overcoat. The biggest challenge was to keep in mind that the sculptures were going to be viewed from a distance, and from below.

"The commission was a result of a previous page we had in *The Guild Sourcebook*, and because of this, the designer of the project was already open to my ideas. The whole thing went without a hitch, and the team at Arrabelle couldn't have been more helpful. The maypole had been standing empty in the middle of the town square, and it was rewarding to observe people's reactions after the sculptures were installed—some people were quite moved, and one woman actually cried."

See more work by Atelier Huck Fisher on page 241.

C Glass Studio

Catherine Woods   515 22nd Street South, Unit E, St. Petersburg, FL 33712   TEL 727.327.3473
EMAIL cathwashere@yahoo.com   WEB www.CglassStudio.com

Left: *State Song*, Kansas City, KS, painted, laminated, and sandblasted glass with metal frame. Photograph: Richard Sprengeler.
Top right: *Arcs in Motion*, St. Petersburg, FL, fused glass and aluminum. Photograph: Michael Rixon.
Bottom right: *Underground Spring*, St. Petersburg, FL, fused, laminated safety glass with slip-resistant surface. Photograph: Michael Rixon.

PUBLIC ART

Teresa Camozzi

The Camozzi Art Studio   1190A Shafter Avenue, San Francisco, CA 94124   TEL 415.822.6222
FAX 415.822.6322   EMAIL tcamozzi@comcast.net   WEB www.teresacamozzi.com

244

Water and the Plow, public art commission, Davis Library, Plano, TX, three revolving dichroic glass sculpture wheels relating to agriculture and high-tech social changes, 8', 6', and 4', created in collaboration with Alan Lee Birkelbach, Texas Poet Laureate.

Teresa Camozzi

The Camozzi Art Studio   1190A Shafter Avenue, San Francisco, CA 94124   TEL 415.822.6222
FAX 415.822.6322   EMAIL tcamozzi@comcast.net   WEB www.teresacamozzi.com

Transitions, Marriott Moscone Hotel, San Francisco, CA, poly-resin sculpture
conceptually relating multi-diversity and social change, 72" x 190" x 4".

Douglas Olmsted Freeman

Doug Freeman Studio   310 North Second Street, Minneapolis, MN 55401   TEL 612.339.7150
EMAIL doug@freemanstudio.com   WEB www.freemanstudio.com

The Mississippi Guardian Birds, Saint Paul, MN. Photographs: Jerry Mathiason.

PUBLIC ART

Douglas Olmsted Freeman

Doug Freeman Studio   310 North Second Street, Minneapolis, MN 55401   TEL 612.339.7150
EMAIL doug@freemanstudio.com   WEB www.freemanstudio.com

The Lion's Fountain, Culver City, CA, bronze, 8'H. Photograph: William Short.

Archie Held

Archie Held Studio   #5 18th Street, Richmond, CA 94801   TEL 510.235.8700
FAX 510.234.4828   EMAIL archieheldstudio@comcast.net   WEB www.archieheld.com

Wings, 2008, St. Anthony's Hospital, Oklahoma City, OK, bronze, stainless steel, glass, and water, 30' x 12.25' x 2'.

Archie Held

Archie Held Studio   #5 18th Street, Richmond, CA 94801   TEL 510.235.8700
FAX 510.234.4828   EMAIL archieheldstudio@comcast.net   WEB www.archieheld.com

Three Waves, 2008, Britannia Oyster Point, South San Francisco, CA, bronze, stainless steel, and water, 35' x 22' x 22'.

Eric Higgs

Higgs Sculpture Studio, Inc. 2245 Fourth Avenue South, St. Petersburg, FL 33704 TEL 727.322.2309
TEL 727.641.5161 FAX 727.321.5640 EMAIL eric@erichiggs.com WEB www.erichiggs.com

Top: *Passage,* 2008, Whitewing at Germann Estates, Gilbert, AZ, basalt and water, 30'H x 90'W x 70'D. Photograph: Chris Booth.
Bottom left: *Love,* 2008, private residence, Sarasota, FL, stainless steel and paint, 6' x 2' x 2'.
Bottom right: *Dignity,* 2008, Sarasota, FL, marble, 8'H x 2'W x 2'D. Photograph: Chris Booth.

Jeff and Sandy Jackson

Jaxon Design Works   444 17th Street #704, Denver, CO 80202   TEL 720.284.1922
FAX 720.548.9830   EMAIL sjackson@jaxondesignworks.com   WEB www.jaxondesignworks.com

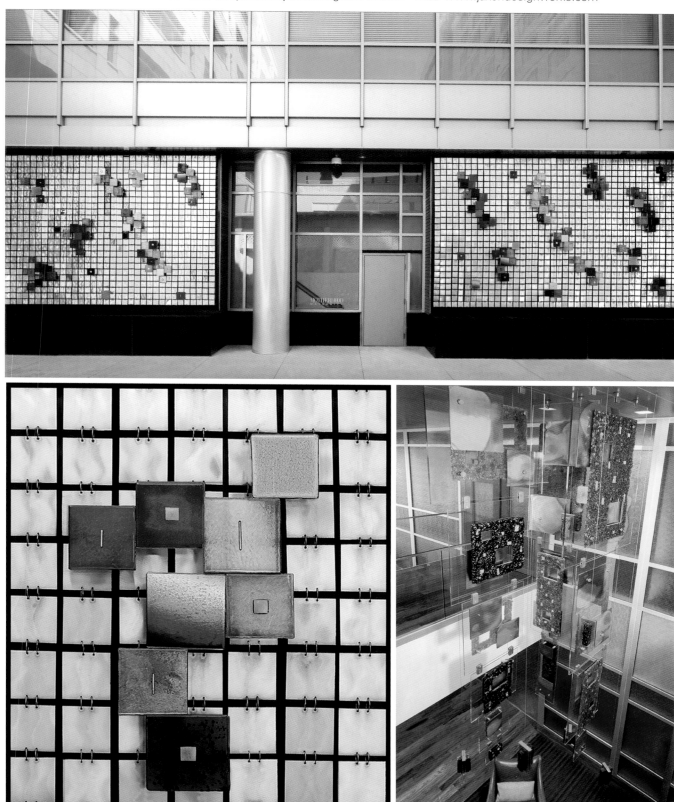

251

Top: *Aqua Rhythms*, 2005, JW Marriott, Denver, CO, kinetic, fused dichroic glass and stainless steel, 13' x 15' and 13' x 19'. Bottom left: *Aqua Rhythms* (detail). Bottom right: *Fusion*, 2006, Coors-Molson, Denver, CO, fused glass, copper, and plexi, 17' x 7' x 7'. Photographs: Linda Nix.

Tuck Langland

12632 Anderson, Granger, IN 46530   TEL/FAX 574.272.2708
TEL 574.360.7946   EMAIL tuck12@comcast.net

252

Top left: *Resting Dancer,* life-size bronze, edition of seven. Top right: *Dance of Awakening Day,* bronze figure, 44"H, edition of ten. Bottom left: *Memory: though they are gone, their impressions remain,* bronze, 8.5'H, edition of seven. Bottom right: *Solitude,* bronze, 50"H, edition of ten. Photograph: Jafe Parsons.

Tuck Langland

12632 Anderson, Granger, IN 46530   TEL/FAX 574.272.2708
TEL 574.360.7946   EMAIL tuck12@comcast.net

Spirits of Commerce and Industry, 2008, Federal Reserve Bank of Kansas City, MO, bronze, 12'H.

Eric David Laxman

Eric David Laxman, Inc.   478 Mountainview Avenue, Valley Cottage, NY 10989   TEL 845.304.7615
FAX 845.429.4454   EMAIL eric@ericdavidlaxman.com   WEB www.ericdavidlaxman.com

Left: *Standing Wave,* 2007, Saunders Farm, Garrison, NY, welded steel and stainless steel, 11'H x 30" x 30".
Top right: *Anahata Fountain,* 1999, private estate, CT, fabricated silicon bronze, 96"H x 36" x 36". Photograph: Stuart Sachs.
Bottom right: *Synergy,* 2008, Summit Medical Group, Berkley Heights, NJ, bronze and stainless steel, 114"H x 48" x 48". Photograph: Sal Cordaro.

Kathleen Lee Meehan

369 Montezuma Avenue #582, Santa Fe, NM 87501   TEL 505.629.9791
EMAIL kathleenmeehan@gmail.com   WEB www.kathleenmeehan.com

255

Palm Desert Community Walk, commissioned by the City of Palm Desert, CA, Art in Public Places program. Art paths and seating with rose poetry etched in tile, abstracted rose mosaic, and painted steel shade sculpture inspired by Cahuilla Indian basket, 90' x 12'.

National Sculptors' Guild

2683 North Taft Avenue, Loveland, CO 80538   TEL 800.606.2015
EMAIL info@nationalsculptorsguild.com   WEB www.nationalsculptorsguild.com

Top left: *Conversation* by Carol Gold, City of Paramount, CA, bronze and granite, 6' x 10' x 3'. Top right: *Fortitude* by Dee Clements, Golden Springs Memorial, Santa Fe Springs, CA, bronze, figures 8', concrete structure 16'. Bottom: *Ladder of the Rising Stars* by Kevin Box, Dalbey Education Institute, Westminster, CO, powder-coated steel, 10' x 3' x 2'. Photographs: John W. Kinkade.

National Sculptors' Guild

2683 North Taft Avenue, Loveland, CO 80538   TEL 800.606.2015
EMAIL info@nationalsculptorsguild.com   WEB www.nationalsculptorsguild.com

Top: *Stars and Stripes* by Kathleen Caricof, War Memorial Stadium, Little Rock, AR, stainless steel and granite, 36' x 40' x 40'.
Bottom left: *Baptismal Font* by C.T. Whitehouse, Our Lady of the Pines, Conifer, CO, bronze and sandstone, 48" x 36" x 36".
Bottom right: *Together* by Mark Leichliter, River Front Park, Little Rock, AR, powder-coated steel, 14' x 10' x 3.5'. Photographs: Alyson Kinkade.

PUBLIC ART

Bruce A. Niemi

Sculpture by Niemi   13300 116th Street, Kenosha, WI 53142   TEL 262.857.3456   TEL 847.971.0845
FAX 262.857.4567   EMAIL sculpture@bruceniemi.com   WEB www.bruceniemi.com

Top left: *Samurai,* 2002, private residence, Indianapolis, IN, bronze, 168" x 52" x 40". Photograph: Pawel Pfludzinski. Right: *Torch,* 2000, Cary Academy, NC, bronze, 15' x 4' x 4'. Bottom left: *Eye to the Soul,* 2002, Niemi Sculpture Gallery, Kenosha, WI, stainless steel, 10' x 9.4' x 5'.

Bruce A. Niemi

Sculpture by Niemi   13300 116th Street, Kenosha, WI 53142   TEL 262.857.3456   TEL 847.971.0845
FAX 262.857.4567   EMAIL sculpture@bruceniemi.com   WEB www.bruceniemi.com

259

Standing the Test of Time, 2008, West Bend Mutual Insurance, West Bend, WI, stainless steel, 17' x 24' x 9'.

Zachary Oxman

Oxman Studios, Inc. Bethesda, MD TEL 301.656.5032
EMAIL studio@zacharyoxman.com WEB www.zacharyoxman.com

260

Soaring Pathways, 2004, lobby installation, Nova Medical Center, Ashburn, VA, stainless steel, 25'H. Photograph: Lightstruck Studio, Ed Whitman.

Zachary Oxman

Oxman Studios, Inc.   Bethesda, MD   TEL 301.656.5032
EMAIL studio@zacharyoxman.com   WEB www.zacharyoxman.com

261

Inspiration, 2006, entry sculpture, Northwest Indiana Times Newspaper, Munster, IN, stainless steel, 18'H. Photograph: Mox Studio.

Ulrich Pakker

RP Art, Inc.   2442 NW Market Street #157, Seattle, WA 98107   TEL 206.789.7454
TEL 206.478.0568   EMAIL info@rpart.com   WEB www.rpart.com

Trivergence Fountain (detail), Everett Events Center, Everett, WA, stainless steel, 20'H x 12'W x 8'D. Photograph: City of Everett.

Matthew Placzek

Placzek Studios, Inc.   3716 Leavenworth Street, Omaha, NE 68105   TEL 402.551.1200
FAX 402.553.1315   EMAIL mplaczek@aol.com   WEB www.matthewplaczek.com

263

Left: *Metamorphosis,* 2008, Henry Doorly Zoo, Omaha, NE, painted aluminum and acrylic, 18'H x 8'W x 10'L.
Right: *Leaves,* 2007, Omaha, NE, painted aluminum water feature, 17'H x 12'W x 50'L.

Ralfonso.com LLC

Ralf Gschwend   301 Clematis Street #3000, West Palm Beach, FL 33401   TEL 561.655.2745
EMAIL ralfonso@ralfonso.com   WEB www.ralfonso.com

264

Top left: *Moving on Up,* kinetic wind sculpture, 2004, St. Petersburg, Russia, stainless steel and fiberglass, 15' x 6' x 6'. Top center: *Bird of Paradise,* kinetic wind sculpture, 2008, 9' x 5' x 1'. Top right: *ExoCentric Spirits,* suspended light sculpture, 2006, Elements mall, Hong Kong, Lucite and aluminum, 30' x 30' x 20'. Bottom: *Dance with the Wind,* kinetic wind sculpture, 2007, Olympic Park, Beijing, China, stainless steel and mirror, polished, 30' x 9' x 9'.

PUBLIC ART

Ray Miller Studio

Raymond A. Miller   7172 Pfeiffer Road, Cincinnati, OH 45242   TEL 513.791.0898
TEL 513.919.5476   EMAIL raymillr@fuse.net   WEB www.raymillerstudio.com

Top: *The Minyon*, 2000, Cincinnati, OH, fabricated and powder-coated steel, each chair approximately 4'–5' x 2' x 2'.
Bottom: *Completion*, 1995, welded steel maquette. Photographs: Tony Walsh.

PUBLIC ART

Barton Rubenstein

Rubenstein Studios   4819 Dorset Avenue, Chevy Chase, MD 20815   TEL 301.654.5406
FAX 301.654.5496   EMAIL bartsher@aol.com   WEB www.rubensteinstudios.com

266

Top left: *Carpe Diem,* 2007, Sidwell Friends School, Washington, DC, stainless steel kinetic wind sculpture, 5.5'H, 6.5'H, and 7'H. Top right: *Field of Dreams,* 2005, Somerset Elementary School, Chevy Chase, MD, stainless steel, 13'H x 11'DIA. Bottom left: *Together, We Stand,* 2008, NSF International, Ann Arbor, MI, stainless steel and water, 10'H, 12'H, and 14'H. Bottom right: *Ray of Light,* 2008, Redwood Shores Library, Redwood City, CA, stainless steel and water, 76" x 38" x 18".

Margo Sawyer

Margo Sawyer Inc.   107 South Avenue C, Elgin, TX 78621
EMAIL margo@margosawyer.com   WEB www.margosawyer.com

Top: *Synchronicity of Color—Blue,* 2008, Discovery Green, Houston, TX, painted aluminum, 12'H x 49'W x 9'D.
Bottom: *Synchronicity of Color—Red,* 2008, Discovery Green, Houston, TX, painted aluminum, 12'H x 49'W x 9'D. Photographs: Kolanowski Studio, Inc.

Michael Szabo

SzaboWorks   1777 Yosemite Avenue, San Francisco, CA 94124   TEL 650.743.3769
EMAIL mike@szaboworks.com   WEB www.szaboworks.com

268

Top: *Arch-Cradle,* 2008, Mitchell Park, Palo Alto, CA, stainless steel and bronze, 8' x 20' x 7'. Bottom left: *Holes,* 2002, Woods Gerry Gallery, Providence, RI, reinforced cement, 40" x 23" x 18". Photograph: Aron Cohen. Bottom right: *Quencheet,* 2006, private residence, San Mateo, CA, bronze, concrete, and water, 58" x 40" x 15".

Luis Torruella

TEL/FAX 787.722.8728 EMAIL luis@luistorruella.com WEB www.luistorruella.com

Pajarera, 2008, Senderos, Montehiedra, PR, painted aluminum, 8'H x 48'W x 12'D.

Ellen Tykeson

1033 Sharon Way, Eugene, OR 97407   TEL 541.687.5731   TEL 541.221.8931
EMAIL etykeson@yahoo.com   WEB www.ellentykeson.com

270

Top: *Fine Balance,* 2008, Peace Health Riverbend Medical Center, Eugene, OR, bronze, 17.5' x 36' x 36'. Photograph: Deborah Weese.
Bottom left and right: *Fine Balance* (details). Photographs: Grady Layman.

Aaron P. Van de Kerckhove

APV Sculpture   PO Box 1777, Watsonville, CA 95077   TEL 831.345.1404
FAX 831.728.2119   EMAIL aaronswork@hotmail.com   WEB www.apvsculpture.com

The Lookout Tower, 2005, Pleasure Point, Santa Cruz, CA, Corten steel, stainless steel, mahogany, Australian cherry, and pine, 16'H x 9'DIA. Photographs: PPD Multimedia. Custom *Lookout Towers* built to your specifications.

James Vilona

James Vilona Sculpture Garden   890 East Hwy 56, Berthoud, CO 80513
TEL 970.532.9801   EMAIL info@jamesvilona.com   WEB www.jamesvilona.com

Echo, 2008, private collection, stainless steel, 8' x 5' x 5'.

Jamie and Jeremy Wells

6817 Flintlock Road Suite A, Houston, TX 77040   TEL 713.466.9990
FAX 713.466.9998   EMAIL hello@jamiejeremywells.com   WEB www.jamiejeremywells.com

273

Top: *Light & Life: The Texas Landscape* (detail).   Bottom left: Three of six triptychs from *Light & Life: The Texas Landscape*, 2007,
Chevron Art Collection, acrylic on canvas with metal sculpture, each triptych: 14' x 30', metal sculpture: 22' x 100'.
Bottom right (from top): *Golden Reflections, Autumn Corridor*, and *Resplendent*, three of six triptychs from *Light & Life: The Texas Landscape*.

Jeannine Young

PO Box 520876, Salt Lake City, UT 84152-0876   TEL 801.467.6692
EMAIL jysculptures@gmail.com   WEB www.jeannineyoung.com

274

Storm's Brewing, 2008, Benson Sculpture Garden, Loveland, CO, bronze, 7.4', edition of nine.

Aaron T. Brown

154 Putnam Hill Road, Lyndeborough, NH 03082 TEL 603.654.6115
TEL 603.654.2933 EMAIL aarontbrown@tds.net WEB www.aarontbrown.com

Order 1, 2008, Lyndeborough, NH, Corten steel, 8'H x 18"W.

Mike Hansel

Mike Hansel Sculpture 354 Purgatory Road, Middletown, RI 02842 TEL 401.225.7083
FAX 401.842.6665 EMAIL mike_hansel@stgeorges.edu WEB www.mikehansel.com

Left: *Cause and Effect*, 2008, Liberty State Park, Jersey City, NJ, aluminum, 24' x 12' x 14'.
Right: *Loosends*, 2007, SUNY, Fredonia, NY, 15' x 6' x 8'.

Sculpture/Non-

Representational

Alex Anagnostou Glass Studio	Lashua Metal Studio	Ted Schaal
Michael Bauermeister	Rob Lorenson	Craig Schaffer
Errol Beauchamp	Cynthia McKean	Patrick Shannon
Jackie Braitman	Stephen Porter	Cheryl Williams
Riis Burwell	Robert Pulley	Richard Yaski
Brian Chessmar	QUINTAL Studio	Guy J. Bellaver
Stephan Cox	Renee Dinauer Sculpture	Philip S. Drill
Barry Entner	Robert Rickard	Jeff Jackson
Eric Holt	Kevin Robb	Sarinda Jones
Dale Claude Lamphere	Brian F. Russell	John Wilbar
Melody Lane	James T. Russell	

Alex Anagnostou Glass Studio

Alex Anagnostou   10 Meaford Avenue, Toronto, ON M8V 2H5, Canada   TEL 416.668.4411
FAX 416.503.2709   EMAIL info@alexanagnostou.com   WEB www.alexanagnostou.com

Top left: *Glaciation* series, 2008, hot sand-cast glass with flameworked inclusions and aluminum frame, 12" x 13" x 13". Center left: *Ovoid Form,* 2007, blown glass with hot-worked glass threads, aluminum base, 16" x 7" x 8.5". Bottom left: *Greenscape* series, 2008, hot sand-cast glass with copper foil, steel frame includes LED lighting, each 12" x 5" x 4". Right: *Golden Spiral,* 2007, blown glass teardrops with hot-worked glass threads, 10' x 32" x 32". Photographs: Kevin Hedley.

SCULPTURE / NON-REPRESENTATIONAL

Michael Bauermeister

6560 Augusta Bottom Road, Augusta, MO 63332   TEL 636.228.4663
EMAIL michael@bauermeister.com   WEB www.michaelbauermeister.com

Left: *Tall Vessels* (left to right), stained birch, 65" x 19"; linden, 40" x 11"; birch, 73" x 20". Top right: *Tall Vessels* (left to right),
walnut, 38" x 12"; oak, 50" x 14"; painted oak, 26" x 11". Center right: *Sprout Vessels,* various woods, 17"–40" tall.
Bottom right: *Two Painted Vessels* (left to right), linden with paint, 34" x 14"; right, birch with paint, 56" x 15".

SCULPTURE / NON-REPRESENTATIONAL

Errol Beauchamp

Beauchamp Sculpture   27135 Mountain Park, Evergreen, CO 80439   TEL 303.378.0932   TEL 303.674.0997
FAX 303.670.4741   EMAIL errolcreates@beauchampsculpture.com   WEB www.beauchampsculpture.com

Top left: *Canyons*, bronze. Top right: *Posing with Sidelight*, bronze. Bottom: *Passages*, bronze. Photographs: Paul Peregrine.

SCULPTURE / NON-REPRESENTATIONAL

Jackie Braitman

Braitman Design Studio, Inc   120 Park Avenue, Takoma Park, MD 20912   TEL 301.891.3800
FAX 301.891.3801   EMAIL jackie@jackiebraitman.com   WEB www.jackiebraitman.com

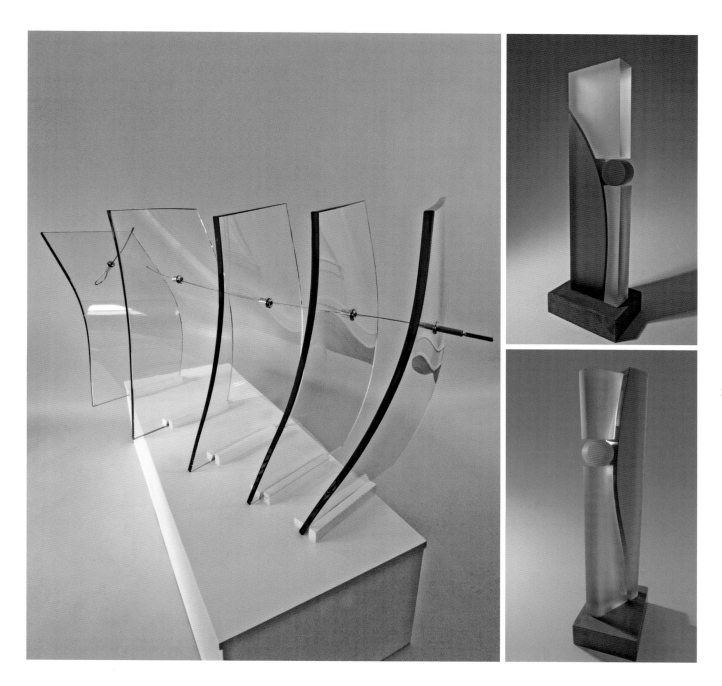

Left: *Jumping Off the Bandwagon* (maquette), 2008, bent glass, 40" x 60" x 30". Top right: *Silo Series IV #19,*
2008, cast glass, 22" x 7" x 5". Bottom right: *Silo Series IV #12,* 2008, cast glass, 22" x 7" x 5".

SCULPTURE / NON-REPRESENTATIONAL

Riis Burwell

Riis Burwell Studio   3815 Calistoga Road, Santa Rosa, CA 95404   TEL 707.538.2676
EMAIL riis@riisburwell.com   WEB www.riisburwell.com

282

Top left: *Synergetic*, 2001, London, England, bronze and stainless steel, 24" x 12" x 8". Top right: *Entropy Series #53*, 2005, Presbyterian Hospital, Denton, TX, bronze and stainless steel, 48" x 32" x 12". Bottom: *Spirit Form Horizontal*, 2007, Wilshire Grand Hotel, Los Angeles, CA, bronze and stainless steel, 16" x 12" x 36".

SCULPTURE / NON-REPRESENTATIONAL

Brian Chessmar

Chessmar Sculpture Studio   1405 Anderson Lane, Santa Barbara, CA 93111   TEL 805.637.7548
FAX 805.845.8558   EMAIL bchessmar@aol.com   WEB www.chessmarsculpture.com

283

Left: *Yin & Yang,* 2006, residence, Malibu, CA, stainless steel, 48" x 30" x 42". Top right: *Vision,* 2007, residence, Malibu, CA, bronze, 41" x 25" x 11".
Center right: *Alliance,* 2007, residence, Montecito, CA, stainless steel, 28" x 32" x 24". Bottom right: *Repose,* 2003, lacquered steel, 38" x 33" x 19".

SCULPTURE / NON-REPRESENTATIONAL

Stephan Cox

Stephan Cox Glass   W8651 690th Avenue, River Falls, WI 54022   TEL 715.425.7006
FAX 715.425.6668   EMAIL coxglass@gmail.com   WEB www.coxglass.com

284

Black Orchid/Black Grasses, 2007, glass, 40" x 14" x 14". Photograph: Don Pitlik.

SCULPTURE / NON-REPRESENTATIONAL

Barry Entner

Barry Entner Sculpture   41 Violet Hill Road, Rhinebeck, NY 12572
TEL/FAX 845.876.3077   EMAIL bentnerglass@aol.com   WEB www.barryentner.com

Top left: *Corona Series, Turquoise and Crystal,* 2008, glass, 24"H x 30"W x 30"D. Photograph: Bob Burrett. Top right: *Flora Sconce,* 2007, glass, 24"H x 16"W x 8"D. Bottom: *Corona Series, Gold to Blue, 2008,* Hunt Corporate Headquarters, Dallas TX, glass, 18"H x 60"W x 60"D.

SCULPTURE / NON-REPRESENTATIONAL

Eric Holt

Eric Holt—Metal Artist   3439 NE Sandy Boulevard Suite 665, Portland OR 97232   TEL 503.710.0711
FAX 503.546.5656   EMAIL grindmeister@yahoo.com   WEB www.emetalsculpture.com

Left: *Machines of Loving Grace,* 2005, Lake Oswego, OR, stainless steel, 144" x 40" x 38".
Right: *Praying Hands,* 2006, stainless steel, 132" x 68" x 30".

SCULPTURE / NON-REPRESENTATIONAL

286

Dale Claude Lamphere

Lamphere Studio   21079 Cardinal Place, Sturgis, SD 57785
TEL/FAX 605.347.5776   EMAIL lampherestudio@dndwifi.net

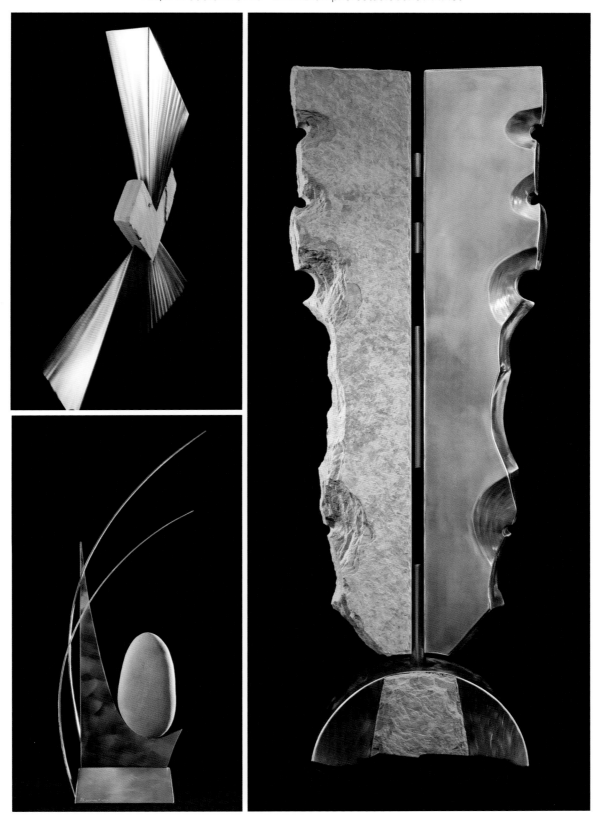

Top left: *Prism,* 2006, stone and stainless steel, 80" x 72" x 15". Right: *Echo,* 2008, stone and stainless steel, 83" x 30" x 17".
Bottom left: *Red Stone Landscape,* 2008, river rock and stainless steel, 36" x 24" x 6". Photographs: Kevin Eilbeck.

SCULPTURE / NON-REPRESENTATIONAL

Melody Lane

Melody Lane, Ceramic Artist   18 East Brocketts Point Road, Branford, CT 06405   TEL 203.481.3182
TEL 203.314.9086   FAX 203.432.8939   EMAIL melody.lane@yale.edu   WEB www.melodylanestudio.com

288

Sun Mandala Sculpture, 2008, Branford, CT, ceramic, glass, and steel, 72"H x 48"W x 18"D.

Lashua Metal Studio

Paul Lashua   4111 Spring Grove Avenue, Cincinnati, OH 45223   TEL 513.615.0594
FAX 513.531.0676   EMAIL paul@lashuametalstudio.com   WEB www.lashuametalstudio.com

Top: *Caring Spirit*, 2008, Hospice Care Center, Grand Junction, CO, formed, forged, fabricated, and painted steel, 108"H x 144" x 144".
Bottom left and right: *Caring Spirit* (details). Photographs: Chad Mahlum Photography.

SCULPTURE / NON-REPRESENTATIONAL

Rob Lorenson

Seven Coombs Street, Middleboro, MA 02346   TEL 508.454.5478
EMAIL rlorenson@bridgew.edu   WEB www.roblorenson.com

Top left: *Red Boxer*, 2007, painted aluminum, 32" x 48" x 48". Top right: *Pulsar*, 2006, stainless steel, 85" x 96" x 96".
Bottom left: *Syosset Series #10*, 2007, painted aluminum, 96" x 72" x 32". Bottom right: *Solar Flare*, 2005, stainless steel, 96" x 70" x 60".

SCULPTURE / NON-REPRESENTATIONAL

Rob Lorenson

Seven Coombs Street, Middleboro, MA 02346   TEL 508.454.5478
EMAIL rlorenson@bridgew.edu   WEB www.roblorenson.com

Top left: *Radio City,* 2005, stainless steel, 140" x 144" x 60". Top right: *Niagara,* 2008, 180" x 72" x 96".
Bottom left: *Maryland Headlong,* 2008, painted aluminum, 72" x 120" x 50". Bottom right: *Autumn Rhythm #19,* 2008, 168" x 96" x 75".

SCULPTURE / NON-REPRESENTATIONAL

Cynthia McKean

cMc Design   1000 Mason Street, Saugatuck, MI 49453   TEL 269.857.4612
EMAIL cmcdesign@cynthiamckean.com   WEB www.cynthiamckean.com

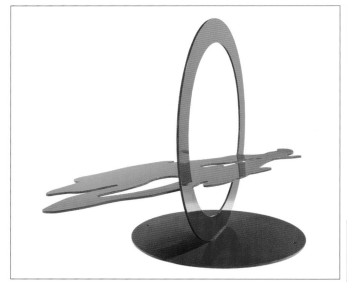

292

Top left: *Untitled*, steel, 3'H. Photograph: Terence Mahone. Right: *Seagulls*,
steel, 21'H. Photograph: Jen Jorgensen. Bottom left: *Untitled*, steel, 10'H.

SCULPTURE / NON-REPRESENTATIONAL

Cynthia McKean

cMc Design   1000 Mason Street, Saugatuck, MI 49453   TEL 269.857.4612
EMAIL cmcdesign@cynthiamckean.com   WEB www.cynthiamckean.com

Family of Man IV, steel, 10'H. Photograph: Gary Burmeister.

SCULPTURE / NON-REPRESENTATIONAL

Stephen Porter

Stephen Porter Studio   50 Peters Road, Searsmont, ME 04973   TEL 207.589.4843
EMAIL sporter@fairpoint.net   WEB www.stephenporterstudio.com

294

Top left: *Southern Bend II*, 2008, stainless steel, 48" x 96" x 65". Top right: *Circle 56*, 2004, stainless steel, 31" x 18" x 12".
Bottom left: *Cube Column 4*, stainless steel, 72" x 20" x 22". Bottom right: *Series 11 #22*, 2008, stainless steel, 73" x 16" x 13".

SCULPTURE / NON-REPRESENTATIONAL

Robert Pulley

Robert Pulley Sculpture   8670 West 450 South, Columbus, IN 47201   TEL 812.342.6475
EMAIL bpulley25@comcast.net   WEB www.robertpulley.com

Top: *Rose Canyon* and *Post,* 2008, stoneware clay, 44" x 106" x 24".
Bottom: *Marker,* 2005, stoneware clay, 23" x 28" x 18". Photographs: Kevin Montague.

SCULPTURE / NON-REPRESENTATIONAL

Admitting

Ross Cooperthwaite

Guild Sourcebooks at Work

Case Study #6

ARTIST: Michael Bauermeister
ARTWORK TITLE: *Water's Edge*
MEDIA: Linden wood with tinted lacquer
SIZE: 96" x 144" x 2"
INSTALLATION: Banner Thunderbird Medical Center, Glendale, AZ

"My experience working with Michael was great! We are strong believers in the importance of 'healing art' in healthcare facilities, and encouraged Michael to use that to develop his design. Michael sent us sketches to present to our client, along with a written proposal. During the process, he also sent us photos of the work in progress. Michael is my favorite artist that I have worked with thus far, and I look for any opportunity to commission him again in the future!

"*The Guild Sourcebook* has been great, especially for commissioning artists. The format is very clean and flattering to the artwork. We actually found another artist with *The Guild Sourcebook,* Goldstein Kapellas [see page 67] for the same hospital project. They were also amazing artists and great to work with. They are another group that I will look for future opportunities to work with."

Angela Lafica, Interior Designer
NTD Architecture
www.ntd.com

"*Water's Edge* is an offshoot of an earlier piece that was inspired by my firewood pile during a canoe float trip in southern Missouri. The textures of the sticks overlaying the smooth stones on the gravel bar just really sang to me. I get some of my best inspiration on trips like this.

"The designer, Angela Lafica, saw that earlier piece and asked if I could do something along those lines but much larger. She liked the imagery and thought it would be peaceful and contemplative, perfect for the hospital.

"The piece is made up of seven linden wood panels. The pebble texture is carved by hand with a gouge, and then painted by hand with tinted lacquer. Then the surface is sanded, stained, and clear coated with lacquer. The sticks are carved over the top of the finished stone texture, then stained, and the whole piece is finished with several coats of clear lacquer.

"The best part of this project was working with my son, Zac. He was home from college for the summer and was responsible for most of the pebble painting and a few other steps. It gave us a lot of time for conversation while working on these quiet, time-consuming tasks."

See more work by Michael Bauermeister on pages 279 and 407.

296

QUINTAL Studio—Fine Art, Glass, and Design

100 El Camino Real Suite 200, Burlingame, CA 94010   TEL 650.348.0310
FAX 650.348.8733   EMAIL quintal@quintalstudio.com   WEB www.quintalstudio.com

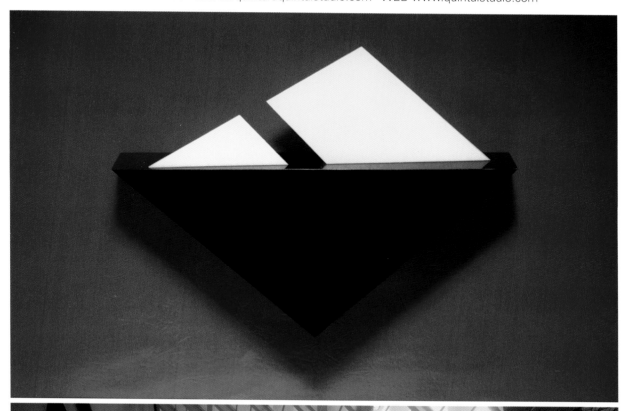

Top: *Convergence*, residence, Hillsborough, CA, spandrel glass and acrylic, 3'H x 4'W x 12"D.
Bottom: *Sheer Illusion*, 2'H, 4'H, and 6'H. Photographs: William A. Porter, San Francisco, CA.

SCULPTURE / NON-REPRESENTATIONAL

Renee Dinauer Sculpture

Renee Dinauer   PO Box 101032, Palm Bay, FL 32910-0132   TEL 321.223.1288
EMAIL renee@reneedinauersculpture.com   WEB www.reneedinauersculpture.com

Top left: *Autumn Loops II,* 2007, private residence, Dunedin, FL, free-form bent wood, 6' x 3'. Top right: *Crayzola Massive III Diagonal,* Palm Beach, FL, free-form bent wood, 75" x 52". Bottom: *Cappuccino Chaos,* Carmel Valley Ranch Resort, CA, free-form bent wood, 6' x 30'.

SCULPTURE / NON-REPRESENTATIONAL

Renee Dinauer Sculpture

Renee Dinauer   PO Box 101032, Palm Bay, FL 32910-0132   TEL 321.223.1288
EMAIL renee@reneedinauersculpture.com   WEB www.reneedinauersculpture.com

Top: *Zebra 5-D,* 2008, Highland Beach, FL, free-form bent wood, 50" x 75".
Bottom: *Oceans One Sea Turtle,* 2008, lobby, Atlantic Beach, FL, free-form bent wood, 4' x 13'.

SCULPTURE / NON-REPRESENTATIONAL

Robert Rickard

Rickard Studio   PO Box 1360, Taos, NM 87571   TEL 575.613.4885
EMAIL robert@rickardstudio.com   WEB www.rickardstudio.com

300

Left to right: *Malabar Pendulum Wall Clock*, 2008, patinaed copper, bronze, and iron over aluminum, 28.5"H x 10.5"W x 1"D.
Comfort, 2008, patinaed copper, bronze, and iron over hand-fabricated steel, 80"H x 24"W x 11"D.
Desert Passage Wall Hanging, 2008, patinaed copper, bronze, and iron over aluminum, 32"H x 52"W x 1"D.

Robert Rickard

Rickard Studio   PO Box 1360, Taos, NM 87571   TEL 575.613.4885
EMAIL robert@rickardstudio.com   WEB www.rickardstudio.com

Left to right: *Playful,* 2008, patinaed copper, bronze, and iron over hand-fabricated steel, 100"H x 45"W x 9"D.
Third Dimension Wall Hanging, 2008, patinaed copper, bronze, and iron over aluminum, 32"H x 52"W x 1"D.
Desk Clock, 2008, patinaed copper, bronze, and iron over aluminum, 7"H x 7"W x 3"D.

SCULPTURE / NON-REPRESENTATIONAL

Kevin Robb

Kevin Robb Studios, LLC   7001 West 35th Avenue, Wheat Ridge, CO 80033
TEL 303.431.4758   EMAIL 3d@kevinrobb.com   WEB www.kevinrobb.com

302

Playing Ball, 2009, stainless steel, 17'H. Photograph: Diane Robb.

SCULPTURE / NON-REPRESENTATIONAL

Brian F. Russell

Brian Russell Studio   10385 Long Road, Arlington, TN 38002   TEL 901.867.7300
FAX 901.867.7843   EMAIL info@brianrussellstudio.com   WEB www.brianrussellstudio.com

Left: *Hemisphere: Nadir,* 2008, cast glass and forged steel, 24" x 13" x 10".
Right: *Hemisphere: Zig Zag,* 2008, cast glass and forged bronze, 28" x 15" x 12".

SCULPTURE / NON-REPRESENTATIONAL

James T. Russell

James T. Russell Sculpture   1930 Lomita Boulevard, Lomita, CA 90717   TEL 310.326.0785
FAX 310.326.1470   EMAIL james@russellsculpture.com   WEB www.russellsculpture.com

304

Zephyr, 2008, Memphis, TN, highly polished stainless steel, 18'H.

SCULPTURE / NON-REPRESENTATIONAL

James T. Russell

James T. Russell Sculpture   1930 Lomita Boulevard, Lomita, CA 90717   TEL 310.326.0785
FAX 310.326.1470   EMAIL james@russellsculpture.com   WEB www.russellsculpture.com

Infinite Spirit, 2008, 10'H. Photograph: Paul Moses.

SCULPTURE / NON-REPRESENTATIONAL

Ted Schaal

Schaal Arts Inc.   1633 South Estrella Avenue, Loveland, CO 80537   TEL/FAX 970.461.2007
EMAIL ted@schaalarts.com   WEB www.schaalarts.com

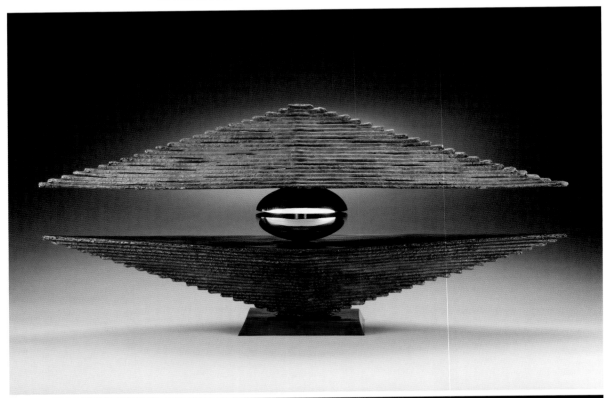

306

Top: *Mirage,* 2007, 15" x 30" x 8". Bottom: *Halved Thricell,* 2007, bronze, 24" x 24" x 30". Photographs: Jafe Parsons.

SCULPTURE / NON-REPRESENTATIONAL

Craig Schaffer

3814 Jocelyn Street NW, Washington, DC 20015   TEL 202.362.4507   TEL 202.360.0020
EMAIL schaffer.sculpture@gmail.com   WEB www.craigschaffer.com

Top left: *Ming Yang,* 2007, steel, 11" x 18" x 11". Top right: *Spiral Squares,* 2008, bronze, 28" x 38" x 10".
Bottom: *Gallo Grande,* 2008, steel, 65" x 54" x 36".

SCULPTURE / NON-REPRESENTATIONAL

Patrick Shannon

Forest Edge   46461 295 Avenue, Vergas, MN 56587   TEL 218.342.2682
FAX 218.342.2680   EMAIL cottagecraftsman@arvig.net   WEB www.forestedgeartgallery.com

Left: *Structure,* 2008, Stone Hearth Restaurant, Frazee, MN, copper and steel, 9.3' x 18". Top right: *Projection,* 2008, copper, steel, and stone, 7' x 24".
Bottom right: *Planters,* 2008, residence, Minneapolis, MN, copper, steel, and stone, 4'–6'H x 30". Photographs: Nathan Lovas.

SCULPTURE / NON-REPRESENTATIONAL

Cheryl Williams

PO Box 1283, Ashland, OR 97520   TEL 541.531.3677
EMAIL info@cherylswilliams.com   WEB www.cherylswilliams.com

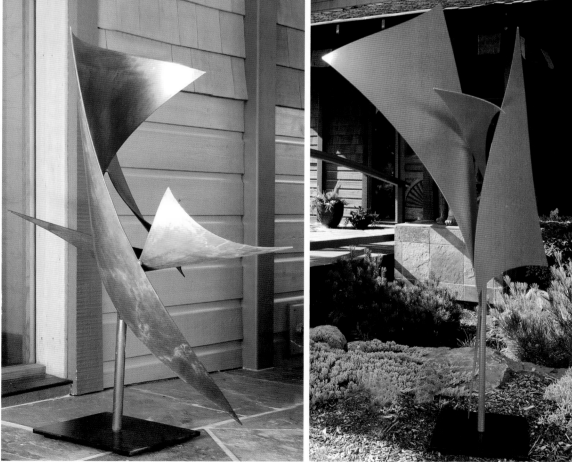

309

Top: *Silver Ring with Stone,* 2008, aluminum and ceramic. Bottom left: *Untitled,* 2008, steel, 4'H.
Bottom right: *Untitled,* 2008, steel, 5'H. Photographs: Stuart Grey.

SCULPTURE / NON-REPRESENTATIONAL

Richard Yaski

6024 Albion Little River Road, Little River, CA 95456   TEL 707.937.0075
223 North Guadalupe #558, Santa Fe, NM 87501   TEL 505.216.7639   EMAIL richard@yaski.com   WEB www.yaski.com

310

Top and bottom: *Concentric Sphere,* Shibui Sculpture Garden, Little River, CA, welded steel and bronze, 20'L x 8'DIA.

SCULPTURE / NON-REPRESENTATIONAL

Guy J. Bellaver

6 Aintree Road, Saint Charles, IL 60174-1415   TEL 630.886.7818
TEL 630.584.4650   FAX 630.377.7045   EMAIL gjb.rteest@gmail.com

Left: *Oriental*, 2006, painted wood, steel, and resin, 12' x 7' x 4'6".
Right: *Quarks III*, 2008, bronze with verdigris patina, 12" x 14" x 6".

Philip S. Drill

80 Main Street, West Orange, NJ 07052   TEL 973.736.9350
FAX 973.736.3776   EMAIL psdrill@aol.com   WEB www.psdrill.com

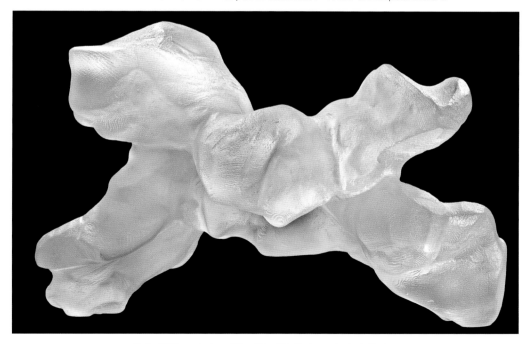

Halic, 2008, cast glass, 14" x 19" x 10". Photograph: Andy Foster.

SCULPTURE / NON-REPRESENTATIONAL

Jeff Jackson

Jeff Jackson Fine Art   11250 East Stallion Drive, Parker, CO 80138   TEL/FAX 303.840.0140
TEL 720.284.1920   EMAIL jeff@jeffjacksonfineart.com   WEB www.jeffjacksonfineart.com

Left: *Multiple Arcs #124,* 2008, stainless steel, 16.5' x 28" x 34".
Right: *Arc #123,* 2008, Parker, CO, stainless steel, 34" x 19" x 9".

312

Sarinda Jones

Reflective Art Studio   TEL 801.835.8611
EMAIL sarinda@comcast.net   WEB www.reflectiveartstudio.com

It is, 2008, Salt Lake City, UT, glass. Inset: *It is* (detail). Photographs: Jan Stevenson.

SCULPTURE / NON-REPRESENTATIONAL

John Wilbar

222 West Abriendo, Pueblo, CO 81004 TEL 719.542.1370
EMAIL jfwilbar@yahoo.com WEB www.johnwilbar.com

O x O, 2007, Pueblo, CO, wood, stucco, and paint, 96"H x 60"W x 40"D. Photographs: Wark Photography.

Sculpture / Non-Representational: Common Terms and Their Meanings

Bentwood A process commonly used in chair-making that uses steam to make wood pliable for shaping into furniture parts.

Casting The process of pouring molten metal or glass, clay slip, etc. into a hollow mold to harden. Some casting processes permit more than one reproduction.

Epoxy A group of thermosetting resins, well adapted to molding and therefore popular with sculptors. Epoxies are also used in adhesives, laminates, enamels, and coatings.

Fabricating Assembling, forming, manufacturing, or otherwise constructing metal products.

Fire-polishing Smoothing the surface of a sharp or rough piece of glass by careful heating in the flame. As the surface of the glass softens, surface tension will draw it into a smooth contour.

Pate de Verre Literally, "paste of glass." A type of glass using a glass "paste" of finely crushed glass that is mixed, heated, poured into a mold, annealed or cooled, and ultimately freed from the mold. Similar to cast sculpture.

Model To shape. In sculpture, an additive process where the artist builds up a form by adding and shaping material.

Verdigris A greenish blue patina that forms on copper, brass, or bronze surfaces. Faux verdigris (or verdi) finishes are common on the metal work of coffee tables, etc.

CASTING

Silo Series IV #19
by Jackie Braitman, see page 281.

Sculpture/

Art, Inc.
Bennett Studio
Bigbird Studios
Erik Blome
Jeanine Briggs
Shelley Tincher Buonaiuto
    and Michael Buonaiuto
Steven Bush
Donna L. Caron
Gesso Cocteau

Bennett Studio

Chris Bennett   26983 Route J40, Keosauqua, IA 52565   TEL 319.592.3228
FAX 319.592.3463   EMAIL cbennett@netins.net   WEB www.bennettstudio.com

317

Top: *Prairie Preening,* 2007, Butler Community College, El Dorado, KS, bronze, 78"H x 30"W x 12"D.
Bottom: *Parade Route,* 2007, Main Street, Shoreline, WA, bronze, 8'H x 24"W x 24"D.

SCULPTURE / REPRESENTATIONAL

Bigbird Studios

Pat Payne   2121 Alameda Avenue, Alameda, CA 94501   TEL 510.521.9308
EMAIL ppbigbird@aol.com   WEB www.bigbird-studios.com

318

Top left: *Heron in Garden*, 2006, welded steel, weathered, 87" x 70" 32". Top right: *Condor II* (detail), 2007,
bronze and powder-coated steel, 45" x 60" x 42". Bottom: *Young Condor*, 2006, bronze and powder-coated steel, 32" x 42" x 21".

SCULPTURE / REPRESENTATIONAL

Erik Blome

Figurative Art Studio LLC   5569 Likins Avenue, Martinez, CA 94553   TEL 925.408.3446
EMAIL emblome@gmail.com   WEB www.figurativeartstudio.com

Top: *Peace* (detail), 2006, Mount Prospect Public Library, IL, bronze and stainless steel, 20'H. Bottom left: *African Elephant*, 2005, Ivory Coast Embassy, Washington, DC, bronze, 12'H. Bottom right: *Mastodon Digger*, 2005, Aurora, IL, bronze, over life size.

SCULPTURE / REPRESENTATIONAL

Jeanine Briggs

PO Box 475441, San Francisco, CA 94123   TEL 415.567.4662
EMAIL jbcreativestudios@yahoo.com   WEB www.jeaninebriggs.com

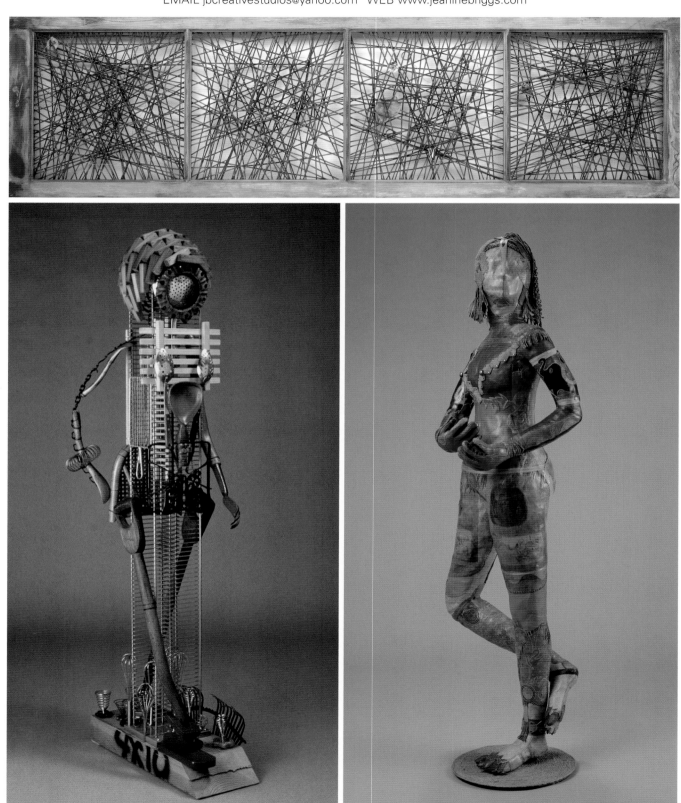

320

Top: *Nexus,* wall sculpture, 2007, discarded steel, wire, and wood, 21.25" x 75" x 3". Bottom left: *Crossing the Planes,* 2006, discarded wood and metal, 68.5" x 16" x 26". Bottom right: *Joie de Vivre,* 2008, reused leather on mixed-media core, 71" x 24" x 16". Photographs: Maximage.

SCULPTURE / REPRESENTATIONAL

Shelley Tincher Buonaiuto and Michael Buonaiuto

Buonaiuto Pottery   13866 Pin Oak Road, Fayetteville, AR 72704   TEL 479.445.6567
TEL 505.470.6770   FAX 479.445.6772   EMAIL goodhelp@cybermesa.com   WEB www.alittlecompany.net

321

Top: *Alternative Energies,* 2006, Loveland, CO, bronze, 37"H. Bottom left: *Wind* (detail), 2006, Loveland, CO, bronze, 24"H x 24"W x 20"D.
Bottom right: *Wave* (detail), 2006, Loveland, CO, bronze, 29"H x 28"W x 23"D. Photographs: Hollis Officer.

SCULPTURE / REPRESENTATIONAL

Steven Bush

smARTwork by Steven Bush LLC   4155 North Waggoner Road, Blacklick, OH 43004   TEL 614.578.0322
TEL 614.855.0419   FAX 614.884.2317   EMAIL stevenwbush@insight.rr.com   WEB www.stevenwbush.com

Left: *Steven Bush Original Flowers*, 2008, Dutt Gardens, Ostrander, OH, steel, 10' x 5' x 4'.
Right: *Steven Bush Original Flowers 2*, 2008, steel, 6' x 4' x 3'. Photographs: Larry McVay.

SCULPTURE / REPRESENTATIONAL

Donna L. Caron

82A Waterhouse Road, Dayton, ME 04005   TEL 207.499.2201
EMAIL donnalcaron@roadrunner.com   WEB www.donnalcaron.com

323

Origins, modified concrete with marine specimens, 85" x 48" x 17". Photograph: J. Michael Gerstner.

Gesso Cocteau

Gesso Cocteau Studio   45565 Williams Road, Indian Wells, CA 92210   TEL 760.341.3988
TEL 760.702.5049   EMAIL gesso@gessococteau.com   WEB www.gessococteau.com

324

Top: *Ode to Love*, 2008, cast bronze, 81" x 64" x 32", edition of twelve. Bottom left: *Kiss of Life*, 2008, cast bronze, 44" x 22" x 20", edition of twelve. Bottom right: *Ti Amo*, 2005, cast bronze, 74" x 72" x 39", edition of twelve.

Gesso Cocteau

Gesso Cocteau Studio   45565 Williams Road, Indian Wells, CA 92210   TEL 760.341.3988
TEL 760.702.5049   EMAIL gesso@gessococteau.com   WEB www.gessococteau.com

325

Endless Celebration, 2005, Bellevue, WA, cast bronze, 51' x 24' x 12', one of a kind.

SCULPTURE / REPRESENTATIONAL

Brent Cooke

CastArt Studio   549 Langvista Drive, Victoria, BC, V9B 5N2, Canada   TEL 250.386.5352   TEL 250.588.5352
FAX 250.391.9966   EMAIL brentcooke@shaw.ca   WEB www.castartstudio.com

326

Top: *Headin' Home,* 2006, bronze, 24"H x 42"W x 35"D.
Bottom: *Wing Speed,* 2001, bronze, 14"H x 33"W x 16"D. Photographs: Perry Danforth.

SCULPTURE / REPRESENTATIONAL

Brent Cooke

CastArt Studio   549 Langvista Drive, Victoria, BC, V9B 5N2, Canada   TEL 250.386.5352   TEL 250.588.5352
FAX 250.391.9966   EMAIL brentcooke@shaw.ca   WEB www.castartstudio.com

Top: *Into the Blue,* 2007, bronze, 14"H x 52"W x 25"D. Bottom left: *Bald Eagle,* 1999, bronze, 9"H x 7"W x 7"D.
Bottom right: *Split Decision 2,* 2004, bronze, 36"H x 18"W x 28"D. Photographs: Janet Dwyer.

SCULPTURE / REPRESENTATIONAL

Randy Cooper

Cooper Creations, Inc.   130 Quincy Street NE, Albuquerque, NM 87108   TEL 505.266.2781
TEL 505.463.9342   FAX 505.266.5701   EMAIL randy@randycooperart.com   WEB www.randycooperart.com

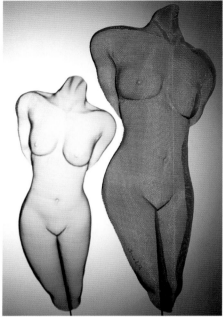

Top left: *Carol,* 1993, The Cathedral of St. John, Albuquerque, NM, bronze, 25"H x 17"W x 12"D. Top center: *Synergy Plus,* 2008, steel wire mesh, 69"H x 28"W x 11"D, created with Darin Cooper. Top right: *Annabelle,* 2008, powder-coated steel wire mesh, 39"H x 17"W x 8"D. Bottom: *Symphony,* 2008, abstract steel mesh, powder-coated steel wire mesh, 75"H x 80"W x 12"D, created with Darin Cooper. Photographs: Tomar S. Flores.

SCULPTURE / REPRESENTATIONAL

Renate Burgyan Fackler

Chrysalis Sculpture Studio, LLC   447 Lakeshore Drive West, Hebron, OH 43025   TEL 614.832.6444   TEL 740.527.2114
FAX 740.527.2116   EMAIL rfackler@columbus.rr.com   WEB www.chrysalissculpturestudio.com

329

Jumping Daisies, 2008, Columbus, OH, bronze, 20"H x 9"W x 12"D. Photographs: Rachel Bowen.

SCULPTURE / REPRESENTATIONAL

Lindsay Feuer

Lindsay Feuer Studio   Cherry Hill, NJ   TEL 215.688.0873
EMAIL lindsay@lindsayfeuer.com   WEB www.lindsayfeuer.com

Top left: *Hybrid Cluster No. 11,* 2007, hand-built porcelain, 11"H x 7"D x 6.5"W. Top right: *Hybrid Flora No. 9,* 2008, hand-built porcelain, 12"H x 7"W x 8.5"D. Bottom: *Large Hybrid Series No. 8,* 2006, hand-built porcelain, 19"H x 30"W x 15"D. Photographs: John Carlano.

SCULPTURE / REPRESENTATIONAL

David J. Holmes

Wolf's Crag Sculpture   974 Ward Hill Road, Plymouth, ME 04969   TEL 207.948.3742
EMAIL wolfscrag@uninets.net   WEB www.wolfscragsculpture.com

331

Top: *Sea Whispers,* 1999, Takaka, New Zealand marble, 4' x 6.6' x 4.5'.
Bottom left and right: *Rose Bowl,* 2005, Ellsworth, ME schist, 12" x 38" x 38".

SCULPTURE / REPRESENTATIONAL

Casey G. Horn

CGH Studios, Inc.   PO Box 805, Brighton, CO 80601
TEL 720.394.7236   EMAIL chorn@cghstudios.com   WEB www.caseyhorn.com

332

Left: *Evening Sunset,* 2008, stainless steel with patina, 12' x 9' x 5', custom sizes available. Photograph: Jafe Parsons. Top right: *Woman,* 2006, stainless steel, 48" x 36" x 24". Photograph: Mel Shockner. Bottom right: *Tree,* 2006, bronze and stainless steel, custom sizes available. Photograph: Jafe Parsons.

SCULPTURE / REPRESENTATIONAL

Dori Jalazo

Dori Jalazo Visions   505 Kemp Road West, Greensboro, NC 27410   TEL 336.299.2517
EMAIL dori@dorij.com   WEB www.dorij.com

Top: *A Diva is Born* (detail), 2007, sculpted ceramic and mixed media, 49" x 29" x 9". Bottom left: *What Do You Pack When You Are Ready to Fly?*, 2007, sculpted ceramic and mixed media, 12" x 14". Bottom right: *Letting Go*, 2007, sculpted ceramic and mixed media, 37" x 19" x 12". Photographs: Innovations Imaging.

SCULPTURE / REPRESENTATIONAL

Jane Rankin Sculpture

Jane A. Rankin   19335 Greenwood Drive, Monument, CO 80132   TEL 719.488.9223   TEL 719.332.5406
FAX 719.488.1650   EMAIL janerankin@magpiehill.com   WEB www.janerankin.com

334

Top left: *Periwinkle*, 2005, Arboretum, Newton, IA, bronze, 40" x 23" x 19". Top right: *Repose*, 2007, private collection, bronze, 24" x 20" x 19".
Bottom: *Abracadabra*, Harvest Community, Fort Collins, CO, bronze, 50"H x 50"W x 24"D.

SCULPTURE / REPRESENTATIONAL

Barry Woods Johnston

SculptureWorks, Inc.   2423 Pickwick Road, Baltimore, MD 21207   TEL 410.448.1945
FAX 410.448.2663   EMAIL barry@sculptorjohnston.com   WEB www.sculptorjohnston.com

Faith, Hope, and Love, 2007, Bellevue, WA, bronze and stone, bronze 8.25'H.

Tuck Langland

12632 Anderson, Granger, IN 46530   TEL/FAX 574.272.2708
TEL 574.360.7946   EMAIL tuck12@comcast.net

336

Left: *Moonbeam*, 2008, English bone china. Right: *Diana the Huntress*, 2007, bronze. Photographs: William G. Healy.

SCULPTURE / REPRESENTATIONAL

Peter W. Michel

185 Brookside Lane, Fayetteville, NY 13066   TEL 315.632.4780   TEL 315.663.5308
EMAIL peter@petermichel.com   WEB www.petermichel.com

337

Top left: *Support Circle Rainbow,* 2006, painted wood wall sculpture, 42"DIA. x 1.25"D. Right: *Peace Garden Totem Maquette,*
2008, painted wood, 37"H x 10"DIA. Bottom left: *Coming Together,* 2008, painted wood, 10"H x 23.5"DIA.

Richard A. Moore III

5515 SE Stark Street, Portland, OR 97215   TEL 503.706.5721
EMAIL rmoore27@msn.com   WEB www.rmooresculptures.com

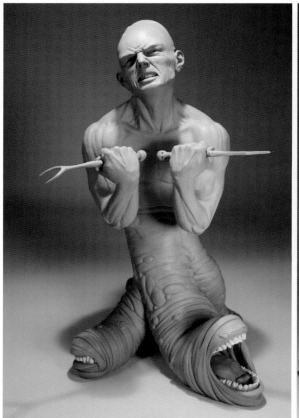

Top left: *I'm So Hungry,* 2006, oil clay, 24"H x 16"W x 14"D. Top right: *Sweet Casey,* 2008, oil clay, 24"H x 18"W x 8"D.
Bottom: *Octohandy,* 2007, oil clay, 12"H x 24"W x 26"D.

SCULPTURE / REPRESENTATIONAL

Amy J. Musia

Musia Fine Art   5625 Pearl Drive Suite F #325, Evansville, IN 47712   TEL 812.459.8833
EMAIL a.musia@att.net   WEB www.amymusia.com

339

Top left and right: *Leaves*, 2009, available in copper, Corten, aluminum, and powder-coated steel in sizes ranging from 3' to 16'.
Bottom: *Lotus in Quiet Waters*, 2008, Deaconess Gateway Hospital, Evansville, IN, wood with 24K gilding, 40"H x 72"W x 56"D. Photograph: John Dawson.

SCULPTURE / REPRESENTATIONAL

Pokey Park

Pokey Park Studios   6396 North Desert Wind Circle, Tucson, AZ 85750   TEL 520.529.6435
FAX 520.749.1338   EMAIL pokey@pokeypark.com   WEB www.pokeypark.com

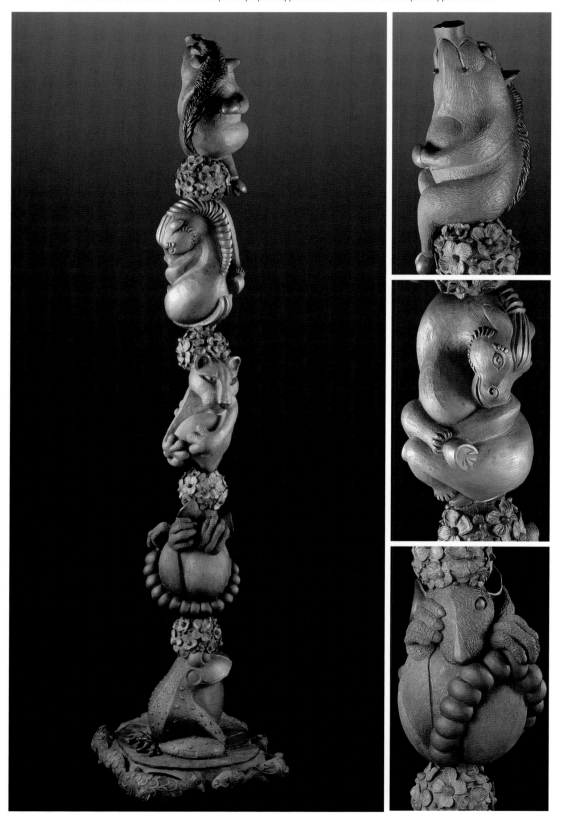

340

Zodiac Totem I, 2008, bronze, 108" x 26". Photographs: Steve Torregrossa.

Louise Peterson

PO Box 67, Guffey, CO 80820   TEL 888.829.0016
EMAIL louise@danesculptor.com   WEB www.danesculptor.com

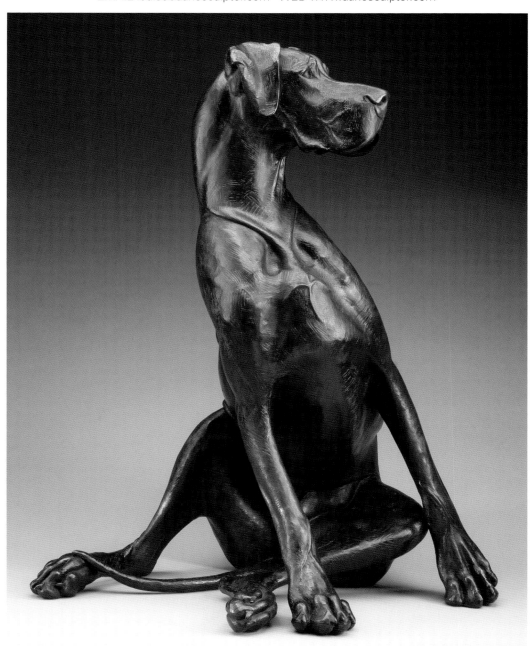

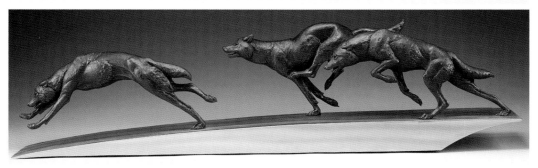

Top: *On the Rise,* bronze, 40"H x 30"W x 24"D. Photograph: Jafe Parsons.
Bottom: *Free Spirits,* bronze and stainless steel, 17"H x 64"W x 10"D.

SCULPTURE / REPRESENTATIONAL

Tanya Ragir

Tanya Ragir Studio   3587 Ocean View Avenue, Los Angeles, CA 90066   TEL 310.390.5919
FAX 310.398.7965   EMAIL tanya@tanyaragir.com   WEB www.tanyaragir.com

342

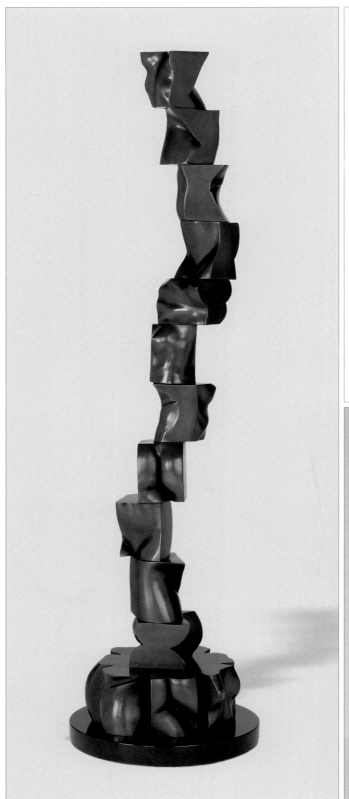

Left: *Building Blocks I,* 1999, bronze, 42" x 10" x 10", edition of nine. Top right: *Curve,* 2003, bronze, 18" x 13" x 8", edition of nine.
Bottom right: *SpaceBetween,* 2001, bronze, 22" x 12"DIA., edition of nine.

SCULPTURE / REPRESENTATIONAL

Tanya Ragir

Tanya Ragir Studio   3587 Ocean View Avenue, Los Angeles, CA 90066   TEL 310.390.5919
FAX 310.398.7965   EMAIL tanya@tanyaragir.com   WEB www.tanyaragir.com

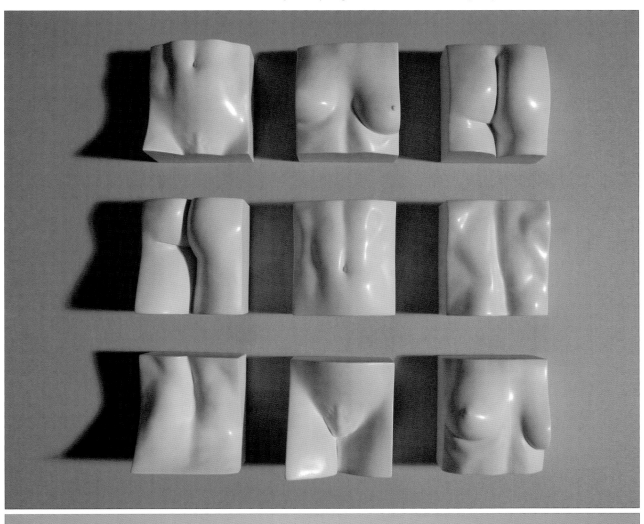

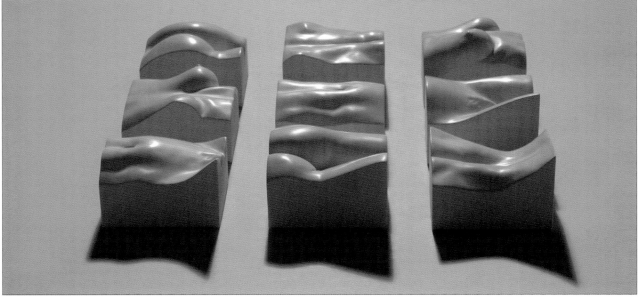

Brick Work, 2009, cast stone, each element 3.25" x 3.75" x 2.5".

SCULPTURE / REPRESENTATIONAL

Rosetta

Rosetta   405 Eighth Street SE #15, Loveland, CO 80537   TEL 970.667.6265
EMAIL rosetta@rosettasculpture.com   WEB www.rosettasculpture.com

344

Top: *Running Cheetah,* 2008, NuVasive, San Diego, CA, bronze, 34" x 115" x 17". Photograph: Nadia Borowski Scott.
Bottom: *On the Alert,* 2008, private residence, Belvedere, CA, bronze, 39" x 36" x 26". Photograph: "Scotty" Scott.

SCULPTURE / REPRESENTATIONAL

Gerald Siciliano

Gerald Siciliano Studio Design Associates   9 Garfield Place, Brooklyn, NY 11215-1903   TEL 718.636.4561
TEL 718.757.2845   EMAIL geraldsicilianostudio@gmail.com   WEB www.geraldsicilianostudio.com

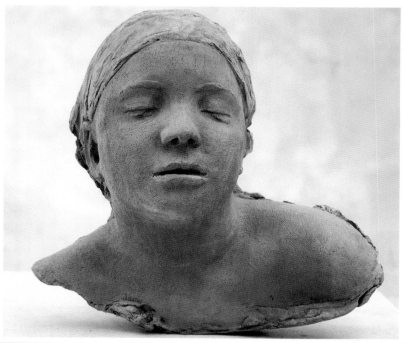

345

Top: *Sara*, terra cotta, life size.
Bottom: *Acier*, stainless steel, competition study, 36.5" (1/10" scale).

SCULPTURE / REPRESENTATIONAL

Ron Slagle

Slagle Studio   2052 Highway 226 North, Bakersville, NC 28705   TEL 828.688.4204
EMAIL ronslagle@hotmail.com   WEB www.ronslaglestudio.com

346

Left: *Female Figure on Pedestal,* 2007, private collection, clay, 35" x 9" x 11".
Right: *Head,* 2007, clay, 37" x 21" x 17". Photographs: Tom Mills.

SCULPTURE / REPRESENTATIONAL

Milon Townsend

Townsend Associates   262 Moul Road, Hilton, NY 14468   TEL 585.392.6476
FAX 585.392.7782   EMAIL milon@rochester.rr.com   WEB www.milontownsend.com

347

Top: *Ciel,* 2008, kiln-cast glass, 24" x 44" x 14".
Bottom: *Esprit du Bois,* 2008, kiln-cast glass, 24" x 44" x 14".

SCULPTURE / REPRESENTATIONAL

Evgeni Vodenitcharov

Icon Sculpting 5119 South Cameron Street, Las Vegas, NV 89118
TEL 702.768.5147   EMAIL evsculpting@yahoo.com   WEB www.iconsculpting.com

348

Left: *V-8 Goddess,* 2008, Bob Drake Productions, OR, fiberglass sculpture, 8' x 4.5' x 3.5'. Photograph: Randy Johnson.
Top right: *Athena,* 1998, Venetian Casino, Las Vegas, NV, 5' x 2.5' x 2.5'. Photograph: Steve Weeks. Center right: *Crucifix,* 2001,
St. Viator Church, 7.5' x 7' x 1.5'. Photograph: Steve Weeks. Bottom right: *Treasure Island,* 2003, Las Vegas, NV, 12' x 25' x 9'.

SCULPTURE / REPRESENTATIONAL

Wanner Sculpture Studio

David Wanner and Jordan Wanner   5828 North 97th Street, Milwaukee, WI 53225   TEL/FAX 414.462.3569
EMAIL info@wannersculpturestudio.com   WEB www.wannersculpturestudio.com

349

Top left: *St. Martin DePorres* (detail), 2005, St. Rose Dominican Hospital, Henderson, NV, cast bronze, 8'H. Bottom left: *Mother and Child,* 2008, St. Jerome Catholic Church, Oconomowoc, WI, cast bronze, 3'H. Right: *Zachary Taylor,* 2008, Leicht Park, Green Bay, WI, cast bronze, 8'H.

SCULPTURE / REPRESENTATIONAL

Bruce Wolfe

Bruce Wolfe Studio   206 El Cerrito Avenue, Piedmont, CA 94611   TEL 510.655.7871   TEL 510.655.7077
FAX 510.601.7200   EMAIL landbwolfe@earthlink.net   WEB www.brucewolfe.com

350

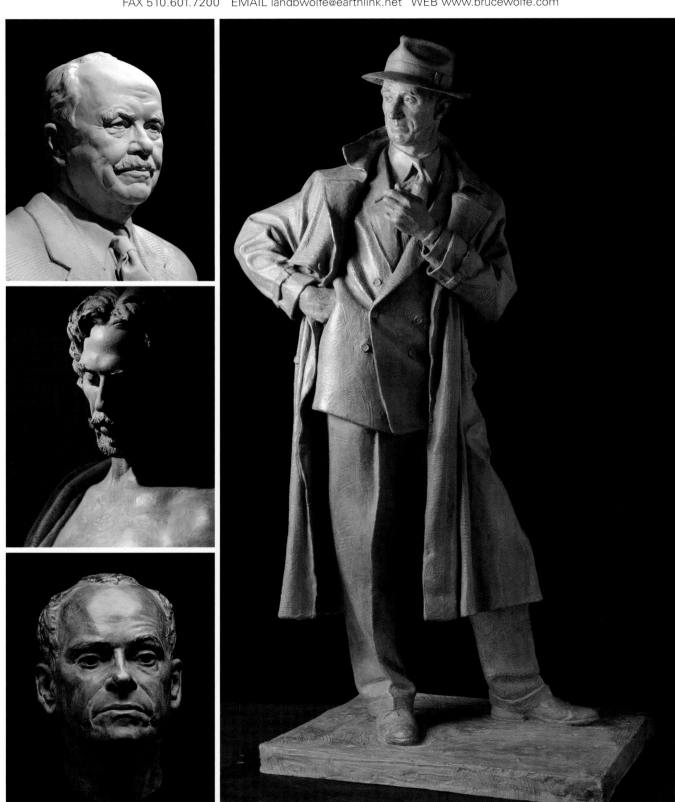

Top left: *Dr. James Potchen,* 2005, Genome Laboratory, Michigan State University, bronze, 1.5 life-size. Right: *Harry Bridges,* 2007, maquette for monument, Harry Bridges Plaza, San Francisco, CA, bronze, one-half life-size, monument 9'H. Center left: *Risen Christ,* 1999, Old Mission, Santa Barbara, CA, bronze, 1.25 life-size. Bottom left: *Joseph Frank, Operatic Tenor,* 2006, Bohemian Club, San Francisco, CA, bronze, life-size.

SCULPTURE / REPRESENTATIONAL

Bruce Wolfe

Bruce Wolfe Studio   206 El Cerrito Avenue, Piedmont, CA 94611   TEL 510.655.7871   TEL 510.655.7077
FAX 510.601.7200   EMAIL landbwolfe@earthlink.net   WEB www.brucewolfe.com

351

Margaret Thatcher, 2008, Hillsdale College, Hillsdale, MI, bronze, 1.4 life-size.

SCULPTURE / REPRESENTATIONAL

Neil Rashba

Guild Sourcebooks at Work

Case Study #7

ARTIST: Pat Payne, Bigbird Studios
ARTWORK TITLE: *Heron*
MEDIA: Weathered welded steel
SIZE: 80" x 70" x 32"
INSTALLATION: Glenmoor Retirement Resort, St. Augustine, FL

 352

"I was in a bind trying to find what I needed. I started thumbing through *The Guild Sourcebook* and found Pat. Pat was so responsive and very professional. She did what she said she would do when she said she'd do it. She was responsive to our inquiries and questions concerning everything from logistics to maintenance.

"The Guild Sourcebooks continue to be a valuable resource for me. In addition to being a great resource for finding the appropriate piece for a project, I find thumbing through the book inspirational. I'm an artist, reachable at www.larrywilsonartist.com, as well as an interior designer, and the Sourcebook is always close by. It has proven to be a consistently professional collection of art resources."

Larry Wilson, IIDA, ASID
DESIGNMIND, LLC
www.designmindllc.com
Former senior principal,
Rink Design Partnership, Inc.
www.rinkdesign.com

"This was a great commission because it was so simple! The designer had seen a similar bird of mine in *The Guild Sourcebook,* called me, and I had a another bird at my studio, so it was a simple process. Many people say that rust belongs outdoors, but the *Heron* looks so wonderful in this indoor resort restaurant.

"I was inspired by my environment when I created this piece; I live near the water and see these magnificent birds all the time. Working in steel allows a lightness of look with a thin strength that you cannot cast in bronze."

See more work by Pat Payne of Bigbird Studios on page 318.

Ann Fleming

West Linn, OR   TEL 503.577.2730
EMAIL a.fleming@comcast.net   WEB www.annfleming.com

A Wild Hare, 2008, bronze, 11.5" x 22" x 7".

Shohini Ghosh

Shohini's Studio   9187 South Madras Court, Littleton, CO 80130   TEL 303.470.6776
TEL 720.217.8516   EMAIL shohinighosh@hotmail.com   WEB www.shohini.com

Left: *How Do You Feel Today,* 2007, bronze, 9"H x 9"W x 9"D.
Right: *Gossip,* 2007, bronze, 11"H x 20"W x 18"D.

SCULPTURE / REPRESENTATIONAL

Bill Hueg

Peacock Studios, Inc.   12919 North Vallejo Circle, Westminster, CO 80234
TEL 720.281.5349   EMAIL billhueg@msn.com   WEB www.billhueg.com

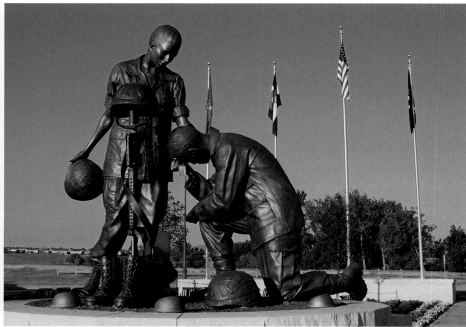

Left: *Terpsichore*, bronze, 14.5" x 5" x 3". Photograph: Ken Trujillo.
Right: *Grieving Friends,* 2007, Armed Forces Tribute Garden, Westminster, CO, bronze, 112.2" x 118" x 96".

354

Sculpture / Representational: Common Terms and Their Meanings

Bronze Traditionally, an alloy of copper and tin widely used in casting. The term is often applied to brown-colored brasses.

BRONZE

Contrapposto A pose in which one part of the body twists away from the other with the weight of the figure balanced on one leg instead of two, exemplified in Michelangelo's *David.*

Edition The total number of impressions an artist makes of any one image or design. In recent times, each impression in an edition is signed and numbered by the artist, but this is a relatively recent practice.

Hand-built Ceramics term referring to a work that is assembled by hand. Finished object may include wheel-thrown, cast, coiled, and/or slab elements.

Lampwork The technique of manipulating glass by heating it with a small flame. An open flame is advantageous in very detailed work.

Maquette French term for three-dimensional model or study for a larger work.

Pinch Forming In ceramics, a method of forming objects by pinching the clay wall with the fingers.

Powder Coating Powder coating is a method of applying a decorative and protective finish by coating an item in the powder mixture of pigment and resin, and then curing that mixture in an oven, resulting in a uniform, durable, fused, and smooth finish.

Blue Heron by Brent Cooke, see pages 326-327. Photograph: Perry Danforth.

Tim Washburn

Washburn Fine Art Sculpture Studio   PO Box 466, Kirtland, NM 87417
TEL 505.598.3085   EMAIL tiwashburn@infoway.lib.nm.us

Left: *Summer Work*, 1998, Indiana limestone, 5' x 4' x 2'.
Right: *Romance*, 2000, white Italian marble, 4' x 20" x 12".

Debra White

Debra White Studio   12535 Township Road 85, Thornville, OH 43076
TEL 740.974.1501   EMAIL mail@debrawhite.us   WEB www.debrawhite.us

Three Fish (front and back views), bronze, 16"H x 15"W x 8". Photographs: Joe Clark Photography.

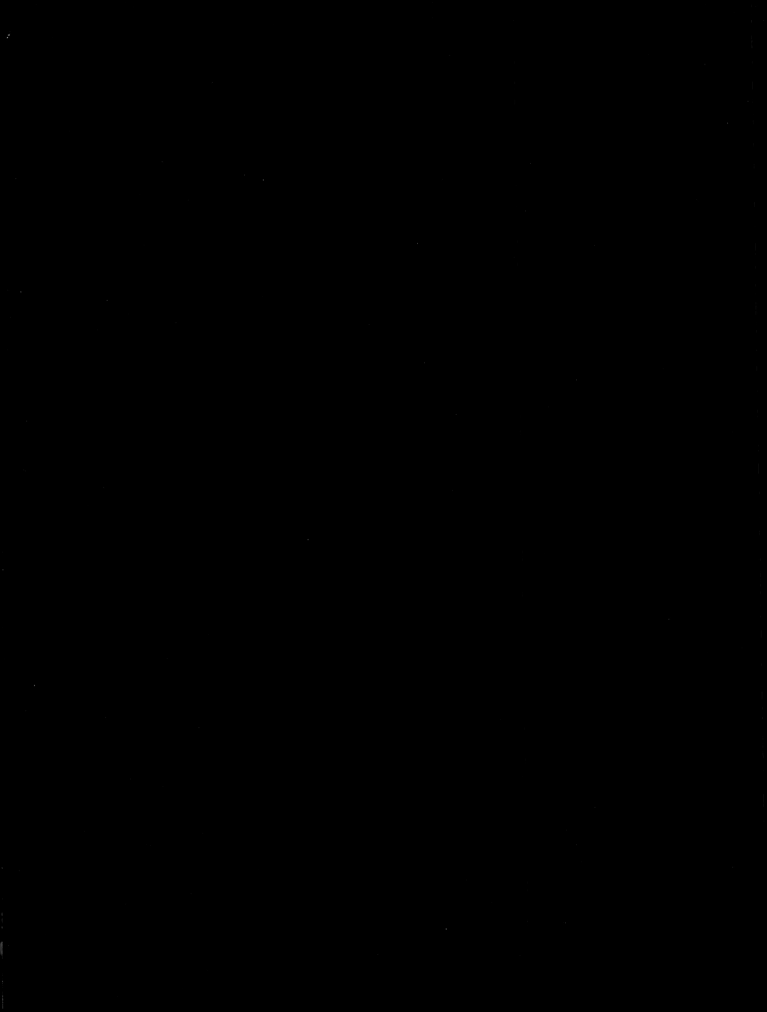

Wall Art/Fiber

Katherine K. Allen

Fiber Art Studio 1   707 SW 14 Court, Fort Lauderdale, FL 33315   TEL 954.253.5224
TEL 954.525.1809   EMAIL softart@mac.com   WEB www.KatherineKAllen.com

358

Top: *Understory*, 2008, private residence, Los Altos Hills, CA, monoprinted and stitched silk, 54"H x 88"W. Photograph: Gerhard Heidersberger.
Bottom: *Many, Many Moons*, 2008, town hall, Los Altos Hills, CA, monoprinted and stitched silk, 57"H x 142"W. Photograph: Gregory Case.

WALL ART / FIBER

Saule and Alibay Bapanov

Art Beyond Borders   164 Boulevard, Scarsdale, NY 10583   TEL 914.713.4494
EMAIL wagner@artbeyondborders.com   WEB www.artbeyondborders.com

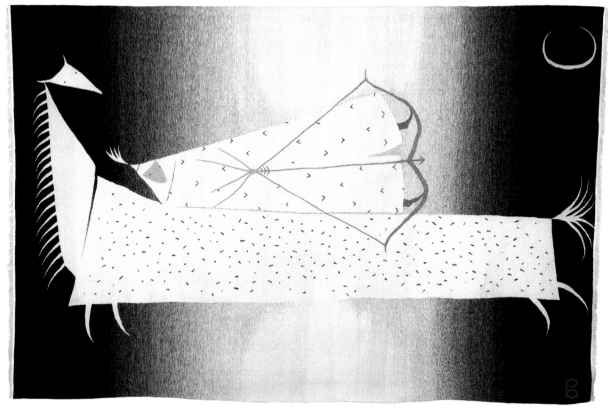

Top: *Night Archer,* 2007, handwoven wool and cotton tapestry, 81" x 116".
Bottom: *Creeping Time,* 2007, handwoven wool and cotton tapestry, 80" x 116". Photographs: Cristophe Randall.

Doreen Beck

100 West 57th Street Apartment 12C, New York, NY 10019
TEL/FAX 212.541.5066   EMAIL dorbec@verizon.net

360

Brahms Op. 40, 2007, contemporary tapestry, 61"H x 41"W. Photograph: Karin L. Willis.

Charlotte Bird

Birdworks Fiber Arts   2633 Reynard Way, San Diego, CA 92103   TEL 619.294.7236   FAX 619.294.6873
EMAIL cbird2400@aol.com   WEB www.birdworks-fiberarts.com

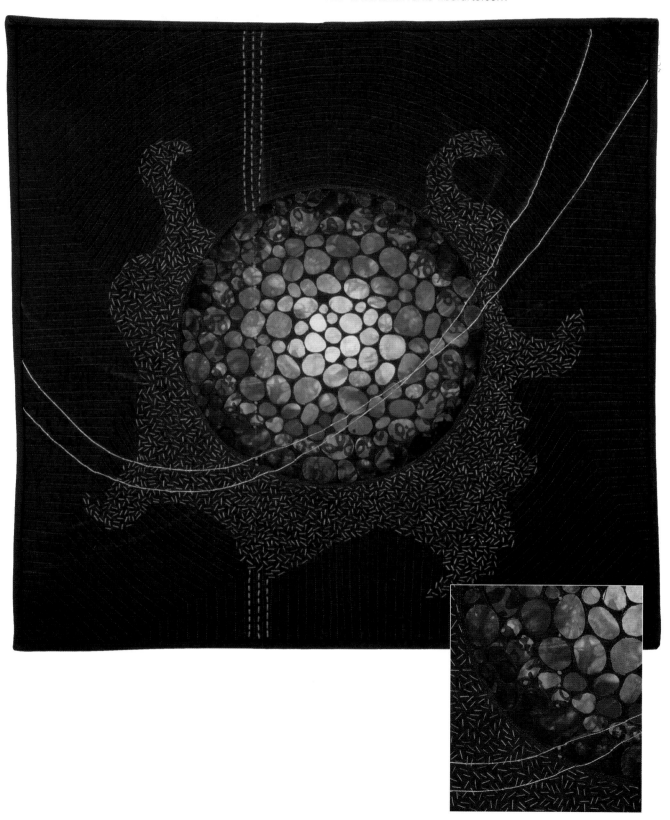

361

New Orbit, 2006, private collection, 19" x 19" x 0.5". Inset: *New Orbit* (detail). Photographs: Jack Yonn.

Susan Eileen Burnes

596 Earhart Road, Rogue River, OR 97537
TEL 541.582.8967   EMAIL seburnes@earthlink.net

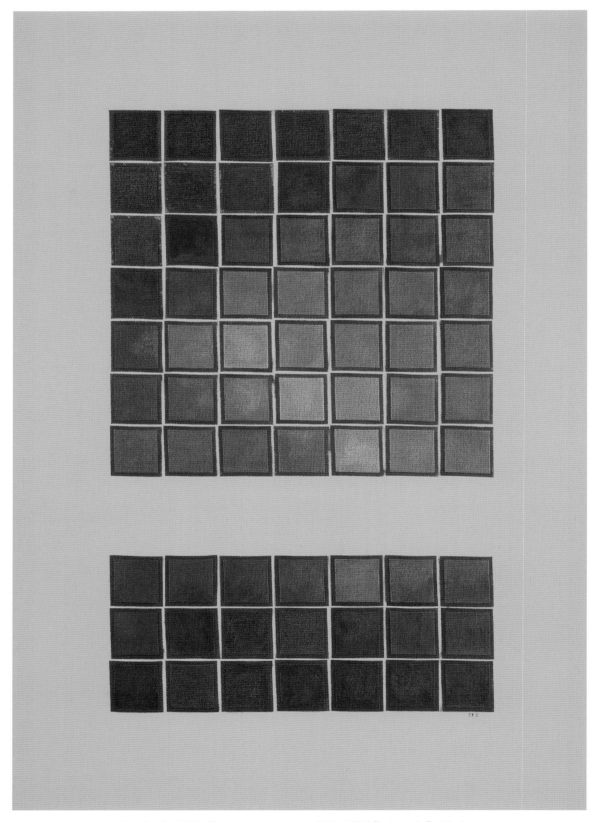

Needing Red, 2008, fiber and pastel pigments, 36"H x 24"W. Photograph: Paul Jordan.

Liz Alpert Fay

10 Evergreen Road, Sandy Hook, CT 06482   TEL 203.426.1845
EMAIL liz@lizalpertfay.com   WEB www.lizalpertfay.com

363

Top left: *Meditations on Color: Earth Meets Water,* 2008. Top right: *Meditations on Color: Annual Rings #3,* 2007.
Bottom left: *Meditations on Color: Annual Rings #4,* 2008. Bottom right: *Meditations on Color: Annual Rings #2,* 2007.
Each is wool on linen, hand hooked, 26" x 18". Four pieces in a series of five. Photographs: Brad Stanton.

Marilyn Forth

Bayberry Art Studio   7658 Haylage Circle, Baldwinsville, NY 13027
TEL 315.638.3666   EMAIL mforth@twcny.rr.com

364

Sunflower Cycle, 2008, painted batik. Photograph: Anthony Potter.

Marilyn Forth

Bayberry Art Studio   7658 Haylage Circle, Baldwinsville, NY 13027
TEL 315.638.3666   EMAIL mforth@twcny.rr.com

365

Tied to the Dock, 2008, painted batik. Photograph: Anthony Potter.

WALL ART / FIBER

Tim Harding

402 North Main Street, Stillwater, MN 55082   TEL 651.351.0383
FAX 651.351.1051   EMAIL t.h@visi.com   WEB www.timharding.com

Top: *Radiance,* 2008, Chapel of St. Thomas Aquinas, St. Paul, MN, textured silk, each panel 18.5' x 5'. Photograph: Cecile Hooker.
Bottom left: *Garden Reflections,* 2007, GGLO Architects, Seattle, WA, textured silk, 60" x 60". Photograph: P. Meyer/C. Hooker.
Bottom right: *Gold Shimmer #4,* 2008, private residence, Asheville, NC, textured silk, 57" x 48".

WALL ART / FIBER

Ellen Mears Kennedy

6500 Broxburn Drive, Bethesda, MD 20817
TEL 301.320.9014   WEB www.ellenmearskennedy.com

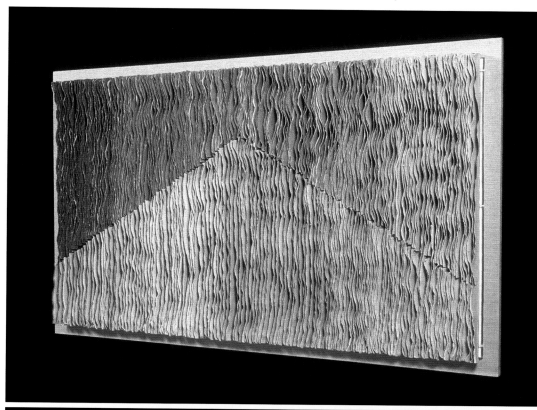

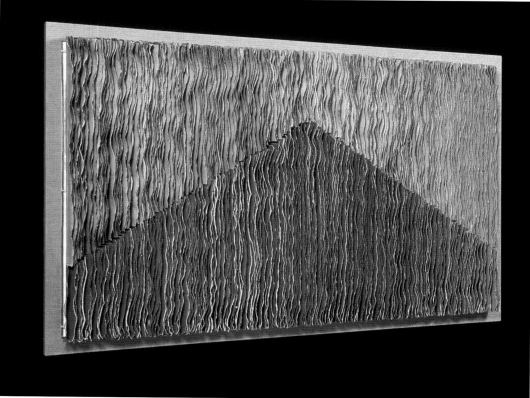

Top: *Peak at Evening* (left view), 2005, handmade paper, 36" x 60" x 3".
Bottom: *Peak at Evening* (right view). Photographs: PRS Associates.

WALL ART / FIBER

Carol LeBaron

Carol LeBaron Fine Art Textiles   2278 Highway 91, Elizabethton, TN 37643   TEL 423.474.2729
TEL 423.534.0063   EMAIL carol@carollebaron.com   WEB www.carollebaron.com

Spring Growth, 2008, Bronson Hospital, Kalamazoo, MI, wool, stitch, resist, and dye, 5' x 8'. Photographs: Mary Whalen.

WALL ART / FIBER

Susan Leslie Lumsden

Rebel Quilter   221 North Third Street, Thayer, MO 65791   TEL 417.274.1561
FAX 417.264.7992   EMAIL susan@rebelquilter.com   WEB www.rebelquilter.com

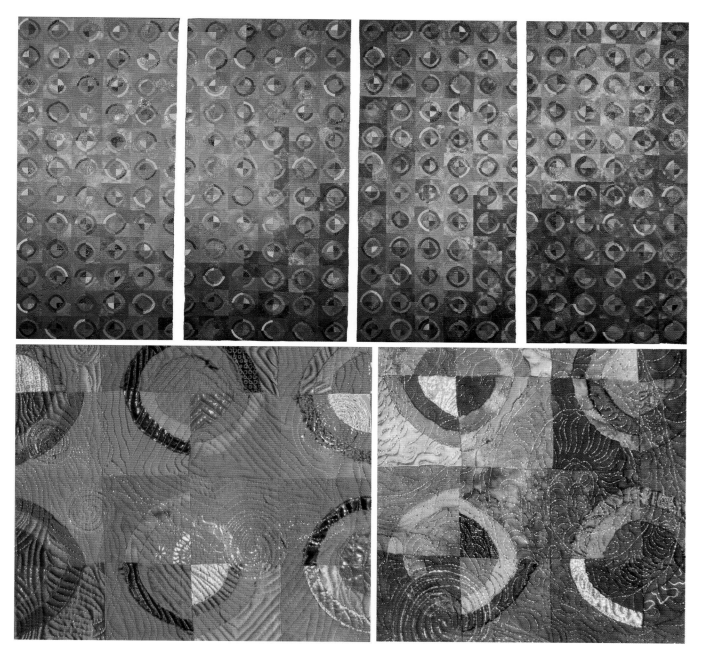

369

Top: *Slipstream Adventure,* 2008, silk and cotton, 84" x 154". Photograph: Bruce Carr.
Bottom left: *Slipstream Adventure* (detail). Bottom right: *Slipstream Adventure* (detail).

WALL ART / FIBER

Mija

Libby and Jim Mijanovich   651 Long Branch Road, Marshall, NC 28753
TEL 828.649.0200   EMAIL contact@mijafiberart.com   WEB www.mijafiberart.com

Flight of Fancy, 2008, Handmade in America, Asheville, NC, pieced vintage clothing. 8' x 8' x 1.5". Photograph: Stewart Stokes.

WALL ART / FIBER

David Nerwen

3333 Henry Hudson Parkway Apt 23B, Riverdale, NY 10463 TEL 718.796.6494
EMAIL nerwenfiberart@earthlink.net WEB www.nerwenfiberart.com

371

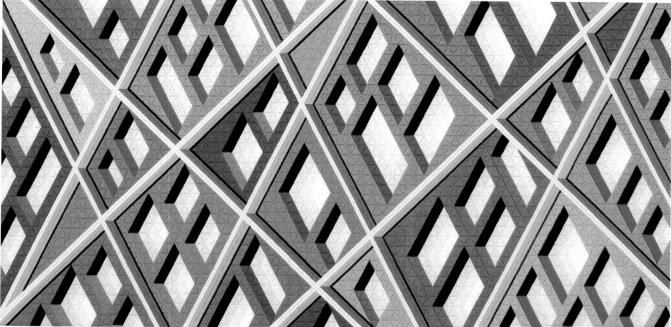

Top left: *Rebuilding O,* 2008, hand-stitched fiber, 55"H x 37"W. Top right: *18 Open Cubes,* 2008, hand-stitched fiber, 52"H x 37"W. Bottom: *Planet D,* 2008, hand-stitched fiber, 30.5"H x 58"W.

Out of the Mainstream Designs, Inc.

Christine L. Kefer   107 South Second Street, Geneva, IL 60134
TEL 630.232.2419   FAX 630.232.2491   EMAIL c.kefer@att.net

Top: *One Green Line,* 2004, private collection, Geneva, IL, handwoven, bias-cut cotton wall piece, 44" x 72".
Bottom: *Pastel Sky,* 2004, handwoven, bias-cut cotton wall piece/rug, 5' x 8'. Photographs: Jay King.

WALL ART / FIBER

Joy Saville

244 Dodds Lane, Princeton, NJ 08540   TEL/FAX 609.924.6824
EMAIL joysaville@comcast.net   WEB www.joysaville.com

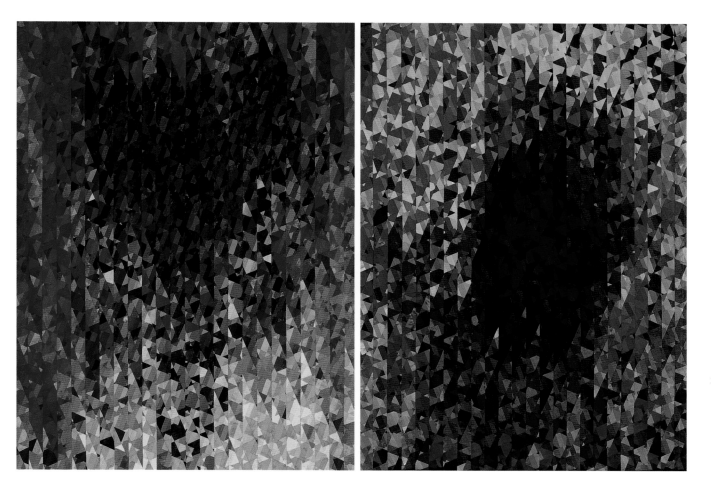

373

Left: *Event Horizon,* 2008, pieced cotton, linen, and silk, 77" x 56" x 1". Photograph: Taylor Photo/Ross.
Right: *Quickening,* 2008, pieced cotton, linen, and silk, 82.5" x 57" x 1". Photograph: William Taylor.

WALL ART / FIBER

Joan Schulze

Schulze Studio   808 Piper Avenue, Sunnyvale, CA 94087   TEL 415.642.8312
TEL/FAX 408.736.7833   EMAIL joan@joan-of-arts.com   WEB www.joan-of-arts.com

374

Mediatation – Place, 2008, mixed-media quilt, 33" x 59". Photographs: Sharon Risedorph.

WALL ART / FIBER

Carter Smith

Carter Smith Ltd   25 Pleasant Street, Nahant, MA 01908   TEL 781.581.9706
FAX 781.581.3267   EMAIL carter@shibori.com   WEB www.shibori.com

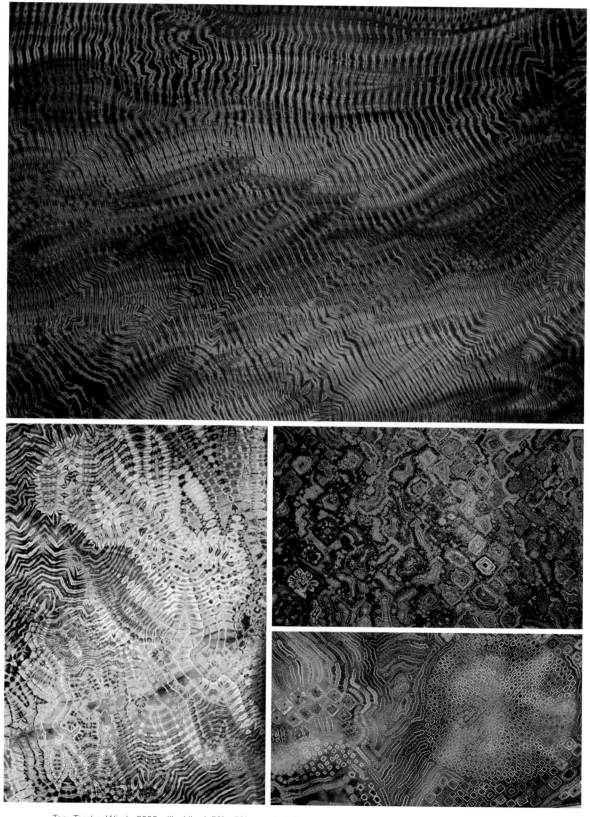

375

Top: *Tambor Winds,* 2006, silk shibori, 56" x 72" stretched. Bottom left: *Tiger Tree,* 2007, silk shibori, 89" x 43" banner.
Center right: *Anemones Garden,* 2008, silk shibori, 53" x 142" banner. Bottom right: *Lantern Parade,* 2008, silk shibori, 43" x 192".

Luann Udell

271 Roxbury Street, Keene, NH 03431   TEL 603.352.2270   FAX 603.358.1056
EMAIL luann@luannudell.com   WEB www.luannudell.com

376

Horse Shrine: The Red Canyons, 2003, fiber with handmade artifacts, 32"H x 12"W. Photographs: Jeff Baird.

WALL ART / FIBER

Karen Urbanek

PO Box 1128, Mendocino, CA 95460-1128 TEL 707.937.0626
EMAIL ku@karenurbanek.com WEB www.karenurbanek.com

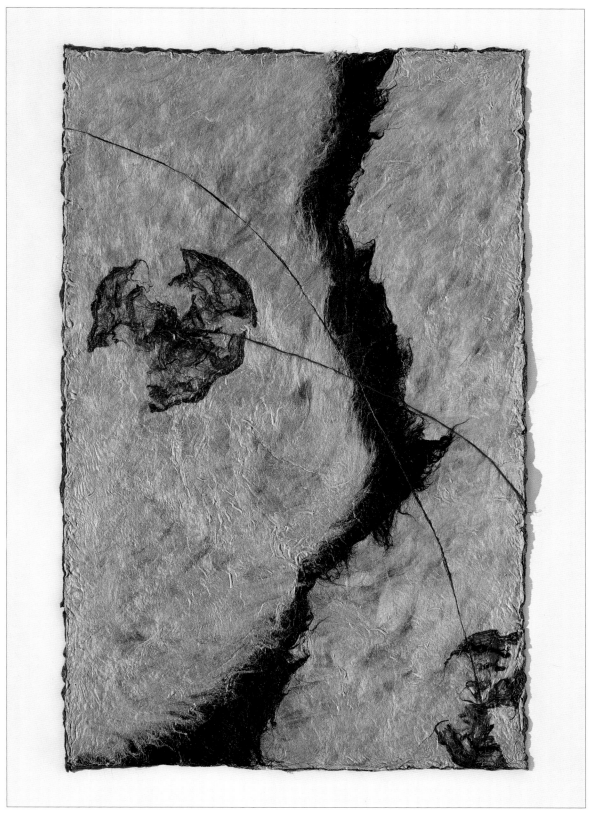

377

Reaches 5, layered, compacted, naturally dyed silk fiber, polymer, 43" x 27". Photograph: Don Tuttle Photography.

WALL ART / FIBER

Wall Art/Glass

DC Art Glass

Robert Wiener   1322 Corcoran Street NW, Washington, DC 20009
TEL 202.234.0171   EMAIL robert@dcartglass.com   WEB www.dcartglass.com

Summer Salsa, from the *Colorbar Murrine* series, 2008, Tyson's Corner Marriott, McLean, VA, kiln-formed art glass, 36"H x 18"W.

WALL ART / GLASS

Domsky Glass

Barbara and Larry Domsky   3720 West Oquendo Suite 104, Las Vegas, NV 89118
TEL 702.616.2830   EMAIL domskyglass@aol.com   WEB www.domskyglass.com

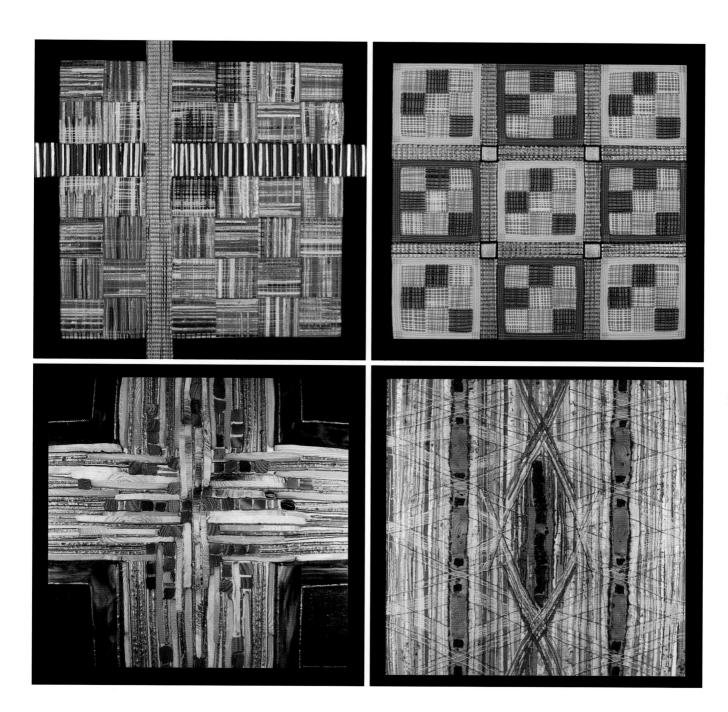

381

Top left: *Xhosa Blanket,* 2008, private residence, Las Vegas, NV, wall-mounted fused glass panel, 42" x 42" x 0.5". Top right: *Ndebele Blanket,* 2008, private residence, Las Vegas, NV, wall-mounted fused glass panel, 42" x 42" x 0.5". Bottom left: *Empowerment,* 2006, law office, Chicago, IL, wall-mounted fused glass panel, 40" x 41" x 0.5". Bottom right: *Kente Cloth,* 2006, private residence, New Zealand, wall-mounted fused glass panel, 40" x 41" x 0.5".

Lisa Mote

Lisa's Glass Studio   421 Meadows Road, Newborn, GA 30056   TEL/FAX 678.625.9983
TEL 770.388.7126   EMAIL lisa@lisamote.com   WEB www.lisamote.com

382

Top: *Uncompromising Burst,* 2008, fused glass, 36" x 58". Photograph: Deborah Karwisch.
Bottom: Lobby room divider, 2007, Kaiser Permanente, Lithonia, GA, fused glass and steel frame encased in Plexiglas, 23" x 56" x 2".

Nicholson Blown Glass

Rick and Janet Nicholson   5555 Bell Road, Auburn, CA 95602   TEL 530.823.1631   FAX 530.823.1070
EMAIL janet@nicholsonblownglass.com   WEB www.nicholsonblownglass.com

383

Top: *Pacheco Pass Wall Installation*, 2008, Hunton & Williams, Dallas, TX, freehand blown glass, 3' x 4.6', 3' x 6', and 3' x 3'. Bottom left: *Pacheco Pass Wall Installation* (detail). Bottom right: *Wheat Fields Wall Installation*, 2008, Weil Gotschal & Manges, Dallas, TX, freehand blown glass, 10' x 15'. Photographs: Craig Blackmon.

Rene Culler Glass LLC

Rene Culler   540 East 105 Street #122, Cleveland, OH 44108   TEL 216.851.5149
EMAIL glass@reneculler.com   WEB www.reneculler.com

Top: *Las Ventanas de Barcelona,* private residence, Bratenahl, OH, fused, carved glass, 50"H x 40"W.
Bottom: *Bloom,* Findley Davies human relations firm, Cleveland, OH, fused, carved glass, 28"H x 54"W. Photographs: Lumina: Daniel Fox.

WALL ART / GLASS

Suna

Designs by Suna   Toronto, Ontario, Canada   Tel 905.875.3180
EMAIL suna@designsbysuna.com   WEB www.designsbysuna.com

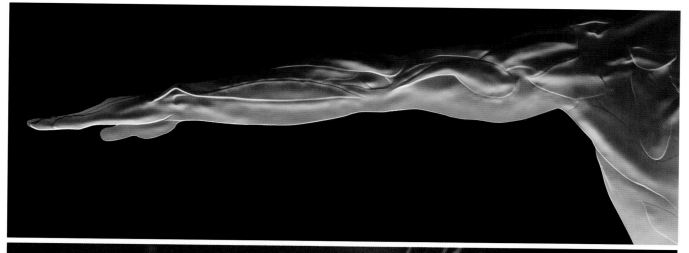

385

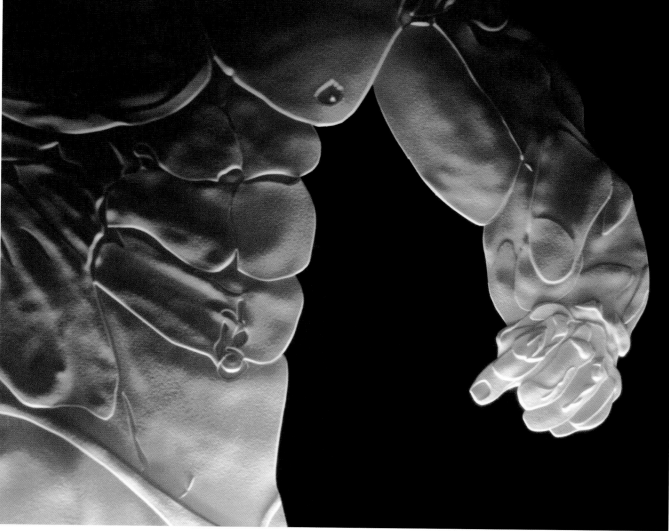

Top: *Muscular Arm*, 2008, Iovate Health Sciences, Oakville, Ontario, carved glass, 21" x 48".
Bottom: *Mr. Olympia* (detail), 2008, Iovate Health Sciences, Oakville, Ontario, carved glass, 5' x 4'.

WALL ART / GLASS

Bonnie Hinz

6715 Ashton Avenue NE, Fridley, MN 55432   TEL 763.571.1552   TEL 763.242.8938
EMAIL bonniehinz@gmail.com   WEB www.bonniehinz.com

Left: *Currents,* 2008, fused glass and metal, 53" x 31.5" x 2".
Right: *Autumn Cascade,* 2008, blown glass and metal, 37" x 30" x 6".

386

Sandy Jackson

Sandy Jackson Fine Art, LLC   444 17th Street #704, Denver, CO 80202   TEL 720.284.1922
FAX 720.548.9830   EMAIL sandy@sandyjacksonfineart.com   WEB www.sandyjacksonfineart.com

Left: *Murano Mix,* 2008, Crown West Corporate Offices, Denver, CO, fused glass and stainless steel.
Right: *Foliage 1 & 2,* 2007, First Commerce Bank, Fort Collins, CO, fused glass with copper inclusions. Photographs: Linda Nix.

Pictures in Glass

Patricia Deere   10650 Carson Highway, Tecumseh, MI 49286   TEL 517.431.2271
FAX 517.431.3605   EMAIL info@picturesinglass.net   WEB www.picturesinglass.net

The River, 2008, private residence, Tipton, MI, stained glass, 22" x 80". Photograph: Lad Strayer, Adrian, MI.

Wall Art / Glass: Common Terms and Their Meanings

Blown Glass Glasswork produced by gathering molten glass onto the end of a blowpipe and forming it into a variety of shapes by blowing air through the blowpipe and manipulating the glass as it is rotated.

Carved Glass Glass that has been sandblasted to different depths. Also called stage-blasted.

Enameled Glass Glass decorated with particles of translucent glass or glass-like material, usually of a contrasting color, which fuse to the surface under heat. Multicolored designs can be created, as well as monochrome coatings.

Fused Glass Glass that has been heated in a kiln to the point where two separate pieces are permanently joined as one without losing their individual color.

Inclusions Particles of metal, bubbles, etc., occurring naturally within glass or added for decorative effect.

Kiln-Forming A glass-forming process that utilizes a kiln to heat glass in a refractory or heat-resistant mold, slump glass over a form, or fuse two or more pieces of glass together.

Murrini A small wafer of glass bearing a colored pattern. Formed by bundling and fusing colored glass rods together and then heating and pulling the resulting cylinder to a very small diameter. When cut into cross-sectioned wafers, each piece bears the original pattern in miniature.

Stained Glass Popular name for leaded glass, the process of forming objects using pieces of colored glass or glass that has been painted with liquid enamel and then fired. Pieces are fitted into channels in a lead strip or joined together using copper or cement.

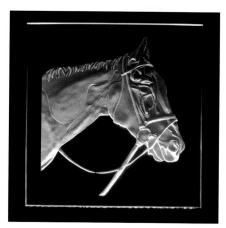

CARVED GLASS

Ginger Brew by Suna, see page 385.

Wall Art/Metal

Anjin Abe

Onishi Gallery, U.S. Representative   521 West 26th Street, New York, NY 10001   TEL 212.695.8035
FAX 212.695.8036   EMAIL info@onishigallery.com   WEB www.onishigallery.com   WEB www.anjin-abe.com

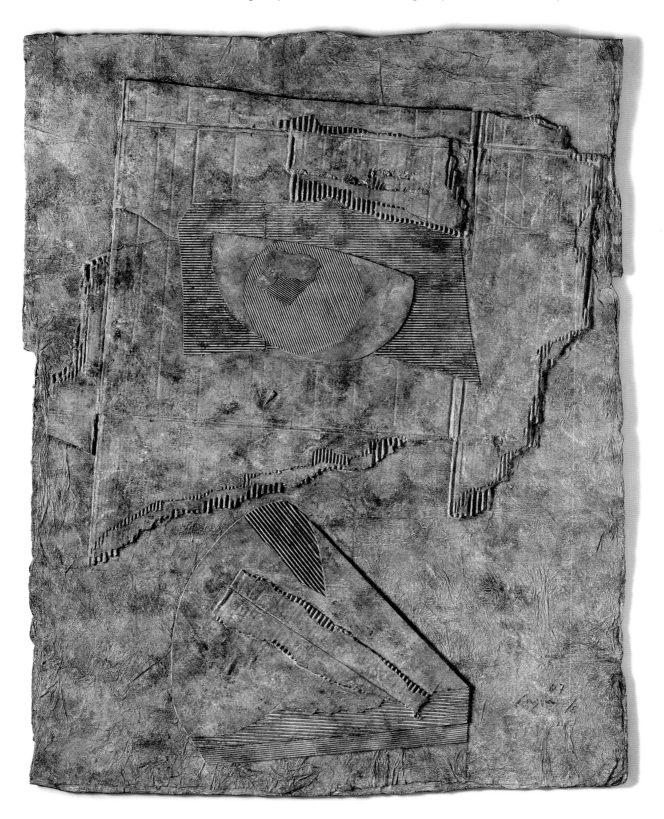

390

07-02, 2007, bronze, 54" x 41".

David M Bowman Studio

David M Bowman and Reed C Bowman   PO Box 738, Berkeley, CA 94701   TEL 510.845.1072
EMAIL david@davidmbowman.com   WEB www.davidmbowman.com

391

Left: *Wallpiece 07.21*, 2007, patinaed brass and copper with repoussé copper face, 45" x 8".
Right: *Stairwell Triptych: Wallpieces 08.18, 08.17* and *08.15* (left to right), 2008, patinaed brass and copper, 90" x 60" overall.

WALL ART / METAL

Linda Leviton

Linda Leviton Sculpture   2747 East Powell Road, Lewis Center, OH 43035
TEL 614.433.7486   EMAIL guild@lindaleviton.com   WEB www.lindaleviton.com

San Clemente installation, private residence, copper, wood, and patina on a curved wall, 8.5'H x 15.5'W x 3.5"D. Photograph: Frohlich Photography.

WALL ART / METAL

Linda Leviton

Linda Leviton Sculpture   2747 East Powell Road, Lewis Center, OH 43035
TEL 614.433.7486   EMAIL guild@lindaleviton.com   WEB www.lindaleviton.com

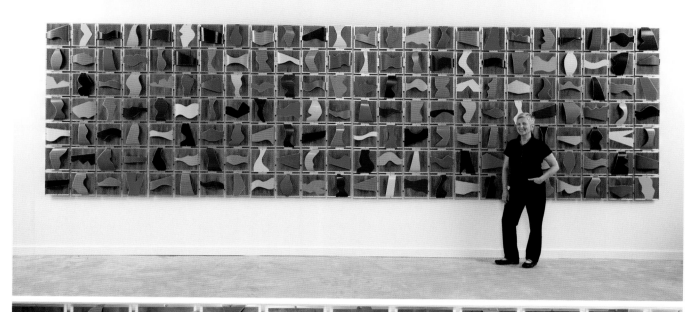

Over and Under, copper, wood, steel, oil, and latex, 6.1'H x 20'W x 3.5"D. Photograph: Flashback Photography.

WALL ART / METAL

Susan McGehee

Metallic Strands   540 23rd Street, Manhattan Beach, CA 90266   TEL 310.545.4112
FAX 310.546.7152   EMAIL metalstrands@aol.com   WEB www.metalstrands.com

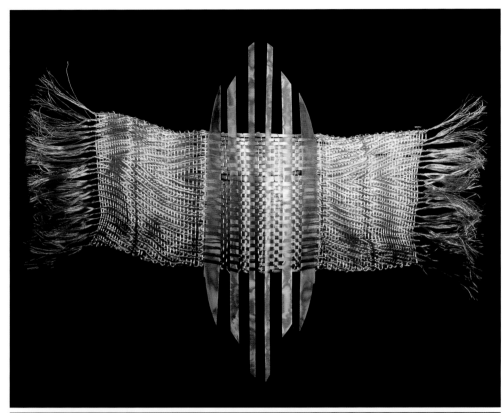

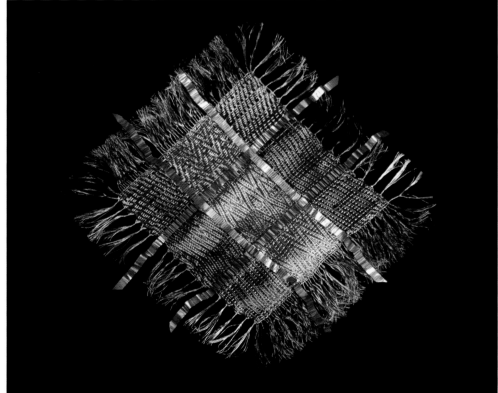

Top: *Sentinel,* 2007, woven anodized aluminum wire, coated copper wire, and titanium strips, 30" x 38".
Bottom: *Copper Twill Quilt,* 2008, woven anodized aluminum wire, coated copper wire, and copper strips, 33" x 36". Photographs: Andrew Neuhart.

WALL ART / METAL

Darcy Meeker

3452 Spur Street, Blacksburg, VA 24060   TEL 540.449.4291
EMAIL darcy.meeker@juno.com   WEB www.darcymeeker.com

395

Top left: *Moon, Tree, Thee,* tooled, flamed copper and paint, oils, 8' x 5'. Photograph: Eliza Hodges.
Top right: *The Girls in Yellow,* tooled, flamed copper, oils, each 60" x 11" x 3". Photograph: John Kline. Bottom left: *Moon, Tree, Thee* (detail).
Bottom right: *Elephant Vine* (detail), General Electric, Schenectady, NY, copper and flexible plywood, 36' x 14' x 2'. Photograph: Glenn Davenport.

Peter Skidd Fine Art

Peter Skidd   Scottsdale, AZ   TEL 480.586.0478
EMAIL info@peterskidd.com   WEB www.peterskidd.com

Solar Tide, 2008, mixed media on steel, 48" x 92.5" x 3.75". Photograph: Artisan Captures.

WALL ART / METAL

Dan Rider

Dan Rider Sculpture   21883 Boonesborough Drive, Bend, OR 97701   TEL 541.647.1532
EMAIL dan@danridersculpture.com   WEB www.danridersculpture.com

397

Top: *Callas on the Wall,* copper mesh, 36" x 72" x 12".
Bottom: *Run River Run Autumn,* copper mesh, aluminum, and copper wire, 30" x 80" x 6". Photographs: Ross Chandler.

WALL ART / METAL

Bette Ridgeway

Ridgeway Studio, Santa Fe, NM   TEL 505.983.4301
EMAIL bridgesfnm@aol.com   WEB www.ridgewaystudio.com

398

Harvest Moon, acrylic with resin on steel panel, 40" x 30".

Jon Michael Route

Frederic, WI   TEL 888.345.2602   EMAIL jon@jonmichaelroute.com
WEB www.jonmichaelroute.com

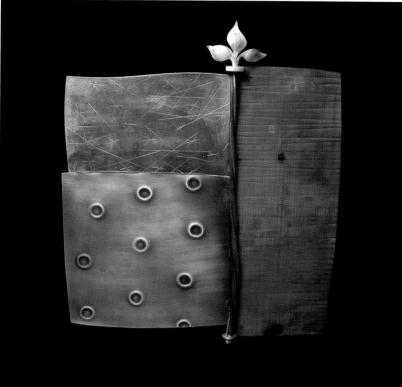

Top left: *Bird with Copper,* 2008, metalwork, 21"H x 11"W x 2"D. Top right: *Three Leaf Twist,* 2006, metalwork, 23"H x 19.5"W x 2"D. Photograph: Deb Route.
Bottom: *Nature's Song,* 2006, St. John's Heart Hospital, St. Louis, MO, metalwork, each 24" x 24" x 3". Photograph: Deb Franke.

WALL ART / METAL

Kurt Shaw

PO Box 16152, Pittsburgh, PA 15242   TEL 412.921.5533   TEL 800.524.SHAW
EMAIL ksfineart@comcast.net   WEB www.kurtshawstudio.com

400

Seasonal Orb, 2006, sculptural clock created for Progressive Medical, Inc., Westerville, OH, polychrome aluminum, 13' x 22'.

WALL ART / METAL

Martin Sturman

Sturman Steel Sculptures   3201 Bayshore Drive, Westlake Village, CA 91361-4233   TEL 818.707.8087
FAX 818.707.3079   EMAIL mlsturman@sbcglobal.net   WEB www.sturmansteelsculptures.com

401

Symbolic Gate, 2008, City of Alhambra Library, Alhambra, CA, stainless steel,
120"H x 96"W x 2"D. Photographs: Barry Michlin Photography.

WALL ART / METAL

Timothy R. Decker

RT Designs   PO Box 823, Grafton, WI 53024
FAX 262.377.7126   EMAIL RTistDESIGNS@yahoo.com

Left: *Christina,* 2007, 22-gauge steel hardware cloth, 24" x 42" x 12".
Right: *Hercules,* 2007, 22-gauge steel hardware cloth, 48" x 24" x 12".

Wall Art / Metal: Common Terms and Their Meanings

Anodizing Method of dyeing an aluminum surface by coating the metal with an anodic film of aluminum oxide while it is in an acid bath. The metal is then washed and immersed in organic dyes, allowing the oxide film to absorb the dye, followed by a final washing, drying and sealing with lanolin.

Cold Connected The joining together two pieces of metal without the use of heat. Rivets or screws are examples of cold connections.

Flamed Copper Copper which has been heated with a torch to produce a natural dichroic patina. As the copper is heated, it first turns orange, then purple, then a silvery blue.

Mokume-gane Japanese for "wood-grained metal." An ancient technique originally used to forge katana blades. Soft metals like copper and silver are pressed together, heated, and rolled to create the distinctive wood grain-like pattern.

Pickle An acidic solution used to clean metal.

Planishing The process of smoothing metal with polished hammers.

Repoussé An ancient process in which sheet metal is hammered into contours from both the front and the back.

Reticulation A process in which metal is heated and shrunk, resulting in a rippled, veiny texture resembling the surface of a leaf.

FLAMED COPPER

Moon, Tree, Thee by Darcy
Meeker, see page 395.

Shohini Ghosh

Shohini's Studio   9187 South Madras Court, Littleton, CO 80130   TEL 303.470.6776
TEL 720.217.8516   EMAIL shohinighosh@hotmail.com   WEB www.shohini.com

Left: *Night Lights,* 2007, copper sheet with patina paint, 2' x 2'.
Right: *Around the Corner,* 2007, copper sheet with patina paint, 2' x 2'.

403

Casey G. Horn

CGH Studios, Inc.   PO Box 805, Brighton, CO 80601
TEL 720.394.7236   EMAIL chorn@cghstudios.com   WEB www.caseyhorn.com

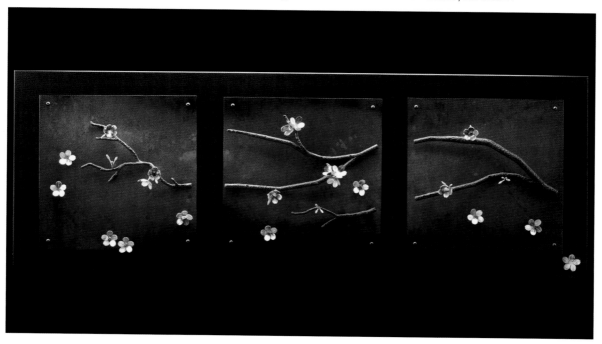

End of Spring Triptych, 2007, wood, metal, bronze, and stainless steel,
24"H x 66"W x 4"D, custom sizes and colors available. Photograph: Jafe Parsons.

WALL ART / METAL

Wall Art/Mixed

& Other Media

Susan Adamé
Michael Bauermeister
Bethanie Brandon Design
John Boak
Laura Militzer Bryant
Myra Burg
Myra Burg and Liz Cummings
Dolan Geiman Inc.
J.A. Nelson Studios

JP Design
LH Originals
Silja Talikka Lahtinen
Raven Lunatic Studios
Craig Robb
Priscilla Robinson
Yvette Kaiser Smith
P.T. Tiersky
Alice Van Leunen

Susan Venable
Kerry Vesper
Libby Ware
Graceann Warn
Laurie Wohl
Fanne Fernow
Grace Hoff
Brigid Manning-Hamilton

Susan Adamé

1235 Garfield Avenue, Albany, CA 94706   TEL 510.524.2990   TEL 510.823.4871
EMAIL susanadameart@gmail.com   WEB www.susanadameart.com

406

Top left: *Coming Together*, 2008, mixed-media collage, 21" x 28".
Top right: *Musical Memories*, 2008, mixed-media collage, 28" x 21". Center right: *Contemplation*, 2008, mixed-media collage, 28" x 21".
Bottom left: *Harmony*, 2008, mixed-media collage, 21" x 28". Bottom right: *Expanding*, 2008, mixed-media collage, 21" x 28".

WALL ART / MIXED & OTHER MEDIA

Michael Bauermeister

6560 Augusta Bottom Road, Augusta, MO 63332   TEL 636.228.4663
EMAIL michael@bauermeister.com   WEB www.michaelbauermeister.com

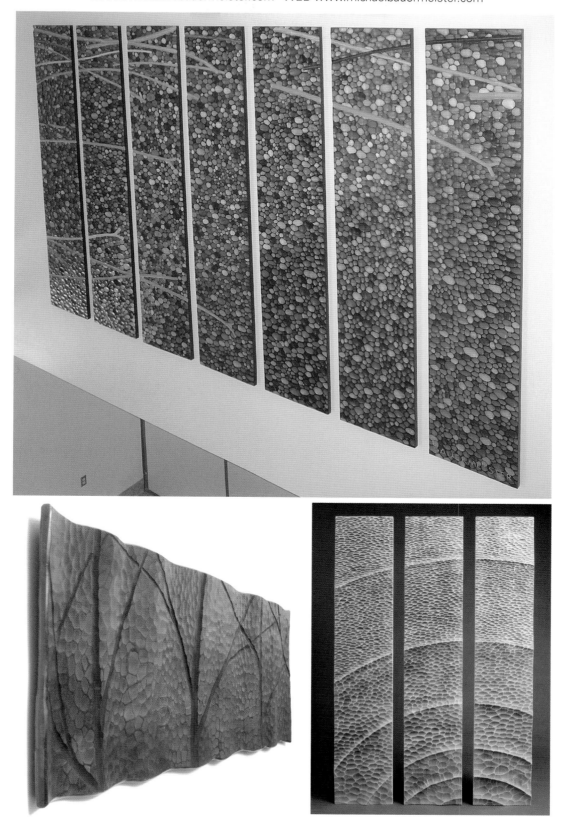

407

Top: *Water's Edge*, 2008, Banner Hospital, Glendale, AZ, linden wood with tinted lacquer, 96" x 144" x 2". Photograph: Angela Lafica. Bottom left: *Sapling Angles*, 2007, linden wood with tinted lacquer, 20" x 75" x 3". Bottom right: *A Stone's Throw*, 2008, linden wood with tinted lacquer, 60" x 40" x 3".

WALL ART / MIXED & OTHER MEDIA

Bethanie Brandon Design

Bethanie Brandon   25 Zephyr Court, San Rafael, CA 94903   TEL 415.492.0809
TEL 415.225.3656   EMAIL bethaniebrandon@aol.com   WEB www.bethaniebrandondesign.com

408

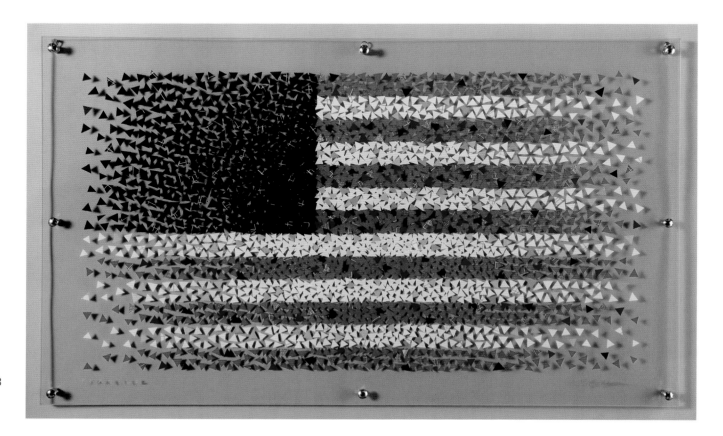

Top: *F R A G I L E,* 2008, painted silk encased in Plexiglas, 32" x 54" x 1.5". Bottom left: *Union Jack,* 2008, silk encased in Plexiglas, 22" x 34" x 1.5". Bottom right: *Tibet,* silk encased in Plexiglas. Photographs: Charles Kennard.

WALL ART / MIXED & OTHER MEDIA

John Boak

1035 South Ogden Street, Denver, CO 80209 TEL 303.777.6226
FAX 303.733.4733 EMAIL johnboak@boakart.com WEB www.boakart.com

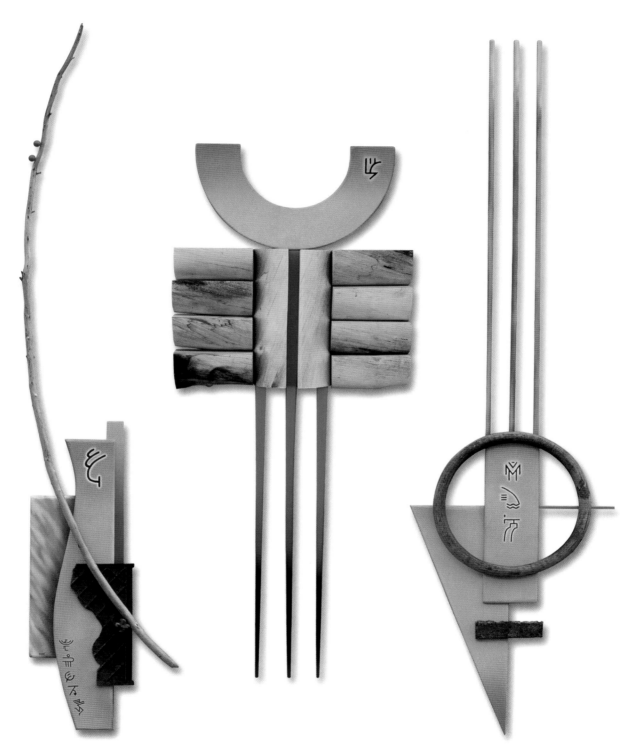

409

Left: *Waffle*, 2003, University of Colorado, Folsom Field Addition, acrylic on wood and metal, 74.6" x 15.6". Center: *Naxos*, 2005, Heitler Development, Denver, CO, acrylic on wood, 37" x 15". Right: *Steer*, University of Colorado, Folsom Field Addition, acrylic on wood and metal, 72" x 18.8".

WALL ART / MIXED & OTHER MEDIA

Joe Carty

Guild Sourcebooks at Work

Case Study #8

ARTIST: Richard Houston
ARTWORK TITLE: Fireplace and Trellis Light Fixture
MEDIA: Stone fireplace with African and American mahogany
                    and low-voltage lighting; mahogany light fixture
SIZE: Fireplace 21'H X 8'W x 5'D; Light fixture
                    14'H x 5'W x 5'D
INSTALLATION: Cape Cod Residence, Brewster, MA

410

"We found Richard in your Guild Residential Sourcebook, which we ordered from the Artful Home website. I had been searching for months for the right artist to create a sculpture for the fireplace, which is a soaring twenty-two foot expanse and the first thing you see when you enter the home. I just happened to stumble upon Richard's work in the book and it was one of those 'Eureka!' moments.

"Richard's work is so unique, I just had to trust him when he said he would create something that would go beautifully in the space. His vision went well beyond just creating wooden light sculptures to mount over the fireplace; he transformed the fireplace itself, reworking the fireplace shape and suggesting specific stone work. When I asked for his help on designing a hanging light fixture, he once again came up with something utterly unique and stunning.

"For me, The Guild Sourcebook was, without a doubt, one of the most inspiring resources for our project. I can't tell you how many ideas we got while going though the book. It made it so convenient to research various disciplines from a single source. And, on the whole, the caliber of the work done by your artists seem to be much higher than those I might find doing a web search."

Joe Carty, homeowner

"The homeowners were building a beautiful, compact house in Cape Cod. They had seen my work in *The Guild Sourcebook,* and after visiting my website, contacted me to create a fireplace for them. I learned that they particularly liked an outdoor light fixture I had built for a home in Ashland, Oregon. The general design character of that light fixture was a perfect match for their contemporary Craftsman-style home.

"The fireplace itself was made of stone selected by the owner and placed according to several sketches I made. The sculptural light fixtures were made of African and American Mahogany and stained glass. These were made in my shop in Oregon, and then shipped to the site for installation. Midway through the project, the owners also asked me to design and build a suspended light fixture for the living room.

"Although we were at opposite ends of the country, we planned from the very beginning how we could communicate via email, telephone, Internet, digital photos, and expedited shipping so that I only had to fly to the East Coast once to install the artwork during the year-and-a-half project. This planning was critical for keeping within the budget.

"A great client can make all the difference in the success of an artwork commission, and these clients were a perfect example of that. Their desire for high quality, follow through with their agreements, and openness to new and creative ideas made for a winning combination. One of the key components of this project was having a visionary client."

See more work by Richard Houston on page 154.

Laura Militzer Bryant

Prism Arts, Inc.   3140 39th Avenue North, St. Petersburg, FL 33714   TEL 727.528.3800
FAX 727.528.3308   EMAIL laura@prismyarn.com   WEB www.lauramilitzerbryant.com

411

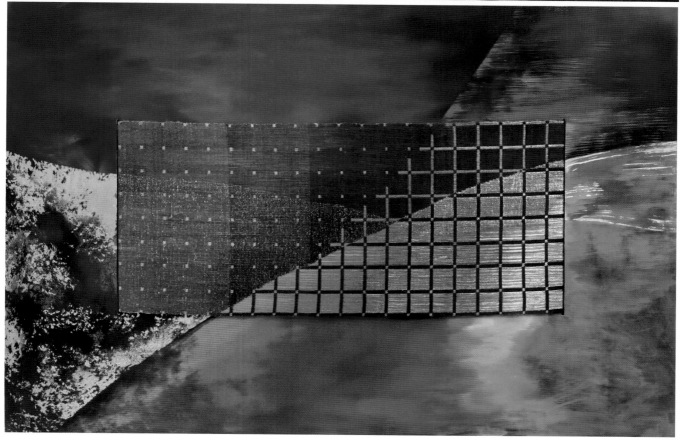

Top left: *Beyond Light,* 2008, wool, rayon, nylon, wood, and acrylic, 20" x 20" x 1". Top right: *Crossing Light,* 2008, wool, rayon, nylon, Lurex, wood, and acrylic, 20" x 20" x 1". Bottom: *Beyond the Blue,* 2008, wool, rayon, nylon, Lurex, wood, acrylic, and copper leaf, 36" x 54"x 1". Photograph: Rob Moorman.

WALL ART / MIXED & OTHER MEDIA

Myra Burg

171 Pier Avenue #353, Santa Monica, CA TEL 310.399.5040 TEL 310.780.0666
FAX 310.317.9208 EMAIL myraburg@yahoo.com WEB www.myraburg.com

412

Top: *Cleveland Curve,* 2008, penthouse residence, Cleveland, OH, wrapped fiber over hollow core, 4' x 7'. Bottom left: *Primarily Eve,*
2008, wrapped fiber over hollow core, 4'x 3'. Bottom right: *A Home for Susan,* 2008, residence, San Diego, CA, wrapped fiber over hollow core, 4' x 7'.
Opposite: *Quiet Oboes in Lemon Citrus* (detail), 2007, wrapped fiber over hollow core, 84" x 3.5"– 5". Photograph: Barry Blau.

WALL ART / MIXED & OTHER MEDIA

Myra Burg and Liz Cummings

Myra Burg (fiber)   171 Pier Avenue #353, Santa Monica, CA 90405   TEL 310.399.5040
FAX 310.317.9208   EMAIL myraburg@yahoo.com   WEB www.myraburg.com
Liz Cummings (oils)   Laguna Niguel, CA   TEL 949.249.2552
EMAIL lizcummings1@gmail.com   WEB www.lizcummings.com

Top: *Beginnings,* mixed media, 72"H x 80"W. Photograph: Barry Blau. Bottom left: *Paradise 3 with Bassoon,* mixed media, 2008, 78" x 32".
Bottom right: *Paradise Green and Purple with Pickup Stix,* 2008, mixed media, 52" x 52". Photograph: Barry Blau and Liz Cummings.

WALL ART / MIXED & OTHER MEDIA

Dolan Geiman Inc.

Dolan Geiman   1137 West Taylor Street #314, Chicago, IL 60607   TEL 773.247.3775
FAX 866.418.1280   EMAIL info@dolangeiman.com   WEB www.dolangeiman.com

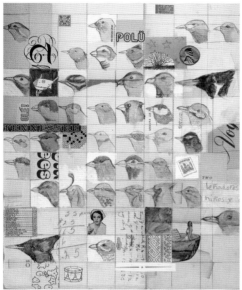  

415

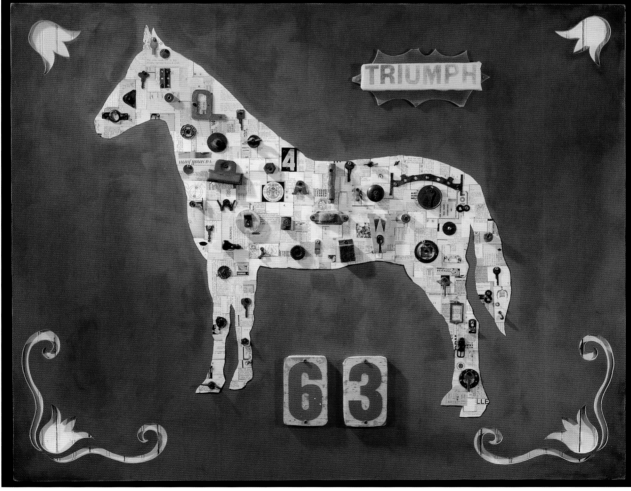

Top left: *Field Guide Tennessee,* 2007, gouache, watercolor, and vintage paper collage on recycled wood, 16.5" x 13". Top center: *American Beauty,* 2008, recycled paint with salvaged wood, 48" x 33". Top right: *Blue Highway, Yellow Cornhusk (Box Print),* 2008, archival, VOC-free reproduction on wood, 33" x 24". Bottom: *Triumph 63,* 2008, recycled paint, vintage papers, found objects, and salvaged wood, 48" x 60". Photographs: David Ettinger.

WALL ART / MIXED & OTHER MEDIA

J. A. Nelson Studios

James A. Nelson   Eureka Springs, AR 72632
TEL 479.253.4314   WEB www.janelsongallery.com

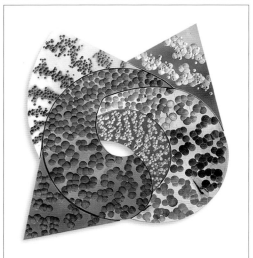

416

Left: *Wally,* 2007, carved wood and acrylic, 96" x 67". Top right: *Big Woody,* 2007, carved wood and acrylic, 96" x 69". Center right: *Borogove,* 2007, carved wood and acrylic, 43" x 37". Bottom right: *Bird Brains,* 2008, carved wood and acrylic, 53" x 58". Photographs: David Harvey.

WALL ART / MIXED & OTHER MEDIA

JP Design

Jeanne Petrosky and Dennis Guzenski   243 Jefferson Avenue Suite 1, Pottstown, PA 19464
EMAIL jp@jeannepetrosky.com   WEB www.jeannepetrosky.com

417

Top: *Courage to Try,* 2008, handmade paper and acrylics, 3' x 8'.
Bottom: *Water, Wind, Fire,* 2008, handmade paper and acrylics, 30" x 50". Photographs: Bill Mason.

WALL ART / MIXED & OTHER MEDIA

LH Originals

Louise Harris   PO Box 390173, Minneapolis, MN 55439   TEL 952.941.1420
EMAIL louise@lhoriginals.com   WEB www.lhoriginals.com

418

Top: *Relief Circles (Recycled Filters),* 2007, residence, Minneapolis, MN, metal, 30" x 30". Bottom left: *Relief Circles (Recycled Filters),* detail, 2006, metal, 10" x 10". Bottom right: *Relief Circles (Recycled Filters)* detail, 2006, metal, 20" x 16".

WALL ART / MIXED & OTHER MEDIA

Silja Talikka Lahtinen

Silja's Fine Art Studio   5220 Sunset Trail, Marietta, GA 30068   TEL 770.992.8380
TEL 770.993.3409   FAX 770.992.0350   EMAIL pentec02@bellsouth.net

Pictures of Deep Nothing series, 2007-2008, Ward-Nasse Gallery, NYC, acrylic and mixed media on canvas, each 32" x 32".

WALL ART / MIXED & OTHER MEDIA

Raven Lunatic Studios

Kamilla White   829 NW 62nd Street, Seattle, WA 98107   TEL 206.650.1263
EMAIL kam@nevermorrigan.com   WEB www.nevermorrigan.com

420

How Do I Look?, 2008, collage and colored pencil, 24" x 21.5". Photograph: Art & Soul, Seattle, WA.

WALL ART / MIXED & OTHER MEDIA

Craig Robb

3470 South Grant Street, Englewood, CO 80113   TEL 303.783.3659
EMAIL craiger@4dv.net   WEB www.craigrobb.com

421

Top: *Heartache*, 2008, wood, steel, dirt, glass, and water, 24" x 43" x 16". Bottom: *Tres*, 2008, wood and steel, 10" x 27" x 6".

Priscilla Robinson

2811 Hancock Drive, Austin, TX 78731   TEL 512.452.3516   TEL 575.758.2608
EMAIL pjr@priscillarobinson.com   WEB www.priscillarobinson.com

Top: *Fringe Between Earth and Sky,* fused glass and acrylic on embossed handmade paper on panel, 30" x 45" x 3".
Bottom: *Ways of Water,* acrylic on embossed handmade paper on panel, 30" x 30".

WALL ART / MIXED & OTHER MEDIA

Yvette Kaiser Smith

2607 West Augusta Boulevard, Chicago, IL 60622   TEL 773.395.2981
EMAIL yvette@kaisersmith.com   WEB www.kaisersmith.com

Top: *Identity Sequence e Black* and *Identity Sequence RW pi,* 2008, Alfedena Gallery, Chicago, IL, crocheted fiberglass and polyester resin, 72" x 92" x 32" and 88" x 112" x 6". Photograph: James Prinz. Bottom left: *Identity Sequence e 4,* 2007, Alfedena Gallery, Chicago, IL, crocheted fiberglass and polyester resin, 121" x 117" x 8". Photograph: James Prinz. Bottom right: *Identity Sequence RW pi* (detail).

WALL ART / MIXED & OTHER MEDIA

P.T. Tiersky

Studio 84 West, Inc   510 El Paseo Road, Ojai, CA 93023   TEL 805.905.3812
FAX 805.640.9359   EMAIL studio84@west.net   WEB www.studio84west.com

424

Top: *Steps*, 2008, Ojai, CA, mixed media on wood panels, 54" x 61".
Bottom: *Slopes*, 2008, Ojai, CA, mixed media on wood panels, 58" x 58". Photographs: Roger Conrad.

Alice Van Leunen

9025 SE Terrace View Court, Amity, OR 97101   TEL 503.835.7717
FAX 503.835.7707   EMAIL avanleunen@msn.com   WEB www.alicevanleunen.com

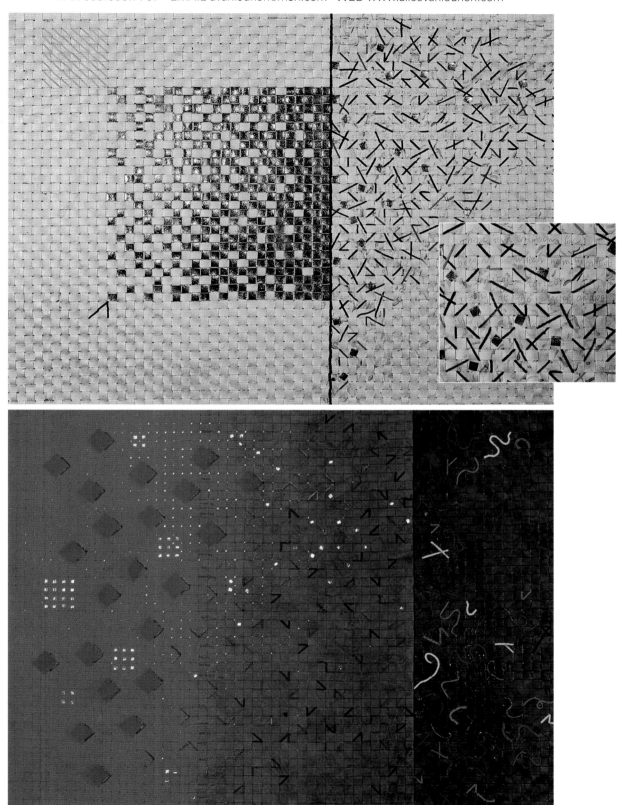

425

Top: *Perimeter*, 2008, woven paper with paint, metallic foil, stitchery, and poetic text, 32" x 40". Inset: *Perimeter* (detail).
Bottom: *That Way Madness Lies*, 2008, woven paper with paint, metallic foil, stitchery, collage, and poetic text, 32" x 40". Poetry by Kelly Gill Holland.

WALL ART / MIXED & OTHER MEDIA

Susan Venable

Venable Studio   2323 Foothill Lane, Santa Barbara, CA 93105   TEL 805.884.4963
EMAIL susan@venablestudio.com   WEB www.venablestudio.com

426

Top left: *Moorea Anciens,* 2008, mixed media, 48" x 48". Photograph: William Nettles. Right: *Alta.Mar,* 2008, San Diego, CA, steel and copper wire construction. Photograph: Fred Gemmell. Bottom left: *Motu I,* 2008, mixed media, 41" x 41". Photograph: William Nettles.

WALL ART / MIXED & OTHER MEDIA

Kerry Vesper

Vesper Sculpture and Design, LLC   116 East Ellis Drive, Tempe, AZ 85282   TEL 480.429.0954
FAX 480.839.5376   EMAIL kerry@kerryvesper.com   WEB www.kerryvesper.com

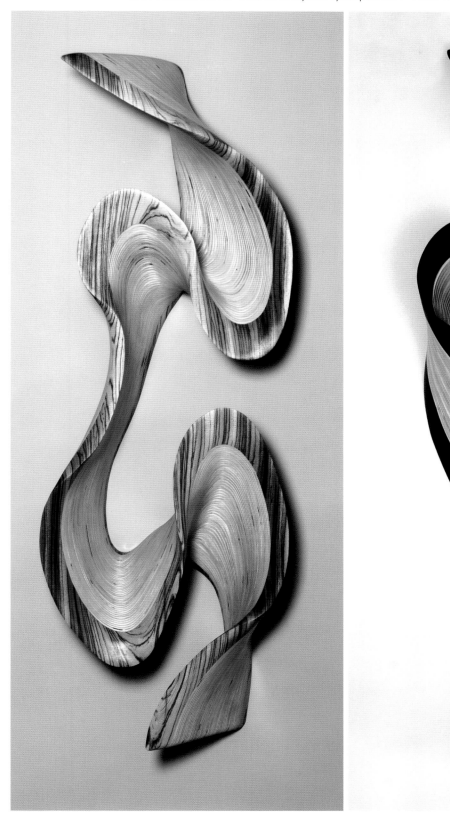 

427

Left: *Newwave Wall Sculpture,* 2008, Zebrawood and Baltic Birch, 56" x 20" x 6".
Right: *Woodwave Wall Sculpture,* 2007, Wenge and Baltic Birch, 56" x 15" x 6". Photographs: Randall Bohl.

WALL ART / MIXED & OTHER MEDIA

Libby Ware

Libby Ware Studios   2005 Pottery Lane, Port Orange, FL 32128   TEL 386.304.6102
TEL 386.871.4318   FAX 386.788.1641   EMAIL libby@libbyware.com   WEB www.libbyware.com

428

Aurora, 2008, private collection, Naples, FL, mixed media, 60" x 48" x 6". Photographs: Jack McCarty.

Graceann Warn

Graceann Warn Studio   1524 Strieter Road, Ann Arbor, MI 48103   TEL/FAX 734.665.2374
EMAIL gwarnart@gmail.com   WEB www.graceannwarn.com

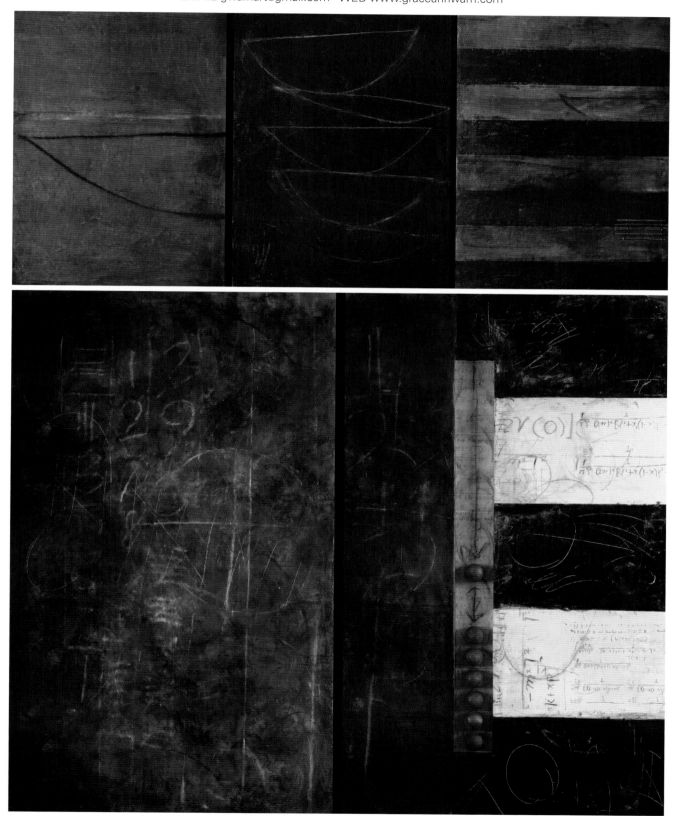

Top: *Quench,* 2008, private collection, Ann Arbor, MI, encaustic painting with paper and objects on wood panel, triptych, 40" x 92" x 2". Bottom: *Chalkboard Cypher,* 2007, private collection, Baltimore, MD, encaustic painting with paper and objects on wood panel, diptych, 58" x 72" x 2". Photographs: William Pelletier.

WALL ART / MIXED & OTHER MEDIA

Laurie Wohl

236 West 27th Street Suite 801, New York, NY 10001   TEL 646.486.0586
TEL 646.522.6753   EMAIL lauriewohl@yahoo.com   WEB www.lauriewohl.com

430

Top: *Out of the Midst of the Fire,* unweaving®, 2007, private collection, Chicago, IL, mixed media, 8'H x 7'W.
Photograph: Tom Van Eynde. Inset: *Out of the Midst of the Fire* (detail). Photograph: Richard A. Smith.

WALL ART / MIXED & OTHER MEDIA

Fanne Fernow

TEL 831.239.1985   TEL 831.465.1463
EMAIL fannefer@gmail.com   WEB www.fannefernow.com

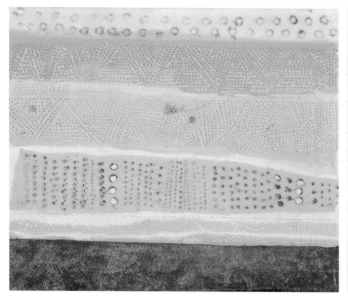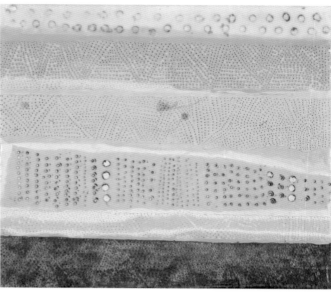

Spring at the Vineyard, 2008, encaustic on panel, 16" x 36".

Wall Art / Mixed & Other Media: Common Terms and Their Meanings

Assemblage The technique of combining various elements, especially found objects, into a three-dimensional work of art.

Casein Paint Also known as Buttermilk Paint, this paint has an opaqe watercolor appearance and uses casein (a glue precipitated from milk by rennin) as a binding ingredient. Casein paint may be used for light impasto on paper or board, for underpainting or wall decoration.

Encaustic From the Greek *enkaustikos,* or "to burn in." A paint medium in which pigment is suspended in molten wax and resin. After applying the paint to a panel or canvas, the artist passes a heat element over the work to fuse the colors into a uniform film. The resin helps to harden the paint as it cools.

Foil A thin, flexible sheet of metal—often aluminum, copper, gold, silver, or tin—used alone or adhered to the surface of other materials.

Gesso A substance made of plaster and glue that may be molded into ornamental shapes that are usually painted or gilded.

Laminated Composed of layers bonded together for strength, thickness, or decorative effect.

Onlay Something laid or applied over something else, creating slight relief. In furniture, to apply a veneer or decorative appliqué.

Resin A plastic that may be bonded to metal or cast in molds.

RESIN

Etude 3.1415 by Yvette Kaiser Smith, see page 423.
Photograph: James Prinz.

Grace Hoff

59-209 Ke Nui Road, Haleiwa, HI 96712   TEL 808.782.7604
EMAIL vickygracehoff@gmail.com   WEB www.vickygracehoff.com

Egyptian Wall Jewelry, 2008, 36" x 60". Photograph: Leroy Douglas.

432

Brigid Manning-Hamilton

I.E. Textiles   1419 South 14th Street Suite 2, Lafayette, IN 47905   TEL 765.471.2956
TEL 317.918.1123   EMAIL ietextiles@comcast.net   WEB www.ietextiles.com

Nightwind, from the *SpiritWear* series, 2007, Pivot Gallery, Indianapolis, IN,
fiberglass screening and machine stitching, 34" x 53" x 10".

Resources

Artist Statements

The pages that follow provide important information on the artists featured in *The Guild Sourcebook of Art*.

Listings in the Artist Statements section are arranged alphabetically according to the heading on each artist's page. These listings include details about the artists' materials and techniques, commissions, collections, and more. References to past Guild Sourcebooks are also included, so that you can further explore the breadth of a particular artist's work. Each listing includes a reference to the artist's page(s) within the book.

As you explore *The Guild Sourcebook of Art,* use the Artist Statements section to enrich your experience. If something in an artist's statement intrigues you—an idea or a past commission—we hope you'll give the artist a call.

434

Artist Statements

Anjin Abe
Wall Art / Metal, page 390

My electrocast works transform paper textures of cardboard and *washi* (Japanese paper) into bronze, embellished with touches of oil paint. They are effective as individual works and, in combination, as extended wall finishings. Born in Osaka in 1938, I began my career as a painter and later established a position as a creator of Bizen ceramics that revive the techniques and the spirit of Momoyama (late sixteenth-century) Japanese pottery. Observers frequently cite a painterly quality in my ceramics and in my bronze wall hangings, which I began creating in the 1990s. I have exhibited throughout Japan and in New York, Paris, San Francisco, Santa Fe, Riga, and elsewhere around the world. My works appear in the permanent collections of the Metropolitan Museum of Art (New York), the Kyoto National Museum of Modern Art, the Ariana Museum (Geneva), and the Mint Museum (Charlotte, North Carolina), among others.

Susan Adamé
Wall Art / Mixed & Other Media, page 406

My artwork begins with the creation of a watercolor painting, which gives the piece a feeling of depth and movement. The nature of my work is to have a strong abstract composition when viewed from a distance and to also draw the viewer in closer by the added depth from the underlying painting and the intricate details of the collage. The use of circle and lines are elements in my work that represent the body and spirit. I feel these elements give my work grounding and strength. Currently, most of my work is created for commissions through art consultants and for sales at art galleries. Sealed with polymer UVLS.

COMMISSIONS: San Francisco, CA, Mill Valley, CA, Walnut Creek, CA

COLLECTIONS: VISA, Foster City, CA

EXHIBITIONS: San Francisco Museum of Modern Art Artists Gallery, 2008, San Francisco, CA; NAWA, 2008, New York, NY; Market Street Gallery, 2007, San Francisco, CA.

Susan Ahrend
Murals, Tiles & Wall Reliefs, page 143

I began Cottonwood Design in 1987, specializing in bas-relief patterned tiles for kitchens and baths. Since 2000 I have focused on creating tile murals for residential, commercial, and public environments. I work in the traditional cuerda seca (dryline) technique with color palettes ranging from vibrant, full-color transparencies to soft, warm mattes. Within each palette I mix and play with the glazes to give my work a painterly or watercolor appearance. Frequent designs include florals, plein air landscapes, animals, and sea life. My murals have also been used as fundraisers for nonprofit organizations.

COMMISSIONS: Twenty-one 6' x 4' murals for shower stalls, Camp Aldersgate, a camp for handicapped children, 2007, Little Rock, AR; Vista Grande Elementary School, 2004, Palos Verdes, CA; Los Angeles Orthopedic Hospital, 2000, Los Angeles, CA; American Heart Association, 2000, Irvine, CA; Rancho Los Alamitos, 1998, Long Beach, CA; Barlow Respiratory Hospital, 1999-2005, Los Angeles, CA

435

Mary Lou Alberetti
Murals, Tiles & Wall Reliefs, pages 144, 145

Throughout my career as a sculptor, I have lived, taught, and studied the architecture of Spain, Italy, France, and Ireland, looking for clues and insights from the fragments left behind. My creative impulse and curiosity has found expression in clay sculptural reliefs—a fusion of classical features that capture the light, texture, and color of ancient walls, arches, and other architectural forms from history and my imagination. Through these multilayered works, I seek to evoke the depth and mystery of the human experience. My works are freestanding or wall hung in individual or multiple groupings and are designed for residential and corporate settings. Original works are available and commissions are welcomed.

COLLECTIONS: Mint Musem of Art, Charlotte, NC; HBO World Headquarters, NYC

EXHIBITIONS: Currier Musem of Art, Manchester, MA

GUILD SOURCEBOOKS: *Designer's 14, 15; Architectural & Interior Art 16, 17, 18, 19, 20; Residential Art 1, 4, 5, 6*

Alex Anagnostou Glass Studio
Sculpture / Non-Representational, page 278

I developed my own technique for creating intricate glass web structures within hollow glass vessels during several years of experimenting with blown glass techniques. Each unique *Filaments* sculpture is inspired by microscopic images and the underlying structures found in nature, a metaphor for the strong and fragile connections found within and between us. *Golden Spiral* is a large sculpture that incorporates multiple forms. My sand-cast glasswork incorporates rich texture and color in topographical framed landscapes for the wall or window, some of which incorporate LED lighting. I have worked on projects with residential and commercial designers. Visit www.alexanagnostou.com or contact me for a consultation. Ships worldwide.

EXHIBITIONS: Solo show, 2009, Galerie Elena Lee, Montreal; Collect, Victoria and Albert Museum, 2008, London; Solo Show, 2007, Material Matters; SOFA Chicago 2007, 2006; Contemporary Craft Museum Gallery, OR; Canadian Clay and Glass Gallery, 2004

COLLECTIONS: Work is held in the Canadian State Fund Art Collection and private collections around the world.

AWARDS: Emerging Glass Artist Award, 2004; Mary Corcoran Award for Craft, 2004; Glass Award, 2005, Toronto Outdoor Art Exhibition; Glass Art Society Scholarship, 2003

Katherine K. Allen
Wall Art / Fiber, page 358

The source of inspiration and material for my unique "soft paintings" is my own tropical garden. From it I create complex mono prints that are then enhanced with paint and stitch. The texture of stitching worked into the semitransparent, graphic layers of printing produces a unique art form. I work in a full range of sizes for both corporate and private settings. Soothing natural subject matter combines with the beauty of stitched silk to offer an elegant, soft counterpoint to hard architectural surfaces.

COMMISSIONS: Florida Atlantic University; All Saints Episcopal Church, Ft. Lauderdale, FL; private residences: Oklahoma City, OK; Easton, MD

COLLECTIONS: University Hospitals Health System, Cleveland, OH; Broward Community College, Ft. Lauderdale, FL; Oklahoma Dance Alliance, OK City, OK; San Jose Museum of Quilts & Textiles, San Jose, CA; private collections

EXHIBITIONS: Stanford Art Spaces, 2008, CA; solo exhibition, 2008, CA; solo exhibition, 2005, Coral Springs Museum, FL; Material Matters, 2008, OH; Fiberart International, 2007, PA; International Fiber Biennial, 2006, China; Quilt National, 2001 and 2005, OH

PRICING: Prices range from $170-$300/square foot

Artist Statements

Michael Allison
Objects, page 166

My work uses a traditional material, wood, in unique and unexpected ways. These are sculptural pieces using the vessel form with a focus on surface, light, and color. Lathe turned from log sections of found local hardwoods, they are extracted rather than fabricated from the material. I select raw material with features (burls, voids, bark decay, parasite damage) that interact dramatically with the color and finish. The visual look involves the unrestrained use of color (dyes and acrylics). I then apply a deep, polished clear coat, resulting in a highly reflective, glass-like finish. The impact of light on this surface gives the wood a vivid depth of color and luminescence. Many pieces are either pierced or carved. These techniques alter the surface of the form, as well as provide access to the interior of the vessels.

GUILD SOURCEBOOKS: *Architectural & Interior Art 23, Residential Art 4*

Amos Fine Art Studios
Public Art, page 240

Bold design, rich colors, and unusual modular formats define the paintings from my studios. Personal involvement in all phases of the project guarantees a timely and successful custom artwork. Past imagery has been thematically diverse, including urban night scenes, national parks, and historical postcards. A maquette is designed and approved in collaboration with the clients. The work is developed on wood, canvas, vinyl, or metal, in paint or photography, and can be shipped worldwide. High-quality materials, expert knowledge, and premium finishes combined with the time-tested techniques of the old masters create artworks that are unique, contemporary, and lasting.

COLLECTIONS: U.S. Library of Congress, Washington, DC; Civic Art Collection, City of Calgary, Canada; Alberta Art Foundation; RBC Dominion Securities; Norcen Energy Resources Ltd; Alberta Energy Corporation; Esso Resources Limited

COMMISSIONS: Cardel Place; Coe & Company International; Applied Communications; Auburn Saloon

PUBLICATIONS: *Legacy Magazine; Galleries West; Artichoke Magazine; Where Magazine; New York Times; Calgary Herald; Avenue Magazine*

Anne Oshman Mosaics
Mosaics, page 130

The art of mosaic is created by combining small pieces of tesserae to form a larger image. I use this ancient medium to capture twenty-first century reflections of ourselves. Using 3/8" micro-mosaic tile, marble, and/or glass, these portraits express the relationship between people and their surroundings. Details that would otherwise go unnoticed are highlighted, yet the feeling of anonymity creates a sense of voyeurism for the viewer. The newest evolution of my work is shifting toward the sculptural, both real and organic; an interesting extraction from materials that are solid and impervious. They, too, have quirky elements that lend context and personality, conveying a story behind them. I welcome the collaborative process to create specific mosaic designs for residential and commercial sites.

COMMISSIONS: Crescent Parking Deck, Montclair, NJ; Thread Clothing Store, Montclair, NJ

EXHIBITIONS: *In The News,* 2008, The Pen and Brush, New York; NJ Arts Annual: CRAFTS, 2008, The State Museum of New Jersey, Trenton; *Body Parts,* 2008, Arts Guild of Rahway, Rahway, NJ

436

Scott E. Armstrong
Furniture & Floor Coverings, page 96

My work is shaped by thirty-five years of artistic and creative living, learning, and working. Growing up in northern Wyoming nurtured my independent spirit and love of natural materials. Getting my B.F.A. from Kansas City Art Institute taught me to direct my creativity and showed me the value of the decorative arts and the beauty of modern design. Working eight years as a senior product designer in the furniture industry gave me an education in production and a respect for traditional forms and ornamentation. For the past fifteen years, I have been running my studio and drawing on this varied background to create graceful, animated, one-of-a-kind, limited-production, and commissioned pieces of fine cabinetry and furniture. I use solid woods for strength and figured veneers for their rare beauty and ecological benefits, then add a touch of inlay for fun.

GUILD SOURCEBOOKS: *Residential Art 6*

Art and Soul
Paintings & Prints, page 176

I was born on December 18, 1972. The techniques in my paintings are many, but there is only one subject matter that I am most intrigued with: the soul. And what is more beautiful and complex than the human body that houses your soul? I want my art to focus on what the world is in desperate need of, and that is unconditional love. Through my art, I can take the world to a place of romance and kindness, a place of unconditional love, a place where the soul is illuminated through poetry and art. A shifting of the consciousness is needed; my art is the portal to that place. I have to stop thinking in order to start creating; art comes from my soul, not my mind. It is time to take the road not traveled and awaken the soul. We have been sleepwalking through life long enough.

EXHIBITIONS: The Florence Biennale International Contemporary Art, 2009, Florence, Italy; Infusion Gallery, 2008, Los Angeles, CA

PRICING: Prices range from $5,000-$75,000 for original work; for wholesale prices to the trade, contact artist.

Art Glass Ensembles
Architectural Glass, page 39

I have been creating custom stained glass and mosaic glass artwork for a variety of clients since 1995. I specialize in creating stained glass artwork for private homes, offices, churches, and public art installations. I also do repair and restoration of stained glass. I work as the primary artist, as the fabrication studio for other non-glass artists, or in collaboration with furniture makers, cabinetmakers, interior designers, and clients. Recent projects include: featured artist on HGTV's *That's Clever;* publication of my fifth CD-ROM of stained glass patterns for Dragonfly Software (www.dfly.com); stained glass mosaics for Immaculate Heart of Mary R. C. Church of Ft. Worth, TX; creation of the world's greatest operas in stained glass for the University of North Texas Lyric Opera Theatre; and numerous large custom stained and leaded glass windows for private homes throughout the U.S. Please see www.ArtGlassEnsembles.com for examples of my work.

Artist Statements

ART, Inc.
Sculpture / Representational, page 316

I specialize in architectural ceramics and clay sculpture for public or private, interior or exterior spaces. Just as nature is diverse, my creations are diverse in subject matter, ranging from realistic to abstract. When on my acreage in northwest Arkansas, I take in the glorious nature that is there. I keep visuals in my mind of things I see, and I take those images back to the studio where they fuel my creativity. It is creating inspired by nature that I have to do. My work has appeared in one-woman shows, galleries, and group shows, and is in private collections.

COMMISSIONS: Benton County School of the Arts, 2008, Rogers, AR; Northwest Arkansas Children's Shelter, 2007 and 2006, Bentonville, AR; Creation Park, 2000, Rogers, AR

EXHIBITIONS: *Art Expo NWA*, 2007, Fayetteville, AR; *Art Expo Retrospective Show*, 2007, Fayetteville, AR.

Atelier Huck Fisher
Public Art, pages 241, 242

Fifteen years of collaboration between artist Laura Fisher and master metalsmith Christopher Huck have produced a highly experienced and powerful design and manufacturing team. The constant flow of commissions, ranging from custom indoor sculptural pieces to large exterior installations, along with our commitment to producing well-made, highly durable and beautiful work, has strengthened and honed our motto: Attention to detail adds strength to design. We create custom work in brass, bronze, copper, aluminum, and stainless and mild steels. Some of the more unique pieces have been hand painted.

COMMISSIONS: Design of exterior railings and gateway to the Sculpture Court of the Art Gallery of Nova Scotia; forty-four permanent fish sculptures on the streets of Lunenburg, Nova Scotia; a thirty-foot Bavarian-style maypole for The Arrabelle at Vail, CO; five seven-foot whimsical fish for the entryway to Coastal Flats restaurant, Tyson's Corner, McLean, VA; entry gate and eight-foot weathervane for a professional riding center in Chester, Nova Scotia; grand bronze chandelier, main lobby, Government of Canada Building, Halifax, Nova Scotia

GUILD SOURCEBOOKS: *Architect's 8, 9, 10, 11, 12, 13, 14; Architectural & Interior Art 16, 18, 19, 21, 23*

Elizabeth Austin
Architectural Elements, page 30

After two decades of exhibitions across the United States and in Europe, I have recently begun producing the series *Illuminated Windows*, to be installed in buildings in corporate, municipal, educational, religious, and residential settings, in place of stained glass. The materials I have used in my work lend themselves to experimentation with transparency, light, and depth, reflecting and refracting light (via iridescent paints and holographic, collaged elements) in addition to transmitting it. The beautiful, visual elements of the painted windows are augmented by the fact that, as being made of plastic rather than glass, the windows are lighter weight and much easier and more economical to install than traditional glass. Windows have already been installed at Crossroads Academy, Lyme, NH; Parkersburg Art Center, Parkersburg, WV; Villa Terrace Art Museum, Milwaukee, WI, as well as private residences in the United States and in England. Please contact me at ElizabethAustin1@ compuserve.com with inquiries.

Saule and Alibay Bapanov
Wall Art / Fiber, pages 357, 359

For over twenty years, my husband Alibay and I have created handwoven and handfelted tapestries using the centuries-old techniques of our nomad ancestors. We find inspiration in blending Central Asian cultural icons with modern artistic expression. We are always seeking new artistic challenges and love opening unexpected horizons with every piece, whether bold color contrasts or fluid color gradation, grand scale or smaller size pieces, ethnic symbolism or universal abstraction. Our tapestries are found in museums and private collections in Europe and Asia. We are very happy to reach an American audience through Meggy Wagner and Art Beyond Borders. Meggy's friendship and enthusiasm for our work has been an inspiration and great source of energy for us for more than a decade! We live and work in Almaty, Kazakhstan, and teach painting and textile art at the Kazakh National Academy of Art. In 2003 Alibay was awarded the Kazakh National Medal of Honor for his lifetime achievements in the arts. In 2007 we were awarded the Platinum Tarlan of the Mécénats' Club of Kazakhstan.

Kathy Barnard
Architectural Glass, pages 40, 41

Glass has intrigued me with its unique properties for more than thirty years. A deep love of nature, commitment to the client's vision, and distinctively detailed design are the hallmarks of my works in glass. I have selected details from *Beauty in the Cycles of Life* at the Grace Covenant Presbyterian Church in Overland Park, Kansas, to be featured in this book. The twelve deeply carved glass sanctuary doors form a forty-foot wall. Five large stained glass windows in abstract designs complement the doors. Four windows depict the elements earth, air, water, and fire. The fifth window incorporates the acorn and oak sapling, the symbol of the church. You can see examples of this stained glass, as well as many other installations, on my website, www.KathyBarnardStudio. com. Each of my pieces touches my heart. Whether abstract or realistic, most of my pieces deal with nature and its magnificent forces. I thoroughly enjoy what I do and immerse myself in each creation. My hope is that the client and the public will find delight in each commission. Please view my past Guild Sourcebooks for a list of commissions and awards.

GUILD SOURCEBOOKS: *The Guild 3, 4, 5; Architect's 8, 9, 10, 13; Architectural & Interior Art 16, 22, 23; Residential Art 6*

Sam Bates
Murals, Tiles & Wall Reliefs, page 163

I use hand-held abrasive lapidary tools to carve rare fine-grained stone. Working with architects, designers, and individual clients, I create original designs for carvings ranging in scale from small hand-held sculptures to large architectural installations. I enjoy the challenge of creating completely original designs within the rigorous discipline of stone carving. Exploring the intrinsic parallels between natural form and abstract design is a vital part of my work. While I am always developing my own artistic vision, I enrich my approach by freely adapting to my customers' requests for original artwork in the diverse traditions of classic art and architecture, from Romanesque to modern minimalism. My work includes, but is not restricted to, carvings incorporating abstract and botanical motifs, free-form and geometric minimalism, wildlife, marine portraiture, landscape and liturgical themes, architectural details, and freestanding sculptures.

COMMISSIONS: Seattle, WA; Bellevue, WA; Spokane, WA; Centralia, WA; Vancouver, BC; Pender Harbor, BC; Woodside, CA; Coeur d'Alene, ID; Sandpoint, ID; Chicago, IL; Cape May, NJ; Philadelphia, PA; Green Lane, PA

PRICING: $1000–$40,000

437

Artist Statements

Michael Bauermeister

Sculpture / Non-Representational
Wall Art / Mixed & Other Media, pages 9, 279, 296, 407

I think of my tall vessels as figures. As such, I'm interested in their personalities and how they relate to one another. These vessels are made from cabinet-grade hardwoods and are finished with lacquer so they will not warp or crack. Most range in price from $1,000 to $3,000. In my wall pieces, I approach the wood as a canvas. These undulating wood panels are carved, sometimes turned, and finished with layers of tinted lacquer, which is partially sanded away before the piece gets a final stain and clear finish. The panel is not quite flat but usually has the flowing quality of draped fabric or the surface of the sea. Collections include: Smithsonian Institution, Renwick Gallery, Washington, D.C.; University of Michigan Museum, Ann Arbor; Mesa Museum of contemporary Art, Mesa, AZ. Exhibitions include: Smithsonian Craft Show, 2003, 2002, Washington, DC; Wood Turning Invitational, 2000-2003, American Art Co., Tacoma, WA; Turned Wood Invitational, 2002, 1999, 1998, Del Mano Gallery, Los Angeles, CA; and Nuances d'ete, 2001, Carlin Gallery, Paris, France. Awards include: 25th Annual Contemporary Crafts Purchase Award, 2003, Mesa Arts Center, Mesa, AZ; Best of Wood, 2002, American Craft Exposition, Evanston, IL; Niche Award, 2002; and the Award of Excellence, 2000, American Craft Council, Baltimore, MD.

438

Beeline Studio LLC

Lighting, page 118

I'm driven by color, light, transparency, and chance. The interactions between colors in a given environment become inspiration for my work. I am ever conscious of the color and light of my surroundings. One such inspiration came from a cup of tea. I was intrigued not only by the color of the tea, but also by the tea bag itself. The use of tea bags in my artwork evolved into the creation of lampshades and allows me the opportunity to explore the many elements of color and light. Taking an innocuous object and transforming it into something with greater presence intrigues me. Each lampshade is handmade from individual 3" x 5" tea bags dyed with acrylic paint, then glued together to create larger compositions. An acrylic polymer medium encases and preserves the sheets. I began BeeLine Studio for my functional, unique lampshades and lamp designs. More images of my work can be found at www.BeeLineStudio.net.

GUILD SOURCEBOOKS: *Residential Art 5, 6*

Errol Beauchamp

Sculpture / Non-Representational, page 280

My bronze sculpture is appropriate for hotel, spa, corporate, healthcare, and private collections. I provide extensive experience collaborating with architects, interior designers, and art consultants to comfortably discuss site selection, sizing to the environment, base material selection, and delivering the appropriate expression of my work for the design intent of the project. Layering, cracking, carving, and casting textures of simplistic form to reflect my expressionistic sculptures is my passion. By exploring the relationship between the clay and my highly stylized bronze forms, I interpret the human gesture and the fluid motion of the Western landscape. For more information please visit www.beauchampsculpture.com.

COMMISSIONS: Walnut Creek Business Park and the City of Westminister, Colorado

COLLECTIONS: Medical Center of the Rockies-Loveland, CO; various private collections in Oregon, Utah, New Mexico, Colorado, Texas, Florida, and Paris, France

EXHIBITIONS: *Colorado: See the New West Like a Local*, 2008-2009, Denver International Airport; *Evergreen Invitational*, 2004, Evergreen, CO

PRICING: Prices for small indoor to large outdoor/public art from $2,000 to $90,000. Please view my website and contact me for pricing information.

Guy J. Bellaver

Sculpture / Non-Representational, page 311

I work in many mediums, but my most recent work has been in bronze or painted steel, and ranges in size from tabletop to monumental pieces over 18' tall. I am fascinated by positive/negative space, and my sculptures attempt to stretch the physics of the medium that I'm working in to occupy those spaces. My work is in civic, corporate, residential, and university settings, both commissioned and spec. I take pride in working effectively with all of those involved in commissioned work to achieve a piece that fulfills an artistic vision. Call for a brochure.

COMMISSIONS: Monumental work: Kane County; City of St. Charles; Prose Orthodontics; Daughters of St. Paul; St. Patrick Church; MCC Technology; Elgin Community College; and others

COLLECTIONS: Armstrong County; Forbes Health System; Graphite Sales; H.J. Heinz; Hiram College; Indiana University; White International; St. Vincent College; and many other public and private collections

Doreen Beck

Wall Art / Fiber, page 360

My contemporary tapestries are created with a rich palette of cottons, damasks, linens, silks, satins, suede, velvets, lightweight wools, synthetics, and metallics in appliqué and piecing; with laces and chiffons for depth and subtlety in layering; buttons, sequins, decorative braiding, and embroidery for fanciful highlights; outline quilting for a soft, sculptural effect. They have been exhibited in the 10th Annual Salon, Williamsburg Art & Historical Center (WAH), Brooklyn, New York, NY, 2009; October Salon 2007/One Hundred Per Cent Design, Pratt Mansion, New York, NY; National Trust for Historic Preservation, Decatur House, Washington, DC, 1992 and 1991; Gallery 500, Philadelphia, PA, 1990; Society of Illustrators, New York, NY, 1989; Art in Embassies Loan Program, U.S. State Department, Washington, DC, 1986; The Metropolitan Museum's Gallery at Lincoln Center, New York, NY, 1985; I Miller/Jaeger Window Displays, New York, NY, 1985. They have been published as limited-edition art prints, 1993; on the cover of *The Flutist Quarterly*, 1991; and in an article in *Creative Quilting*, 1990.

BellFlower Design Studio

Murals, Tiles & Wall Reliefs, pages 146, 147

BellFlower began as a dare. I'm best known for my signature flower-based work and was challenged by Captain V.J. Bell, one of the most sought-after sport fishing boat captains throughout Florida and the Caribbean, to paint a fish. Since then, V.J. has been an inspiration to my new line of fine art and, in turn, has led to the development of Bell Flower Design Studio. With V.J.'s wealth of experience and knowledge of open waters, and my natural ability to use color, shades, and light to paint serene images and bring them to life, the BellFlower line of fine art is born. BellFlower: where dreamlike art, secrets of the waters, and a love of nature come together.

Artist Statements

Bennett Studio
Sculpture / Representational, page 317

I specialize in classically rendered sculptures of human figures, animals, and wildlife. Works include more than fifty public works of art for parks, colleges, liturgical settings, memorials, corporate headquarters, hospitals, and private residences. I have successfully worked in collaboration with architects and other professionals to implement large-scale designs and site developments. Venturing beyond the simple definition of sculpture as an object in space, an effort is made to incorporate or define the entire space that surrounds the central or peripheral sculpture being presented. This can be enhanced with a water feature, stone, metal, or other materials. All budgets are accommodated.

COMMISSIONS: *Parade Route*, 2007, Main Street, Shoreline, WA; *Prairie Preening*, 2007, Butler Community College, El Dorado, KS; Ames Veterans Memorial, 2006, Fifth and Grand Street, Ames, IA; *Athletic Heroes of Iowa*, 2006, Iowa Events Center, Hall of Pride, Des Moines, IA; Douglas Hoeft Memorial, 2005, Riverside Park, Elgin, IL

AWARDS: Pollock-Krasner Foundation, 1999

GUILD SOURCEBOOKS: *Architect's 12, 13, 14; Designer's 12, 13; Architectural & Interior Art 20, 22*

Lanny Bergner
Atrium Sculpture, page 64

I am a mixed-media sculptor, fiber and installation artist who creates ethereal suspended organic constructions out of wire mesh and glass frit. By employing inventive, yet simple construction techniques, I transform common materials into otherworldly sculptures and installations. My goal as an artist is to use my work to enliven and enhance a space, and to inspire the viewer.

COMMISSIONS: Skagit Valley College, 2008, Mount Vernon, WA; Island Hospital, 2007, Anacortes, WA; Giaudrone Middle School, 2005, Tacoma, WA; Anacortes Public Library, 2003, Anacortes, WA; Philadelphia International Airport, 1994, Philadelphia, PA

COLLECTIONS: Museum of Art and Design, New York, NY; Cheongju International Craft Biennale, Cheongju-City, Korea; Seattle Art Museum, Seattle, WA; Philadelphia Museum of Art, Philadelphia, PA

AWARDS: Gold Prize, 2005, 4th Annual Cheongju International Craft Biennale, Cheongju-City, Korea; Artist Trust Fellowship, 1997, Artist Trust, Seattle, WA; Seventeenth Annual Betty Bowen Memorial Award, 1995, Seattle Art Museum, Seattle, WA

Karen Berman
Paintings & Prints, page 233

For nearly two decades, watercolor painting has been my passion. I paint what I think is beautiful. I am mesmerized by color, movement, and light, and have a strong drive to personally interpret the beauty around me. My goal is to express my response to the natural world through brushstroke, texture, color, light, and composition, rather than control of photographic detail. My large florals and landscapes have been called beautiful and spiritual. I believe my work fits into the needs of healthcare, corporate, hotel/spa, and academic facilities, as well as private ownership. My work ranges from 15" x 20" to larger pieces up to 6' wide. Commissions welcome. "Karen Berman's description of her painting process, '...if I'm very lucky, the painting takes on a life of its own, and all the world is silent and at peace while I paint,' makes you want to be out there yourself and enjoying that peace." Katheryn Almy, *Redwood Arts Guide*

Bethanie Brandon Design
Wall Art / Mixed & Other Media, page 408

Political events and personal experiences, the hues of Italy, ancient artifacts from rural Japan, and the geometry of modern architecture inspire my designs. Textiles have been a part of my life since childhood, when I explored the mills of industrial upstate Pennsylvania where my father wove seatbelt webbing for the automakers of Detroit. As a teen I earned an income and developed a sense of color in a New Jersey design studio, painting production canvases for a renowned needlepoint artist. My goal is to turn my love of fiber into an expression, to create everyday objects as well as refined art pieces that engage the user in a substantive experience, both gratifying and continuous.

COLLECTIONS: Crump's, Fresno, CA; Herzog, Tiburon, CA; Matloff, Paradise Valley, AZ; Cerf, Tiburon, CA; Sawbridge Studios, Chicago, IL; Kopol Bonick, Napa, CA; Millman, Palo Alto, CA

EXHIBITIONS: Museum of Craft and Folk Art, San Francisco, CA; Silver Fox Gallery, Hendersonville, NC; The Gardener, Berkeley, CA; Palo Alto Art Center, Palo Alto, CA; Marin Arts Salon, San Rafael, CA; ASID Designer Showcase, Atherton, CA

PUBLICATIONS: *Marin Independent Journal*, 2008; *American Art Collector*, 2007, 2006; *American Style*, 2004; *Niche Magazine*, 2004, 2003; *San Francisco Chronicle*, 2002

Matthew Bezark
Architectural Glass, pages 38, 42

Growing up near Chicago, I gained a great appreciation for glass in architecture. Influenced in part by many visits to the Frank Lloyd Wright houses in the area, my exploration of glass design based on light and color began. A move to the foothills of Colorado added nature to the forces that inspire me to create. Building the Mountain Glassworks studio here has provided a place for this exploration to continue. One of my strengths is the ability to collaborate with other artists, as well as architects and designers, to exchange ideas and help a project become reality. The *Repeated Travel* project for the Jacksonville International Airport shown in this book is the beginning of a new direction for me. That project was a rewarding and successful expansion of the scope of my work to include fabricated elements. In addition to my newest fabricated work, hand-poured glass castings are still prominent in my designs. The immediacy, movement, fluidity, and drama inherent in working with hot glass captivates me. Hand-poured castings are very dynamic. Color and surface texture work is done while the glass is still hot and helps ensure the uniqueness of these works. Please view my web site for examples of commercial and residential installations.

Bigbird Studios
Sculpture / Representational, pages 318, 352

I love steel, its strength, immediacy, even its tendency to fight back before yielding to form. Its structural limits seem boundless. With steel and direct sculpting, the sculptor's imprint, and the immediacy of method is not changed in processing. Currently, I am also combining steel, bronze, and other materials using the best qualities of these materials to enhance the sculpture. I have had the pleasure of creating one-of-a-kind sculpture for the public and private sectors for over twenty-five years. The majority of my sculpture is suitable for both indoor and outdoor placement.

COLLECTIONS: Robin Williams, Gary Larson, Cypress Gardens, Broadway Plaza

EXHIBITIONS: Los Angeles Natural History Museum; El Paseo, Palm Desert; One Bush, San Francisco

Artist Statements

Charlotte Bird
Wall Art / Fiber, page 361

Annie Dillard writes of a fellow sitting in a cabin teaching a stone to talk. The Incas taught stones to speak of shape and fit. In the American Southwest, stones express sunlight, chemistry, and time. I explore the speech of stones in shapes, colors, and value changes. My stitches percolate among the stones, seeking their words. I have been featured on *The Carol Duvall Show*, and *Simply Quilts* on HGTV, Commissions are welcome. Prices range from $200 to $300 per square foot.

COLLECTIONS: Neutrogena; Luce Forward, The Thomas Contemporary Quilt Collection; and numerous private collections

EXHIBITIONS: Solo shows, 2005, 2001, 1999, La Jolla Fiber Arts Gallery, La Jolla, CA; Mingei International Museum, 2008, San Diego, CA; Leepa-Rattner Museum of Art, 2008, Tarpon Springs, FL; Visions Art Quilt Gallery, 2007, 2008, San Diego, CA; Quilt Visions 2004, San Diego, CA; John Wayne Airport, 2004, Long Beach, CA

GUILD SOURCEBOOKS: *Architectural & Interior Art 19, 20; Residential Art 4, 5*

Erik Blome
Sculpture / Representational, page 319

My studio produces custom sculpture work that encompasses everything from small-scale sculpture and drawings created for display in galleries to publicly commissioned monumental-size bronzes for stadiums, forest preserves, and cities. Born and raised in the Chicago area, I have shown my work extensively and completed numerous private commissions and impressive monumental public figurative sculpture works. My studio has handled everything from monumental bronze sculpture projects to restoration projects on commission. We provide all aspects of design, fabrication, bronze casting, maintenance, and installation services for all works produced. Work has been featured in major media like *The New York Times, the Wall Street Journal,* and CNN.

COMMISSIONS: *Oscar De La Hoya: The Golden Boy,* 2008, Staples Center, Los Angeles, CA; *Mississippi Harvest,* 2007, Muscatine, IA; *African Elephant,* 2006, Embassy of Cote D'Ivoire, Washington, DC; *Wayne Gretzky: The Great One,* 2003, Staples Center, Los Angeles, CA; *Jack Benny,* 2002, Waukegan, IL; *Ms. Rosa Parks,* 2000, Montgomery, AL; Six life-size hockey players, 2000, United Center, Chicago; *John Sturdivant,* 1999, U.S. Department of Labor, Washington, DC; *Dr. Martin Luther King Jr.,* 1997, YWCA, Greater Milwaukee; *Thurgood Marshall,* 1996, Chicago

John Boak
Wall Art / Mixed & Other Media, page 409

Living as we do in a world of highly refined and powerful objects, we are trained to approach unknown objects as if their meaning will soon be revealed. My sculptures encourage the anticipation of function and meaning. While waiting for that revelation, the pleasures of mystery and speculation remain. The glyphs are my own; I have drawn and collected them for over thirty years. I have worked closely with architects and designers, creating art that joins the architecture. Projects have included sculpture, oil paintings, etched glass, water-cut bronze, aluminum, steel and slate, acetylene-cut steel panels, porcelain enamel on steel, and bronze in concrete.

COMMISSIONS: University of Colorado, Folsom Field Addition, 2003, Boulder; Colorado Department of Transportation, El Moro Rest Area, 2000, Trinidad; Colorado Welcome Center, 1992, Dinosaur; City and County of Denver, Harvard Gulch, 1992, CO; Colorado Welcome Center, 1988, Burlington and Fruita

440

Carl Borgia
Paintings & Prints, pages 177, 233

My art is not formally learned and has no intention of imparting deep meanings. I paint because I am drawn personally to the subject and its beauty. I work until I'm pleased with the proportions, colors, and details of the painting. My work focuses on city subjects from the heritage countries of Portugal, Italy, and Brazil. But I also enjoy creating works inspired by other beautiful places like China and Greece. Please take a voyage through my world at www.carlborgia.com. The geography is familiar yet different, real yet transcending, personal yet universal.

PRICING: The wholesale price range of my prints is $500 to $2,000, depending on the dimensions and quantity purchased. Print sizes are customized according to the client's needs. Original oils are also available and range from $15,000 to $60,000. Call or email me for more information or quotes.

Boykin Pearce Associates
Furniture & Floor Coverings, pages 11, 97

"Sensitively designed and carefully crafted": a simple phrase we use defining furniture created by Boykin Pearce Associates. It describes an intense drive for technical and design excellence. Our concepts are developed in CAD and built with loving care, melding historically proven techniques with the best of today's advancements. Our palette consists of the world's finest materials, including hardwoods carefully selected for grain pattern and color to yield furniture with beauty, balance, and strength. We're inspired by the quest for excellence and the endless possibilities of design and technique. The result is lovingly developed heirloom-quality furniture built to be passed on for generations. The work appears in numerous private, commercial, and liturgical collections. We teach, consult with design professionals, and serve on advisory boards at the Art Institute of Colorado and the Denver Art Museum. You are invited to see more at boykinpearce.com.

GUILD SOURCEBOOKS: *Residential Art 6*

Kathy Bradford
Architectural Glass, page 43

Sandblast carving and etching remain the major forces in my glass art. Over the years I have created many unique techniques to achieve certain imagery not found in the work of other glass artists. Attention to detail is especially important, giving the viewer a special glimpse into the private world of nature. The majority of works are in the public art realm, but commissions are also created for corporations and individual residences throughout the nation. Imagery is split between nature-derived compositions and energetic contemporary abstract designs. Everything is taken into account to create beautiful art glass that will work in concert with the architecture of the location.

COMMISSIONS: Westside Police Station (public art), 2007, Tucson, AZ; Burien Library/Town Hall (public art), 2008, Burien, WA; Abramson Center for Jewish Life, 2008, Philadelphia, PA; Wildlife Experience, 2008, Denver, CO; Aurora Firehouse #3 (public art), Aurora, CO

GUILD SOURCEBOOKS: *Architect's 12, 13, 14, 15; Architectural & Interior Art 16, 17, 18, 19, 20, 21, 22, 23*

Artist Statements

Jackie Braitman
Sculpture / Non-Representational,
pages 281, 313

My artwork investigates how emotional tension is magnified in the rhythm of our movements. I work in series; each series within this infinite topic explores different aspects of motion or tension. I sculpt site-specific work that focuses on building continuity with the site, institution, and future direction. I work at both architectural scale and the intimate scale of indoor sculpture. In addition to my sculpture studio, I own a Design/Build business specializing in residential remodeling, spending each day at the intersection of art, architecture, and design. Paradoxically, it is the daily rigors of meeting the engineering demands of construction that helps me understand and meet my own artistic voice.

COMMISSIONS: Include publicly installed art at the Bradley Hills Presbyterian Church and for many private residential clients

EXHIBITIONS: Solo exhibits 2008: RedSky Gallery, Charlotte NC; Glenview Mansion Art Gallery, Rockville, MD; BlackRock Art Center, Germantown, MD

AWARDS: Niche Award, 2008, fused glass; twice a finalist in Bullseye Glass e-merge competitions; architectural awards for remodeling work in Montgomery County, MD

PUBLICATIONS: *InSight Montgomery*, Nov. 2008; *AmericanStyle Magazine*, Apr. 2008; *Washington Post*, June 2007, Feb. 2007

Aaron T. Brown
Paintings & Prints
Public Art, pages 13, 234, 275

Art for me is an improvisational dance, its movement caught on paper, wood, and steel. The movement is born out of my love of rhythm and form, coming mysteriously out of an unknowing frame of mind. In the moment of creation, something is happening, something is being born. I watch as I draw with pen or cut with saw, an impromptu dance, here fluid motion, now staccato, twisting, turning, stopping, starting, watching as the wonderful forms appear. Art is an exploration. An exploration that leaves in its wake a record that others can behold. This is one of art's gifts to the world, this record left behind, this inner journey revealed. Finally, a piece of writing from an artist who has been an inspiration for me, Jean Arp:

"Anyone who tries to shoot down a cloud with arrows will soon exhaust his quiver. Many sculptors are like these foolish hunters. Here is what one should do: charm the cloud with the tune of a violin played on a drum, or with the tune of a drum played on a violin. Then before long the cloud will come down and take its ease on earth until, full of happiness, it turns to stone. Thus in the twinkling of an eye the sculptor realizes his most beautiful works."

From *The Art of Jean Arp* by Herbert Read.

Ursula J. Brenner
Paintings & Prints, page 178

My paintings reflect a wide range of moods, from light and playful to deep and mysterious. I am influenced by old-world museums, music, and architecture. My art makes a strong, bold statement, yet it can be very ethereal as well. I want people who look at my art to be transported to another realm, to transcend the normal human experience. I like to focus on the fundamental nature of a scene—the values, colors, and shapes—using "notan" study, a Japanese method of examining lights and darks. My paintings are in private and corporate collections worldwide. I have worked with interior designers and art consultants, and accept commissions in a broad range of sizes. Prices range from $600 to $10,000.

Bruce Middleton and Co.
Murals, Tiles & Wall Reliefs, page 148

Specializing in theme rooms, murals, and "extreme makeovers," I bring a wealth of artistic knowledge and experience to every job. I possess a very unique and masterful sense of color and design, paying great attention to detail as is evident in every piece that I do. I use my extreme sense of imagination and extensive knowledge of material and fabrication to make each piece a truly unique work of art. My illustration background makes each piece look good not only from a distance but even more amazing close up. I am well versed in such a wide variety of styles and mediums that there is nothing I can't do. I love a challenge. To view more of my work, please visit www.brucemiddleton.com.

Jeanine Briggs
Sculpture / Representational, pages 21, 22, 320

Seeing different things and seeing things differently, I begin transforming discarded materials into art. My imagination takes form through freestanding sculptures, wall sculptures, and paintings. Environmental sensibilities influence my constructive processes as well as my choice of materials. Just as nature inspires my work, I hope my work in some way serves nature by suggesting creative and conservational solutions to consumer practices. Appearing in galleries, museums, public spaces, trade shows, corporate collections, and government offices, my work has been exhibited extensively in California and most recently in New York City. Commissions of any scale welcome. Imagine the possibilities.

AWARDS: Artist in Residence, 2000, SF Recycling & Disposal, San Francisco, CA

PUBLICATIONS: *Show & Tell: The Art of Harmony*, 2007, Zimmer Children's Museum, Los Angeles, CA

GUILD SOURCEBOOKS: *Designer's 15; Architectural & Interior Art 16; Residential Art 6*

441

Laura Militzer Bryant
Wall Art / Mixed & Other Media, page 411

The intent of my work can be seen in poet Mark Strand's stanza:

"In a place that is not a place, but where the mortal beauty of the world is stored."

I create richly layered and detailed complex double weaves of wool, rayon, nylon, and Lurex that reflect an inner landscape, of this world and others. These landscape-inspired geometric images are interpreted in free-hanging large weavings or as more intimate textiles floating on wood or metal panels. Visual integration of woven surface to panel involves processes ranging from patination on copper to acrylic paint and metal leaf on wood. All threads are hand painted and dyed with high-quality light-fast dyes, and metal or wood surfaces are sealed. I welcome collaboration with clients to achieve the perfect enhancement for their environment, and enjoy the synergy that is created during the commission process.

GUILD SOURCEBOOKS: *Designer's 10, 11, 12, 13, 14, 15, Architectural & Interior Art 16, 17, 18, 19, 20, 21, 22, 23*

Artist Statements

Fran Bull
Paintings & Prints, page 179

Season of Bones is a suite of four works, plus two related images, and eventually may include more pieces since the series is still in progress. A photograph that appeared in *Archeology* magazine was the starting point for these works. It is a powerful photograph of two skeletons, male and female, entwined in an embrace. We see them embedded in soil, carefully exhumed by archaeologists at an Italian site where they had lain for four millennia, their almost-intact bones overlapping, their legs and arms piled together like sticks on a forest floor. Their heads, now skulls, are turned towards each other, giving the impression that they died gazing into each other's eyes. We love and we die. Nothing has changed. The image of human bones, 4,000 years old, literally locked in an embrace, moved me to make my etching series.

Shelley Tincher Buonaiuto and Michael Buonaiuto
Sculpture / Representational, page 321

Michael and I have worked together for thirty-seven years. After studying in college, we began working in clay at Chardavogne Barn, a group studying Gurdjieff, and our education continued in combining art with our spiritual studies. We work in clay, bronze, and resin. Some of the work is representational and some is stylized. The subject is the human figure, usually two or more figures in relationship. At present, I do most of the sculpture and focus especially on women, the elderly, and a diversity of races, with an emphasis on positive and loving interactions. The bronzes are cast in a local foundry, and I do the patinas. The bronzes shown here, *The Alternative Energies*, have been chosen to be displayed at a park in Loveland, CO, and at an apartment building in Little Rock, AR. The clay and resin figures can be seen on our website.

Myra Burg
Wall Art / Mixed & Other Media, pages 412, 413, 414

Somewhere between tapestry and jewelry, *Quiet Oboes* and sculptural installations adorn spaces in a free-floating, peaceful way. Hand-wrapped fiber and burnished metals are combined to create inspired sculptural pieces that meet clients' needs and wants within the requirements of the space. The bigger the challenge, the more the fun. Collaborations are welcome.

COMMISSIONS: The Buffett Foundation, NE; Western Asset, London, England; Boston Children's Hospital; *Japonaise*, Universal Studios, Japan; *Galactic Curve*, Universal Studios, Japan; *Quiet Oboes*, Caribé Hilton, Puerto Rico; *Travelocity*, Dallas, TX

EXHIBITIONS: American Craft Council; SOFA, Chicago; Los Angeles County Museum of Art, CA; Howard Hughes Center, Los Angeles, CA; Orange County Museum of Art, CA

GUILD SOURCEBOOKS: *Designer's 10, 13, 14, 15; Architect's 14, 15; Architectural & Interior Art 16, 17, 18, 19, 20, 21, 22, 23; Residential Art 1, 2, 3, 4, 5, 6*

Myra Burg and Liz Cummings
Wall Art / Mixed & Other Media, page 414

At long last, we have done it! We are now celebrating our collective fifty years of artistic experience by producing a whole new art form that begins on the wall and blooms, becoming spatial elements as well. Liz, with twenty-five years of experience as an artist painting romantic architectural and scenic images, and Myra, moving from the practice of architecture to creating architectural wrapped wall elements, have joined efforts in their respective specialties. We are combining lustrous oils on canvas, creating two-dimensional color fields that provide an environment for sumptuous wrapped fiber. The planar canvases and dimensional cylinders work in tandem, engaging one another in this brand new and highly versatile mixed-media format. Somewhere between the image and the imagination, these combinations give new life to the act of placing color in a living space.

GUILD SOURCEBOOKS: *Architectural & Interior Art 20, Residential Art 6*

Susan Eileen Burnes
Wall Art / Fiber, page 362

My work is about the experience of light and color, illuminations of the spirit. Using a traditional hand-stitching technique, I establish a textural base of cotton thread on even-weave fabric. As paint and pastel pigments are applied over the fiber, layers of color emerge and flow. These simple geometric forms relate to each other as they evolve into rhythmic patterns of light and shadow. Each element is then attached to painted canvas. These original wall pieces have been featured in juried exhibitions around the country.

GUILD SOURCEBOOKS: *Designer's 8, 9, 10, 13, 14; Architectural & Interior Art 19; Residential Art 4, 6*

Riis Burwell
Sculpture / Non-Representational, page 282

My work is an exploration—emotional, spiritual, and physical—of what is seen and unseen in nature. Process and the gradual, though constant, change of things from one state of being to another fundamentally inform my artwork. My focus is to bring attention back to sculpture as a finely crafted object. Bronze, steel, and stainless steel are my materials of choice because of their permanence and inherent beauty. They lend themselves well to both tabletop and monumental sculpture, and are appropriate indoors and out.

COMMISSIONS: Lumiere Palace Casino, St. Louis, MO; Wilshire Grand Hotel, Los Angeles, CA; TCC International Holdings Ltd., 2006, Hong Kong; The MGM Mirage, 2005, Las Vegas, NV; Presbyterian Hospital of Denton, 2005, TX; SAS Institute World Headquarters, 2005, Cary, NC; The District at Green Valley Ranch Resort, 2004, Henderson, NV; Hyatt Hotel & Convention Center, 2002, Santa Rosa, CA

COLLECTIONS: Hotel Vue Plage, La Baule, France; Neuberg International Ltd., Hong Kong; Fresno Museum of Art, CA

GUILD SOURCEBOOKS: *Architect's 12, 13, 14, 15; Architectural & Interior Art 16, 17, 18, 19, 20, 21, 22, 23*

Artist Statements

Steven Bush
Sculpture / Representational, page 322

I am a third-generation ironworker with a strong work ethic. It has been my passion and talent to work with iron since I first began welding at the age of eight. While studying painting and fine art at Columbus College of Art and Design, I realized that I must be true to myself and follow my roots. Upon graduation I worked for fabrication shops to hone my craft and better learn my trade. In 1998 I opened my studio, smARTworks, which specializes in site-specific pieces designed and created for the client. I work for corporations, associations, schools, and hospitals, as well as the private sector. My pieces range in size up to thirty feet. I use steel and stainless steel, accented with painted, patinated, or natural finishes. I pride myself, and build smARTworks's reputation, on being punctual and on budget. My pieces are durable, long lasting, and timeless.

Betty Butler
Paintings & Prints, pages 180, 181

My abstract acrylic paintings are a juxtaposed collection of images that I observe in the natural world. Softly floating clouds, flowers, and foliage find their way into the imagery; yet, I strive for a balance between the sweetness of nature and its inevitable entropy. The earth moves with each seedling, gardens bloom, rain falls, and eventually the cold wind blows life into its seasonal hibernation—all to my fascination. Pastel shapes of sage, purple, and teal contrast the splashes of bright pink, orange, and yellow that one finds in nature's narrative. My work is found in public and private collections, and I am represented by the Illinois Artisans Program. My paintings are available as giclée prints, and I welcome commissions. See more of my work at www.responsiveart.com

PUBLICATIONS: *American Art Collector, Juried Competition of New Work*, 2007

GUILD SOURCEBOOKS: *Residential Art 6*

C Glass Studio
Public Art, page 243

I specialize in site-specific installations with an emphasis on glass. My public artworks are included in collections around the country and have been featured in several notable publications, including *Public Art Review, Sculpture Magazine, Florida Design*, and S*t. Louis Magazine*. Before turning to art full-time, I enjoyed a career in advertising as an award-wining art director, creating television campaigns for national clients. My experience as a former A.D. brings a distinct graphic sensibility to my work. I find that the skills honed in advertising dovetail perfectly with those needed to successfully execute public art projects: providing creative ideas, presenting ideas to groups, assembling talented fabrication partners, managing the process of turning ideas on paper into award-winning projects, and bringing those projects in on time and on budget.

COLLECTIONS: Whole Foods Corporate Office, 2006, Boca Raton, FL; First Jersey Credit Union, 2005, Wayne, NJ; Grand Center, 2004, St. Louis, MO; Smackover Bank, 2004, El Dorado, AK

EXHIBITIONS: Arts Center, 2008, St. Petersburg, FL; Florida Craftsman, 2008, St. Petersburg, FL; Bullseye Gallery, 2006, Portland OR; Xen Gallery, 2004, St. Louis, MO

Teresa Camozzi
Public Art, pages 244, 245

Inspiration for my work is drawn from a passion for ecological ideals. In collaboration with architects and art and design professionals, I create intimate to monumental-scale commissions for hospitals, hotels, and corporate collections. Working with nature photography, sculptural elements, painting, and chiffon mobiles, I strive to achieve a unique complexity that leaves a lasting impression. My work addresses the fragility of our environment, its beauty, and its desecration. My core belief is that the beauty of nature lifts us toward a higher state of spirituality and consciousness; by basing my art in the mathematics of nature, I seek to achieve a balance of mind and heart. This is termed the "biophilic experience." My objective is to assist viewers in attaining inner equilibrium so that they may make wise choices in their everyday lives and salvage our ecology.

COLLECTIONS: Marriott Moscone, San Francisco; Davis Library, Plano, TX; Mills-Peninsula Health Services, Burlingame, CA; St. Vincent's Hospital, Indianapolis, IN; Metropolitan Club, Chicago, IL; Mayo Clinic, MN, IL, and FL; Four Seasons Hotels; Nemacolin Woodlands Resort, Farmington, PA; Fluor Daniel; Bellagio Hotel, Las Vegas, NV; Kaiser Permanente; Canon Corporation

PUBLICATIONS: *HealthCare Design*, Vol.7, No 3

Carina
Paintings & Prints, page 182

I paint with oils on canvas, using a palette knife to create texture and brushes to add details. My subject is water in its natural settings. The combination of reflection, translucence, and movement offer a sense of momentum and beauty ever changing, often bringing us into a meditative state. As we all are profoundly connected to water, existentially and spiritually, I aspire to capture the liquidity of the subject in its essence.

EXHIBITIONS: ARTERRA Gallery, 2008, Belleview, WA; Truckee River Gallery, 2007-2008, Reno, NV; Sausalito Art Festival, 2007-2008, Sausalito, CA; La Quinta Art Festival, 2006-2008, La Quinta, CA; Scottsdale Art Festival, 2008, Scottsdale, AZ; La Jolla Art Festival, 2008, La Jolla, CA; Palo Alto Art Festival, 2006-2008, Palo Alto, CA

PRICING: Originals from $3,500 to $14,000. Giclée prints from $1,100 to $1,600. Call 775.240.6312 for more information or visit my website, www.carina-art.com.

Donna L. Caron
Sculpture / Representational, page 323

Presently, my work is centered on the human form. From an initial perception of the figure's rudimentary forms, the viewer is drawn into ever-increasing surface detail. This process reveals an interaction between the figure and elements that mirror the natural world. The impressed natural materials, including vegetation and marine specimens, describe a sense of fusion between humankind and nature. The human scale of these sculptures allows the viewer to be drawn into a relationship. Composed of modified concrete, the sculptures are relatively lightweight, with the majority of the weight concentrated in the base. They are constructed as modules that can be disassembled for ease in handling. For more information please visit donnalcaron.com.

EXHIBITIONS: NAWA Gallery, 2008, New York, NY; Ames Museum, 2007, North Easton, MA; Kraft Center, Columbia University, 2007, New York, NY; Berkley Art Center, 2006, Berkley, CA; Center for Maine Contemporary Art, 2005, Rockport, ME

PRICING: Available upon request

Artist Statements

Lee Carver
Fine Art Photography, page 91

I began making multi-image three-dimensional murals in 2000 on commission for a Silicon Valley entrepreneur—*The Golden Gate Bridge & San Francisco* for his lobby. Viewing landscapes in a new way has brought creative insight. It captures the imaginations of youth and adults. My work ranges in size from 24" to works exceeding 6' in length. The style lends itself to even larger works. I work with clients and trade professionals to meet their space requirements. Each work is unique. The images are fine giclées. My work hangs in homes, conference rooms, and the lobby walls of collectors from coast to coast and internationally. I travel extensively to capture compelling scenes to exceed expectations. I was elected to Professional Photographers of America in 1985. I endeavor to bring vision, insight, and technical excellence to all I do.

PRICING: Wholesale prices for my work ranges from $275 to $20,000. See www.leezwebgallery.com.

Brian Chessmar
Sculpture / Non-Representational, page 283

I have always been interested in the physical, spiritual, and emotional balance that is present in life. As an artist I deal with these issues through finely crafted sculptural forms in order to create a dialogue between the work and the viewer. I choose to use bronze, steel, and stainless steel because of their permanence and strength, which allow me to explore and push the physical limits of balance. Although I am interested in dealing with issues such as physical, spiritual, and emotional balance through form, texture, color, and composition, I am equally focused on creating work that is visually pleasing in and of it itself.

COMMISSIONS: Public Art competition award commission, 2009, City of San Luis Obispo, CA; Western Open; Velicity Sports and Entertainment

COLLECTIONS: Ken Chiate; Frank and Parm Williams; Steve O'Grady; Bryan Gianson; Santa Barbara City College

EXHIBITIONS: Atkinson Gallery, Magnificent Mile, 2002, 2001; Chicago Art Institute, 2005; Diana Bottoms Gallery, 2008, 2007

PUBLICATIONS: *Dining and Destinations*, 2007

ClayGal
Murals, Tiles & Wall Reliefs, page 149

It is difficult for an artist to pick out an absolute reason for making his or her art, but one of the most important reasons for me is that I enjoy doing it. Nine years ago while in college, I got hooked on clay; today I cannot imagine doing anything else. With a background in painting, I find my ceramic work consistently manifests itself in hybrid forms, with relationships to both painting and sculpture. I'm committed to quality, integrity of design, consistency, and a sense of professionalism. Color catalog is available upon request.

444

Clowes Sculpture
Atrium Sculpture, pages 65, 74

We design sculpture for healthcare, corporate, hospitality, and academic facilities, as well as private residences. We enjoy excellent relations with architects, designers, and consultants to achieve a balance of art, architecture, and interior design. We are skilled at developing exceptional design, on time and within budget. Our distinct shapes and flowing curves formed in wood, metal, or composite contrast with the color and texture of blown glass, stone, and other materials. A Clowes sculpture will serve as an enduring and welcome ambassador whose gracious gestures invoke the presence of serene seas and soft winds.

COMMISSIONS: Verizon Wireless Arena; St. Vincent's Hospital, IN; L.L. Bean; St. Mary's Hospital; Michigan State University; Memorial Hermann Hospital; Kingsbury Cancer Center; Wells Fargo; St. Vincent's Hospital, AL; The Lodge at Woodloch; American Lawyer Media; White County Medical Center; Phelps Dunbar; Hope Hospice; Pfizer; Royal Caribbean International; Tokyo Hilton Hotel; Indianapolis Museum of Art; Visalia Convention Center; Manchester, NH, District Courthouse; Antioch New England Graduate School

Gesso Cocteau
Sculpture / Representational, pages 324, 325

We create art to remember who we are, to reach back into our primordial genetic thoughts. Art always consists of our memories and usually a prayer to imitate something we remember in nature. There is, as Stanley Romaine Hopper wrote, "a mythological consciousness that inspires us to create." Every human has her own personal intelligence, her own authentic and ancient dream. Dreams and art transform us into our own conversation, our own individual existence. We are freed from stereotypical labels by reclaiming our own mythic function. Art helps us to do just that. I create sculpture for corporate, private, and public collections. My dancing figures have been placed in hospitals, performing art centers, and private and public gardens all over the world. My newest body of work is angels. My angels are messengers for humanity. They symbolize healing and compassion. In this day and age, we can all benefit from strong symbols depicting hope. Among my commissioned works is the tallest standing cast bronze sculpture in America, commissioned by Kemper Freeman Jr. and installed in Bellevue, Washington. Recent projects include: Hard Rock Cafe, Boston, MA; and Eisenhower Hospital, Rancho Mirage, CA

GUILD SOURCEBOOKS: *Architectural & Interior Art 20, 21, 22, 23*

Lester Coloma
Murals, Tiles & Wall Reliefs, page 150

The distinctive art form of mural painting can prominently showcase a client's product, history, or simply serve as a decorative element to enhance a unique space. With over a decade of experience in the production of custom interior murals, distinguished clients include Caesars Windsor, Whole Foods Market, and Paramount Canada's Wonderland. All works are highly detailed and meticulously hand painted. The excellence in craftsmanship of these murals has been utilized in various art projects across North America, ranging from restaurant and hospitality to world-class casinos. Proudly represented by www.chistineprapas.com.

Artist Statements

Brent Cooke
Sculpture / Representational, pages 326, 327, 354

In designing and creating sculptures of birds and marine animals, I try to impart a sense of movement to engage and intrigue. It's important to me that my works tell a story easily envisioned, such as with my birds-of-prey pieces, which leave to each viewer's imagination the outcome of the chase and their own choice of the victor. At the same time, I hope my works are engaging beyond the visual so that viewers want to touch them, thus adding a tactile enjoyment to their art appreciation. My works have been featured at the prestigious Sculpture in the Park show in Loveland, Colorado; Chicago's One of a Kind Show; Jackson Hole's Art Fest; the Tempe Art Festival in Arizona; and, in March 2009, the La Quinta Art Festival in California. Pieces are currently shown at The Peninsula Gallery, Sidney, BC, and at the Webster Gallery, Calgary, AB.

Diana Zoe Coop
Paintings & Prints, page 183

I am an expressionist painter. The sensuous quality of luscious colour ignites my passion for making art. Painting connects me with the land. My inspiration is the real environment; it is intrinsic to my intimate exploration of the Japanese garden, its authentic water features, and the landscape of growth specific to the Pacific Northwest. The essence of my work is a visual dialogue between line, variations in texture, fluid acrylic, and lustres. Applications of my ideas have evolved into novel collaborative and commissioned corporate and residential works in architectural glass, banners, wood, and canvas.

COMMISSIONS: Marine Foods, Den Haag, Holland; City of Vancouver; Steelcase, Vancouver; Hope Breast Cancer Resource Centre, Manitoba; Temple Sholom, Vancouver; The Beaches Synagogue, Toronto; Ocean Fisheries, Vancouver; Weinberg Residence Courtyard, Louis Brier Seniors Home, Vancouver; Positive Women's Network, Vancouver, Yaletown Headquarters, Vancouver

COLLECTIONS: Canada Council Art Bank; University of Manitoba; Mount Allison University, New Brunswick

Randy Cooper
Sculpture / Representational, page 328

I am an internationally recognized sculptor with continuing exhibitions in galleries in France, Canada, Sweden, Mexico, Israel, New Zealand, and major art centers in the U.S., including New York, Sausalito, Santa Fe, New Orleans, Laguna Beach, and Fort Lauderdale. My medium is wire cloth (steel, stainless steel, and bronze). I've created more than 4,000 handmade *Shadow Sculptures©* in the past fifteen years, gracing the homes and offices of many collectors. I'm excited to announce that my son Darin Cooper is collaborating with me! Recently, I've taken the graceful lines of my nudes and created mysteriously sensuous abstracts. I also play, as shown in my brightly colored clown fish (with personalities), sharks (with none), brains for surgeons, feet for podiatrists, a pug for my daughter, and wearable art. I live for challenges and new projects!

COMMISSIONS: Major exhibition for Los Angeles County Museum of Natural History

EXHIBITIONS: Galleria Bella, 2005–2009, New Orleans, LA; Miva Galleri, 2005–2009, Malmo, Sweden; Galleri Scandinavia, 2007, Gotenborg, Sweden; Art Symbol, 2007–2008, Paris, France; Nuances et Lumière, 2006, Lyon, France; Wyland Gallery, 2005–2006, Niagara Falls, Canada

Jesse Corning
Paintings & Prints, page 184

Much I feel about painting is in keeping with the thoughts and theory of American Abstract Expressionism. While my compositions closely relate to an artistic tradition, my media are entirely original. I employ unique media even though they are challenging to work with because they endow my work with presence and an impression of weight. The paintings have the depth of landscape and a monumental quality about them. Describing the world in any literal way would limit the meaning of my painting. Instead I strip away reference, relying on the language of color and form. Only by avoiding representation is it possible to articulate emotional concerns directly. An aesthetic consciousness gained through the process of painting is means to understanding and expressing the human experience. For me, imperfection is at the heart of beauty. It is the something askew that attracts us. I seek to evoke these mysterious and intriguing revelations within the surfaces of my paintings. My artwork investigates both the subjective and universal meanings of the visual elements surrounding us all. The paintings intend to connect each of us with the evocative elements within our lives.

Stephan Cox
Sculpture / Non-Representational, pages 2, 284

My work is an ongoing study of the interplay of form, color, texture, and light, and I love the "frozen moment" I can achieve working with molten glass. I imagine, design, and make my work with the purest intention and a rampant imagination, using the finest materials in the world. I know that all art is rooted somewhere, at least partially, but I try to transcend the previous and make things that are new under the sun. I am interested in designing art for the wall, niches, pedestals, hanging, or freestanding, and I will work with residential, corporate, or public clients within any budget on site-specific glass sculpture.

GUILD SOURCEBOOKS: *Residential Art 1, 5*

DC Art Glass
Wall Art / Glass, page 380

As a warm glass artist, I strive to achieve individual style through personal expression with emphasis on structure and technique. My most recent work, the *Colorbar Murrine* Series, affords me the opportunity to experiment with color and fusing temperatures, and to express a personal style that reflects simplicity with a close attention to detail. I developed my *Colorbar Murrine* series by joining the hot glass techniques perfected in Murano during the late nineteenth century with the kiln-formed, or warm glass, techniques popular today. I transform the art glass into cane, or "Colorbars," based on the overall project design. The cane is eventually cut into many small pieces, called *millefiori* or *murrine*. Each *murrine* is meticulously arranged by hand and then fired together to produce the final piece. The *Colorbar Murrine* series is a sculptural collection that is comprised of table and pedestal pieces, as well as wall panels and sconce lighting. Each wall panel is unique; some include up to nineteen color selections, 3,000 individual handmade *murrine*, and more than 425 *murrine* designs.

AWARDS: Best in Fused Glass, 2006, NICHE Award; Best in Show, 2005, Creative Craft Council

PUBLICATIONS: *500 Glass Objects, A Celebration of Functional and Sculptural Glass*, 2006

Artist Statements

David J. Lunin Furniture Maker
Furniture & Floor Coverings, page 98

I work in a small studio creating original, one-of-a-kind pieces of furniture in wood. My background in eighteenth-century American antiques has deeply influenced my work. When I first opened my shop, I made very strict reproductions of important antiques. More recently, I desired to make my own mark in the world of furniture design. I begin with traditional designs and give them a contemporary twist. What has never changed is the level of craftsmanship that was employed by colonial craftsmen. Hand-cut dovetails, as well as mortise-and-tenon joints, are used throughout. I also prefer the use of traditional finishing material, such as shellac and varnish.

GUILD SOURCEBOOKS: *Residential Art 6*

David M Bowman Studio
Wall Art / Metal, page 391

Work at our studio is a father-and-son collaboration. The two of us design and build patinaed brass table accessories, tables, and abstract sculptural compositions for the wall. Our wall pieces appear massive, but are actually quite light and can be hung on any wall. The patinaed surfaces are durable and weather well outdoors. Every wall piece is individually designed and will not be repeated. We have made wall pieces on all scales, for intimate corners and three-story atrium walls, and we enjoy each new project for its design possibilities and challenges. Please visit our website, www.davidmbowman.com, to learn more about the range of our work, to see all of our wallpieces (both sold and available), or to take the next steps in commissioning a piece for your space.

PUBLICATIONS: *The Artful Home,* 2007

GUILD SOURCEBOOKS: *Designer's 8, 11, 13; Architectural & Interior Art 19; Residential Art 5*

David Wilson Design
Architectural Glass, page 44

Known for my successful collaborations with architects on large-scale works for both public and private buildings, I pursue the goal of designing glass that adds to and enriches architecture. By emphasizing the importance of visual harmony in the built environment, I create designs that are the result of reducing forms to their simplest solution. My design process firmly relies on clear and thoughtful communication with both the architect and those who will use the building. This reciprocal exchange is a delicate balance that requires mutual respect for the integrity of all involved.

COMMISSIONS: St. Isaac Jogues Catholic Church, 2008, Hinsdale, IL; St. Mary's Catholic Church, 2008, Richmond, VA; Greystone Park Psychiatric Hospital, 2007, Morris Plains, NJ; St. Theresa Catholic Church, 2007, Tuckerton, NJ; College of Education Building, Rowan University, 2005, Glassboro, NJ

AWARDS: AIA Connecticut Design Awards Program, 2006; Merit Award, Decorative Glass, Stamford Courthouse, CT

GUILD SOURCE BOOKS: *The Guild 1, 2, 3, 4, 5; Architect's 6, 7, 8, 9, 11, 13, 14, 15; Architectural & Interior 16, 17, 18, 19, 20, 22*

446

Barbara De Pirro
Paintings & Prints, page 185

Within the calm serene layers of my work lies a deeply emotional and nurturing whisper of my perceptions. I find a complexity of imagery in the simple echoes of our world. Colors, textures, and patterns flow through the stream of my imagination, creating my own soft and gentle language. Acrylic is my predominant medium; it allows me to create depth and texture within the many transparent layers. Painting and printing my own papers, I embed them onto a textural plane, building up clear layers, then developing imagery and pattern within the structure. Looking into my paintings is very much like peering into a pool of water.

Timothy R. Decker
Wall Art / Metal, page 402

RT Designs hand forms 22-gauge steel hardware cloth into original creations. With an electrical and technical background, I have transformed the medium of my work into an obsession and explosion of Renaissance art using modern materials. Many colors are available for powder coating. I have also refined my technique to create portraits using wire and other metals.

COLLECTIONS: Private collection, Scottsdale, AZ; private collection, Niles, IL

EXHIBITIONS: Art One Gallery, 1995, Scottsdale, AZ; *One of a Kind Show,* 2006, Chicago, IL; *Gold Coast Show,* 2005, Chicago, IL; *Thunderbird Artists Scottsdale Fine Art and Chocolate Festival,* 2002, AZ; *Thunderbird Artists Scottsdale Celebration of Fine Art,* 1997, AZ; *Thunderbird Artists Fountain Hills Fine Art and Wine Affaire,* 1996, AZ

Dickinson Designs
Lighting, pages 117, 119

Simple and bold is what I strive for in my work. The potential that comes from combining porcelain and wood is exciting. The challenge of taking a single simple shape and creating a range of distinctly different yet familial work from it is fun. The journey began with lamps and now expands to tables. All are classically contemporary in look and feel. For the lamps there are custom-made shades and sometimes matching finials to complete the sentence. Tables are topped with rich, simple clear glass. The opportunity to custom design your table is a given; the fundamental building block is a 5" pyramid of porcelain that can be glazed and fired in oxidation, reduction, or soda atmospheres. The possibilities are nearly endless. Additional information can be found at www.dickinson-designs.com.

Artist Statements

Dolan Geiman Inc.
Wall Art / Mixed & Other Media, pages 405, 415

With a style blending rural iconography and contemporary techniques, I produce mixed-media works using acrylic, silkscreen, found objects, and recycled materials. Works range from intimate collages under glass to large-scale works on wood and, together, reflect a body of work and general business mission focused on sustainability. My most popular collection, archival reproductions on wood called *Box Prints,* offer an affordable and ready-to-hang alternative to traditional paper and canvas prints. Custom *Box Print* editions are available for hotel guestrooms, sustainable and LEED-certified projects, and real estate developers. For more information and to request a proposal, visit dolangeiman.com.

COMMISSIONS: Hyatt Regency, 2008-2010, Jersey City, NJ; Elway's, 2007, Denver, CO; Marina Grand Resort, 2006, New Buffalo, MI, Rockit Bar & Grill, 2004, Chicago, IL

PRICING: Competitive trade and volume discounts available. Complete the online application at dolangeiman.com for access to trade pricing and other resource pages. Trade brochures available.

Patricia Dreher
Funiture & Floor Coverings, page 99

After obtaining my M.A. in classical painting and art history, I worked with textile design in Sweden as a Fulbright fellow and in England as an artist in residence. The floorcloth—a canvas painting made for the floor—embodies my love of combining the beautiful with the functional. My favorite challenge is to collaborate with a client, designer, or architect to create an installation that resonates with the larger concept for the space. My designs can harmonize or they can dominate, as the client chooses. My repertoire is broad and diverse, from classical antiquity, Asian themes, and ethnic designs, to modern abstracts and geometrics. I make wall-to-wall installations and rug-format pieces of any size or shape, using the very best materials. Floors I made twenty years ago retain their color clarity and remain fresh and beautiful. I sign all my pieces.

GUILD SOURCEBOOKS: *Residential Art 4, 5, 6*

Domsky Glass
Wall Art / Glass, page 381

Working in the mediums of hot glass, fused glass, and metal, we hold over thirty years experience as professional artists. Our artistic focus is in creating large-scale glass panels, sculptures, and chandeliers for architectural and residential installation. Every commission custom created to the unique needs of the client and their environment. We encourage you to visit our website or our 5,000 square-foot studio located in Las Vegas, NV, to witness the range and quality of our work. We welcome architects and designers to collaborate in creating site-specific, residential, and commercial commissions.

COMMISSIONS: Manhattan West Project, 2009 installation; McCarran International Airport, 2011 installation; International: Sweden, India, Australia, New Zealand, Germany, Mexico, and South Africa; Nike; Mandalay Bay Hotel; Wynn Hotel; Cirque Du Soleil; Bellagio Hotel; City of Hope Hospital; Charlie Palmer Restaurants; Shark Reef; Luxor Hotel; Monte Carlo Hotel; Storm Theater; Neiman Marcus

EXHIBITIONS: Cirque Du Soleil; Guggenheim Young Collectors; Wynn Hotel; Palos Verdes Art Center, CA; *Circle of Life,* Kansas City, MO

PRICING: All budgets considered

GUILD SOURCEBOOKS: *Architectural & Interior Art 22, 23; Residential Art 6*

Philip S. Drill
Sculpture / Non-Representational, page 311

I am intrigued by natural forms. My sculpture combines structural integrity with the sensual curvilinear grace of found natural objects, such as leaves, shells, or bone fragments. A walk in the woods, a stroll on the beach or a city street, and even the remains of a meal have served as catalysts for my designs. An engineer by training, I began my career as an artist working with welded metal. My interest in organic form led me to explore the expressive possibilities of plastic media such as clay, wax, or plaster, then casting each sculpture in bronze, acrylic, or stainless steel. My work has been exhibited in juried exhibitions, one-man shows, art festivals, museums, and universities. To view more of my sculpture, please visit my website at www.psdrill.com. I welcome the opportunity to discuss commissions.

Sally Dougan
Fine Art Photography, pages 78, 79

I am fascinated by the beauty and subtle qualities of nature's simple treasures —flowers, wildflowers, leaves, grasses, seeds, weeds, vegetables, and fruits—and feel that their unique characteristics are shown more richly through my process of direct live scanning than via traditional photography. My compositions highlight the intricate details of color, shape, texture, and habit of petals, leaves, veins, stems, etc., and bring out what I see as the essence of the subject's true character and "spirit." I offer giclée prints, available in a variety of sizes to suit the installation setting. The consistency of the black background treatment allows the prints to work well together in groups or series as well as individually. White mattes and black frames help the images "pop."

COLLECTIONS: Private collections in the U.S. and U.K.

EXHIBITIONS: Salmagundi Club, 2007, 2006, 2005, NYC; Ansonia Windows Show, 2007, NYC; Lamington Art Show, 2008, 2007, 2006, 2005, NJ; Somerset Art Association, 2008, 2007, NJ; Tinicum Arts Festival, 2007, 2006, Bucks County, PA; TTN Creativity Showcase, 2008, NYC

Eccentric Luxuries
Lighting, page 120

Our mission is to combine innovative lighting with art and woodworking. Handmade paper, combined with organic material, is used to create light boxes, tabletops, bartops, and room dividers. Transforming space with elegance and a sustainable twist is our forté; capturing and preserving nature's unique beauty is our vision and continusous inspiration. Other areas of specialty include hand-painted silk bedding, upholstery, custom furniture, and silk and paper wall hangings. Handmade paper paintings can be made up to twenty feet and make an amazing impact in any space. This environmentally friendly art form is tactile and uses texture and layering to create interest that is not easily achieved in other art forms. Whatever your project or vision may be, we have a variety of work to suit all tastes and styles. Please check our website periodically for updates: www. eccentricluxuries.com.

447

Artist Statements

Joline El-Hai
Architectural Glass, page 45

I fill my glass panels with a sense of movement, rich coloring, and bold, detailed imagery of a narrative quality. The drama of the natural world often informs my designs. My reductive glass painting technique gives depth and mystery with a graininess reminiscent of mezzotints and old photographs. I incorporate glass fusing for complexity of color and texture. In addition to naturally lit stained glass windows and door lights, my work has also been electrically illuminated when set into wooden frameworks. These "light boxes" have ranged from large murals set into walls to small, intimate glowing sculpture for the table or shelf. I began creating leaded glass panels in 1975. Over the years I have expanded the scope of my work to include glass jewelry, fused glass wall sculpture, giclée prints of pastel drawings, and a nationally known and popular production line of decorative lights for the home.

GUILD SOURCEBOOKS: *Architectural & Interior Art 22; Residential Art 6*

Elizabeth Embler
Paintings & Prints, pages 23, 234

My paintings are a rich mix of realism and abstraction. I am drawn to both the detailed and formal nature of realist painting and the loose, physical, and intuitive feel of abstract expressionism. My work combines both styles. The primary medium is oil, into which I incorporate monoprints, photography, copper, paper, and other media in a brisk, layered, and painterly way. They bring a sense of serenity and calm to an increasingly chaotic and challenging world. Many of my pieces are diptychs and triptychs. The canvas is usually gallery wrapped and unframed, and ranges in size from 4" to 6' and larger. Prices range from $100 to $10,000. For more information visit my website at www.elizabethembler.com.

Barry Entner
Sculpture / Non-Representational, page 285

My sculptural glass represents an idealized continuum of otherworldly botanical and sentient life. I devise unique processes to attain this concept. The techniques employed range from hand and steam blowing to poured casting. The resulting work is alternately sleek, saturated with color, or roughly textured with characteristics of primitive forms. Exhibitions include the International Exhibition of Glass Kanazawa and the International Exposition of Sculptural Objects and Functional Art. Commissions include the Hale Koa Hotel, Honolulu, HI, and the Langham Place Hotel, Hong Kong.

GUILD SOURCEBOOKS: *Residential Art 4,5*

Renate Burgyan Fackler
Sculpture / Representational, page 329

Whether through my figurative or abstract sculptures, I invite you to experience an emotionally intimate expression of life. As owner of Chrysalis Sculpture Studio, LLC, I am located in Hebron, Ohio. Although a graduate of The Ohio State University School of Journalism, I have found communicating through sculpture supercedes the written word. In addition to over twenty years of experience in all phases of the lost wax bronze casting process, I have studied at The Columbus College of Art and Design, Johnson's Atelier, Columbia University, and with patina expert Ron Young of Sculpt Nouvea.

COLLECTIONS: The Ohio State University; The Herb Society of America; Charity Newsies; Wendy's International; The Museum of Women in the Arts, Washington, DC; The White House

PUBLICATIONS: *The Well-Designed Mixed Garden; Midwest Living* magazine, June 2001

Liz Alpert Fay
Wall Art / Fiber, page 363

I gather colors from all around me: the brilliance of the zinnias in my garden, the unexpected splash of orange in the woods, the clear blue of the sky on an autumn day: I carry these images with me as I approach the dye pot. Here, I hand dye new and recycled fabrics, striving for a feeling of spontaneity. By working in an improvisational style, I combine many traditional textile techniques in new ways to create a lively and contemporary feel. While some of my pieces are purely explorations of color, others tell stories and comment on issues of importance. I have worked extensively with individual collectors and enjoy the collaborative process.

COMMISSIONS: Numerous private commissions in the U.S., Canada, and New Zealand

COLLECTIONS: Museum of Arts and Design, New York, NY; Fairfield Processing Corporation, Danbury, CT; Dietche and Field Advisers, New York, NY; The White House, Washington, DC

GUILD SOURCEBOOK: *Architectural & Interior Art 23*

Constantine Fedorets
Furniture & Floor Coverings, page 100

I completed my classical art education in the Ukraine. For ten years I focused my work on painting in different media. Having always admired fine furniture makers and their art, I was inspired to study and build furniture. In my work I reflect classical styles and movements in a modern interpretation. When working with special commissions, I collaborate closely with the client in order to bring their vision and ideas to life. My work can be viewed on my website at www.constantinesinteriors.com. It is also shown at the annual Providence Fine Furnishings show in Rhode Island.

GUILD SOURCEBOOKS: *Residential Art 4, 5, 6*

448

Artist Statements

Lori Feldpausch
Paintings & Prints, page 186

The beauty of nature inspires me daily. I am a plein air painter because I love to capture the natural scenes that nature itself paints with colors and light. The effect of light reflecting on water just amazes me. I capture that nuance, that essence of a moment in time. In nature when I really see my surroundings, the contrast, hues, and values come together like a poem. I paint that feeling of being in nature, and often I make a larger painting of that study in my studio. Hospitals, businesses, non-profits, and private homes have collected my paintings. Several Michigan galleries and my web site represent my work. I have studied under many of the contemporary masters of today. My experience also includes commercial mural work for hotels, businesses, and residences. I now enjoy painting and creating my own body of work for sale.

Fanne Fernow
Wall Art / Mixed & Other Media, pages 26, 27, 431

I am a theologian, lover of media, and seeker of justice. I live near the Pacific Ocean and the redwood forest. I love Buddhism, but I am not a Buddhist. This is all very important to me. If I had more patience, I would be a quilt maker. I love the way fabrics work together, and the way quilting stitches enhance the top and bottom designs of a quilt. I use many of the qualities of quilts—grids, repetition, simplicity. I began to use encaustic paints in 2007. As I entered the work, I realized that making wax art requires more patience than making quilts. I see quilting in the dots—mantras repeating songs or prayers of dots, circles—paper fused to wax with hot tools. I work intuitively, one step leading to the next. My process is not exact, so I must risk and trust.

Lindsay Feuer
Sculpture / Representational, page 330

Suspended in the realm between fantasy and reality, my sculptures explore the organic processes of growth, replication, and locomotion. Deliberately ambiguous combinations of biological imagery reflect the perfect integration of form and function found in the natural world. Through an intuitive process, I allow these elements to respond to one another, creating "hybrid" forms with movement and fluidity. Porcelain is an ideal medium for my work because its white luminescence showcases rich surfaces and curvilinear components. The strength and responsiveness of this clay also enable me to achieve whimsical and delicate sculptural elements. Hidden building techniques allow my sculptures to exist in a space of seamless illusion where they appear "born" rather than "made." Inspired by the mysteries of nature, these pieces deliver an animated and fantastical view of our biological surroundings. I invite my audience to draw upon their experience and imagination, and to discover a unique reality for each piece.

GUILD SOURCEBOOKS: *Residential Art 6*

449

Bonnie Fitzgerald
Mosaics, pages 129, 131

Mosaics are a perfect architectural enhancement. Infused with texture and color, my mosaics complement the environments in which they reside with a lovely blend of classic and contemporary design. Honoring the craftsmanship and tradition of classical mosaics, I use high-quality glass, including Italian and Mexican Smalti, vitreous tiles, stained glass, and in many instances blending these materials together in my design palette. My creations are one of a kind and whenever possible show a lightheartedness and sense of humor. Working under my studio name Maverick Mosaics, my artwork ranges in size from small decorative appointments to large exterior and interior architectural installations. My works have been featured on HGTV, and in *Southern Lady* and *Elan* magazines. Many reside in private collections. Large-scale architectural commissions include Whole Foods Market, Inc. (2007 and 2008) and Rockville Town Square (2007), Rockville, MD, and Hunters Woods Elementary School, Reston, VA (2009). I currently serve as Executive Committee member and President-elect for the Society of American Mosaic Artists.

GUILD SOURCEBOOKS: *Residential Art 6*

Ann Fleming
Sculpture / Representational, page 353

My work tells stories. Many of these stories are symbolic of the needs and desires, hopes and experiences that we all share. Some are stories alive in the mythology of different cultures or talk of the belief in something greater than ourselves. They are the universal stories that connect us to each other and to what it means to experience life. When I began to sculpt, I thought I had left my years as a production potter behind. I now can see that my work speaks of those years. The smoothness and subtlety of form reflects the potter's eye for the minute changes that occur with the repetition in the making of a mug or a bowl. The hand-building technique of coiling used in creating the original pieces reflects back to early cultures and creates figures that are full and grounded. I had my first pieces cast in bronze in 2005 and now have pieces in private collections across the United States and in Europe. My body of work currently includes twenty-four sculptures in the round and four bas-relief pieces that can be either freestanding or grouped for wall mounting. Each piece lends itself to monumental scale.

Marilyn Forth
Wall Art / Fiber, pages 364, 365

The art I present to the world is large and unique. The painted dyes are modulated and layered. You can actually see the layers in some instances. White lines are a very important part of my work. Many of my pieces are based on natural forms taking on a human context. The pieces entitled *Singing Flowers* and *Wild Flower Waltz* are examples. My prices range from $950 to $4,500, depending on size and complexity. Photos of completed commissions are sent to the client for final approval. I have exhibited in many national shows and created art for corporate and residential clients. I have also taught fiber art classes at Syracuse University. My pieces are light resistant and guaranteed.

GUILD SOURCEBOOKS: *Architect's 6; Designer's 6, 7, 8, 10, 11, 12, 13, 14; Architectural & Interior Art 16, 20; Residential Art 2, 5, 6*

Artist Statements

Ronald R. Franklin
Objects, page 167

A pot reflects the actions that create it. The effect of two types of reduction, kiln atmosphere and post firing, are essentially evident. Red/bronze glaze responds beautifully to kiln reduction. Its bright reds and greens reflect circulation. Patina and matte-type glazes produce wonderful flashing effects by post firing. Copper, a key ingredient to both of these glazes, becomes mystical under such conditions. The touch of fire, temperature, atmosphere, and circulation, are all beautifully recorded by copper's keen responsiveness. Through precise craftsmanship and the probity of the fire, the mystery of smoke, flash, and crackle communicate a beauty beyond the elements of a simple pot. My work has been shown in numerous galleries and museums. Exhibitions include the First World Ceramic Biennale 2001 International Competition, Ichon, South Korea, and the Cheongju International Craft Competition, both 2001 and 2003, in Cheongju, South Korea. I am honored to be in the permanent collection of the World Ceramic Center in Ichon, South Korea.

GUILD SOURCEBOOKS: *Residential Art 6*

Franz Mayer of Munich, Inc.
Architectural Glass, pages 46, 47

From our very beginning in 1847, it has been Franz Mayer of Munich's goal to continuously develop new artistic and architectural expressions. The studio (now owned and operated by the fourth and fifth generations) and its self-conception of quality and workmanship, combined with the ability to explore and improve, has made us one of the leading international studios for stained glass, architectural glass, and mosaic. Craftsmanship of highest skill and vision, together with the finest-quality material, create a product that guarantees the best artistic solution for the various clientele: artists, architects, designers, and the private art connoisseur.

Douglas Olmsted Freeman
Public Art, pages 239, 246, 247

Based in Minneapolis, I create sculpture and design spaces that invite visitors to participate, play, and imagine. My work focuses on commissioned public art—particularly places for people, such as fountains, memorials, plazas, and parks. Trained as a figurative sculptor with additional study in landscape architecture, I often collaborate with landscape architects and other design professionals. I have worked with clients in this country and Japan to create public art that has become a lasting part of their communities.

Cheri Freund
Paintings & Prints, page 187

I think of my work as a unique communication between the art and the individual viewer. I create with a surrealistic and ethereal flair, intending to invoke inner feelings and emotions. Visible within my abstract work is a hint of realism, which provides the viewing audience with multiple interpretations. My inspiration comes from color, everyday objects, and most importantly, music. I approach each image as a challenge and strive to create something completely different from the previous image. Creating within the digital realm (with occasional blending of traditional art) takes my work in unexpected directions, allowing for unlimited possibilities. As any artist will tell you, it is a "knowing" when the image is complete. As a diversified artist, I am able create in a multitude of directions. My work has been commissioned by the publishing, software, and music industries. I was an exhibitor in the New York "Prevailing Human Spirit – 911 Tribute" hosted by the Society of Illustrators, and have been featured in: *PEI* (Photo Electronic Imaging magazine) and the 2009 edition of *The Big Black Book of Contemporary Illustration* (Anova Publishing – UK). Additionally, my giclée prints have been shown internationally. To view additional samples of my work, please go to: http://www.pixel-artist.com.

GUILD SOURCEBOOKS: *Residential Art 6*

Fusio Studio Inc.
Architectural Glass, page 48

As an artist and an architect, I find inspiration in both the human-made environment and in the vast landscape of the American west where I live. I am fascinated by the paradigm of the constructed and the natural. It is critical to my existence to make things with my hands, using real materials. Fusio Studio glass work includes architectural installations and design elements such as lighting, tiles, and windows; freestanding and wall hung panels; and functional objects.

COMMISSIONS: Memorial Sculpture, St. John's Mercy Medical Center, 2009, St. Louis, MO; Wall Panels, Hyatt Regency Chesapeake Bay, 2009, Cambridge, MD; Wall Panels, Northwestern Mutual Life, 2008, Franklin, WI; The Children's Hospital Chapel, 2007, Aurora, CO; Bozeman Public Library, 2007, Bozeman, MT

EXHIBITIONS: *Narrative: 2008 Glass Invitational*, Curator and Exhibitor, TurmanLarison Contemporary, Helena, MT; *SOFA Chicago*, 2007; *Strata*, 2006, Solo Exhibition, Bullseye Gallery, Portland, OR

AWARDS: Best Artist, Accents, Western Design Conference Exhibition, 2008; Selected for the Corning Museum of Glass's *New Glass Review 27*, 2006; American Craft Council Award of Achievement, 2003

Deborah Garber
Paintings & Prints, page 188

My work reflects a long-standing interest in landscape and how it is affected by light, weather conditions, and the influence of humans. Some images hint at the human role by depicting houses, roads, and cultivated fields. Others reveal a fascination with cloud formations or atmospheric effects. In all of them, landscape is the vehicle for the expressive use of color. My works are created in pastel or oil and employ numerous layers of rich, saturated color and simplified form. My goal is to create something of beauty, harmony and mystery that is direct and accessible, and that speaks to the viewer without verbal explanation.

COLLECTIONS: AT&T, Chicago, IL; HBO Corporation, New York, NY; Citigroup, Chicago, IL; IBM, San Francisco, CA; Korbel Winery, Guerneville, CA; Kaiser Permanente, San Francisco, CA; Marriott Corporation, Boston, MA; Prudential Life Insurance Co., New York, NY; Quaker Oat Co., Chicago, IL; 3M Corporation, Minneapolis, MN; U.S. Dept. of State, Washington, D.C.

EXHIBITIONS: *Small Works*, 2008, Arts Council of Sonoma County, Santa Rosa, CA; Marin Art Festival, 2008, San Rafael, CA; *Landscapes—Real and Imagined*, 2005, The Living Gallery, Ashland, OR

PRICING: Prices range from $250–$4,000 for prints, pastels, and oils

Artist Statements

Gasch Design
Mosaics, page 132

My name is Michael Gasch. I create a contemporary style of mosaic art using a variety of techniques and materials to accommodate many different projects and locations. This particular project is created with stones collected by the client from around the world. In the form of abstract waterfalls, these stones were meticulously placed with copper as a reminder of foreign travels and past adventures. As always, this work has an overall balance and beholds significant meaning for the client. Both smaller commissions such as this and large-scale commercial projects are welcome at Gasch Design. These commissions are designed to enhance the existing architectural concepts and functionality while also creating a meaningful and artistic viewpoint. Please feel free to take a look at my website, www.gaschdesign.com, to find out more about Gasch Design.

Josephine A. Geiger
Architectural Glass, page 49

Imagine a landscape: a forest of brilliant fall colors, a mountain stream surrounded by towering pines, a quaking stand of aspen, or a waterfall frozen in time. Now imagine these shades of nature recreated in glass, dancing with color and assembled as if seen through a fractured lens. My leaded glass panels create an abstract collage, which at first glance appears as a myriad palette of colors and elusive forms, but upon closer examination is revealed as a landscape. My artwork is inspired by a love of architecture, Frank Lloyd Wright's Prairie style, the Arts and Crafts movement, the Impressionists, and even crazy quilts—a mix of tradition and history. Continually challenging myself to push the envelope of design, I incorporate unusual materials such as copper mesh or unique glass, and frequently mix techniques to add depth and texture. Structure, design, and exceptional craftsmanship are hallmarks of my work.

Suzan Germond
Murals, Tiles & Wall Reliefs, page 133

My mosaics are colorful and whimsical. I purposefully use a variety of materials including glass, tile, ceramic, jewels, collage, and found objects to create a rich contrast of texture and an element of the unexpected. I enjoy participating in juried fine art festivals to see the public reaction and explain my process of layering and transforming bits and pieces into a mosaic whole. When I'm not at an art show, I run a full-service commercial mosaic studio with classes, commissions, and gallery. My work includes decorative wall pieces, mosaic furniture, garden sculpture, and residential and commercial installations. Please visit my website, www.majormosaics.com, to view the variety and workmanship of my mosaics. I am a member of the Society of American Mosaic Artists. I have been filmed for HGTV and my work is published in *Creative Garden* (2003) and *500 Chairs* (2008). I recently wrote my own book, *Found Art Mosaics*, Sterling Publishers, 2007. I am represented at the gallery Artisans at Rocky Hill in Fredericksburg, Texas. My pieces are in numerous private collections and displayed in public art venues in Austin, Texas.

Shohini Ghosh
Sculpture / Representational
Wall Art / Metal, pages 353, 403

My name is Shohini Ghosh. I was born in New Delhi, India, in 1970, before moving to Colorado in 1998. I am one of the few women sculptors of Indian origin living and creating in the United States. I began my career as a lecturer in metallurgy and the history of art at Sir J.J. School of Art, University of Mumbai, India, and this eventually evolved into a career as a professional sculptor. Bronze is my metal of choice. My style evolved from the combination of a naturalistic style to a more structured impressionist style called Synthetism. My murals are unusual as I use copper patina as paint to color the surface of the metal. I paint cityscapes on copper. I have observed that the vibrancy of the city sets the basic character and the identity of a people. I chose copper sheet as my canvas as it is a pure metal and has a live surface, reacting with the atmosphere, like most cities..

Glassic Art
Architectural Glass, pages 50, 51

True connoisseurs, collectors, curators, and discriminating buyers appreciate the outstanding quality of Glassic Art's creations—unique glass products developed from twenty-five years of experience. Our studio offers completion within deadlines, service beyond compare, and one-of-a-kind pieces that have been receiving rave reviews from investors and viewers for years. The "glassic art" created at the studio is a multidimensional medium made by sandblasting, painting, welding, fusion, kiln-formed glass, metal, and bonding techniques. From fine art to functional, our pieces are used for murals, bars and countertops, staircases, waterfalls, room dividers, entries, and free-form sculptures.

COMMISSIONS: Golden Door Spa, Puerto Rico; Red Rock Station/Casino, Las Vegas, NV; Golden Moon Casino, Meridian, MS; MGM High Limit Gaming, Las Vegas, NV; Bellagio Casino Resort, Las Vegas, NV

AWARDS: First Place Glass Artist, 2005, Artv Awards; Gold, First Place Countertops, Designer's Home Excellence Awards

GUILD SOURCEBOOKS: *Architect's 12, 14, 15; Architectural & Interior Art: 16, 18, 20, 22, 23; Residential Art 2, 5*

Glassics
Objects, page 168

Using glass as a means of artistic expression is a practice as old as measured time, and I feel privileged that it is my life's work to continue this ancient tradition. The artworks created in my studio are simply the latest effort, brought forth from a lifetime fascination with form, color, and texture. I am currently exploring various multimedia collaborations. Assisted by my talented husband, I have been able to open up many exciting new avenues of expression and creativity. My award-winning work can be seen at several shows across the western United States. This year also marks my twenty-fourth anniversary as an exhibitor at the renowned Festival of Arts in Laguna Beach, California.

GUILD SOURCEBOOKS: *Residential Art 4, 5, 6*

Artist Statements

Goldstein Kapellas Studio
Atrium Sculpture, pages 66, 67

We have collaborated with architects and designers for over twenty years on public, private and corporate commissions of all sizes. Our site-specific sculptures and mobiles are lightweight, durable, and reflective. The kinetic pieces move gracefully and require minimal air currents to set them in motion.

COMMISSIONS: Ritz Carlton Hotels, Shenzhen, China; Banner Hospital, Glendale, AZ; Memorial Hospital, Modesto, CA; Sallie Mae Corporation, Reston, VA; California Department of Health Services, Richmond, VA; AstraZeneca, Wilmington, DE; BART, Colma, CA.

COLLECTIONS: Fine Arts Museums of San Francisco; Art Institute of Chicago; Brooklyn Museum; Museum of Contemporary Religious Art, St. Louis.

EXHIBITIONS: Durban Art Gallery, South Africa, 2009; Fowler Museum of Art, UCLA, 2008; Durka Chang Gallery, 2002; Brauer Museum of Art, Valparaiso, IN, 2000.

GUILD SOURCEBOOKS: *Architect's 7, 8, 10, 11, 12, 13; Architectural & Interior Art 17, 19, 20, 21, 22, 23*

PUBLICATIONS: *Beyond Belief: Modern Art and the Religious Imagination*, 1998; *Reliquaries*, 1994

Gordon Auchincloss Designs, LLC
Atrium Sculpture, page 68

Finding balance in the mobiles I create is an energizing and challenging venture. Creating a sculpture, piece by piece, and watching it become alive, I find joyfully fulfilling. I am driven further by introducing custom sculptures into specific architectural settings, and forming relationships with those spaces and the people using them. Materials chosen for projects are dependent on the sites, my clients' requests, and what I am excited to work with at any given time. The dynamics of the setting are paramount. Colors, shapes, and textures are all taken into account, as well as lighting, airflow, and structural engineering. Communicating clearly is an important aspect of completing the work in a streamlined fashion and an integral part of the total project. My goal, and that of my clients, is to enhance a location and generate a creative, intriguing, and thoughtful stimulus for those who inhabit the space or for those who just happen through it.

Nancy Gong
Architectural Glass, page 52

The energy and spirit of living things have always intrigued me. It continues to be at the very core of my art. I constantly strive to capture the grace, movement, and dimension of life in a simple, yet powerful style. Facets of nature by way of lyrical abstractions are the soul of my art. With a rich personal style and an impressive command of my medium, I create sensitive, responsive, and enduring glass designs with quality craftsmanship for architectural installations and art collections.

COMMISSIONS: ArtWalk Artistic Bus Shelter Competition, Rochester; Port of Rochester; Lidestri Foods Inc.; State of Vermont Sharon Vietnam Honorial; American Institute of Architects; Constellation Brands Inc.; Cornell University; Corning Tropel Corp.; Garcia's Restaurant SPI; Genencor Intl.; Highland Hospital; Lifetime Care; Oakhill Country Club; Paetec; Paychex; Rochester General Hospital; NTID, Rochester Institute of Technology; Rochester Philharmonic Orchestra; Strong Memorial Hospital; University of Rochester; Virgin Atlantic; Virgin Vacation U.S.; Duke University's Fuqua School of Business, NC; Other commissions and private residences in IL, NC, NJ, NY, SC, TX, VT, and Austria

EXHIBITIONS: *SOFA Chicago* 2004, *Crafts National 38/27, ArtForm International* 2003

Carol Green
Objects, page 169

Like you, my heart catches in my throat when I encounter scenes of great natural beauty. It's a feeling that we've shared with our ancestors throughout the world and over the millennia. Artists have always created objects for utility, pleasure, and symbolic meaning. My goal is to combine the beauty of the natural world with objects that serve. The *Gourd Vessel* series is wheel thrown using mica-impregnated earthenware and is raku fired. The lids are copper and cast bronze and finished with a hot patina. The *Candle Branch* series is cast bronze and finished with a hot patina. Commissions include The Palace Hotel, Beijing, China; Allegany Power, Hagertown, PA; and Kaiser Permanente, Cleveland, OH. You can see more of my work at www.carolgreen.com.

Lynn Goodpasture
Architectural Glass, page 53

Solar Illumination I: Evolution of Language, Pearl Avenue Library, San Jose, CA, is the first permanent public art in the United States to combine building-integrated photovoltaics with architectural art glass. This innovative installation demonstrates the practical application of renewable forms of energy. One hundred forty-four PV (solar) cells, embedded in art glass windows located in the children's section, generate electricity that illuminates the art glass lamp suspended at the library's entrance. The windows' imagery explores the evolution of ancient alphabets from languages that are predominant in the library's collection: Latin, Russian, Vietnamese, and numerous Indian languages. The lamp is illuminated with color-changing LEDs, custom programmed to move subtly through the color spectrum every thirty minutes, giving a time-keeping aspect to the lamp, and visually manifesting the solar energy. "We are all one" is engraved in cuneiform on the lamp. I create site-specific work in glass and mosaic for public and private clients.

GUILD SOURCEBOOKS: *Architectural & Interior Art 17, 18, 20*

Katherine Greene
Paintings & Prints, page 189

Painting is all about trusting the process and my intuition, while being open to the unpredictable. Each painting begins with layers of texture that serve as the ground to which I respond. Colors are layered with repeated building up and rubbing off. Where they overlap, a new color is created and often shifts the direction of the painting. I embrace these surprises, which lead me down a challenging new path. Investigating the layers of my painting serves as a metaphor for exploring an energy or spirit beyond the physical world. Shapes are imbued with meaning. As a universal symbol, the circle represents nature's cycles, no beginning/no end, unity, the limitless, and the boundless. The square symbolizes perfect balance, stability, the four seasons, the four directions, the four noble truths, and point to universal truths passed down through the ages.

452

Artist Statements

Carol Griffin
Paintings & Prints, page 191

I delight in exploring color. For my *Series* paintings, I use a limited palette and one design, and let the improvisation on the theme of that palette take its own course. *Series 6* is actually a series of six paintings—two of which are shown on my page—using the same color palette for each painting. The palette for a painting is often based upon the colors that occur in natural stone. I find that nature, and particularly stone, provides a superb source of inspiration for my work. My palettes are inspired by imposing mountains, the colors of a flower, or dramatic sunsets. I often choose colors that evoke memories of a special place visited, as a way to remember the experience. My paintings are well suited to residential and corporate settings, as well as textile designs. My work has been exhibited in New York City and East Hampton, New York. Commissions are welcomed. To view my website, please visit http://web.mac.com/cgriffin6.

GUILD SOURCEBOOKS: *Residential Art 6*.

Christopher Gryder
Murals, Tiles & Wall Reliefs, page 151

The lineage of my meticulously carved ceramic relief tiles traces back to the architectural terra cotta tradition of organically inspired facades. My work reinterprets natural objects and processes them into a new visual language of form. I have developed a sort of "dimensional drawing" technique that is incorporated within a modular tile framework to form elegant compositions at both the level of the individual tile and that of the larger assemblage. Suitable for both indoor and outdoor installations, the tiles come alive in strong light, creating a mesmerizing play of shadow. My skills as an artist and an architect allow me to seamlessly integrate my artistic vision with the unique needs of the space and client. I produce initial studies as detailed photo-realistic images, which allow others to have a clear understanding of what the artwork will eventually become.

GUILD SOURCEBOOKS: *Architectural & Interior Art 20, 22 .23; Residential Art 2, 4, 5*

Mike Hansel
Public Art, page 275

Through my sculpture I attempt to distort traditional assumptions relating to purpose while also suggesting a conceptual relationship between life and industry. Taking common objects out of context gives them a different identity, which may lead the viewer to make unanticipated comparisons. These visual metaphors point people away from what they might take for granted towards a view of an oddly humorous world that is made up of vaguely familiar elements. My intention is to create durable, low-maintenance, site-specific sculpture that stimulates the imagination and initiates interest in the viewer. Work can be commissioned in all scales from 1' high to monumental in stainless steel, aluminum, Corten, and bronze. For more information please visit www.mikehansel.com.

COMMISSIONS: Oak Park, IL; DeCordova Museum, Lincoln, MA; Goldenvoice, Los Angeles CA; The Newport Museum, Newport, RI; St. George's School, Newport, RI; SUNY, Fredonia, NY

Tim Harding
Wall Art / Fiber, page 366

My wall pieces are done in layered, stitched, and cut silks, and are characterized by vibrant, lustrous colors and richly faceted textures. These large-scale, semi-abstract compositions complement architectural interior spaces by adding a warm, inviting visual element. I have a great deal of experience working collaboratively with clients on their specific color requirements. The dense textural relief of my work also adds the important function of acoustic dampening. I am influenced by impressionists and color field painters, primarily for their ability to create luminous color. My use of their painterly techniques, such as simultaneous contrast, within my unique fiber medium, achieves a rich visual presence of intense color and texture with an almost lit-from-within quality.

COMMISSIONS: Mayo Clinic; MCI; SeaWorld; Kaiser Permanente; Neutrogena; Cargill; Nokia; Banner Aerospace; GMAC; Hyatt Regency Hotels; Lawson Software; Minneapolis Institute of Arts; St. Paul Companies; Westlaw; U.S. Embassy, Bangkok; Northwest Airlines; Wells Fargo; Ecolab

GUILD SOURCEBOOKS: *Architectural & Interior Art 16, 22; Residential Art 3*

Mary Hatch
Paintings & Prints, pages 192, 193

My work is about the beautiful social surface of America. Like Tom Wolfe and Robert Altman, I love looking at small sections of our lives. My current work, the *Wedding Book* series, is part of this exploration. Based on wedding photographs borrowed from family and friends, these are not meant to be portraits but daily evidence of "this time" as change and tradition merge. Please visit my website to see more of this ongoing series, as well as other paintings, prints, and my resumé. I'm always happy to answer questions and/or send a price list.

Yoshi Hayashi
Paintings & Prints, page 194

I was born in Japan and learned the rigorous techniques of Japanese lacquer art from my father. I carry the spirit, history, and inspiration of this process with me today as I reinterpret the ancient lacquer tradition for my screens and wall panels. My designs range from delicate, traditional seventeenth-century Japanese lacquer art themes to bold, contemporary geometric designs. By skillfully applying metallic leaf and bronzing powders, I add both illumination and contrast to the network of color, pattern, and texture. Recent commissions include works for private residences in the United States and Japan.

EXHIBITIONS: *Lost Art for the Modern World*, 2004, San Francisco, CA; *Japanese Screens Revisited*, 2003, San Francisco, CA

GUILD SOURCEBOOKS: *The Guild 3, 4, 5; Designer's 6, 7, 8, 9, 10, 11, 12, 13, 14, 15; Architectural & Interior Art 16, 17, 18, 19, 20, 21, 22, 23*

453

Artist Statements

Rhonda Heisler
Mosaics, pages 24, 25, 134

My mosaic art is grounded in my fascination with the color, patterning, and textural properties of fine opaque and metallic stained glass. My technique is akin to painting in hand-cut art glass. I draw my inspiration from the material itself, and as I cut into the glass, I edit the sheet for the choicest bits, creating tesserae that vary in size and shape. In laying the tiles, I juxtapose surfaces that are matte, shiny, or iridescent; color that is solid, shaded, or streaky; textures that are smooth or irregular. In my abstract compositions, I sketch only minimally and work spontaneously and expressively, using modulated color progressions and variations in shape, scale, and texture to create visual metaphors for complex ideas. Commissioned mosaics may be abstract or representational, single- or multi-panel, to bring drama and dimension to any living space. I am an officer in the Society of American Mosaic Artists.

GUILD SOURCEBOOKS: *Architectural & Interior Art 21, 22; Residential Art 4, 5, 6*

Archie Held
Public Art, pages 22, 248, 249

I work primarily in bronze and stainless steel, often incorporating water as a central element. I enjoy using contrasting materials, surfaces, and textures in my work. My many site-specific commissions require collaboration with design committees, architects, engineers, and building contractors to develop a piece of sculpture that is compatible with the site, both aesthetically and technically. My philosophy of public art is one of inclusion; I have found it important to take a team approach and encourage input from all parties involved in the project. Through the simplicity and elegance of my sculptural designs, I strive to enhance and complement the environs and the architecture while making a dynamic statement that will draw people to the location and reward them with an exciting visual experience.

COMMISSIONS: Florida International University, Miami, FL; Genentech Corporation, South San Francisco, CA; Charles Krug Winery, St. Helena, CA; St. Anthony's Hospital, Oklahoma City, OK

Doris K. Hembrough
Fine Art Photography, page 80

It is the light that is special, and it is with us always, everywhere. I see it, am sensitive to it, and wait for it. Like the Mississippi River that I lived by and watched every day, I cannot stop it from moving, and I cannot see the end. I photograph the rocks as people. They have seen all, heard everything, and their stories are there. I have been following the stories for twenty-five years in the sacred places of Ireland, Nova Scotia, the American West, the Southwest, and elsewhere. I work with natural light and do not manipulate the scene, the subject matter, the exposure, or the printing process. I will always continue to use film. Through these images I show the remarkable in the mundane, the unfamiliar in the commonplace, as in my series called *Images from Another World*. My work has been exhibited in galleries spanning the country and is found in numerous private and corporate collections. Please visit www.hembrough gallery.com.

GUILD SOURCEBOOKS: *Residential Art 6*

454

Stephen Henning
Paintings & Prints, page 195

I enjoy quiet, natural surroundings that are far away from the noisy demands of everyday life. I strive to capture impressions of the fleeting beauty of such places that are uncluttered by man, whether it be a wilderness waterway illuminated by the morning light or an abandoned pasture bathed in the colors of evening. My primary artistic goal is to provide a pleasing, peaceful image that can be brought indoors, a sort of escape portal where one's mind is free to stretch and dance. I prefer to create large paintings that make a big impact and are easy to "step into." Once your eye has entered one of my paintings, you will be entertained by a wide spectrum of colors that are built up in many overlapping layers or intertwining brushstrokes, a playground of hue, value, and varying texture that gives a rich depth to a seemingly simple scene.

AWARDS: Signature status, 2008, Oil Pastel Society

GUILD SOURCEBOOKS: *Architectural & Interior Art 23; Residential Art 2, 6.*

Henry Domke Fine Art
Fine Art Photography, page 81

Believing that patients exposed to nature are less stressed and heal faster, I specialize in creating nature art for healthcare settings. My work, which is known for its fresh views of nature, can be found in hospitals across the country. I enrolled in art school while I was still in high school, but I never made it. At the last minute, I decided to pursue medicine, and was a family physician for twenty-five years. But the desire to create art never went away, so I entered the M.F.A. program in the mid 90s. As my art career took off, I pulled back from medicine and finally decided to be a full-time artist in 2007. Also important in my art is the 600-acre property that I live on. It is called the Prairie Garden Trust, and it is a nature restoration project started by my family. I photograph many of my nature images in my "backyard," but increasingly I draw inspiration from nature found from coast to coast

Kevin Heram
Furniture & Floor Coverings, page 114

With over thirty years of experience working with domestic woods and exotic veneers, I craft furniture that represents all of the creative elements of style, design, and quality that my customers have come to expect. I enjoy working with architects, interior designers, and individuals to create hand crafted pieces of art that are unique and distinct. From airy, ethereal tables to the flowing lines of curved vanities, secret spaces, and mahogany libraries, my work encompasses the broad spectrum of "custom original design." I specialize in heirloom-quality furniture and cabinetry using curved lines, exotic woods, and veneers. My desire is to make your concept a reality.

COMMISSIONS: Dresbach, MN; Chicago, IL; La Crosse, WI; Minneapolis, MN; Pittsburg, PA; Shell Lake, WI; Sylmar, CA

PRICING: Please view my website, www.heramcw.com, and contact us for pricing.

Artist Statements

Karen Heyl
Murals, Tiles & Wall Reliefs, pages 142, 152, 153

My award-winning mural relief sculpture combines old-word stone carving techniques with contemporary design, lending itself to a variety of architectural applications, both monumental and small. Using varied textural surfaces, I create aesthetic sophistication with simplified, sensual form.

COMMISSIONS: *Ecological Sampler*, 2002, six limestone panels, each: 5' x 3.5' x 3", mounted on 30'H steel easel, Orange County Convention Center, Orlando, FL; *Nature's Guardians: Endangered Land Animals, Endangered Sea Life*, 2003, limestone, each of two panels: 8' x 4' x 10", Art in Public Places Program; MBK Homes, Brea, CA; *Fight To Freedom*, 2004, six limestone panels, various sizes; The National Underground Railroad Freedom Center, Cincinnati, OH

GUILD SOURCEBOOKS: *Architect's 9, 12, 13, 14, 15; Architectural & Interior Art 16, 17, 18, 19, 20, 21, 22, 23; Residential Art 1, 2, 3*

Eric Higgs
Public Art, page 250

Utilizing various combinations of stone and metal, I strive to create intriguing and architecturally bold sculpture. My designs embody abstract symbolism inspired by the architecture, history, context, and purpose of the locale. I focus on site-specific commissions for public, corporate, and private clients, and welcome collaborations of all types.

COMMISSIONS: Element Building, 2009, City of Tampa, FL; Whitewing at Germann Estates, 2008, Gilbert, AZ; Planned Parenthood Regional Headquarters, 2008, City of Sarasota, FL; City of St. Petersburg, FL, 2007, an OPUS South development

COLLECTIONS: Mitsui Corporation, Tokyo, Japanl Chateau Musee De Vallauris, France; A.I.R. Valluaris, France; private collections in the United States, Japan, and France

EXHIBITIONS: Gallery Seiho, 2009, Tokyo, Japan; PIE Gallery (Best of Show), 2008, Jacksonville, FL; *Miniaesculptures*, 2007, Seiho Gallery, Tokyo, Japan; Fete Picasso, "Allumons Vallauris" Vallauris, 2007, France; Tokyo Mid-town Art and Design Exhibition, 2007, Tokyo, Japan; Stonearium Gallery, 2007, Seattle, WA

GUILD SOURCEBOOKS: *Architect's 14, 15; Architectural & Interior Art 20, 23*

Bonnie Hinz
Wall Art / Glass, pages 7, 386

My work incorporates fused or blown glass and metal. The strong, industrial, and durable nature of metal and how it can work in harmony with the fragile, organic nature of glass captivates me. I enjoy combining the two materials into seamlessly integrated designs. Color and movement in the work are also very important to me. As a former interior designer, I am passionate about making sure my artwork blends perfectly with the client's space, and welcome custom commissions.

COMMISSIONS: Minute Clinic Corporation, Minnesota Life College, and many private residences in the Minneapolis/St. Paul area; Duluth, Minnesota; Madison, Wisconsin; and Texas

Grace Hoff
Wall Art / Mixed & Other Media, page 432

My primary passion is exploring color and texture. I have an artistic flair that transforms the appearance of paper into the luster of metal or the texture of raku. I created these current assemblages with a harmonious blend of paints, inks, washes, and composition leafing, as well as various found natural objects, glass, sticks, and pottery shards. The pieces can be made in any color desired, and in any size necessary.

David J. Holmes
Sculpture / Representational, page 331

I have always believed that art serves two purposes: that of giving its creator a sense of accomplishment in fulfilling the need to create, and secondly, attempting to touch the human condition, bringing about positive and possibly thought-provoking reactions. Although I try to stay away from grandiose symbolic descriptions, I find that my pieces sometimes develop their own stories before, during, and after their creation, whether I mean them to or not, as they take on a life of their own. The history and the symbolism of my work are intended to come together to create an emotional reaction in the viewer. Combining the laws of good design and using the natural magnificence of wood, stone, and metal to their best advantage is where I start and the stories begin.

GUILD SOURCEBOOKS: *Architect's 11, 13, Architectural & Interior Art 23*

Eric Holt
Sculpture / Non-Representational, page 286

In so far as my choosing to sculpt metal, the metal originally chose me. The fascination with it flows in my veins, just as it has through my family for generations. I heat and form and strike the metal, bending it to my will. It, in return, cuts and burns and breaks me, reminding me always of its quiet, magnificent power. It is not a union of adversaries, but rather a labor of both joy and pain. I honor the metal and expose its beauty as I shape it into a tangible figment of my imagination. I have been schooled in many ways in many places, from books, to fists, to the irrefutable genius of a child's logic. I am a graduate with honors from the University of Good Art Sense, and my masters thesis is a declaration of my reverence for the power and beauty of the simple organic form. As an unrefined mineral, the metal longs for its visual beauty to emerge. It is in this moment where I find my calling. Just as the bud is coaxed to bloom by soil and water, through my hands and mind the metal experiences a transformation, the fruit of which is my art.

Artist Statements

Erling Hope
Liturgical Art, pages 123, 124

Versed in a wide range of materials and techniques, I use a multidisciplinary approach to explore the influence of objects, images, and the built environment on the contemporary liturgical experience. I serve as director of the Society for the Arts, Religion and Contemporary Culture, and have served as artist-in-residence at Andover Newton Theological School's Institute for Theology and the Arts.

COMMISSIONS: 14 Bronze Stations of the Cross, Immaculate Heart of Mary Catholic Church, Grand Junction, CO

COLLECTIONS: Good Shepherd Episcopal Church, Silver Springs, MD; Trinity Evangelical Lutheran Church, North Bethesda, MD; Insurance Board Disciples of Christ, UCC

AWARDS: Merit Award, 2003, *Inform Magazine;* Religious Arts/Visual Arts Award, Interfaith Forum on Religion, Art and Architecture

GUILD SOURCEBOOKS: *Architect's 13; Architectural & Interior Art 16, 19*

Casey G. Horn
Sculpture / Representational
Wall Art / Metal, pages 332, 403

I contemporize the two-dimensional art form of calligraphy into three-dimensional sculptures. Skillfully and brilliantly communicating the human emotion behind the ancient art form, I enhance my bronze creations with accents, colors, and textures that outwardly express each character's insightful meaning. With over eighteen years of sculpting experience, I have worked on both public and private collections. My *Essential Kanji* series has been exhibited throughout the United States and is gaining popularity and recognition, including a Best of Show Award in Salem, OR, and first place in sculpture at the Sedona Art festival in AZ. Visit www.CaseyHorn.com.

COMMISSIONS: One-of-a-kind bronze and stainless steel sculptures, including smaller, limited editions in cast bronze, are created to meet the specific size requirements of any interior or exterior space.

Richard Houston
Murals, Tiles & Wall Reliefs, pages 154, 410

My clients are looking for something truly out of the ordinary. Whether the need is for a singular marketing identity for a commercial project or an expression of individuality in a beautiful home, they want artwork that is unique and innovative, with significant impact. My most important service to the client is to offer that creative vision. Coming from a background as a builder and certified professional building designer, I find it easy working as a team with architects, interior designers and builders since I fully understand their unique concerns. In addition to the layered murals shown in this sourcebook, I also create other architecturally integrated artworks such as light fixtures, fireplaces, bridges, trellises and doors. For the smaller budget, I also offer a line of catalog items such as portable murals, light fixtures and mirrors that can be purchased from inventory. To view my online portfolio, visit www.richardhoustonart.com.

456

Brian A. Hubel
Furniture & Floor Coverings, pages 16, 101

The satisfaction of designing and creating furniture by hand is the driving force behind my work. Much of my inspiration comes from the wood itself. I truly appreciate my ability to transform a raw natural resource into a functional and timeless piece of art. It's kind of my way of leaving my mark in this world. As I see it, every piece has a purpose. I believe a piece of furniture should stand on its own. It should be graceful, yet strong, something you never tire of viewing.

EXHIBITIONS: *Masters in the Art of Furniture,* 2006, Shidoni Gallery, Santa Fe, NM; *Fabric, Furniture and Furnishings,* 2006, Steamboat Springs, CO; Collector's Event, 2003-2006, 2008, Shidoni Gallery, Santa Fe, NM; Denver International Airport, 2005, Denver, CO; Pioneers Museum, 2002-2004, Colorado Springs, CO

AWARDS: Design Portfolio 2007-2008, CWB; Fine Woodworking Exhibition 2004, Colorado Springs Pioneers

PUBLICATIONS: *Source & Design Magazine,* 2008; *Luxe Magazine,* Vol. 4, 2008; *CWB Magazine,* Feburary 2007; *Woodworker West,* November/December 2005

GUILD SOURCEBOOKS: *Residential Art 6*

Bill Hueg
Paintings & Prints
Sculpture / Representational,
pages 235, 354

I create images using painting and sculpture in a representational, imaginary style. All of my work is influenced by mathematical relationships found in nature, offering a wonderful sense of harmony. The scale of my work ranges from small paintings and sculptures for the home or office to large murals and monumental sculpture for commercial and public places, all of which are exceptionally crafted. The composition of my work is the key factor, along with the belief that a story should be revealed to the viewer. I have worked with interior designers, architects, contractors, and corporate clients on a national level. My scope of services includes design and fabrication.

COMMISSIONS: Armed Forces Tribute Garden, Westminster, CO; Paris Casino, Las Vegas, NV; Arts Council, Belvidere, IL; Joe's Garage, Tustin, CA; McDonald's, Belvidere, IL

COLLECTIONS: Private and corporate collections in California, Colorado, Hawaii, Idaho, Illinois, Minnesota, New Mexico, New York, and Oregon

Douglas Hyslop
Paintings & Prints, page 196

My artistic strong suit has always been drawing, particularly the human figure. Handling the human figure well usually requires a certain amount of articulation. And when I paint the human figure, I try to include the articulation of the pencil's line, as well as the emotion of the brush stroke and pigment. A number of years ago, I was taken by the Comedy of Art, and have clung to it ever since. The Comedy deals with the happenings of old and well-worn characters, including Harlequin, Columbine, and Pierrot. To depict them necessitates inclusion of narrative elements. In my paintings, I try to raise the narrative element to a level commensurate with the formal composition. I think I have been so taken by the Comedy because it seems to refuse to let go of humanistic values. As a friend of mine said, "You make paintings for people who read."

GUIILD SOURCEBOOKS: *Residential Art 5, 6*

Artist Statements

Illuminata
Lighting, pages 23, 121

Allow me to introduce myself and my work. My name is Julie Conway, and I am the owner, designer, and artist behind Illuminata, specializing in extraordinary lighted glassworks, sculpture, and unique installations. I create glassworks from blown, lampworked, and cast glass techniques. My studies with traditional European and American glass masters, combined with my passion for contemporary design, result in glasswork that is dynamic and revolutionary. I have received several awards for design, lighting, and artistic accomplishments. Pieces in my collection are displayed in showrooms, galleries, restaurants, hotels, museums and private collections. Studio Illuminata offers functional and sculptural work and welcomes custom commissions. I am extremely dedicated to the development of bio-sustainable fuel sources to produce glass and a new energy initiative, thereby helping to protect the environment and the future existence of glass arts. Lighted works use low-energy LED components, and I have introduced the use of alternative fuel sources and recycled materials in my studio.

J. Gorsuch Collins
Architectural Glass
Architectural Glass, page 54

I produce works in leaded, fused, carved, cast, optically laminated, and beveled glass for corporate, health care, hospitality, public, and residential settings. Commitment to excellence and extensive dialogue with the client are distinguishing aspects of my work. Creative design solutions, often involving unique combinations of other materials with glass, provide a fresh approach to design and technique for each project and can result in a complete departure from prior work. Every project is installed on time and on budget.

COMMISSIONS: Ustick Public Library, Boise, ID; CareSource, Dayton, OH; Park Central Office Complex, Denver, CO; 1290 Broadway, Denver CO; Park Hyatt Spa, Beaver Creek, CO; Mercy Medical Center, Des Moines, IA; Kaiser Clinic, Fontana, CA; Kaiser Permanente Rock Creek, Lafayette, CO; Marriott Hotel, Denver, CO; Newmont Gold World Headquarters, Denver, CO; Charles Schwab, Englewood, CO; Wells Fargo Complex, Denver, CO: Avon Public Library, Avon, CO; Hilton, Washington, DC

GUILD SOURCEBOOKS: *THE GUILD 4, 5; Architect's 7, 8, 9, 10, 11; Architectural & Interior Art 20, 21, 22, 23*

J. A. Nelson Studios
Wall Art / Mixed & Other Media, page 416

These sculptures are like multidimensional puzzles, and I treat each piece of the puzzle as an individual work of art. I enjoy the intimacy of working with wood by hand. Being covered in sawdust and wood chips is a joyful part of the process. These sculptures are created from many kinds of wood: bass, birch, catalpa, western cedar, pine, fir, and maple. I select each piece of wood from a small family-run sawmill in rural Oklahoma. The 1.5" to 2" thickness of these wooden slabs adds a substantial look and feel to the finished work. I refer to my current wooden wall art series as *Instrumentals,* that is, without figurative representation. I feel fortunate to have stumbled onto a way to combine my woodworking, painting, and drawing into a unique, personal expression of what I find beautiful.

JP Design
Wall Art / Mixed & Other Media, page 417

Lightweight paper sculptures with an attitude of strength focusing on subtle to vibrant colors and textures. Abstract minimal design and bold areas of color bring a thoughtful, meditative spirit to any corporate or residential environment. Layers of acid-free papers are created by spraying cotton fibers onto anodized aluminum mesh. Surface is embellished with colorants of lightfast acrylics and various textures. Papers are then applied to a gently curved armature allowing the deckled edge intrinsic to handmade paper to be accentuated. This unusual presentation brings a contemporary, sculptural appearance to traditional wall décor. The work is a collaborative effort of Jeanne Petrosky, a papermaker since 1987 and Dennis Guzenski, a faux finisher also since 1987. We have been working together since 2002. Commissions are welcomed. For more information, please visit our website, jeannepetrosky.com.

Jeff Jackson
Sculpture / Non-Representational, page 312

My work in sculpture is an exploration of form, light, and material. I want my viewer to be engaged in and interact with my work. As I evolve so does my art. I find that organic and graphic lines of nature are what drive the concepts of my work, an organized chaos. I follow the simple rules of balance, volume, and space. My materials allow me to project my ideas upward and outward, allowing each piece to interact with its surroundings and the viewer. I have found that sculpture was where my real creative energy could be found. I pull my many themes from dozens of sketchpads; within these concepts I find a fluid idea and strive to develop an organized and cohesive direction. By using a minimalist perspective, I choose materials to interact with light and capture that fleeting moment found in nature. For further examples please visit www.jeffjacksonfineart.com.

Jeff and Sandy Jackson
Public Art, page 251

As an artist team, we have designed, created, and installed numerous successful large-scale commissions. We excel in working with art consultants, designers, architects, and community teams. We believe that multiple viewpoints and parameters coming together create unique and wonderful pieces of art that otherwise would not have come to fruition. We enjoy and are proficient in working with many different forms of media in our sculpture. We are most recognized for our works combining different types of metals and fused art glass to create large-scale contemporary works. Past commission projects include large-scale wall sculpture, hanging atrium sculpture, and large-scale freestanding sculpture, as well as water features. We also welcome smaller scale commissions. We have a reputation for maintaining extremely high standards of quality and creativity, and always honor the budget and time lines set forth by our clients. For a listing and examples of commission work, please visit www. jaxondesignworks.com.

Artist Statements

Sandy Jackson
Wall Art / Glass, page 386

I create contemporary sculpture using a combination of fused, iridescent, and dichroic art glass, often incorporating various metals into my sculpture. My sculptural and architectural glass works grace many corporate, public, and private collections. I excel at commission work, which includes large-scale wall art, freestanding sculpture, atrium sculpture, and architectural glass work. The unique nature of my work complements its surroundings and can be executed in custom color palettes and sizes. I enjoy and have many years of experience working with art consultants, designers, and architects. I maintain an excellent reputation for giving my clients what they have envisioned and I always deliver on time and within budget. I am continually experimenting with new ways to utilize glass and metal in corporate and public settings, and I am developing work that fits the new LEED certification standards. For a listing of commissions and further examples, visit www.sandyjacksonfineart.com.

Bill Jacobs
Furniture & Floor Coverings, pages 12, 102

Over the past three decades, we at W. T. Jacobs Inc. have developed a unique ability to design and build furniture and cabinets to any style or scale. From design to completion, we realize the vision that our clients desire to bring the artistry and skills to fulfill a masterful and professional product. Each piece is magical in its color and figure. We transcend specific styles; our furniture is contemporary as well as Asian or craftsman in design. Maintaining the integrity of the wood, accentuating the shape and grain, combined with sophisticated design elements gives a contemporary yet grounded feel and appearance. High tech and holistic, we provide for the hospitality industry, as well as residential. We feel it is important to not only deliver a beautiful product but also a memorable experience.

Adam Jahiel
Fine Art Photography, pages 82, 83

I like to look, and I like to share what I see. But I like to do that sharing wordlessly. Over the years some of my peers have accused me of being mostly interested in the "fringe" people. Maybe so. But I like to think I am drawn to those who seem to exist outside of time in forgotten corners and cultures. They seem somehow more in touch with, or part of, the human condition. I try to document people, places, and life in an honest, straightforward, respectful, and intimate way. And preserve it forever. I work in black-and-white because it allows me to boil elements down to their very essence—shape, lines, and light. Light can be indescribably beautiful and fascinating. I love to watch it completely transform something. The same scene can go from being unremarkable, to extraordinary, and back to unremarkable in a heartbeat. Even after all these years of working, the ability to freeze a moment in time and preserve it forever, although mostly science, to me is really like magic. More details available at www.adamjahiel.com.

458

Jaimi Novak Photography
Fine Art Photography, page 91

I received my first camera when I was eight and have loved photography ever since. My *Through the Viewfinder* photographs combine digital photography with a vintage viewfinder camera to highlight the dust and scratches that make vintage photos so unique. This is an ongoing project with new images added regularly. My photographs are available in various sizes, and I'm happy to create custom sizes. Please visit www.jnovakphotography.com for more information..

Dori Jalazo
Sculpture / Representational, page 333

My art tells the story of the travels we all take through this journey of life. The symbols reflect the pain and joy we celebrate through the years. There is a healing, a meditative calm that infuses the energy of the space where this art dwells. Specific *Life Story* pieces, by commission, are available to specially honor someone's life. The awards and honors are not what matters. People's stories fill my heart and fuel my passion. "There is no other work like this" I have been told repeatedly. My work resides in the collections of Henry Winkler, Harry Connick, Jr., Dr. Bernie Siegel, Dr. Ruth, Joshua Malina, and many others throughout the world.

GUILD SOURCEBOOKS *Residential Art 3, 4, 6*

Jane Rankin Sculpture
Sculpture / Representational, page 334

I create limited-edition bronze sculpture and specialize in life-size and tabletop figures, mostly of children and child-related things.

COMMISSIONS: Cerritos Plaza, 2003, City of Cerritos, CA; Harvest Community, 2002, Ft. Collins, CO; Town Hall, 1999, Cary, NC; Morse Park, 1998, Lakewood, CO

COLLECTIONS: City of Cerritos, CA; Newton, IA; Pueblo Public Library, Pueblo, CO; Dogwood Festival Center, Jackson, MS; Waukegan Public Library, IL; Colorado Springs Fine Art Center, CO; Buell Children's Museum, Pueblo, CO; Lincoln Children's Museum, NE; Creative Artists Agency, Beverly Hills, CA

EXHIBITIONS: Pueblo Street Gallery, 2001-2004, Pueblo, CO; American Numismatic Association, 2000-2002, Colorado Springs, CO

GUILD SOURCEBOOKS: *Architect's 14, 15; Architectural & Interior Art 16, 17, 18, 19, 20*

Artist Statements

Nicolette Jelen
Paintings & Prints, page 197

What inspires me is the way light travels through veils of color, enhancing one while the others stand by. Like mists, they are all part of each other. My work reflects this balance, starting with one dark red and layering transparent and opaque veils of color that build upon each other to form the final image. When I paint, I think about the travels of light and time.

GUILD SOURCEBOOKS: *Residential Art 6*

Jensen & Marineau Ceramics
Murals, Tiles & Wall Reliefs, page 155

We think of our work as functional art for everyday life. Our tile installations add the warmth of the human touch to a room, creating spaces so beautiful they become central to the life of the home. Our tile is made entirely by hand from the raw clay to the finished glaze. Applied with a slip-trailer and brush, the whimsical blue and white images are slightly raised under the clear glaze. We offer a variety of styles and images suitable for the most intimate to the most public spaces. We are happy to work with clients to create original installations reflecting their vision. Visit us at www.jensenandmarineau.com to tour our hand-made home and studio, visit a gallery of finished installations, and browse our catalogue to view our complete tile line, from contemporary to classic.

Randy Johnson
Paintings & Prints, page 198

I intend for these images of *Directed Chaos* to capture the ethereal and to trigger the recognition of patterns that mimic the underlying structure of life. Viewers sense in these paintings a familiarity akin to natural phenomena like cloud formations, eroded landforms, swirling liquids, and life forms. My palette is largely tropical; the compositions are of a bold simplicity. The hybrid paintings begin as blended and layered films of acrylic paint on illustration board applied with non-traditional manual painting techniques. I then digitally recompose and repaint them, and finally make archival giclée prints on canvas. The prints are the end product of an art-making process similar to the complex series of steps that leads to a multi-layered stone lithograph or serigraph. The hybrid paintings are produced in short limited editions of twelve to thirty prints.

PUBLICATIONS: *Architecture+* magazine, 2004, Vol. 7

Barry Woods Johnston
Sculpture / Representational, page 335

My job is to visualize and then breathe life into inert clay, bronze, or stone. My sculptures, often light and lively in sentiment, are generally upbeat. I seek to complement an architectural setting while adding levity, movement, and humanity. Clothing is rendered in faithful detail, with flowing movement and compositional unity. My degree in architecture gives me a regard for aesthetics and the ability to integrate art into its architectural setting. I view public commissions as an opportunity to capture the vision of the community. My subjects are derived from mythology, religion, literature, psychology, and the contemporary dilemma.

COMMISSIONS: Govan's Presbyterian Church, Baltimore, MD; Catholic College of Notre Dame, Baltimore, MD; White River Medical Center, AR; City Hall, Hampton, VA; Lafayette Center, Washington, DC, Evanston Women's Hospital, IL

EXHIBITIONS: Schedel Arboretum and Gardens, 2009, Elmore, OH; Art Barn, 2009, Gaithesburg, MD; Circle Gallery, 2009, Annapolis, MD; Riverspan Show, 2009, Cincinnati, OH

GUILD SOURCEBOOKS: *Architect's 13, 14, 15; Architectural & Interior Art 16, 18, 19, 20, 21, 22, 23; Residential Art 3, 5*

Jolino Architectural Mosaics
Mosaics, page 135

Welcome to Jolino Architectural Mosaics: creating hand-crafted contemporary *pique-assiette* (peek-assyet) mosaics for public and private spaces—mosaics filled with humor and imagination that intrigue and even dare the viewer not to touch. But the hope is that you will touch—that's half of the fun! There is a uniquely mysterious beauty and many levels of visual depth to be discovered upon multiple viewings. A single fragment or an arrangement of objects can draw you into the composition. As you glide your hand and eyes over the mosaic, you become surrounded with what feels to be personal stories and memories. As these recycled objects are given new importance or are used in unexpected ways, they make the viewer appreciate everyday items in a whole new context. I am very excited and proud to be continuing in the ancient tradition of an extraordinary artisanal form, reinterpreting it to suit the contemporary aesthetic.

Jonathan Mandell Designs Inc.
Mosaics, page 136

My goal in my art is to push the craft of mosaic as a fine art medium. I create tactile paintings, incorporating my thoughts in spatial design and color compositions. The mosaic's grout lines act as drawing lines, helping to define the mosaic's imagery. I am always seeking different directions to push the medium, hence my portfolio is very eclectic. It includes portraits, landscapes, sports scenes, Judaica, and much more. My mosaics are made using ceramic tile, glass shards, and semi-precious stones and minerals. In my glass shard mosaics, the glass pieces are convex and concave. This creates a topography, or bas relief effect, across the mosaic surface. I have also explored mosaic in three dimensions, wrapping the imagery around sculptural forms. Mosaic for me is the perfect fusion of sculpture, paint, and drawing.

459

Artist Statements

Sarinda Jones
Sculpture / Non-Representational, page 312

I create sculpture for corporate, hospitality, and academic facilities, as well as private and gallery installations. The scale ranges from small tabletop works to pieces over five feet high using steel, aluminum, and glass to create a contemporary feel that illuminates the simple beauty of glass. I enjoy collaborating with architects, designers, and art consultants. My motivation is to capture that moment when time stands still, condensing the elements of my work to their essence—to a sense of space that has a concentration of spirit, character, and physical presence. Each piece is designed with meticulous care and thought. While the placement of color and individual elements may appear random, there is a formula involved. For more information, please visit reflectiveartstudio.com.

EXHIBITIONS: Sweet Library, 2008, Salt Lake City, UT; American Craft San Francisco Show, 2008, San Francisco, CA; Utah Arts Festival, Invited Artist, 2008, 2007, and participant 2006, Salt Lake City; Palm Springs Museum of Fine Art, 2008, CA

Julie Boehm Photography
Fine Art Photography, page 92

For twelve years, it has been my passion to capture images that evoke mood and feeling by showing the beauty of the world. It wasn't until I picked up a camera that I discovered how we see things differently. By composing images, I see how the art of photography can bring meaning to the simplest of details in this world. I love getting lost for hours in the micro and macro world behind a lens, and I am inspired by light's ability to bring such beauty and life to a scene like no other element on this planet. As the reflection of the light in my photos travels through the images from one side of the frame to the other, the viewer gets a very clean and pleasing subject to look at; the images come alive and are able to evoke the deepest of meanings, even in the smallest details of life. As an artist I am constantly balancing the changes and transformations that surround my life. It is with great joy that I am able to share my vision of life, through my photography, with you.

PRICING: Giclée Print
Prints are limited edition of 150
Signed and numbered on the reverse side
16" x 20" $500 plus S+H $20
20" x24" $700 plus S+H $30

Scott Kahn
Paintings & Prints, page 199

I consider my work to be a visual diary of my life. I am especially drawn to painting landscapes because it allows me the opportunity to express my response to the vastness and mysteries of nature. If I am successful, the painting will have depth, poetry, and honesty. To achieve this result, a creative person calls upon every tool available—technical, emotional, intuitive, and intellectual. The act of creating teaches us and reveals to us who we are and our relationship to life. This is why I paint. All paintings available as giclée prints. Visit www.scottkahnpainter.com.

COLLECTIONS: AT&T, Somerset, NJ, and Chicago, IL; Chase Manhattan Bank, NYC; Metropolitan Life Insurance Company, NYC; Philip Morris Corporation, NYC; numerous private collections in the U.S. and abroad

EXHIBITIONS: American Embassy, Moscow, 2006, Art in Embassies Program; Arthur Ross Gallery, 2004, University of Pennsylvania, Philadelphia

AWARDS: Pollock-Krasner Foundation Grant, 1995

460

BJ Katz
Architectural Glass, page 55

Working closely with design professionals, collectors, and end users, I create art glass to complement design elements and to create a conceptual framework for the space that celebrates the client's identity and purpose. Originality, elegance, and scale define my body of artwork; nature and spirituality inform it. I begin each work with concept and design, and intuitively follow my muse. An idea is coaxed into being by hand molding, coloring, and shaping glass in large industrial kilns. Evocative, subtle, nuanced monumental artworks are thus created.

COMMISSIONS: Bellagio Hotel, Las Vegas; Baylor University Medical Center, Dallas; Georgia Aquarium, Atlanta; Midwestern University Chapel, Chicago; Disney World, Orlando; Sky Harbor Airport, Phoenix, AZ

AWARDS: Arizona Artist of the Year, 2008, Art Renaissance; Top 10 Healthcare Product Designers, Healthcare Design; Crystal Achievement Award for Art Glass in Architecture, 2008, Glass;

PUBLICATIONS: US Glass, August 2008; profiled on "Women Artisans," HGTV's Modern Masters

GUILD SOURCEBOOKS: Architect's 14, 15; Designer's 11, 12, 14, 15; Architectural & Interior Art 16, 17, 18, 19, 21; 22, 23; Residential Art 1

Kim Ellen Kauffman
Fine Art Photography, page 84

Aura, a limited-edition photo collage created from multiple scans of original objects, is from my botanically inspired body of work titled Florilegium that utilizes a cameraless imaging technique. Cameraless images are as old as photography itself, begun with Henry Fox Talbot's photogenic drawings of plants and Anna Atkin's cameraless studies of algae. Today's tools have facilitated my new direction in this tradition. Begun in 1998, Florilegium is now one hundred images and growing. Through it I hope to not only share the beauty of plants but also nurture in the viewer reverence for the natural world. See synecdochestudio.com to view the entire collection.

COLLECTIONS: Cleveland Museum of Art, Cleveland, OH; University of Louisville Photographic Archives, Louisville, KY; The Kresge Museum at MSU, East Lansing, MI; McNeese State University, Lake Charles, LA; Dennos Museum, Traverse City, MI; Bowling Green State University Firelands, Huron, OH; Duke Integrative Medicine, Durham, NC; Umstead Hotel, Cary, NC; Northwestern Mutual Life Insurance, Milwaukee, WI

GUILD SOURCEBOOKS: Residential Art 5, 6, Architectural & Interior Art 22, 23

Shelby Keefe
Paintings & Prints, pages 18, 200

I am a contemporary Impressionist specializing in architectural subjects, whether it be urban or rural landscapes. I use my own photographs as references, as well as painting en plein air. I intend to put the viewer in the scene, transporting them to the location and transforming their mood in a positive way through color and composition. I'm attracted to scenes where the subjects are dramatically lit. This adds a vibrancy and a sense of immediacy to the paintings. I like to apply the oils freely and liberally over brilliant acrylic underpaintings, creating a subtle juxtaposition of contrasting colors that vibrates and excites the eye. I believe that a work of art has a longer lasting "wall life" if the viewer continually finds something new in the work and the paint is allowed to do the "talking." I enjoy doing custom work for clients and can paint large-scale corporate works as well as smaller, intimate pieces for private collectors. For more information please visit www.studioshelby.com.

COLLECTIONS: Northwestern Mutual; Foley & Lardner; Acuity; The Bradley Foundation; Ozaukee Country Club; The Radisson Hotel; WE Energies

GUILD SOURCEBOOKS: Residential Art 4.

Artist Statements

Guy Kemper
Architectural Glass, page 56

I work closely with master craftsmen to translate my paintings directly into blown glass. This imbues my compositions with the depth, richness, and refractive qualities of pure blown glass and distinguishes my work from mere painted or stained glass. The techniques are ancient, but I use them in a way to make work that is unique. When laminated to clear tempered glass, the material is nearly indestructible and maintenance free. Every project is installed on time and on budget.

COMMISSIONS: St. Petersburg/Clearwater International Airport; Mt. Baker Station, Seattle SoundTransit; Baltimore/Washington International Airport; The Catholic Memorial at Ground Zero, New York, NY; Orlando International Airport; St. Peter auf dem Berg, Bleidenstädt, Germany; Public cemetery chapel, Engenhahn, Germany

EXHIBITIONS: *100% Design Tokyo,* Japan; *Painting in Music,* Idstein Jazz Festival, Germany; German National Museum of Glass Painting permanent collection, Linnich; *Internationale Glaskunst,* Freudenstadt, Germany; *El Arte De Las Vidrieras: Luz, Color y Espacio,* Valencia, Spain

Ken Roth Studio
Paintings & Prints, pages 175, 201

My paintings are derived from direct contact with nature. Light, pattern, color, and texture, combined with memory and imagination, are the driving forces in my work as an artist. I strive to create paintings that invite the viewer into dialogue with the literal surface of the work, as well as their own sense of memory and place. Paintings range in size from small intimate pieces to large architectural installations. My work is included in many private and corporate collections throughout the country and has been exhibited in numerous gallery shows. I also work with design professionals and art consultants to collaborate on pieces for specific private or public settings. Commissions are welcome. For a complete list of available paintings, workshops, shows, and resume, please visit my website at www. kenrothstudio.com.

COMMISSIONS: The Clubhouse at Pronghorn, Bend, OR; The Lake House at Caldera Springs, Sunriver, OR; Mercato Development, Bend, OR

AWARDS: Best Emerging Artist, 2002, *Art and Antiques;* Artist to Watch, 2002, *Southwest Art*

GUILD SOURCEBOOKS: *Architectural & Interior Art 23*

Ellen Mears Kennedy
Wall Art / Fiber, page 367

My artwork is constructed of hundreds of double-sided papers, all handmade in my studio from pigmented pulp. Each paper has a left and right side that displays a unique shade. When the paper is folded, one color shows on the left side and a second color shows on the right. As viewers walk past each construction, the colors subtly change as they see alternating sides of the design.

GUILD SOURCEBOOKS: *Designer's 15; Architectural & Interior Art 16, 17; Residential Art 2*

461

Anne Kessler
Paintings & Prints, page 202

I have a passion for landscapes that bring light and color into a room. I believe people need landscapes as a reminder of where the stillness of the earth meets the human eye. Something in our nature needs to experience the ancient outer ease of the world to remember who we are. Water surfaces are my specialty, also florals in clear bright color. My larger architectural paintings often read well as abstracts. Commissions are welcome. I grew up in Cambridge, Massachusetts, and attended Radcliffe College. I currently live on the wild North Coast of California. I have shown my work in galleries in San Francisco, Scottsdale, New York City, Paris, and Zurich. When Masako Owada was married to Prince Naruhito, the Crown Prince of Japan, one of my paintings was presented to the royal couple as a wedding present and hangs in the private collection of the Japanese Royal household.

GUILD SOURCEBOOKS: *Residential Art 6*

Kessler Studios, Inc.
Architectural Glass, page 57

For over twenty-five years, we have designed contemporary stained glass windows that soften and humanize the built environment. Our dramatic influence on the ambiance within a space is achieved by designing works that touch the human spirit while respecting the architectural character of each site.

COMMISSIONS: The Salvation Army, Ashland, OH; The Clare at the Water Tower, Chicago, IL; McGuffey Hall, Miami University, Oxford, OH; Peru State College Library, Peru, NE; St. Mary's Hospital, Saginaw & Standish, MI; Central DuPage Hospital, Chicago, IL; Florida Department of Transportation, Miami, FL; Old St. Mary Catholic Church, Chicago, IL; Wheeling Hospital, Wheeling, WV; University Place Retirement Center, West Lafayette, IN; Ohio Department of Agriculture, Reynoldsville, OH; St. Michael's Catholic Church, North Canton, OH; University of Cincinnati, Cincinnati, OH; Good Samaritan Hospital, Cincinnati, OH.

AWARDS: Religious Art Awards, 2004, 1994, American Institute of Architects Visual Art Awards, 2004, 2003, 2002, *Ministry & Liturgy Magazine;* Best of Show Bene Visual Art Award, 2003, *Ministry & Liturgy Magazine;* Ohio Artist Fellowship, 1998, Ohio Arts Council

Kevin Sink Photography
Fine Art Photography, page 92

As a full-time natural landscape photographer, I spend several months per year in the field capturing my unique vision of America's landscape. Extensive field work, use of high-end, medium-format equipment, and personally making all of my prints elevate my photographs to fine art. I'm proud of our consistent production of incredible-looking prints, even at very large sizes, up to 96" wide. I print on either a semi-gloss photo paper, watercolor paper, or on canvas that is then coated with a protective giclée veneer. We have a very successful twenty-year history working with the design industry and share a commitment to superb quality, dependability, and timeliness in order fulfillment. My work is characterized by a prominent contemplative component, and the use of line and color as emphasized compositional elements. On top of all this, my company is fun to work with!

COLLECTIONS: St. Luke's Hospital; Lathrop & Gage LLC; EPA Headquarters, Kansas City; Center for Rheumatic Disease

EXHIBITIONS: Office of Kansas Governor Kathleen Sebelius, 2008; Kansas City Public Library, 2008

PUBLICATIONS: Widely published in many national magazines and books including *National Geographic Traveler, Nature Conservancy* magazine, and Sierra Club books and calendars

Artist Statements

Kirschling Studios, Inc.
Liturgical Art, page 125

We are a second-generation studio that has evolved through the years, honing our focus as we continue to grow. We work with some of the top independent stained glass designers in the country to best meet our clients' needs. Whether architects, liturgical designers, or committees, you can realize your vision with the help of our custom design work. Or, if you would like, we can work with you in the creation of a work of art that will not only meet a specific construction need, but will inspire and root generations to come. From conceptual design to physical creation to finished installation, we work with the best glass and fabrication methods so that we may offer our clients a full range of options—from traditional painted windows to modern abstract color fields.

PRICING: Contact us directly for price quotes and budget options.

Vitali Komarov
Paintings & Prints, page 235

The purpose of my work is to make beautiful things. Working from nature, I am inspired by its beauty. When I paint simple things, I vitalize them and fill them with sense. Trying to reproduce exactly the light and the mood of the subject, I experiment with composition, tone, and color. I balance composition, so that onlookers can breathe easily. I make contrast convincing, and colors fresh and pure. Feelings and mood play an important role in my paintings, more so than the form. It is not the technical side of art that interests me; hence, I do not experiment with styles or medium. I am simply excited by the process of painting itself. Technical skills together with inspiration are not enough to be a good artist if you do not work constantly and estimate your results soberly and strictly. I regard each new work as a serious search. This produces a picture that is not an imitation of reality, but a new reality in itself. Nature is the teacher and it is nature that teaches me to see the subject and gives me an immense feeling of love.

Kristin DeSantis Contemporary Metal
Architectural Elements, page 31

Each piece of art that we create is custom designed to fit its architectural space. We design indoor and outdoor sculpture for healthcare, corporate, hotel, and private homes, and enjoy collaborating with architects, designers, and art consultants. With standard sheets of aluminum, we begin creating the "metal canvas." This involves a process of cutting the metal with a plasma torch, welding to build up layers, and carving the metal to achieve a bas-relief. Many hours go into working the metal before any color is applied. The color is achieved with several layers of transparent oil stains and then clear coated to give a glass-like look. Our work is very large and thrives on the light that plays with its surface textures and gives it a luminous three-dimensional illusion. This process is one that we developed on our own: we call it "Industrial Elegance."

COMMISSIONS: Renown Health, 2008-2009, Reno, NV; RAA Radiology Associates of Albuquerque, 2005-2008, Albuquerque, NM; Presbyterian Hospital Pediatric Urgent Care, 2007, Albuquerque, NM; Rady Children's Hospital, 2007, San Diego, CA; Porter residence, 2007-2008, Albuquerque, NM; numerous private residences, indoors and outdoors, Chicago, New York, Seattle, Palm Springs, Miami, and Philadelphia

462

LH Originals
Wall Art / Mixed & Other Media, page 418

This original artwork is created out of recycled metal from Mexico. The initial circles are punched out of a flat sheet of metal to produce bottle caps. The remaining metal sheet is then sent to a manufacturing plant in Illinois to be made into furnace filters. I then take used furnace filters and recycle the metal for a third time to create whatever abstract idea that emerges in the moment, using color and dimension to capture the simplicity and intrigue of each piece. My intention when designing each one-of-a-kind piece is to inspire one's imagination to see the endless possibilities and images that exist among the shadows. The scale of the pieces range from as small as 6" x 6" to as large as 5' or more, and they are often installed as sets. Profits are donated to non-profit organizations around the world. Commissions are welcome. For more information, please visit lhoriginals.com.

Al Lachman
Paintings & Prints, pages 5, 203

Each painting begins with a premise, and I rarely use the same one twice. It is based on what I see and what I am feeling at that moment. I do not think that painting is about technique. It is about a particular perception of the world around us. The premise creates the periphery of my intent. It is a limitation that gives birth to the creative forces within me. (Necessity is the mother of invention.) This approach takes us into uncharted waters with each new painting; adventure awaits us and we are not limited by our knowledge or lack of it.

COLLECTIONS: The Walt Disney Corporation; Northwest Airlines, Inc.; Domino Pizza Corp. Collection; Detroit Tigers Executive Offices; Sun Bank; Hershey Corporation; Ford Motor Corporation; Ortho Pharmaceuticals; Central Library of Denver, CO; President, Disneyland International

Silja Talikka Lahtinen
Wall Art / Mixed & Other Media, page 419

My work draws from the myths, landscape, folk songs, and textiles of my native Finland. I am especially inspired by Lapland Shamanism in my paintings, collages, wall panels, prints, and drums. I am always trying to do a better painting today than what I did yesterday. Prices range from $400–$30,000.

EXHIBITIONS: Solo exhibition, 2009, Amsterdam-Whitney Gallery; Solo exhibition, Summer Show, Ronnvik Vinery, Laitikkala, Finland; WCA Group Artwaves International, 2008, College Art Association Conference, Dallas, TX; Temple Gallery, 2007, Decatur, GA; OIA Salon Show, 2007, Brooklyn, NY; Ward-Nasse Gallery Year-Round Salon, 2008, Summer Salon, 2007; ARTEXPO New York, 2008; Viljamakasum, 2006, Finland; Turnout 2006, De Detoor Centre, Atlanta, GA; One-person show, 2006, Vilja-makasiini, Ruovesi, Finland

PUBLICATIONS: *Who's Who of American Artists Gallery*, 2009; *Who's Who in American Art*, 2009; *GRANDI MAESTRI, Edizione 2008*; *New Art International Vol XII*, 2008; *Art Acquisitor Magazine*, Spring 2008, Vol.6

GUILD SOURCEBOOKS: *GUILD 1, 2, 3; Designer's 9, 10, 11; Architectural & Interior Art 17, 19, 20, 21, 22, 23*

Artist Statements

Dale Claude Lamphere
Sculpture / Non-Representational, page 287

Working with stainless steel, copper, stone, and bronze, I create sculptures that enhance the architecture and landscape of public and private spaces. My inspiration comes from the sweeping, lyric forms that exist in my mountain and prairie environment. I often use natural stones that evoke a context, which I create in beautifully finished and textured metals. I enjoy collaboration with clients, architects, and contractors. With three decades of experience and over fifty large-scale public works completed, we have the capacity to create projects of any scale that are well engineered and sensitive to public interaction and the surrounding environment.

COMMISSIONS: City of Burbank, CA; Benson Park Sculpture Garden, Loveland, CO; Archdiocese of Chicago, IL; City of Edmond, OK; Eisenhower Medical Center, Palm Springs, CA; Basilica of the National Shrine of the Immaculate Conception, Washington, DC; Fenske Media, Rapid City, SD

Melody Lane
Sculpture / Non-Representational, page 288

My art encompasses clay and glass. The clay is smoke-fired to evoke an ancient stone-like finish. The glass allows the light to create its own fire, changing as the light of the day changes. This is a combination of earth and fire that resonates with references to other cultures and civilizations. My aim is to bring the motifs of ancient cultures into a contemporary form, connecting the past and the present. In 2004, I was awarded an Artist Fellowship Grant from the Connecticut Commission on the Arts. In 2006, I was invited to participate in the ART in Embassies Program for the South African embassy. My work is shown in galleries throughout the country, and I have exhibited at the Smithsonian Craft show, the Paradise City shows, and the American Craft Council Trade shows, among others. To see other work, please visit my website at www.melodylanestudio.com or call for a catalog. Prices range from $20 to $4,500.

GUILD SOURCEBOOKS: *Residential Art 4, 5, 6*

Tuck Langland
Public Art
Sculpture / Representational,
pages 252, 253, 336

Although I specialize in large-scale figurative bronzes, in which there is give and take with architects and owners, I also make garden sculptures and small pieces for the home and office, where the ideas come totally from within. As I simplify a portrait, a figure, or clothing, I remove the extra wrinkles that clutter and keep us from seeing the essential shape. Along with this simplification, there is always a solid human form underneath the clothing or drapery. I never lose sight of the principals of line, balance, or form, which are essential to art in every medium. Allegory is also important; it speaks about our human condition.

COLLECTIONS: Ten museums in the U.S. and Europe; Schedel Gardens, Ohio; Brookgreen Gardens, SC; Meijer Sculpture Gardens, MI; private gardens; Town Hall, Arzberg, Germany; Orkney Islands Council Collection, Scotland

463

Lashua Metal Studio
Sculpture / Non-Representational, page 289

The work of Lashua Metal Studio combines my formal education in Architecture (B.Arch.) and Metalsmithing (M.F.A.) with over fifteen years of hands-on design and fabrication experience. In the tradition of a collaborative studio spirit, I welcome the opportunity to work with other architects, designers, and artisans in the process of creating unique sculptural solutions to architectural elements. The goal of the studio is to meet the needs of the client while exceeding their expectations through the high standards of innovative design and craftsmanship. The works of the studio include interior and exterior sculpture, furnishings, fountains, sculptural railings and gates, and architectural details. I work primarily with steel, stainless steel, copper, and bronze. Clients include corporate, commercial, residential, and private commissions.

COMMISSIONS: *Chalice Sculpture,* 2008, Northern Hills Fellowship, Cincinnati, OH; *Caring Spirit* Sculptural Fountain, 2007-2008, Hospice & Palliative Care of Western Colorado, Grand Junction, CO; *Reflections* Donor Wall, 2007, Congregation Beth Adam Synagogue, Loveland, OH; *Branching Out* Sculpture, 2006, Towers of Kenwood, Duke Realty Corporation, Cincinnati, OH

GUILD SOURCEBOOKS: *Architectural & Interior Art 23*

Eric David Laxman
Public Art, page 254

I am a sculptor and custom metal fabricator working in a range of materials to produce elegant museum-quality sculptures and functional artworks. I work closely with architects, designers, and art consultants to develop designs and choose materials that will best serve the client's particular needs. Inspiration may be drawn from the surrounding architecture and landscape, the local history and culture, and the nature and function of the setting. From detailed drawings or scale models to finished pieces, my hands-on approach results in one-of-a-kind, site-specific works that add style, elegance, and energy to any environment.

COMMISSIONS: Hamilton, Ohio—City of Sculpture, Journal Square; Summit Medical Group, NJ; Greenwich Hospital, CT; Rockland County Art in Public Places, NY; numerous private residences

GUILD SOURCEBOOKS: *Architectural & Interior Art 18, 20; Residential Art 1, 2, 3*

Greg Leavitt
Architectural Elements, page 32

In the thirty-seven years that Leavitt Studios has been exploring the limitless possibilities of forged metal as sculpture, we have turned steel into flocks of birds, clouds of butterflies, and gardens bursting with flowers. We draw from a wide palette of visual reference and our commissions address a client's desires with bold and creative design solutions. We embrace the dualities inherent in sculptural form: masculine and feminine, hard and soft, cold and hot, mass and space. When the integration of these oppositional forces is achieved, it leads to a successful work of art.

COMMISSIONS: Lincoln Park Zoo, Chicago, IL; Governor's Mansion, Harrisburg, PA; Mt. Cuba Estate, DE; Hyatt Hotel, Philadelphia, PA; Upper Chesapeake Medical Center, MD; Le Bec-Fin and Brasserie Restaurants; Westminster and Swarthmore Presbyterian Churches; Oaklands Corporate Center; Philadelphia Park System; Waterloo Gardens; Swarthmore College; and many private estates

GUILD SOURCEBOOKS: *The Guild 2; Architect's 9, 10, 11, 14, 15; Architectural & Interior Art 18, 21, 23*

Artist Statements

Carol LeBaron
Wall Art / Fiber, page 368

The inspiration for my fine art textiles comes from forms and colors found in nature. I use these elements to create pieces that guide the atmosphere of interior spaces through color and the inherent sound-absorbing qualities of fiber. The materials I use allow a full-range color palette, from brilliant tones to muted shades. Because the themes in my work center around the beauty of the natural environment, my working process incorporates green practices of water conservation and natural energy to produce long-lasting, beautiful works of art. The imagery and materials combine contemporary aesthetics, modern technology, and ancient processes. I keep a stock of one-of-a-kind pieces available, and I enjoy working directly with consultants and clients to meet the requirements of specific sites.

GUILD SOURCEBOOKS: *Architectural & Interior Art 20, 23; Residential Art 5*

Lederer Studio Furniture
Furniture & Floor Coverings, page 103

Lederer Studio was formed in the summer of 1978 to provide fine furniture, wood carving, and sculpture to select individuals. We are committed to delivering the highest- quality product. Our approach is timeless. Our designs are a synthesis of enduring traditional designs including Arts & Crafts, Art Nouveau, Art Deco, and Oriental designs, with an emphasis on simplicity and subtle, elegant lines. With a philosophy of structure, fine select materials, elegant lines, fine carving, and beautiful finishes, I design each piece with patience, care, and an artistic approach, with extensive design consultation to meet the goals of each client. We believe in using the best hand-selected materials and hardware. All furniture is constructed using domestic and exotic hardwoods and veneers, and executed in traditional fine joinery techniques, including mortise and tenon, mitre-spline, etc. All carving and sculpture is hand carved in original designs.

Vincent T. Leman
Furniture & Floor Coverings, page 114

I create abstract traditional furniture. My love for craft lies in giving form and life to conceptual designs that are conceived in my sketchbook. Traditional furniture is the medium through which I have chosen to embody my work. My main focus is on design; the materials play a supporting role by adding texture, depth, and helping my work retain its identity as furniture. While design is my priority, I also strive to maintain functionality in my pieces because I value the interaction my furniture evokes from people. It's the functionality and traditional design elements that keep the furniture approachable, even though I've pushed it past the orthodoxy of traditional furniture design. This allows my work entrance into daily life, where the pieces are intended to reside.

Marlene Lenker
Paintings & Prints, page 204

My work reflects my response to nature and time. My paintings express my love for landscape, light, and mood. I am governed by my intuition and instinct, capturing a moment felt. I work with acrylic, mixed media, and collage on canvas, paper, and board. Commissions are welcomed. Collections include: Arthur Young; Oppenheimer Fund; Lever Bros.; PepsiCo; Kidder Peabody; Warner-Lambert; Merrill Lynch; Horcht; Pfizer; Hoffman-Laroche; and Johnson & Johnson. Publications include: *Bridging Time and Space*, 1999; *Who's Who in America; American Artists; Women Artists; World Women; International Art*; and *The Art of Layering: Making Connections*. My work has been featured in previous Guild sourcebooks. The Winn Devon Art Group, international art publishers, publish my work as limited editions and open-end editions.

GUILD SOURCEBOOKS: *Designer's 10, 11, 12, 13, 14, 15; Residential Art 1, 2, 3, 4, 5, 6*

Mark S. Levin
Furniture & Floor Coverings, pages 95, 104

I build furniture because I love the process; from the gestation and first sketch to the hours of sanding—if I'm sucking wood dust I'm living my dream. I work with solid hardwoods because of their intrinsic value and prowess as a raw material. Hardwoods also give me room for error and spontaneity as I sculpt. The theme that runs through my work is the perfection of nature's small wonders; leaves, flowers, fruit, seashells, etc. A good day is when I look at one of my pieces, then at an acorn on my collection shelf and think, not bad, I did okay...That little acorn still humbles me though.

COLLECTIONS: D. & N. Wolf, Cincinnati, OH; P. & E. Snyderman, Chicago, IL; L. Garfunkle, Nashville, TN; Occidental Petroleum, Oklahoma City, OK

EXHIBITIONS: *Outside the Ordinary*, 2009, Cincinnati Art Museum; *SOFA Chicago*, 2008, 2006, Chicago, IL; *Show Me Your Drawers*, 2006, Furniture Society, Indianapolis, IN;

AWARDS: *American Craft Council Juror*, 2004, New York, NY; *NICHE Awards, First Place Furniture*, 2003, 2002, Philadelphia, PA;

PUBLICATIONS: *Woodwork*, Spring 2009; *500 Tables*, 2009, Lark Publications

GUILD SOURCEBOOKS: *The Guild 2; Residential Art 1, 2, 3, 4, 5, 6*

Linda Leviton
Wall Art / Metal, pages 389, 392, 393

Shown are two installations: One from the *Patterns of Nature* series, which combines etched metal and curved wood frames, and the other from the *Over and Under* series. Both installations are designed in a modular format, which allow them to be customized for their respective settings.

COMMISSIONS: The Federal Reserve Board, St. Louis, MO; The Glimcher Group, Columbus, OH; The World Bank, Washington, DC; Northeastern University, Boston, MA; One Shell Square, New Orleans; Wells Fargo, Des Moines, IA; The Hartford Insurance Company, Hartford, CT; Abbott Northwestern Hospital, Minneapolis, MN; Shades of Green, Walt Disney World, Orlando, FL; Boulder Community Hospital, Boulder, CO; Ross Heart Hospital, Columbus, OH; Kaiser Permanente, Pasadena, CA; Northwestern Mutual, Milwaukee, WI; Nestle/Ralston, St. Louis, MO; State of Ohio, Columbus; Med Central Hospital, Mansfield, OH; Akron/Summit County Public Library, Akron, OH; Kansas University Medical Center, Kansas City, MO; Northwest Airlines, Detroit, MI; Columbus Metropolitan Library, Columbus, OH

EXHIBITIONS: SOFA Chicago, 2004–2008

PUBLICATIONS: *Color on Metal*, 2001

Artist Statements

Lisette T. Lichtenstein
Paintings & Prints, page 205

My background is in graphic design, and I work in encaustic and oil. Encaustic is a pigmented beeswax and damar resin mixture that is applied to and subtracted from a stabilized surface in sheer, multiple layers that are each fused together with a heat source. It is a medium that dates back to the Egyptians, predating oils. My paintings are a body of changing ideas, with a focus on form, color, and composition. Other constant concerns are illusion and the question of beauty, figurative versus abstraction, motion, and texture. I am working toward an honest and serious expression of art. My work has been privately collected. Please visit my website, www.lisettelichtenstein.com, to see more of my paintings.

GUILD SOURCEBOOKS: *Architectural & Interior Art 21; Residential Art 4, 5*

Åndria Linn
Paintings & Prints, page 206

I fill my canvases with fields of colors, shapes, and textures, aiming to preserve the joy and beauty of life, artistically enhancing the environments in which we live, work, and play. Although objective in nature, each piece symbolizes stories about relationships, social and community issues, or matters of the heart. The titles I choose imply these themes. With acrylic mediums I create paintings of varying sizes and styles reflecting my present journey, or fulfilling clients' guidelines and requests. My works have been commissioned for both residences and businesses across the U.S. and abroad. My paintings are available as original works and also as giclée reproductions. I am able to work within every budget. I welcome challenge and love interacting with my clients during the creative process. To view my catalogue, resume, awards, shows, and work history, I invite you to visit my website, andrialinn.com.

Lisa Kesler Studio
Paintings & Prints, page 207

I earned my B.F.A. from the University of Illinois, where I majored in painting. I have created original acrylic paintings, mixed-media paintings, and linoleum block prints in my unique signature style for twenty years. In my artwork, I explore color, surface pattern, and texture. My most recent paintings, with stylized images of nature, reflect the rural environment where I live. I find inspiration in my environment, as well as in the creative process and the materials I use. My art can be found in private and corporate collections throughout the country.

COLLECTIONS: Carle Clinic, Champaign, IL; Carle Cancer Center, Urbana, IL; Herman Miller Marketplace, Zeeland, MI; Golden Nugget Casino, Las Vegas, NV; Alexis Hotel, Seattle, WA; Riversoft Corporation, San Francisco, CA; Eli Lilly, Indianapolis, IN; Overlake Medical Center, Kirkland, WA

PRICING: Wholesale prices range from $150 to $4,000. Call for specific quote.

Fred Lisaius
Paintings & Prints, page 208

In my paintings I use both naturalistic imagery and manmade pattern to represent nature and human nature. It shows how they coexist and overlay, how they are different yet the same. One of the most satisfying things for me as an artist is when someone makes a connection to my work. I strive for the universal in my paintings because I want my work to resonate with everyone at some level. My paintings have shown in museums and art galleries around the country. I have completed over sixty-five corporate and private commissions. I strive to create artwork that brings something special to the project and fulfills the clients' desires.

COMMISSIONS: Evergreen Hospital, Kirkland, WA; Nordstrom, Chicago, IL; Amazon, Seattle, WA; Hilton Hotels, Hilton of America; University of Washington, Seattle

COLLECTIONS: Boston Scientific, Natick, MA; Swedish Hospital, Seattle, WA; Ex Officio, Seattle, WA; American Contract Designers, New York, NY

Cathy Locke
Paintings & Prints, page 209

I explore the colors and textures in nature. My work is all about transformation. By distilling down the elements I find in nature, I am able to transform reality into more of an abstraction. I work in oil, cold wax, mixed media, acrylic, and pastel. Movement and expression are an important part of my work. I will often let paint run down a canvas and even destroy a completed part of the painting. The emotional concept of not being able to control a situation is all part of my painting philosophy. In my work I often use modeling paste, acrylic polymer, or cold wax products to build up textures. I will then layer a painting with thin washes of paint. My painting process has to do with the building of layers of paint to create depth and rich color.

Margaret Lockwood
Paintings & Prints, page 210

My paintings are about noticing and caring. They are responses to my appreciation of the fragile beauty of remembered trees and the peacefulness of fleeting light and color across the fields and in the clouds above. I am deeply concerned with the layers of connection between our external world and that of our inner worlds, and how we relate to and are informed by our precious environment and each other, as well as our hopes and memories. I am continually seeking a voice to communicate through my work, as well as my life. The choice to be a vital part of my community and to maintain wonder for my surroundings informs and enriches my work. I want to make visible the mysterious atmosphere of landscapes and spaces within us, our spiritual homes. Each of us is alone, ultimately. Understanding this solitude may bring feelings of sadness, but knowing that this is common to all of us can be profoundly reassuring. We can feel connected to our world if we notice. We can feel connected to those who are with us now, along with those who came before and those who are yet to be, if we care. I hope there are some who can feel this mysterious yearning mixed with wonder in my work.

Artist Statements

Rob Lorenson
Sculpture / Non-Representational, pages 290, 291

My studio produces works in stainless steel, Corten®, painted aluminum, and bronze. The scale ranges from small tabletop works to pieces over sixteen feet high. The methodology behind my work is to create a compositionally rich interplay of modernist elements that are exceptionally crafted, removing the hand of the artist. The purpose of this is to further emphasize the compositional qualities of the work. I also intend to make the work look manufactured, as though it were itself an industrial product, like the industrial forms that originally influenced it. Works have been placed in over seventy-five collections in residential, corporate, municipal, and educational settings. My scope of services includes design, fabrication, transportation, and installation of all works that I produce. The wholesale price range of my works is from $1,000 to $100,000. Call for a printed catalog.

COMMISSIONS: Boca Raton, FL; Sarasota, FL; Arlington, MA; and Culpepper, VA

Susan Leslie Lumsden
Wall Art / Fiber, page 369

My large-scale work is appropriate for most public facilities as well as the voluminous spaces in many homes today. I work primarily in silk and high-quality cottons that I dye and print. The use of textiles helps tame bouncing acoustics while providing a powerful aesthetic message. The bull's-eye design I often utilize affords a homogenization of hues creating soothing color blends that travel and direct the eye. Closer inspection delivers another layer of detail in my well-executed, award-winning free-motion stitching. Where appropriate, the backs are as exciting as the faces, often incorporating dynamic surface design techniques that wow the viewer. My extensive exhibition history has garnered many awards while building an appreciative audience nationally for my distinctive style.

COMMISSIONS/COLLECTIONS: Barnes Jewish Hospital, St. Louis, MO; Missouri State University, Springfield, MO; Missouri Dept. of Conservation, West Plains, MO

PRICING: $200-275/ SF

GUILD SOURCEBOOKS: *Residential Art 5*

Elizabeth MacDonald
Murals, Tiles & Wall Reliefs, pages 156, 163

I produce tile paintings that suggest the patina of age. Layering color onto thin, textured stoneware achieves a surface that combines the subtlety of nature with the formality of a grid. These compositions are suitable for either in or out-of-doors and take the form of freestanding columns, wall panels, or architectural installations. Attached to 0.25" luan with silicone, the tiles (often 3.5" square) weigh approximately 1.75 pounds per square foot, are durable, and require a minimum of maintenance. I enjoy working with the requirements of clients and can produce small- or large-scale work. In 1999 I was presented with the Governor's award for visual art. During the last twenty years, my commissions include private installations, as well as the following: Dartmouth-Hitchcock Hospital, Lebanon, NH; Conrad Hotel, Hong Kong; Mayo Clinic Chapel, Scottsdale, AZ; and Nobu Restaurant, New York, NY.

466

Bettina Madini
Paintings & Prints, page 211

I was born in Berlin, Germany. In 1992, I started a career in the corporate world in Luxemburg. The year 1998 was a turning point in my life as I started taking art classes at the Ecole des Arts Contemporains in Luxemburg. In 2003, I moved to New York City, where I continued my art education at the National Academy School of Fine Arts. I have been living and working in Wisconsin as an artist since 2004. Most of my work is abstract and has a dreamlike and expressive quality. Color is my inspiration and passion. My art comes from inside, as energy manifesting through me on the canvas. The "orchestration" often shows powerful hues standing next to delicate pastels, provoking the light and leading the viewer into an inspiring world. I work in acrylics, watercolors, and pastels. My paintings can be found in corporate and private collections in Europe and the United States.

Marc Maiorana
Architectural Elements, page 33

Iron Design Company was established to promote modern designs in hand-formed iron objects, transforming bold materials into items that are inviting and inspirational to live with. The design process and results are influenced by the reverent sequence of steel manufacture, beginning with mass and drawing down and down and down into endless line. Similar to a smithy, with a number of modern technical conveniences, we use heat, hammer, and hydraulics to form raw materials into shapes rooted in our design principles. Special attention is given to line uniformity and edge treatment, resulting in an elegance often unassociated with a structural building material.

Judy Mandolf
Fine Art Photography, page 85

Although eclectic in subject and palette, my work tends to be peaceful and uncluttered, perhaps to offset an often chaotic world. (Someone once wrote, "Every doctor should prescribe take two Mandolfs in the morning.") Most images are photo based. They are then computer manipulated, printed on watercolor paper, mounted on wood panel, and coated with acrylic gel. Some are combined with encaustic (hot wax) painting and collage. I strive to produce art that doesn't look "digital."

EXHIBITIONS: Sony International Fine Art, 2006; Adobe Digital Imaging, 2004–2006; MacWorld Digital Art, 2003 and 2001; Seybold Digital Art, 2002

PUBLICATIONS: *Design Graphics Portfolio*, 2006, 2005; *Going Digital*, 2005; *Advance Guide to Digital Photography*, 2005; *Photography* (college textbook), 2002; *Secrets of Award Winning Digital Photographers*, 2002; numerous digital photography and fine art magazines in the U.S. and China

GUILD SOURCEBOOKS: *Residential Art 6*

Artist Statements

Brigid Manning-Hamilton
Liturgical Art
Wall Art / Mixed & Other Media, pages 127, 432

In my textile-based mixed-media art I make decorative work to please the eye,; contemplative art to provide focus for thoughts or worship, and functional objects to add joy to daily life and rituals. I push the synergy between materials and technique to give shape to visions, feelings, and stories. My signature use of transparent layers and shifting light brings my work to life and reflects the idea that each viewer of my work will see it slightly differently. I have created pieces for houses of worship, schools, and individuals in Indiana and beyond. I enjoy working with clients, within their parameters, to develop their ideas and wishes for artwork to enhance their lives and space, realizing those ideas in forms that speak to their beholders. I'm pleased when the occupant of an interior corporate space tells me that looking at my work transports her to the Maine woods.

COMMISSIONS: Trinity Episcopal Church, IN; Fanning/Howey Associates, IN; 1st Presbyterian Church of Monticello, IN

PRICING: Single-sided wall-hung works from $115/sf. Stoles from $250, chasubles from $1000. Other pricing available on request.

Mark Eric Gulsrud
Architectural Glass
Architectural Glass, pages 37, 58

A self-employed artist/designer for thirty-five years, I work primarily in architectural, cast, and laminated glass. Integrated harmoniously with the architectural statement and the natural environment, art has the potential to ease stress, induce a sense of calm, and enrich lives. I am personally involved in all phases of design, fabrication, and installation. Whether in a public, corporate, or liturgical space, I seek to use a blend of the best traditional and state-of-the-art techniques. Accustomed to collaborating with clients, architects, committees, and general contractors—often with different agendas—I strive for all to arrive at a unified goal without sacrificing the aesthetics of a commission. I consider my artwork a visual point of departure, as each individual brings his or her own perspective. As with cloud watching, one is free to discover an unanticipated aspect, to see something new within the familiar.

GUILD SOURCEBOOKS: *GUILD 3, 4; Architect's 7, 8, 9, 10, 11, 12, 13, 14, 15; Architectural & Interior Art 16, 17, 18, 19, 20, 21, 22, 23*

Marie Martin
Paintings & Prints, page 236

My artistic goal is to enhance lives by causing dynamic reactions through use of color. Color is a catalyst for a wide range of emotional responses: attraction, joy, comfort, aggression, to name only a few. Color plays an important role in the continuation of life. Birds' feathers, camouflaging, eye color, body blushing—all are powerful sparks. Colors have proven effects on behavior, including red as agitator, blue as soother. My hope is to convey the power inherent in color so that people feel a range of emotions while viewing my work. Contact martin.art@mac.com.

COLLECTIONS: Allstate, Aliso Viejo, CA; Judicate West, Santa Ana, CA; Merrill Corp., Irvine, CA; Sarnoff Legal Technologies, Irvine/San Diego, CA

EXHIBITIONS: Second City Council Gallery, Long Beach, CA; Bistango Gallery/Studio, Irvine, CA; Borders, Costa Mesa, CA; Huntington Beach City Hall, CA; Lauryn Taylor Art, Carmel, CA; Marriott Hotel Fashion Island, Newport Beach, CA; Studio Gallery, Irvine, CA; Wells Fargo, Laguna Beach, CA; Whittier Law School, Santa Ana, CA

Barry Masteller
Paintings & Prints, page 212

When I begin a painting, I am rarely sure how it will resolve. It is in itself a part of a greater whole; that is, it has something in it of the work before it. In this I believe painting is like language and paintings like words, each making up a kind of vocabulary whose meaning becomes clearer or at least more complete with each subsequent work. Please visit my website for additional images and information: www.barrymasteller.com.

COLLECTIONS: Palm Springs Art Museum; Crocker Art Museum, Sacramento, CA; San Jose Museum of Art; Seven Bridges Foundation, Greenwich, CT; Monterey Museum of Art, Monterey, CA; Pebble Beach Co; Prudential Insurance, NYC; Roche Bioscience / Syntex Corp; San Jose, CA; Bank of America World Headquarters, San Francisco, CA; Price Waterhouse, NYC; Sapporo Royal Hotel, Japan; Crowne Plaza Hotel, NYC; Cypress Inn, Carmel, CA; Santa Cruz Museum of Art; Siemans AG, Beijing; Veritas Software; National Steinbeck Center, Salinas, CA

Bill Masterpool
Furniture & Floor Coverings, page 105

An important aspect of my work is not to make furniture in the usual sense of the word but to create unique sculptural pieces that are aesthetically interesting. Of equal importance, however, is that the structural integrity and functional nature of the piece not be sacrificed for its aesthetic appeal. The result is a never-ending search for maximum correspondence between structure and art, and form and purpose.

EXHIBITIONS: Western Design Conference, 2007, Jackson Hole, WY; 2006, 2004, Cody, WY, and 2005, Santa Fe, NM; National Ornamental and Miscellaneous Metals Association, Ernest Wiemann Top Job Award (Gold), forged furniture, 2005

GUILD SOURCEBOOKS: *Residential Art 6*

Matteo Randi Mosaics
Liurgical Art
Mosaics, pages 127, 139

My work is born out of a combination of longtime interests and ongoing investigations into the three-dimensionality of mosaic and the effects of mixing natural with semi-natural elements, such as marble, pebbles, and shells with glass and metal. I create mosaics in both classical and modern designs while adhering to traditional mosaic working methods—each tessera is cut by hand with the hammer and hardie, the same tools used by Roman craftsmen over 2,000 years ago. I feel this is the only way to maximize the natural variations found in stone and glass, creating a distinct light and texture unique to each piece. Having worked with mosaic for over twenty years, I can provide my clients with the knowledge and the experience to create successful custom projects for homes, places of worship, and public spaces.

AWARDS: Best 2-D, 2008, Mosaic Arts International, Miami, FL; Vincent Palumbo Prize, 2005, Italian Cultural Society, Washington, DC

467

Artist Statements

Bonnie McCann
Fine Art Photography, page 86

For me, the starting point for each image occurs in the field. Once I return to my studio, I let the photographic image tell me where to go next. Using both Photoshop and Corel Painter, I can subtly or dramatically alter each photograph, striving to create images that will evoke memories for my viewers. From layering techniques to alteration of colors and intensities to blending and painting, I find within the digital toolbox an endless array of techniques. Additionally, digital creation allows the end user to choose final size and printing medium. Popular choices are heavy watercolor paper and canvas. I also do commissioned portrait paintings. Starting with a photograph, I work closely with my clients to ensure their final painting is just what they were hoping for. These future heirlooms are for the discriminating clients who wants more than a captured moment.

Jennifer C. McCurdy
Objects, page 170

I work with high-fire translucent porcelain because it has a smooth, stony surface, and it can convey the qualities of light and shadow that I wish to express. I work with terra cotta clay with a saturated metallic black glaze because it is a visual opposite of the porcelain and because I can create pieces in a larger scale than what is feasible with the porcelain. After I throw my vessel on the potter's wheel, I alter the form to set up a movement of soft shadow. When the clay is leather hard, I carve patterns to add energy and counterpoint. I fire the porcelain to cone 10, where it becomes non-porous and extremely hard. I fire the terra cotta to cone 4. I received a B.F.A. from Michigan State University and have been working as an artist ever since. I currently maintain my studio in Vineyard Haven, Massachusetts. My work is priced from $150 to $3,000.

COLLECTIONS: The Smithsonian's Renwick Gallery, Washington, DC; Everson Museum of Art, Syracuse, NY; Museum of Art & Archeology, University of Missouri, Columbia, MO; Tweed Museum of Art, Duluth, MN; Racine Art Museum, Racine, WI; Lancaster Museum of Art, Lancaster, PA

Susan McGehee
Wall Art / Metal, page 394

Instead of fiber, I weave with wire and metals. I continue to employ the traditional tools, techniques, and patterns from when I worked in fiber. Weaving metals allows me to form a piece into a dimensional shape that will retain its form and undulating vitality. I primarily weave with anodized aluminum wire because even though a piece looks like copper, the anodized aluminum wire has the advantage of being lightweight while maintaining a vibrant color and shine. The pieces are easy to install and maintain. I enjoy the fact that people will assume a piece is fiber and then are astonished to discover it is woven metal.

COMMISSIONS: Nokia, Burlington, MA; Wells Fargo, Minneapolis, MN; American Family Insurance, Madison, WI, and Phoenix, AZ; Lawson Commons lobby, St. Paul, MN; St. Joseph's Medical Center, Milwaukee, WI; Fantasy Springs Convention Center, Indio, CA; Pauma Valley Golf Club, Pauma Valley, CA.

GUILD SOURCEBOOKS: Designer's 12, 13, 14, 15; Architectural & Interior Art 16, 17, 18, 19, 20, 21, 22, 23; Residential Art 1, 3, 4, 5, 6

PRICING: Trade professionals, please call. Retail prices are listed on my website.

468

Cynthia McKean
Sculpture / Non-Representational, pages 292, 293

I grew up in the West—Montana and Wyoming. The West is where there are so few people that everyone counts. It is also where one is inclined to be more in tune with one's own natural environment because one is closer to it. The horizon there is chiseled out against the sky. Lines are sharp. Space is forever. Colors are strong. I believe that all of this influences my art. In my work I dream of natural and built environments, and how they might interact. Sometimes the results lean toward Mother Nature and sometimes they are meant to complement Her. Many ideas frolic without particular meaning, but a few are very serious. I think in terms of cutting through space, blocking space, and what the results might be. Sometimes I see the object, sometimes it's the space around the object, but it's usually a combination of the two. Steel is a marvelous medium. Strong and pliable, it speaks to me. If I work it, respect it, and treat it gently, it will reward me by telling my story to others as well. If people walk around, touch, and occasionally climb my work, I consider it a success. It means they have connected with it. It is talking to them.

Megan McKeithan
Murals, Tiles & Wall Reliefs, page 157

I paint big beautiful murals on walls or ceilings, in homes or businesses, in the public sphere, or with community participation. More than just paintings, these pieces create the atmosphere, energy, and environment my clients desire. With a background in public and community art, I have worked all over the country with clients, architects, designers, and community members to create beautiful art that is perfect for the client and ideal for the architectural location. I paint murals on site or on canvas for installation anywhere.

COMMISSIONS: Carmel and Monterey, CA; Evergreen, CO; Panama City Beach, FL; Acworth, Atlanta, Alpharetta, Decatur, Duluth, Fayetteville, Gainesville, Kennesaw, Lawrenceville, Marietta, Norcross, Roswell, Savannah, Stone Mountain, Suwanee, Thomasville, and Woodstock, GA; Natchez, MS; Lawrence, KS; Boston, Cambridge, and Wellesley, MA; Newburgh, ME; Asheville, Greensboro, Harker's Island, High Point, Raleigh, and Winston-Salem, NC; New York, NY; Cincinnati, OH; Chattanooga, TN; Campbellsport, WI; Fortaleza, Ciera, Brazil

Kathleen Lee Meehan
Public Art, page 255

As a pragmatic, seasoned public artist, I believe public art should have layers of information that appeal to a broad range of ages, cultures, and intellects. Each new project begins with extensive research about area history, site use, and the local community. Material considerations include regional climate, maintenance issues, and vandalism potential. During my twenty-year career, I have completed over twenty-five site-specific public art commissions with budgets up to $800,000 in a variety of materials and processes, including fire, water, glass, mosaic, steel, concrete, and granite, often with text. On budget and on time: that's my mantra, and I have a perfect record due to finely tuned project management skills and attention to detail. I can read blueprints, communicate well both orally and in writing, and respect every member of the team: public art manager, architect, engineer, facilities personnel, landscape architect, and subcontractors.

Artist Statements

Darcy Meeker
Wall Art / Metal, pages 395, 402

Flame gives my copper a shimmering, iridescent patina that changes throughout the day. Detailed hand tooling twinkles over harmonious shapes, and paint highlights the design. My goal is lively experience for both a passing glance and leisurely perusal. I also work and design in stone, clay, fabric, neon, and fiber optics and write, speak, and give workshops on these art forms and healing through making art.

COMMISSIONS: *Shall We Gather*, 2006, Lutheran Church, Blacksburg, VA, copper, 18' x 10'; *Shifting Sun with Birds*, 2005, Seattle, WA, copper, 8' x 8'; *Mountain Spirit*, 2003, Fincastle, VA, copper, 13' x 5'; *Elephant Vine*, 2000, General Electric, Schenectady, NY, 36' x 14' x 2'; *Peace, Love, and Serenity*, 2004, Yucaipa, CA, aluminum; *Wedding Present* and *Source*, 1993–4, Blacksburg, VA, stone

EXHIBITIONS: Galleries, colleges, and art centers in VA, OR, TN, CO, PA, NY, FL, SC, AZ, TX, KS, NC, and Washington, DC

PUBLICATIONS: *Southwest Art, Dwell, Sculptural Pursuit, Best in U.S. Sculptors and Artisans, Fine Art Connoisseur*

GUILD SOURCEBOOKS: *Architectural & Interior Art 20, 21, 23, Residential Art 5*

Peter W. Michel
Sculpture / Representational, page 337

My work represents a stand for the possibility that art is for the expression of joy, aliveness, love, and relationship. Through color, humor, the play of ideas, and the effects of light and space, the viewer is invited to access his own spirit of playfulness and relatedness. From small tabletop and wall pieces to monumental outdoor public art, my work is refined with the aid of computer software and produced with computer-controlled waterjet or laser-cutting methods.

COLLECTIONS: Oakton Sculpture Park, Des Plaines, IL; Wandell Sculpture Garden, Urbana, IL

EXHIBITIONS: Art In Public Places—Stamford Downtown, 2006; Sculpture Internationale, 2002, Atlanta; Pier Walk, 2000, 1999, Chicago; Chesterwood Museum, 1994, Stockbridge, MA

PUBLICATIONS: *The Sculpture of Peter W. Michel*, 2008; *Fall in Love with Your Community*, 2007; *Educational Psychology, 8th Edition*, 2002

GUILD SOURCEBOOKS: *Architectural & Interior Art 16, 20, 22; Residential Art 6*

Mija
Wall Art / Fiber, page 370

Mija recycles vintage clothing to create intricate and involved "green" fabric art that is alive with depth, motion, and the illusion of radiance. Our one-of-a-kind contemporary fiber art adds texture and beauty to any environment, creating stunning visual focal points. Mounted on stretcher frames, the three dimensionality of the work is enhanced and allows for a variety of display options. We specialize in large installations and have extensive experience with commissions in all palettes and sizes. We enjoy collaborating with clients, are particularly skilled at matching and developing color schemes, and are adept at communicating with customers. Our goal is to interpret their vision into art that coherently integrates an environment and complements the space. For more information please visit www.mijafiberart.com.

COMMISSIONS: Private commissions nationwide

COLLECTIONS: 60 North Market, Asheville, NC; Acupuncture Center of Asheville

AWARDS: Winner, Fiber-pieced/quilted, 2005, NICHE

GUILD SOURCEBOOKS: *Architectural & Interior Art 18; Residential Art 3*

Richard A. Moore III
Sculpture / Representational, page 338

When sculpting, I prefer to render my work in a highly realistic way, often combining elements of surrealism and stylization. I try to find the perfect balance of classic sculpture, blended with a modern twist, to create a seamless style unique to myself. The size of my work has a wide range, from something you could hold in the palm of your hand, to my largest creation, which is well over nine feet tall. Along with trying to capture the physical grace of the human form, I also try and keep things interesting by capturing one of the more primal emotions that all people are capable of expressing. All of my pieces are traditionally cast in eternal bronze, for a true classic feel. To see the rest of my work, obtain pricing, propose commissions, or just get more information about my work, please visit www.rmooresculptures.com.

Lisa Mote
Wall Art / Glass, pages 379, 382

My art glass creations fuse color, light, texture, and depth with fluid movement that stimulates the senses and excites the imagination. The unique, sculptural effect of certain pieces is accentuated by the integration of metal supports. As an artist I am committed to working closely with my clients to create distinctive designs that express individuality. I have been fortunate to have had the opportunity to create numerous large-scale corporate installations, as well as works of art for private collectors.

COMMISSIONS: Reid Hospital, 2008, Richmond, IN; Ciba Vision, 2008, Johns Creek, GA; AIG, 2008, Wilmington, DE; Coca Cola, 2008, Atlanta, GA; Kaiser Permanente, 2007, Lithonia, GA; Fleetcor, 2007, Norcross, GA; Brightworth Company, 2007, Buckhead, GA; Sprint/Nextel, 2007, Norcross, GA

Sabiha Mujtaba
Architectural Elements, page 34

Pupils dilate, eyes soften, a subtle smile appears, the heart is moved, and the hand reaches out to touch: that is how we experience beauty. That's how I want my work to be viewed. My design approach is intuitive; an idea appears, and I allow it to gel. Through osmosis, I draw inspiration from a collective knowledge base. For commissioned work I enjoy partnering with my clients in the design process, keeping their needs at the forefront. I respectfully interpret cultural images, and take guidance from nature and the "anthropomorphic behavior" of furniture itself. Using traditional joinery, as well as hand and power tools, I create a sturdy, uninterrupted flow of form in the functional piece. I have participated in American Craft Council Shows and various invitational and juried national shows. I am a recipient and finalist of several NICHE awards.

PRICING: $1,000 to $20,000

Artist Statements

Joseph Murphy
Furniture & Floor Coverings, page 115

I design and build wood furniture by hand, one piece at a time. My work features clean lines, subtle curves, and unexpected touches. Whether I'm using a pencil, bandsaw, or spokeshave, I love to create the countless details that add up to a harmonious mix of form, material, and presence. These details, such as delicate drawer pulls, hand-planed surfaces, or artful inlays, are a delight to explore up close, as much with the hand as with the eye. Whether it is a table, bench, or any other form, I strive to make pieces that I would want to hang out with for a long time.

COMMISSIONS: St. Anne's School of Annapolis, 2007

COLLECTIONS: Private collections in Maryland, Pennsylvania, and California

EXHIBITIONS: Philadelphia Museum of Art Craft Show, 2008

AWARDS: Wharton Esherick Prize for Excellence in Wood, Philadelphia Museum of Art Craft Show, 2008

Murphy Kuhn
Fine Art Photography
Fine Art Photography, pages 6, 87

Said of my work: "Glorious forms, bursting with electric color and energy, these wondrous digital images materialize into being as if from another world, we look upon an entire macrocosm of the artist's own making. The mirror of our collective minds are pure and vast, as we are reminded by his images. One wonders from where they emerge." I realized I had frustration with objects as they exist, and I needed to make them as I wanted them to be. I live in this world, but another lives inside me.

COMMISSIONS: UBS Financial (permanent installation), 2008, Santa Barbara, CA

EXHIBITIONS: Palm Loft Gallery, 2008, Carpentaria, CA; Corridan Gallery, 2007-2008, Santa Barbara, CA; Faulkner Gallery, 2007-2008, Santa Barbara, CA; Oxygen Gallery, 2006, St. Paul, MN

AWARDS: Best of Show, 2008, International Photography Awards; Second Place (Digitally Enhanced) 2008, International Photography Awards; Third Place (People's Choice), 2008, PX3 Paris; Juror Awards, 2008, Faulkner Gallery; Honorable Mentions (Landscape and Digitally Enhanced), 2007, International Photography Awards; Honorable Mentions, 2007, PX3; Juror Award, 2007, Faulkner Gallery; Third Place (Digitally Enhanced and Fine Art), 2006, Intl. Photography Awards

Amy J. Musia
Sculpture / Representational, page 339

For over thirty years, I have successfully worked with art committees, architects, engineers, and designers in creating works of art for healthcare, institutional, public, and corporate clients. Noted as a versatile designer/craftsman, I am known for contemporary columns and capitals. Because site-specific works call for different approaches, I work in many styles and mediums. Whether working in two or three dimensions, wall or free standing, my work is primarily organic, architectural, representational, and symbolic in nature—somtimes minimal and abstract. I have experience working in a variety of environments, and expertise in working with building codes and complex budgets. I am a seasoned arist working in myriad media and approaches. Green art, public art, and healing art are of special interest. I always welcome new challenges and approaches for works of art in any environment.

COMMISSIONS: Evansville, IN: Vectren, Old National Bank, Signature School, VNA Hospice, Deaconess Hospital, Evansville-Vanderburgh Public Library, and others

COLLECTIONS: City of Evansville, IN; Tochigi City, Japan

GUILD SOURCEBOOKS: *Architectural & Interior Art 22, 23; Residential Art 6*

Musickstudio
Murals, Tiles & Wall Reliefs, page 158

Brilliant, non-fading colors, varying effects according to angle of light, and weatherproof durability characterize large-scale enameled metal artworks. Enameling involves applying powdered glass to metals, firing, and repeating the process multiple times, creating layers of images. Integrating architecture, setting, media, and concept, my site-specific murals evoke a spirit and sense of place. My pieces are in exterior and interior academic, nature center, liturgical, hotel, and residential exterior and interior spaces. I carry out all design, research, and fabrication. I value working closely with clients and collaborating with design professionals. From studies and work abroad I have gained an international perspective. My work is grounded in celebration of and service to wild nature and human culture.

COMMISSIONS: Colorado State University; Mesa State College; Fairmont State University; Cheyenne Mountain Zoo; Great Sand Dunes National Park; Michelham Priory, England

COLLECTIONS: Grand Canyon National Park; De La Salle Novitiate and School, Dublin, Ireland; private collections

Natalie Blake Studios
Murals, Tiles & Wall Reliefs, pages 141, 159

My new line of undulating porcelain wall tiles are handcrafted and individually carved. Twelve or fourteen-inch square and wired for eight possible points of orientation, they can be hung in any formation you create, diagonal or square. The studio can assist you in creating an abstract or contiguous design of your own choosing. Flat-edged tiles are also available for grouting installations. I've been working with the lidded vessel for the past fourteen years. My designs are inspired by aquatic, botanical, industrial, and mythical elements. My pieces are thrown, carved, and handbuilt in porcelain, and fired with stone-matte surfaces in rich colors of ivory, celedon, bronze, red, turqoise, and black/brown. My work has been acquired by the San Angelo Museum of Art, the Wheaton College Museum, has received several awards, and is currently shown in New Zealand, Australia, the Caribbean, and across the continental U.S. View my entire body of work at www.natalieblake.com. Large-scale wall sculptures by commission.

GUILD SOURCEBOOKS: *Residential Art 6*

Nathaniel Hester Fine Arts
Paintings & Prints, page 213

These abstract images, which are rare visual delicacies, feature bold compositions, jeweled surfaces, and a luminous, vibrant palette. They embrace highly contemporary design motifs and, at the same time, are created with the most time-honored traditions of extensive successive layerings of opaque scumbles and translucent glazes. These pictures are exquisite additions to any public or private space and are available in any color and size.

COLLECTIONS: Fogg Art Museum; The University of Miami, FL; Amity Art Foundation; Wunderman Group; New York Public Library; Allen Memorial Art Museum, Oberlin College, Newark Public Library

EXHIBITIONS: Olin Gallery, Roanoke College; Faulkner Gallery, Louisburg College; The Gallery at Penn College, Pennsylvania College of Technology; Mooney Center Gallery, College of New Rochelle

Artist Statements

National Sculptors' Guild
Public Art, pages 256, 257

The National Sculptors' Guild is an association of its design team and nationally recognized sculptors chosen for their outstanding artistic abilities and varied style. Working as a team under the leadership of Executive Director John Kinkade, NSG artists closely coordinate with cities, municipalities, corporations, and private institutions across the country to successfully enhance indoor and outdoor venues with creative design and innovative artwork since 1992. NSG members are: Gary Alsum, Kevin Box, Kathleen Caricof, Chapel, Tim Cherry, Dee Clements, Jane DeDecker, Carol Gold, Bruce Gueswel, Denny Haskew, Mark Leichliter, Leo E. Osborne, Louise Peterson, Sandy Scott, Michael Warrick, and C.T. Whitehouse.

GUILD SOURCEBOOKS: *Architect's 9, 10, 11, 12, 14, 15; Architectural & Interior Art 16, 17, 20, 21, 22, 23*

David Nerwen
Wall Art / Fiber, page 371

My main interest in my art of thirty-eight years has always been symmetrical and asymmetrical hard-line geometrics. I have a color palate of 480 commercially dyed wool tapestry yarn, which I hand stitch onto cotton mesh canvas. There is no machinery or any equipment involved except for a needle and wool yarn in my hand. When completed, I stretch and frame my art. Viewed from a distance, my designs have the appearance of paintings. Closer examination reveals subtleties of texture and light. The viewer discovers an intricately woven surface created by patterns of hand stitching. I use a variety of stitches to build my abstract/geometric compositions. Ranging in scale from 9" x 15" to 6' x 6', my framed one-of-a-kind fiber art wall hangings are well suited for both larger corporate interior spaces and smaller intimate settings within the home or office. I create commissioned work and can develop designs to suit a client's individual needs and preferences. I have exhibited in many art galleries and juried art shows, including the Smithsonian Craft Show in Washington, DC, in 2008 and 2006.

GUILD SOURCEBOOKS: *The Guild 5*

Nicholson Blown Glass
Wall Art / Glass, page 383

Our dedication to glass is evident in our attention to detail and quality. We have worked together successfully with galleries since 1979 and have expanded into creating projects for public art, hotels, corporations, churches, and residences. Rick has attended Pilchuck Glass School frequently since 1981, and Janet collaborates with color and design. Our team is prepared to fabricate and install custom commissions from your design or ours on time and within any budget. Our work includes figurative sculpture, sculptural lighting and fountains, and elegant, asymmetrical platter forms for the table, wall, or ceiling. Skills include freehand blowing, hot sculpting, kiln casting, glass fusing, and metal fabrication. Visit www.nicholsonblownglass.com.

COMMISSIONS: Art in Public Places, Sacramento Arts Commission; Twelve Bridges Library, Lincoln, CA; Hunton Williams, Dallas, TX; Weil Gotschal & Manges, Dallas, TX; Ritz Carlton, Shenzhen, China; Kaiser Hospital, Roseville, CA

Bruce A. Niemi
Public Art, pages 258, 259

The stainless steel and bronze sculptures I create are characterized by an uplifting positive nature of aesthetically powerful, graceful forms that create the illusion of movement. My purpose is to stimulate the mind of the viewer, as well as to create a sculpture that complements and harmonizes with its environment. Craftsmanship, structural strength, and public safety are also important elements. My sculptures range from small tabletop pieces to large-scale public art. Currently, I have placed twenty-eight public sculptures throughout the country, as well as numerous private collections. I work well with architects, designers, and developers, and am able to meet budgets and timelines.

COMMISSIONS: West Bend Mutual Insurance Company, West Bend, WI; City of Blue Island, IL; St. Charles Public Library, IL; Mt. St. Mary's Park, St. Charles, IL; Escena Golf Club, Palm Springs, CA; Northern Illinois University, DeKalb, IL; Liberty Property Trust, Hunt Valley, MD

Anthony Novak
Murals, Tiles & Wall Reliefs, page 160

Original designs and transcendent forms in relief sculpture. Some have spiritual themes in the Jewish and Christian faiths. My wall sculpture evokes the Modernist aesthetic where representation is expressed with emotional style and design. With a background in architectural sculpture and ornamental restoration, I am a fabrication specialist, creating works in cast stone and FRGC (Fiberglass Reinforced Gypsum Cement) composites that are less expensive alternatives to bronze. I create all my own molds, casts, and custom patinas. Commissions are welcome for indoor and outdoor works. Prominent commissions include wall sculpture for Christian hospitals and statuary restoration for Belmont University. Catalog at www.anthonynovak.com

COMMISSIONS: Belmont University, Saint Thomas Hospital, Baptist Hospital, and Middle Tennessee Medical Center

EXHIBITIONS: Centennial Arts Center, 2004, Nashville, TN; Union University, 2002, Jackson, TN; The Parthenon, 2001, Nashville, TN

Xavier Nuez
Fine Art Photography, pages 77, 88

Long after dark, I venture deep into mysterious urban settings, seeking out their elusive beauty and splendor. These old, neglected spaces offer up a rich, gritty drama and power that is unknown elsewhere. With the city humming in the background, I find inspiration where there should not be any. Despite their danger, my outings inspire in me a child-like sense of adventure and fantasy—they are determined and intense explorations where, ironically, I find moments of peace in a hectic life.

EXHIBITIONS: Marin Museum of Contemporary Art, CA; Farmington Museum, NM; Virginia Museum of Transportation; Stanford Art Spaces, Stanford University, CA; Schneider Gallery, Chicago; Biddle Gallery, Detroit; Peak Gallery, Toronto

COLLECTIONS: Norfolk Southern Collection; University of Richmond Museum; University of Michigan; City of East Lansing, MI; City of Roanoke, VA; Arts Commission of Greater Toledo, OH; President Vicente Fox of Mexico; Angela Lansbury; Danny DeVito

GUILD SOURCEBOOKS: *Residential Art 6*

Artist Statements

Susan Ogilvie
Paintings & Prints, page 214

Painting the landscape provides the opportunity to explore my connection with nature while creating a personal statement about the beauty I see. The shapes and patterns are what first attract my attention. Fields, structures, waterways—evidence of our partnership with the land—are frequent subjects, although nothing is off limits when there are powerful and interesting shapes to paint. Whether working on location or in the studio, my goal is to capture the soul of the subject with a fresh and emotionally honest approach to composition and color. For me, painting is all about listening, letting go, and enjoying the ride

COLLECTIONS: Totem Lake Hospital, Kirkland, WA; Christidis Lauster Radu Architects, New York, NY; E.C. May & Company, Alexandria, VA; WA State Department of the Military, Olympia, WA; Marriott Corp., Scottsdale, AZ

PRICING: Wholesale prices range from $400 to $4,000

Out of the Mainstream Designs, Inc.
Wall Art / Fiber, page 372

My textiles are contemporary handwoven tapestries, rugs, and wall pieces, individually designed with sensitivity to architectural context, embellishment, and hand-finishing techniques. Each adds warmth, vitality, and a colorful focal point, and facilitates the expression of the client's taste and personality. I have been designing and weaving for more than twenty-eight years and continue to work in traditional and non-traditional fiber techniques. Research in historic textiles, twentieth-century graphic design, and architecture continue to influence my work. The densely interwoven cultural and human histories of my family members and their spontaneous, thoughtful, and happy natures help shape, direct, and inspire my creative process. Currently, my projects involve deconstructing the woven cloth when removed from the loom in an effort to design a surface that changes in texture and line. Prices and samples available through the studio.

GUILD SOURCEBOOKS: *Residential Art 3, 4, 5, 6; Architectural & Interior Art 20, 21, 22, 23*

Zachary Oxman
Public Art, pages 260, 261

For the past twenty years, my goal as a professional artist has been to create extraordinary sculpture that connects the viewer to each work on a visceral level. I combine representational and iconic imagery and infuse a surreal juxtaposition of those elements to create an experience that is at once universally recognizable, yet transcends its literal meaning. Creating in diverse mediums such as stainless steel, bronze, woods, and glass allows me to integrate each sculpture into its distinctive surroundings when working with architects, designers, public art agencies, and synagogues. This approach allows me to capture and give life to the unique qualities that define the client's space or identity. My works range in scale from tabletop to monumental and are collected both publicly and privately.

COMMISSIONS: Eighteen-foot stainless steel exterior entry sculpture, The Times Newspaper, Munster, IN; Twenty-foot stainless steel plaza sculpture, D.C. Arts Project, Washington, DC; Life-size bronze of city founder, Reston, VA; Thirty-foot stainless steel lobby installation, Nova Medical Center, Ashburn, VA; Ark Doors, Washington Hebrew Congregation, Washington, DC

472

PJ Boylan Photography
Fine Art Photography, page 89

My image inventory contains an amazing variety of people, places, and things resulting from my dual passions of travel and photography. Using primarily natural light, I aim for a unique perspective, and one that evokes emotion. My photos have earned more than 50 awards in various categories from the PhotoPictorialists of Milwaukee and Wisconsin Area Camera Clubs Organization. In addition to marketing photos at juried art fairs (examples--Art Fair on the Square, Madison, Wisconsin, sponsored by Madison Museum of Contemporary Art, and the Art Festival sponsored by Boca Raton Museum of Art in Florida), I have participated in many juried art and photography exhibitions. I enjoy working with clients, using the best quality materials to provide limited-edition photos appropriate for healthcare facilities, corporate offices, and residences. I also accept location assignments.

GUILD SOURCEBOOKS: *Residential Art 6*

Ulrich Pakker
Public Art, page 262

Cycles, circles, rejuvenation, and re-use have always been part of my sculptural work. I work to bring together each site's characteristics with my sculpture, joining the surroundings and the art in ever-widening circles to create a different perception of that piece of the earth. My work illustrates the circular qualities of life, the magical transformative powers of water, and the need to capture each moment until it fades away. The universal form of the circle draws the viewer into curvilinear movements of spinning wheels and cyclonic water swirls. The metal circles "dissolve" into water flows. The surge of water completes the circles and evokes an alchemy as stainless steel transforms into liquid and back into metal. The water of my fountains is recycled to fall again—wheels within wheels, circles within circles. With the *Glassflow* series, the "flow" of glass arrests the movement, creating a striking tableau for the viewer.

Pamela Gleave Fine Art
Fine Art Photography, page 93

Chemistry as art does not occur to most people; it is not generally thought of as artistic in nature, but since chemicals are the basic building blocks of our world, why would they not be beautiful? Through my work I have discovered that beauty can be found in the most unlikely places, and may be coaxed out by people who are willing to go beyond the mundane to take a very unique look at the world. I make simple photographs of chemicals and other common household substances taken through a microscope, a process called photomicrography. The photographs, titled *Chemscapes,* are beautiful, otherworldly, and sometimes very surreal. Each viewer has a different vision of what the elements are, how to orient them, and what they mean. They invoke visceral responses, sending viewers off into fantastic landscapes from which they are always reluctant to return.

Artist Statements

Pokey Park
Sculpture / Representational, page 340

My inspiration comes from myths and cultural symbols repeated throughout history, connecting disparate people. My style reflects my belief that life needs to be celebrated with whimsy and attitude. I use the flow of lines and surface patterns to create positive and negative spaces in my sculpture. This creates movement and balance between the parts. I look for the underlying joy in the world to express in my sculpture.

COMMISSIONS: Apponaganset Vineyard, MA; Chanticleer Arboretum, Wayne, PA; Freedom Bank, West Chester and Media, PA; Pyramid Hills Gardens, OH; Sioux Falls Outdoor Campus, SD; Peace Arch Park, Blaine, WA

EXHIBITIONS: *Art for the Mountain Community Sculpture Walk,* Evergreen, CO; *Sculpture on Main,* Marble Falls, TX; *Avenues of Art,* Gillette, WY; *Art on the Plaza,* Sheridan, WY

AWARDS: Honorable Mention, 2008, Impressions, NU Jeannette Hare Art Gallery, West Palm Beach, FL; First Place, 2007, Pot Pourri, Cornell Museum of Art, Delray Beach, FL; Best in Show, 2007, Response to the Muse, West Palm Beach, FL

PUBLICATIONS: *Southwest Art Magazine,* April 2009; *Fine Art Magazine,* Spring 2008; *Telluride Style Magazine,* Winter/Spring 2005-2006

Louise Peterson
Sculpture / Representational, pages 19, 341

Although canine subjects are the basis of most of my work, in recent years I have expanded my subject matter to include horses, cats, bison, and other animals. I often contrast my realistic but stylized animals with abstract architectural elements. My animals are cast in bronze and combined with steel, stone, or wood elements. Sizes range from miniature to monumental.

COLLECTIONS: Numerous museum and public collections including Brookgreen Gardens and the City of Greenville, SC; Benson Sculpture Garden, Loveland, CO; and the Cites of Northglenn and Colorado Springs, CO, Chattanooga, TN, and Gillette and Sheridan, WY

AWARDS: Over one hundred awards including four Best in Shows. Professional memberships include the National Sculpture Society, the Society of Animal Artists, Allied Artists of America, and Hudson Valley Art Association

Pearl Glassworks Ltd.
Architectural Glass, page 59

We are a fine art glass company incorporated in 1987, which specializes in designing and producing custom made, kiln-cast, sandblasted, and painted architectural glass windows and panels. We are accustomed to working closely with architects, interior designers, and private clients to create artwork that speaks to the particular environment, is unique and simply beautiful. Our professional team takes you through the process of design, manufacture, and installation to ensure a lasting and wonderful work of art. Aesthetics, skilled craftsmanship, and transformation of space and light are paramount in our desire to create a magnificent piece, which will settle upon you like the fragrance of freshly mown grass . . . not to be forgotten. Margery Pearl Gurnett, of Pearl Glassworks Ltd., is a nationally recognized glass artist whose public and private commissions can be found everywhere from the White House to major airports in the United States and Canada.

COMMISSIONS: Roberts Wesleyan College, Rochester, NY; Strasenburgh Planetarium, Rochester, NY; Delta Airlines, Salt Lake City, Pittsburgh, Jacksonville, Washington National Airport, Seattle, Houston, Montreal-Dorval Airport; Hyatt Hotels, Puerto Rico; Frontier Communications, Rochester, NY

Tom Philabaum
Atrium Sculpture, page 69

My first contact with glass was in 1971 at the University of Wisconsin-Madison. Since that time I've made my living primarily as a glassblower, starting with art fairs in the 70s and early 80s. Soon, however, my work turned more toward one-of-a-kind pieces for gallery representation. I have always been mindful of the economic role that "production" work played in the development of my personal work. I have also been a student of monadology, and believe in the power of parts. My piece, *Another Way to Fly,* at the Tucson International Airport, is composed of thirty glass carpets in an upward spiraling vortex.

COMMISSIONS: 28' x 28' lighting installation, McMahon's Restaurant, Tucson, AZ; Lobby of Performing Arts Center, Baseline Bouquet, South Mountain Community College, 30' x 30', 210 parts

Peter Skidd Fine Art
Wall Art / Metal, page 396

I provide work in steel and plexi for interior and exterior placement. All design, fabrication, and finishing is done by me to ensure a top-quality product. I work closely with designers, art consultants, galleries, and private clients to achieve dynamic displays within prescribed dimensions and budgets. Please visit PeterSkidd.com for ideas and more information.

COMMISSIONS: Ruth's Chris Steak House Restaurants, 2008, New Orleans, LA, Princeton, NJ, and South Barrington, IL; ABC television network's *Extreme Makeover Home Edition,* 2007, Pinon, AZ

PRICING: Call or email me for an estimate

Pictures in Glass
Wall Art / Glass, page 387

My inspiration comes from life experiences and my interpretation of them. My goal when working with clients is to make sure they are left with feelings when entering a room that they didn't have before my glasswork was installed. Glass is my medium. The play of light on it, how the sun affects the colors and textures throughout the day, the story told within, and the feeling derived from it cannot be duplicated by any other source. With twenty-five years of experience and whether designing or fabricating new windows, repairing or restoring old stained glass, sandblasting, or creating a mosaic design, I am inspired by the people I work with and the journey they are on. Their project will be a reflection of who they are, communicating their beliefs, expressing their thoughts without words. Commissioned projects can be found in churches, public buildings, and private residences throughout Michigan. Please visit my blog at www.PicturesInGlass.blogspot.com.

RECENT PROJECTS: St. Johns Lutheran Church, Farmington, MI; St. Joseph Catholic Church, Adrian, MI; St. Dominic Catholic Church, Clinton, MI; Blessed Savior Lutheran Church, Blissfield, MI

GUILD SOURCEBOOKS: *Architectural & Interior Art 21, 22*

473

Artist Statements

Pinter Studio Inc.
Mosaics, pages 14, 137

A working artist for over twenty-five years, I have mastered a variety of materials, including ceramic, glass, and now mosaics, but I always consider myself a painter. I am most recognized for my bold color use and gestural style. The creative inspiration comes from nature, resulting in works that are transformative, effervescent, spiritual, and provocative at the same time. I like to create intimate views of gardens and ponds that transcend the three-dimensional world we live in, moving the viewer into a higher level of feeling and experiencing nature.

COMMISSIONS: Five large-scale private mosaic murals, 2007 and 2008, Philadelphia, PA, Worcester, MA, and Atlanta, GA; Hughes Spalding Children's Hospital, Atlanta, GA; McDonalds Corporate Headquarters, Chicago, IL; HBO Corporate Headquarters, New York, NY; RCA Corporate Staff Center, Princeton, NJ; Portland Museum, Portland, ME; and Canton Museum, Canton, OH

EXHIBITIONS: Quinlan Visual Arts Center, Gainsville, GA; Vibrantz Gallery, 2006, Half Moon Bay, CA; City Art, 2005, York, PA; Riverview Gallery, 2005, Portsmouth, VA

PUBLICATIONS: *Koi USA,* Jan/Feb 2005; *Southern Homes; Arts Southwest*

Matthew Placzek
Public Art, page 263

I design and create sculptural installations that invite the viewer to interact with and explore the work. My work concentrates on creating an image for a public arena, whether a plaza, office park, or monument, providing the space with a unique identity. Over the last twenty years, my sculptures have ranged from single figures cast in bronze to extensive multimedia installations using steel, acrylic, color, and light. The commissioning entities were able to express their goals, and together we were able to create works of art that fit their needs. I have an extensive team assembled to design, engineer, fabricate, and install my artwork. My latest project, *Illumina,* at Qwest Convention Center and Arena in Omaha, creates visual imagery that people can relate to, as well as be entertained by—the ever-changing spectacular light show. Please feel free to visit this and other works at matthewplaczek.com.

GUILD SOURCEBOOKS: *Architectural & Interior Art 23*

Glenys Porter
Paintings & Prints, page 215

I am inspired by the coexistence of man's ingenuity and nature's patience, seemingly incongruous and yet harmonious. My work seeks to interpret this connection with color, texture, composition, and balance. I start a painting by creating a textured surface. I then build up the paint layer upon layer, alternating opaque with translucent and thick with thin. I often embellish my work with additional acrylic material that I mold or sculpt. The result offers not only visual depth and interest, but also a tactile quality that almost invites the viewer to touch.

COLLECTIONS: Time Warner Telecom, Littleton, CO; MGM Grand at Foxwoods, Mashantucket, CT; Jackson Life Insurance, Denver, CO; Paradise Valley Medical Plaza, Paradise Valley, AZ; U.S. Pharmacopeia, Rockville, MD.

GUILD SOURCEBOOKS: *Residential Art 3, 4, 5*

PRICING: From $150 to $175 per square foot, wholesale.

Stephen Porter
Sculpture / Non-Representational, page 294

My sculpture is based on a formal vocabulary of geometric shapes arranged in ordered configurations that contain a right sense of balance, size, and proportion. These sculptures are concerned with the harmony created by these relationships and are an attempt to create beauty in formal structures.

COMMISSIONS: John Deere, 2003, Cary, NC; SAS Institute, Inc., 1995, Cary, NC; A.W. and Sons Enterprises, 1988, State College, PA

COLLECTIONS: Herbert F. Johnson Museum of Art, Cornell University, Ithaca, NY; Pennsylvania Academy of the Fine Arts, Philadelphia; Southern Alleghenies Museum of Art, Loretto, PA; Storm King Art Center, Mountainville, NY; Worcester Art Museum, Worcester, MA

EXHIBITIONS: Sculpture at Maine Audubon, 2007, Falmouth; Maine 2006, Coastal Maine Botanical Gardens, Boothbay Harbor; Robert Kidd Gallery, 2003, Birmingham, MI; Butters Gallery, 2000, Portland, OR

Robert Pulley
Sculpture / Non-Representational, page 295

My hand-built stoneware sculptures reflect the forces and structures of nature, organic growth, geologic age, and gesture of the human figure superimposed in works of strength and powerful presence. I like to see the sculptures in the garden, where they resonate with the changing colors and textures of nature. When installed indoors they bring the energy of nature in with them. Outdoors the work is unaffected by weather. I can answer questions about installation. My work is in private and public collections around the world, including The Canton Art Institute, Wright State University Art Museum, and McDonalds Corporation, and has been featured in publications such as *Sculpting Clay* and *Smashing Glazes.* Prices range from $500 for tabletop-sized pieces, to $3,000 for typical garden scale, to $15,000 for public-scale work.

GUILD SOURCEBOOKS: *Residential Art 2, 3, 4*

Joni Purk
Paintings & Prints, page 216

When creating art I am completely taken away from my surroundings. Being a part of the painting, capturing the delicate beauty of nature, the complexity of everyday life while feeling every brush stroke exhilarates me. Described as the Artist of Diversity® by public and press, I incorporated this trademark in 2007. An award-winning artist with twenty years of experience, I am diverse in subject. Fauna, flora, figure, still life, landscapes, and cityscapes are available. Representational in style, a traditional oil layering method is used, building up composition, color, light, and shadow until the feeling/mood I want to convey is achieved. Listening to and creating for the client is extremely important. With over 700 clients to date, I meet and/or exceed expectations. Awards, exhibitions, and client referrals available upon request.

COMMISSIONS: Hilton Garden Inn; Coldwell Banker Heritage; Fifth/Third Bank

PUBLICATIONS: *Art Magazine, CarolinaArts, Charleston Review, Cincinnati Magazine, Who's Who 2008 Top 101 Experts*

PRICING: Full range. Small- to large-scale residential and public art

Artist Statements

QUINTAL Studio—Fine Art, Glass, and Design
Sculpture / Non-Representational, page 297

Glass design for specific locations is my passion. With thirty years of experience, I bring contemporary style to the timeless material of glass for corporate, commercial, residential, and retail environments. With precision engineering and skillful execution, QUINTAL provides effective responses to projects of all sizes, with timely worldwide service and delivery.

COMMISSIONS: Entrance to Billiard Room, San Carlos, CA; Entrance to Home Theatre, Portola Valley, CA; Thermo King Corporation, Minneapolis, MN; Tanforan Business Center, So. San Francisco, CA; White House, Washington, DC; Entrance to Concert Theatre, Minot, ND; other public and private commissions

EXHIBITIONS: San Francisco, New York, Paris, Berlin, Honolulu, and other cities

GUILD SOURCEBOOKS: *The GUILD 1, 2, 3, 4, 5; Architect's 6, 7, 8, 10, 11; Designer's 8, 11, 13, 14,15; Architectural & Interior Art 16, 17, 20, 21; Residential Art 1*

PRICING: Interested professionals and private collectors may view our website, www.quintalstudio.com, and contact Quintal for pricing.

Carl Radke
Objects, pages 20, 171

I am an American glass artist and designer. I first touched glass in 1970 while going to art school. I immediately felt called to it, and now, 38 years later, by the grace of God the calling continues. My studio was open to the public for twenty years; two years ago I moved my studio to my home. I am now blessed to be able blow glass in solitude. This solitude has breathed new life into my work. I am essentially a one-man studio; however, my wife, Stephanie, helps me when I need assistance. The art glass colors I use in my work are similar to the Favrile glass made by Tiffany Studios around the turn of the twentieth century, although the colors are personalized by me. Over the years I have worked with many designers, consultants, and restorers of vintage homes. Custom commissions are welcome. For more information, please visit www.carlradke.com .

COMMISSIONS: Harmony Cellars Lighting, 2008, Harmony, CA

PRICING: Wholesale prices range from $55 to $15,000.

Tanya Ragir
Sculpture / Representational, pages 342, 343

My life and my work are about overcoming limitations. Some are cultural, some political, some sexual—many are self-imposed. I embrace the gravitas, the depth and breadth of the beauty of women, which is limitless. I sculpt from life—sometimes deconstructing the body to go beyond the limitations of figure-as-nude. My ongoing current project is life-size sculptures of women ranging from twenty to seventy-five years old. This most personal work is about love, vulnerability, self-revelation, and self-acceptance.

Ralfonso.com LLC
Public Art, pages 10, 264

Kinetic art for private collections and public places. I primarily design wind, water, and light sculptures for public places, such as restaurant, hotel, and corporate interior lobbies or atriums, as well as for outdoor plazas, fountains, and parks. Private and site-specific commissions, as well as numerous ready designs are also available. Please contact me for a free Ralfonso DVD.

COMMISSIONS: *Ad Infinitum,* 21' outdoor kinetic wind sculpture for ZhengZhou, China Public Park; *ExoCentric Spirits,* 20' x 30' indoor kinetic suspended light mobile for new MTR Elements Mall in Hong Kong; *Dance with the Wind,* 30' outdoor kinetic wind sculpture for the Olympic Games, Beijing; *Exo #3* for the main lobby of the new Pittsburgh Children's Hospital

EXHIBITIONS: *MomentuM,* New Jersey Grounds for Sculpture Park; *Sculpture in Motion,* Atlanta Botanical Garden; Cuadro Gallery Inaugural Exhibition, Dubai, UAE; *Homo Ludens,* Leeuwarden, the Netherlands. My moving sculptures have been exhibited or permanently installed in Switzerland, Germany, the Netherlands, Russia, China, Hong Kong, United Arab Emirates, and the U.S.

PRICING: From $10,000 to $450,000

Raven Lunatic Studios
Wall Art / Mixed & Other Media, page 420

The crows continue to act as my muses. They provide a connection to nature and to ancient human traditions. Their keen intelligence and amazing adaptability inspire and guide their human admirers on the journey into an exciting future, both collectively and individually. Raven Lunatic Studios provides visual art in a variety of media, corvid-themed and otherwise. Commissions are most welcome. For more information, please visit my website, www.nevermorrigan.com.

EXHIBITIONS: *Pacific Northwest Art Annual,* 2008, Eugene, OR; *Crow: The Bird of a Thousand Faces,* 2008, Art/Not Terminal Gallery, Seattle, WA; *Think Inside the Box,* 2007, Gallery OK, Seattle, WA; Pacific Northwest Ballet Nutcracker March, 2007, Seattle, WA

GUILD SOURCEBOOKS: *Residential Art 6*

Ray Miller Studio
Public Art, page 265

I approach my work with a commitment to being accessible and evocative while injecting a sense of joy. My work is executed with a trained eye and a skilled hand. Looking at my work brings a smile to the viewer and a sense of appreciation for the interpretation presented. To me art is joyful and a free self-expression. I see art as a relationship between the artist and the world, a conversation, a partnership. In working with clients, I am committed to distilling their vision with mine so there is a connection between us and the work created. Whether it is large-scale public sculpture, sanctuary art, or a piece of furniture, I approach each project with the same level of importance. I respect congregations, individuals, and corporate clients for their commitment to the visual aesthetic.

Artist Statements

Red Iron Studio
Furniture & Floor Coverings, page 106

My work is about the movement of metal and line quality. I create one-of-a-kind and custom pieces of furniture, lighting, and other interior architectural elements. Please contact me about ironwork for residential and commercial spaces. For more information visit www.redironstudios.com or call 715.371.0034.

Rene Culler Glass LLC
Wall Art / Glass, page 384

I specialize in working with architects and designers to create imaginative, site-specific architectural glass. My versatility in innovative glass-working methods makes it possible for me to produce fused, cast, or enameled glass to suit a client's specific need. Original, contemporary imagery is either abstract, narrative, or realistic. In my fusing/casting processes, multiple layers of glass yield dimensionality and depth. Painted or drawn images can be encased within the layers of glass. Blown glass elements, fused within the panels, distinguish the work and are often added as graphic and dynamic patterns. A photographic technique allows for the inclusion of text or precise imagery. Surface techniques, including sandblasting and engraving, add detail or a rich texture. Please visit my website to see examples of wall work, sculpture, and blown glass.

COMMISSIONS: Forest City Enterprises Science and Technology Park, Chicago; The Cleveland Clinic Intercontinental Hotel; The Ohio State University; Robert Woods Johnson Hospital, NJ

COLLECTIONS: The Corning Museum of Glass; Luce Center/Renwick Gallery, The American Museum of Art, Smithsonian

PUBLICATIONS: *500 Glass Objects*, 2006; *Women Working in Glass*, 2003; *International Glass Art, 2003*

Renee Dinauer Sculpture
Sculpture / Non-Representational, pages 298, 299

I create a plethora of unique, sweeping, free-form lightweight sculpture from steam-bent hardwoods often colored in subtle naturals to vibrant colors. I create sculpture for public, corporate, hotels/resorts, casinos, cruise ships, and residences, providing personal service, and teaming with owners, architects, and designers to achieve symbiosis with architecture, and interior design. The unique use of sweeping bent wood often becomes a compelling icon, providing its edifice with a lasting impression. My ubiquitous creative interests flourished while studying for my degree at UCLA.

COMMISSIONS: My work resides in numerous residential, corporate, and public sites including: Hilton Hotel, Deerfield, IL; Chapel Hill School, Indianapolis; Beverly Hills; City Hall, Buffalo Grove, IL; City Center, Texas Tech University; University of Wisconsin; Ashford Hotel, Atlantic Beach, FL; Carmel Valley Resort, CA; The Aspen Hotel; The Anthem, Las Vegas; Le Parc, Naples, FL; Elton John, NYC; Macy's NY; Orlando; Washington, DC; Houston; Hilton; Houston Omni Hotel; Venetian Casino Resort, Las Vegas

GUILD SOURCEBOOKS: *Architectural & Interior Art 23; Residential Art 5, 6*

476

Richard Hall Fine Art
Paintings & Prints, page 217

I am inspired by nature's settings, from serene sunrises and sunsets to the ominous strength of storms and dark clouds. I incorporate the lessons I've learned in my years of painting while weaving new ideas into my latest creations. My paintings bring a balance of space and light, giving a sense of tranquility that goes beyond a literal translation of the landscape. The oil paints are applied in thin layers, alternating colored washes and tinted glazes, which result in subtle changes in tone and depth. Each layer must dry between applications, and painting sixty or more layers is not uncommon. The paint particles suspended in the glazes catch the light and reflect it back to the viewer, creating a luminescent finish and translucent quality. My work has been published and collected internationally for almost thirty years. Original paintings and giclées are available. Custom commissions welcome. Visit my website at www.richardhallfineart.com.

GUILD SOURCEBOOKS: *Residential Art 6*

Robert Rickard
Sculpture / Non-Representational, pages 300, 301

I am fortunate to work in a mountain studio surrounded by the natural beauty of Taos, New Mexico. This lends my work a certain quiet and calmness. My work reflects my love of geometry, movement, and color. I use industrial tools to challenge the immutable properties of metal. I take metal and twist it, bend it, weld it; I cut designs into it with a hand-held plasma cutter. I polish some portions; other portions I treat with metal coatings, dyes, and patinas. The Internet makes it easy to work with clients anywhere in the world; however, I also enjoy having clients visit the studio to collaborate on the design and execution of large pieces. This gives them a direct involvement with the creation of their work, and the rich culture of Taos provides a wonderful background for their visit.

COMMISSIONS: Scottsdale, AZ; Mary Esther, FL; Annapolis, MD; Potomac, MD; Charlotte, NC; Morris Township, NJ; Jenkintown, PA; Kutztown, PA; Philadelphia, PA; Fairfax, VA

EXHIBITIONS: The American Craft Show, 2004–2009, Baltimore, MD

GUILD SOURCEBOOKS: *Architectural & Interior Art 22, 23; Residential Art 6*

Dan Rider
Wall Art / Metal, page 397

My art is about representing nature in the most organic sense, using the interaction of materials and space. I begin with sketches so that I am allowed the freedom of unlimited imagination before proceeding to the practicality of fabrication. I am always considering not only the basic form, but also the play of light and shadow on my work and its surroundings. I continue to answer the challenge of creating movement with minimal elements that appear to have grown into the composition. Working in a collaborative relationship with collectors, designers, art consultants, and architects on a variety of commissions, I have readily adapted my sculpture to both commercial and residential spaces. My work can be found in galleries, private collections, corporate offices, hospitals, and in the television and movie industry..

Artist Statements

Bette Ridgeway
Wall Art / Metal, page 398

In my work on metals, I explore the relationship between the smooth, slick surface and the layering of translucent flows of paint, which reveal a kind of mythic, subterranean history. Similar to ceramic glazing, the alternating of layers of color with resin suggest biomorphic form as well as the natural processes of accumulation and erosion. In my thirty plus years of painting and teaching, I have never felt so rewarded for taking risks. The panels are impervious to moisture; therefore they are perfect for spas and cruise ships! Using a series of panels in multiple sizes, the artwork can be designed to fill any space! I enjoy working with clients to transform their spaces, both commercial and residential. My website, ridgewaystudio.com, provides information on galleries, instruction, and upcoming exhibitions.

GUILD SOURCEBOOKS: *Residential Art 4, 5, 6*

Craig Robb
Wall Art / Mixed & Other Media, pages 20, 421

Within my sculptures I include houses, chairs, and other objects that, with their inherent symbolism, develop metaphors about issues that are important to me. The combination of wood and curved steel are utilized as both compositional elements and to create spaces for these objects to reside. I have always been interested in how objects function within a given space, how they occupy it and the relationships created with the other objects in that space. Because of the broad range of symbolism, these sculptures can speak on many different levels and to many different people.

GUILD SOURCEBOOKS: *Residential Art 4, 5, 6*

Claude Riedel
Liturgical Art, pages 18, 126

"It belongs in this place!" Such sentiments should greet the unveiling of your synagogue's *Ner Tamid*. The light of God radiates from the *Ner Tamid* and blesses all it touches. A client proclaimed, "Your work emanates an aura of spirituality." My *Eternal Lights* marry timeless, ancient traditions with modern sensibilities. I seek to render the essence of my client's vision with the sensitivity and fine craftsmanship appropriate to the architectural setting. A famous designer recently wrote, "Your Ner Tamids are supurb! Seldom have synagogues in the United States had such beauty."

COMMISSIONS: 2008: *Ner Tamids* for Beth Tfliah, Baltimore, MD; Congregation Gates of Heaven, Schenectady, NY; Ohev Shalom of Bucks County, Richboro, PA; Rodeph Sholom, New York, NY; Temple Bet Yam, St. Augustine, FL; Temple Sinai, Reno, NV; Temple Emanuel, Tempe, AZ; Temple Israel, West Bloomfield, MI; Temple Rodeph Torah, Marlboro, NJ; Temple B'nai Torah, Monterey, CA; Temple Shaarei Tikvah, Scarsdale, NY; Temple Ner Tamid, Bloomfield, NJ; Temple Israel, Tallahasse, FL; Beit Knesset Migdal Hashoshanim, Jerusalem, Israel

PUBLICATIONS: *Minnesota Architecture*, March 2004

GUILD SOURCEBOOKS: *Architect's 15; Architectural & Interior Art 17, 20*

Kevin Robb
Sculpture / Non-Representational, page 302

I have made my mark on the national and international art scene with my unique, free-flowing sculptural expressions in bronze and stainless steel. These contemporary pieces work equally well in intimate environments or large-scale public areas. My natural curiosity and integral understanding of how positive/negative space and shadow/light work together manifest themselves in these pieces, bringing life, energy, and beauty to the spaces they occupy. I pride myself on the high-quality craftsmanship, as evidenced by the smooth-to-the-touch edges and seamless metal intersections.

COMMISSIONS: Azle Memorial Library, 2008, Azle, TX; City of Oklahoma City, 2008, Oklahoma City, OK; Hanover Companies, Acoma Lofts, 2008, Denver, CO; COPT, Patriot Park, 2008, Colorado Springs, CO; Gateway at Torrey Pines, 2007, San Diego, CA

EXHIBITIONS: Sculpture in the Park, 2008, Loveland, CO; RiverSpan Sculpture and Exhibition, 2008, Cincinnati, OH; Sculpture on the Green Invitational, 2008, Cashiers, NC; Amsterdam Whitney International Fine Arts, 2007, New York, NY

GUILD SOURCEBOOKS: *Architect's 12, 13, 14, 15; Architectural & Interior Art 16, 17, 18, 19, 20, 21, 22, 23*

Rob Fisher Sculpture, LLC
Atrium Sculpture, pages 63, 70, 71

JetStream is a sculpture that Rob Fisher designed before his death in 2006. It was installed in 2008 by Rob Fisher Sculpture, LLC, under the direction of Talley Fisher. Our studio produces artworks that reference nature and are made of stainless steel and anodized or powder coated perforated aluminum. The suspended sculptures that I designed and installed in 2008, *Alhambra Archetype and Transformation, Sea Turtles,* and *Mountain,* honor my father's artistic legacy and are inspired by his design direction, aesthetic, and creative sensibility. I work closely with art consultants, architects, designers, fabricators, engineers, and installers. See other artworks at www.robfishersculpture.com.

COMMISSIONS 2008: *JetStream,* Indianapolis Airport; *Alhambra Archetype and Transformation,* Old Sauk Trails Office and Research Park, Madison, WI; *Sea Turtles,* One Ocean Resort, Atlantic Beach, Jacksonville, FL; *Mountain,* Bedford Residential Building, Hong Kong. Future suspended sculptures: Las Vegas Airport; Hong Kong Apartment Building; Ritz Carlton Hotel, Shenzhen, China

GUILD SOURCEBOOKS: *Architect's 9, 11, 12, 13, 14, 15; Architectural & Interior Art 16, 17, 18, 19, 20, 21, 22, 23*

477

Priscilla Robinson
Wall Art / Mixed & Other Media, page 422

My art pieces are about texture and color and are created from handmade paper and kiln-cast glass. Inspired by nature, the work is a personal voice exploring translucency, contrasts of materials and chroma saturation within the motifs of land, leaves, and light. Because my unique techniques work well for specific requirements of size and color, they have been created for a wide range of commissions, from residential to large public art installations. The acrylic-saturated, embossed fibers are durable and suitable for public spaces. I welcome the opportunity to create unique artwork for commissioned projects.

COMMISSIONS: Lobby, School of Hospitality, Boston University, MA; University of Massachusetts, Worcester; St. Anthony's Hospital, St. Louis, MO; Broadwing, Austin, TX; Lobby, Frost Bank Plaza, Austin, TX; Lobby, Stafford Performing Art Center, Houston, TX

COLLECTIONS: Chevron Pipeline, Houston, TX; The Royal Library, The Hague, The Netherlands; The Abbey at Spineto, Tuscany, Italy; Komazawa House, Tokyo, Japan

Artist Statements

Ken Roby
Architectural Elements, pages 29, 35

My assistants and I create a variety of custom metalwork in forged iron, copper, bronze, and other metals. Projects and installations range from fire screens, furniture, lamps, and sculptural pieces to railings, gates, balconies, and other significant architectural works. I enjoy the process of figuring out how to make things work visually and functionally perhaps as much as I enjoy making them. My personal interest is largely in the art of the blacksmith. Most work continues to be done by hand in the forge and is signed and dated; however, plenty of current technology and machinery can be used in conjunction with traditional forging and joinery to accomplish the goals of any given project. Fortunately, my shop is well equipped for the wide variety of metalwork and installation work needed in bringing various works to fruition.

Kim Rody
Paintings & Prints, page 218

I have always been connected to the sea. I think the creatures that live near and below the ocean, with their intricate detail and vibrant coloring, are fascinating and compelling. Using acrylics, I work on large (up to 100") canvases and have established markets for my paintings and giclées in the Bahamas and on the eastern Atlantic coast in hotel lobbies, restaurants, primary residences, and second homes. My work is appealing to clients looking for a dramatic, bright, colorful, and tropical feel. My website, www.fishartista.com, showcases hundreds of images categorized by subject. In addition to original art, images are also available as limited editions on heavyweight watercolor paper and open editions on canvas.

PRICING: Retail price for originals: $1,200–$12,000. Retail price for reproductions: $1 per square inch. Call or email for informational folder and DVD.

GUILD SOURCEBOOKS: *Residential Art 5, 6*

Ron Cook Studios
Objects, pages 165, 172

I produce one-of-a-kind hand-carved figures and musical sound sculptures for homes and businesses. Distinctive carvings, often known for their subtle humor, are the hallmark of my works. Figures from history, legend, and mythology are the most popular. I work with the client to create pieces based on historical sources, yet related to today's artistic attitudes, sensibilities, and values. The scale ranges from small two- to six-inch tabletop or cabinet pieces, to large four-foot wall-hangings or floor-standing works. I design and construct my work through traditional and modern methods of the woodworking and luthier's crafts. Each piece is comprised of salvaged, recycled, or sustainably harvested woods. For artwork with a personal connection, I carve realistic figures based on submitted photos.

EXHIBITIONS: Sausalito Art Festival, 2008, Sausalito, CA; American Craft Council Shows, 2004-2008, Baltimore, MD, San Francisco, CA, and Charlotte, NC; Scottsdale Arts Festival, 2005–2009, Scottsdale, AZ; Bellevue Arts Museum ArtsFair, 2007, 2008, Bellevue, WA; Baulines Craft Guild Masters Exhibition, 2007, San Rafael, CA

PUBLICATIONS: *Renaissance Magazine,* 2008; *American Woodworker,* 2008; *Woodwork,* 2006; *Plenty,* 2006; *Guitarmaker Magazine,* 2006

478

Rosetta
Sculpture / Representational, page 344

My subjects are animals, but it is their life force in all of its visual splendor that inspires my stylized interpretations. My work ranges from miniature to monumental and has been exhibited nationally and internationally in museums and galleries, and in juried and invitational exhibitions.

COMMISSIONS: Peru State College, NE; NuVasive, CA; Azle Public Library, TX; Chapman University, CA; Cities of Loveland, CO, and Dowagiac, MI; The Shops at Walnut Creek, CO; Meridian Commons Retail, CO; Lincoln Park Zoo, Chicago, IL

COLLECTIONS: Brookgreen Gardens, SC; Leigh Yawkey Woodson Art Museum, WI; Florida Institute of Technology; Ella Sharp Museum of Art, MI; Bennington Center for the Arts, VT; Neville Public Museum, WI; Cities of Lakewood, Steamboat Springs, and Loveland, CO

AWARDS: Founder Award, 2008, National Sculpture Society; Award of Excellence, 2007 and 2001, Society of Animal Artists; Western Rendezvous of Art People's Choice Award, 2006 and 2005; National Sculpture Society Silver Medal, 2003

Jon Michael Route
Wall Art / Metal, page 399

Combining metal's ageless appeal with vibrant "hot process" patinas gives these fabricated wall pieces a very current design presence for healthcare, corporate, or institutional environments. Three-dimensional elements are set on layered landscapes or patchwork fields of rich surface textures, patterns, and colors. Finely crafted from copper, brass, bronze, aluminum, and pewter, these sculptural wall pieces are custom made to your color schemes, with varying themes from natural to architectural, and to your size requirements. They are built on a wood or metal framework that lifts them off the wall and allows them to be securely and easily hung. Please refer to my website, www.jonmichaelroute.com, for contact information, resume, and complementary work. Commissions and site-specific projects welcomed.

GUILD SOURCEBOOKS: *Residential Art 6*

Barton Rubenstein
Public Art, page 266

I create indoor and outdoor sculpture with and without water for public and private spaces. These include city and state projects, corporate, commercial, and academic institutions, as well as private residences. I typically work with stainless steel, bronze, stone, and glass. Fascinated with various elements of nature, I focus on water, kinetics, light, and suspension to create sculptures that surprise and challenge the viewer. The goal of my artwork is first to create a level of intrigue, and then to allow for the gradual discovery of its secrets and complexities.

COMMISSIONS: National competition-awarded commissions: University of Massachusetts, Dartmouth, 2010; University of Connecticut-Waterbury, 2009; Redwood Shores Library, 2008, Redwood City, CA; Summit Behavioral Healthcare, 2006, Cincinnati, OH; Owens Community College, 2005, Findlay, OH; Boone County National Bank, 2005, Columbia, MO; Jefferson at Congressional Village, 2004, Rockville, MD; University of Central Florida, 2003, Orlando. Other commissions: Prescott Condominiums, 2008, Arlington, VA; NSF International, 2008, Ann Arbor, MI; Van Ness East Condos, 2008, Washington, DC; Sidwell Friends School, 2007, Washington, DC

GUILD SOURCEBOOKS: *Architectural & Interior Art 18, 22*

Artist Statements

Brian F. Russell
Sculpture / Non-Representational, page 303

I create works that will live harmoniously in the world as independent functionaries of society. I draw inspiration from forms and rhythms in nature, the human body, ancient artifacts, mathematics, and science, distilling these influences into abstract points of intersection. My aim on a public scale is to involve the viewer, to interject into the world points of beauty, interest, and spontaneity. I want people to use my sculpture as an excuse to mentally shift to another level of consciousness above the daily hubbub, even for a moment, and to reconnect with themselves via that primal, emotional, cortex-controlled spasm of an encounter with an unexpected oasis in a visual desert.

COLLECTIONS: Mobile Museum of Art, Mobile, AL; First Tennessee Bank, Memphis; Red Rock Hotel, Las Vegas; Energy Partners, New York; Piedmont Gas, Charlotte, NC; Cafesjian Museum, Minneapolis, MN; Rhodes College, Memphis, TN; Tennessee State Museum, Nashville

James T. Russell
Sculpture / Non-Representational, pages 304, 305

The concept of my sculpture is based on the juxtaposition of contrasting contours. Opposites attract opposites. I use highly polished stainless steel because it is alive with reflective energy. Through this medium I transform my inner emotion into permanent form. I have edition sculptures that range from $5,000 to $50,000. Monumental sculptures start at $60,000.

COMMISSIONS: Coast Aluminum and Architectural, 2003, Santa Fe Springs, CA; Astra Zeneca Pharmaceuticals, 2002, Wilmington, DE; Chico Municipal Airport, 2001, Chico, CA

COLLECTIONS: Four Seasons Hotel, Hong Kong; City of Cerritos, CA; Bellagio Hotel, Las Vegas, NV; Motorola Corporation, Beijing, China; Riverside Art Museum, Riverside, CA; A.T. Kearney Inc., Chicago, IL

EXHIBITIONS: *Impact,* 2004, Tadu Contemporary Art, Santa Fe, NM; *Miniatures,* 2004, Albuquerque Museum of Art, NM

PUBLICATIONS: *Santa Fe Reporter,* Oct. 2004; *Leaders* magazine, Sept. 2004

GUILD SOURCEBOOKS: *Architect's 7, 8, 12, 14; Architectural & Interior Art: 16, 17, 18, 19, 20, 21, 22, 23; Residential Art: 1, 5, 6*

Victoria Ryan
Paintings & Prints, page 236

Saturated color and a dramatic sense of light and mood are the hallmarks of my landscape paintings. Soft pastel is my medium of choice to create my dreamlike compositions. In recent years I have produced a series of oils on canvas to add to my portfolio. In 1982 I completed my B.F.A. in painting and drawing from California State University at Long Beach. Since that time I have been exhibiting consistently in featured exhibitions and group shows nationwide. I have a history of working successfully with art consultants on projects of all sizes. Commissions are always welcome.

COLLECTIONS: Northwestern Prentice Women's Hospital, Chicago, IL; Sacred Heart at Riverbend Hospital, OR; Providence Everett Medical Center, Everett, WA; Clorox Corp, Oakland, CA; Delta Faucet Company, Indianapolis, IN; Mayo Clinic, St. Mary's Hospital, Rochester, MN

PRICING: Please contact me through my website for information on pricing.

Sable Studios
Atrium Sculpture, page 72

Sable Studios has been creating kinetic mobiles and stabiles for over forty years. Collaborating with art consultants, architects, and designers, our custom-designed sculpture has enhanced private, corporate, and public spaces. Whether transforming an interior atrium or an exterior location, the artwork integrates color, light, and movement to create a multidimensional experience. Our studio creates work that truly graces the world with exquisite beauty.

COMMISSIONS: Children's Hospital Boston, Waltham and Boston campuses; Union City Senior Center, CA; Lucent Technologies, CO; Boys Town National Research Hospital, Omaha, NE; Metro Plaza Building, San Jose, CA; Syntex Corporation, Hayward, CA; Berklee Performance Center, Boston, MA; Quantum Corporation, San Jose, CA; 3 Comm Corporation, Sunnydale, CA; Cadence Corporation, San Jose, CA

GUILD SOURCEBOOKS: *Architect's 11, 12, 13, 14, 15; Architectural & Interior Art 16, 17, 18, 19, 20, 21, 22, 23*

Joan Skogsberg Sanders
Paintings & Prints, page 219

"Draw what you see and paint what you feel" is an artist adage that applies to my artwork. They are emotional responses to places influencing my art, such as the Middle East and California. I use a colorist-expressionist approach heavy with sensuous application of paint and vibrant colors with minimal visual references, and I depend on color relationships and fresh compositions to give the work its vivid internal energy. I want to give the viewer a sense of pleasure, and most important, make the artwork accessible to the viewer in its directness and spontaneity.

EXHIBITIONS: International Society of Acrylic Painters, 2008, Santa Cruz, CA; NOAPS *Best of America,* 2006, Bolivar, MO; *Arizona Aqueous XII,* 2006, Tucson, AZ; ISAP Exhibit, 2006, Cornell Museum, Del Rey Beach, FL; European Bieniel, FNAM Art Space, 2001, Paris, France

GUILD SOURCEBOOKS: *Residential Art 5*

Joy Saville
Wall Art / Fiber, page 373

Have you ever had your breath taken away by the color of dogwood trees, autumn leaves, a sunset, or the view of the landscape as you drive over a hill? Or recall the depth of emotion one feels over a life experience, the death of a loved one, or a global disaster? These are the frozen moments I strive to express in my work. Piecing cotton, linen, and silk in an impressionistic, painterly manner, I use the inherent quality of natural fabrics to absorb or reflect light, producing a constant interplay of light, texture, and color. In so doing I want to connect the passion I feel with the often-chaotic reality surrounding us in our daily living.

COMMISSIONS: The Jewish Center, Princeton, NJ; Johnson & Johnson; Ortho Pharmaceutical

COLLECTIONS: Museum of Arts and Design, NY; The Newark Museum; Southfield Public Library, MI; Bristol-Myers Squibb; Time-Warner Inc; H.J. Heinz; PepsiCo; Art in Embassies, 2000, Brunei, 2008, Namibia

EXHIBITIONS: Solo and group exhibitions throughout North America and internationally since 1976.

GUILD SOURCEBOOKS: *The Guild 3, 4, 5; Architectural & Interior Art 17, 18, 19, 23; Residential Art 2*

Artist Statements

Margo Sawyer
Public Art, page 267

I am particularly interested in how the relationship between space and transcendence functions, where architecture and ritual converge in creating unique spaces for contemplation. Creating spaces that focus on an equivocal nature of space, where installation art, architecture, and landscape architecture converge. My installations have produced spaces that have an animate nature to them, casting new meaning to the experiential nature of spatial transitions, such as walls, stairs, plazas, and entrances, that become membranes and vehicles to other worlds. Using color and light, I investigate the sublime—and contemplation—in contemporary art.

COMMISSIONS: Discovery Green, Houston, TX; Austin Convention Center, Austin, TX; Whole Foods World Headquarters, Austin, TX; San Antonio International Airport, San Antonio, TX

COLLECTIONS: Austin Museum of Art, Austin, TX; El Paso Museum of Art, El Paso, TX; McNay Art Museum, San Antonio, TX; and many national corporate and private collections

Karen Scally
Fine Art Photography, page 93

I love to capture the ethereal beauty of our Earth. Photographing its mysteries enriches my life. I hope the images speak to you as well. My work includes landscapes, seascapes, florals (including some with special effects and oil or pastel enhancement), sailboats, montages, and abstracts. These magic moments in time can be preserved on canvas, fabric, metal, acrylic, or wallpaper. My art has been displayed since 1983 in healthcare, corporate, and residential environments.

COLLECTIONS: Chevron Corporation, San Ramon, CA; Veterans Administration, Martinez, CA; Tosco Oil, Martinez, CA; Shell Oil, Martinez, CA; St. Mary's Hospital, San Francisco, CA; John Muir Health, Walnut Creek, CA; Kaiser Permanente, Bay Area locations

EXHIBITIONS: Domaine Chandon Winery, Yountville, CA; Ariel Gallery, New York, NY; Spectrum Gallery, Lake Tahoe, CA; York & Associates, Philadelphia, PA; Miller Gallery, Carmel, CA; Sandpiper Gallery, Tiburon, CA; Boundary Oak Country Club, Walnut Creek, CA

PUBLICATIONS: Harcourt Brace Jovanovich Books; *Travel & Leisure* magazine; *This is Canada;* Travel brochures, San Francisco

Ted Schaal
Sculpture / Non-Representational, page 306

I am exploring minimalist nonfunctional vessels for my latest bronze sculptures. My goal is to create strong geometric forms that are a new and exciting aesthetic. A departure from the purely ornate, these new designs incorporate polished stainless steel juxtaposed against a coarse, corrugated texture. I am moving in a more sculptural direction in an effort to do more massive public placements in sculpture gardens and parks. These pieces can be scaled up to fit any room, landscape, or monumental corporate setting. I hope that you enjoy looking at them as much as I have enjoyed creating them.

GUILD SOURCEBOOKS: *Residential Art 6*

Craig Schaffer
Sculpture / Non-Representational, page 307

My sculptures are inspired by the shapes formed by natural processes over time. I try to emulate, but not copy, the rhythms and proportions found in dynamic systems. Nature is non-linear, and I am fascinated by the ways different reflexive processes create similar complex patterns, such as fractals and spirals. Partly because these shapes are universal, my sculpture is found in many types of art venues. I have completed commissions for universities, research centers, hospitals, religious institutions, corporations, and private homes. I create sculpture in all materials and sizes, for indoor and outdoor placement. Prices vary with size and material.

COMMISSIONS: Brown Hall Math Tower, The Ohio State University, Columbus; Princeton Institute for Advanced Studies; Robins Center for Philanthropy, Columbus, OH; Baptist Hospital DeSoto, Memphis, TN; Mathematical Association of America, Washington, DC; Hualien Cultural Center, Hualien, Taiwan

Joan Schulze
Wall Art / Fiber, page 374

I love the idea of quilt. The layering, the fact that it can be reversible, that you can plug into this great and varied history of bed covering, and with a little push, you can enter a new world of walls, ceilings, or installations. It is the best of all worlds for me. My quilts are created through combining photo-transfer processes and paint with the cottons and silks more commonly associated with quilt making. New processes lead me to new ideas, and new ideas lead to new processes such as the alternative photographic processes I've adapted for her own uses over the years. Collage is my favorite way to think and work. Collect, cut up, layer, glue, paint again, reposition, cut up, photograph, print, add, and subtract until the materials and ideas become something greater than the original impulse to begin.

COLLECTIONS: Adobe Systems, Inc, San Jose, CA; A.G. Edwards and Sons, St. Louis, MO; John Walsh, III, NJ; Kaiser Permanente, CA and CO; Musée ArtColle, France; Museum of Arts & Design, NY; Oakland Museum of California; Renwick/Smithsonian American Art Museum

GUILD SOURCEBOOKS: *THE GUILD 4, 5; Designer's 8, 9, 10, 12, 13, Architectural & Interior Art 17, 20; Residential Art 6*

Marsh Scott
Atrium Sculpture, page 73

Working in pierced metals allows me to combine the narrative, symbolic, or abstract in a sculptural context. My work is often a collaborative expression reflecting geographic and cultural diversity to provide a site-specific installation. The positive and negative piercing defines the design while creating dynamic shadows. The hand-brushed surface reflects the colors of the surrounding environment.

COMMISSIONS: Art in Public Places (2), Brea, CA; Art in Public Places (3), Laguna Beach, CA; Kaiser Permanente: Downey, Pasadena, Palmdale, Irvine, West LA, Venice, CA; Hoag Memorial Hospital, Newport Beach, CA; Pfizer, Irvine, CA; Canal Plus US, CA; Discovery Museum, Santa Ana, CA; Edison, NV, CA; Flowers Hospital, Dothan, AL; Four Seasons, NV; Orange County Airport, Irvine, CA; Torrance Memorial Hospital, CA; Providence Hospital, Mobile, AL

EXHIBITIONS: Los Angeles County Museum of Art, CA; *Design for Living,* Millard Sheets Gallery, a Smithsonian affiliate, Pomona, CA; Affaire in the Gardens, Beverly Hills, CA; La Quinta Arts Festival, CA; Sawdust Art Festival, Laguna Beach, CA

GUILD SOURCEBOOKS: *Architectural & Interior Art 17, 18, 19, 20, 21, 22, 23*

480

Artist Statements

Mary Scrimgeour
Paintings & Prints, pages 15, 237

My work expresses my fascination with exploration, navigation, invention, science, mathematics, and flying machines. I have been influenced by the drawings of my inventor/industrial designer father, as well as the notebooks of Leonardo da Vinci. My style is spontaneous and contemporary. Using oil and mixed media, I create many layers of bold color, often referencing specifications, numbers, formulas, and text, using them as graphic elements to create whimsical and thought-provoking images. A favorite commission was the creation of a series of paintings telling the story of the Wright Brothers, now in the permanent collection of Townsend and Townsend in Denver, Colorado. To see more work, please visit maryscrimgeour.com.

COLLECTIONS: Children's Hospital, Denver, CO; Jon Stewart's *The Daily Show*, Denver office; Centennial Airport, Parker, CO; Armstrong Oil & Gas, Denver, CO; Barkley Advertising, Kansas City, MO

EXHIBITIONS: Salon de Musee, Denver Art Museum, 2008

PRICING: My price range is from $3,000 to $10,000.

Roy Secord
Paintings & Prints, page 220

Based on a tradition of mid-twentieth century fine art Modernism to present-day contemporary modes of Abstraction, I create large-format abstract paintings on canvas (usually in series) that are design oriented, ultra-modern, and precisionist based. Utilization of geometric shape and structure (and their interrelationships), as well as lineation, are key to the creation of these nonrepresentational colorist compositions. These dynamic paintings deny the eye visual stasis with compositional mutations and draw upon ambiguous—or equivocal—pictorial space to disallow a finite interpretation. The eye dances. The feel of these modernist works vary from lyrical and tranquil meditative objects to dynamic mesmerizers and colorful, powerhouse abstractions with contemporary punch. I am Manhattan-based and exhibit/sell internationally. Website: RoySecord.com

PRICING: $2,500-$25,000. Commissions welcome and professionally executed on time. Trade discounts on multiple purchases.

Patrick Shannon
Sculpture / Non-Representational, page 308

I have been a full-time working artist for most of my adult life, with a history in hand-built ceramic sculpture. I have been working in metals for many years. The materials—steel, copper, bronze, aluminum, and stainless steel—are used and combined to build wall pieces and small to large indoor and outdoor sculpture. The work is a result of many different techniques and usually involves the incorporation of a multiformity of materials, including such things as natural reed, wood pieces, stone, etc. We also design water features for a number of applications.

COMMISSIONS: U.S. Bank, ND and MN; Meritcare Hospital, ND; Mercy Hospital, MN; North Dakota State University; Bison Football Headquarters, ND; Vergas State Bank, MN; Midwest Bank, MN

PRICING: The wholesale price range of my work is from $500 to $10,000 plus.

Kurt Shaw
Wall Art / Metal, page 400

I have been creating custom artwork for corporate spaces, healthcare facilities, and the hospitality industry since 1992. My work includes some of the largest wall-mounted sculptures in the United States, ranging from an atrium filled with multiple sea-themed pieces in Toms River, NJ, which I completed in 1995, to a massive clock I built for a corporate multi-use space in Westerville, OH, and installed in the spring of 2006. I attended both Carnegie Mellon University in Pittsburgh, PA, graduating summa cum laude with a B.F.A. in 1989, and the Hobart Institute of Welding Technology in Troy, OH, where I received G.M.A.W. certification in 1995. In addition to studio work, I have published hundreds of art reviews on regional, national, and international art exhibitions primarily in the capacity of art critic for the Pittsburgh Tribune-Review, where I have been a regular twice-weekly contributor since June of 2001.

GUILD SOURCEBOOKS: *Designer's 9, 10, 12, 13; Architectural & Interior Art 22*

Michael Shemchuk
Paintings & Prints, page 237

My paintings are abstract landscapes of color, shapes, lines, and textures, synchronized to create their own rhythm. I observe the quality of the color and light in the natural and manmade environments that are all around us (e.g., the pattern created in a grove of Aspen trees or the grey somber light of a concrete parking garage). My responses to these environments inspire me to create these "surfaces of navigation" to awaken the memories of color and light that are evident in all of us, and to inspire a vis-à-vis dialog with those memories.

COMMISSIONS: Camino Medical, 2007, Mountain View, CA; Health Management Solutions, 2006, Orinda, CA; eBay Inc., 2004, San Jose, CA; Accenture, 2000, San Ramon, CA; Metro Café, 2000, San Francisco International Airport, CA; and many private residences across the U.S.

COLLECTIONS: Rockwood Design; Endymion Systems; Francisco Partners; Wells Fargo; Neuret Design; Adobe Systems; Werner Design Group; Half Moon Bay Country Club; Joseph Giereck Fine Art; Hawkins Design Group

AWARDS: Silver Award, 1996, *Art of California* magazine; California Design Award, 1996, *Sunset* magazine

Showcase Mosaics
Mosaics, page 139

We are a mosaic artist team that uses vitreous and stained glass, ceramic, and semi-precious stones to create beautiful art that will last indefinitely. We love the medium for its durability, resistance to graffiti, ability to withstand all kinds of weather, and its suitability to so many settings. Mosaics can add unique style and color both as indoor fine art and outdoor installations. It's wonderful the way a piece will change as the glass absorbs the light that plays across its surface.

COMMISSIONS: 400 sq. ft. mural, State Welcome Center, Missouri Department of Transportation; 50 sq. ft. mural, Philharmonic House of Design, Irvine, CA; Fine art commissions, Bronx, NY; *Sum of All Parts* mosaic show, Hillsboro, OR; Anniversary portrait, NJ; Custom backsplash in residence, Boulder, CO, and Anacortes, WA; Lucille Umbarger Elementary School mosaic in conjunction with the Washington State Arts Commission; Thirty-square-foot commissioned mosaic for shower installation, private residence, CO; Pool surround project, CA; Book cover art, *Mosaics in Communication*, Thomson Learning; *Beneath the Surface*, mosaic exhibition, Chicago, IL; *A More Perfect Union: Mosaic Aspirations*, 2005, Arlington, VA; *Opus Veritas: Fragments of Truth*, 2004; Museo ItaloAmericano, San Francisco, CA

Artist Statements

Gerald Siciliano
Sculpture / Representational, page 345

Gerald Siciliano has created a full range of unique and limited-edition sculptures for the discriminating collector. Attractively priced, these elegant and enduring works are offered in bronze, marble, granite, and stainless steel. Available in sizes ranging from the intimate to the monumental, they will enhance any collection or setting. His classically inspired figurative and non-representational sculptures are meticulously crafted to the highest standards for discerning collectors worldwide. We invite your inquiries, via telephone, email, or the Internet, for our featured sculpture or for your personalized commission.

COMMISSIONS: American Airlines; American Axle & Manufacturing de Mexico; Bristol-Myers Squibb; Brooklyn Museum; Canon Corporation; Chang-Won Provincial Government, Korea; Dong Baek Art Center, Korea; John Templeton Foundation; Mozart Companies; Pusan Olympic Park, Korea; Saint Jane Frances de Chantal RC Church, MD; Sparks Exhibits & Environments; Tangiers Waterfront Park, Morocco

Yvette Sikorsky
Paintings & Prints, page 221

After years of experimentation, I came upon a technique of sensuous abstraction that explores color and form. The images strike the viewer visually to reveal a true sense of design. The use of luminous colors plays across the spectrum while balancing a complex tension in design. I received an honorable mention and bronze medal from the City of Paris, France, my native country, and an Award of Excellence from Manhattan Art International. From 1985 to 2006, I showed my work in Paris, New York, Colorado, California, and The Schacknow Museum of Fine Arts in Florida. My work may currently be viewed in the World Fine Art Gallery in New York City. Sizes begin at 18" x 24". Prices range from $500 to $8,000. Work on commission, large or small, is welcome! I have also designed textiles for upholstery.

GUILD SOURCEBOOKS: *Residential Art 2, 3, 4, 5, 6*

Ron Slagle
Sculpture / Representational, page 346

I have produced forms in clay for almost four decades, the sculptural pieces being the accumulation of those skills learned. The human form is my main concentration, and allows recognizable gestures and feelings that most viewers understand. The surfaces are textured with the process of building up. The tones are earth colored and subdued, giving the images a peacefulness that will complement any area and allows them to be placed in gardens, pathways, entrances, and many indoor spaces. Sizes vary from tabletop to pedestal to floor-mounted pieces. I like to use a wood-fired kiln for the best finishes, and to yield a variable tone of flame flashes and pathways that add warmth to the very textured surfaces. Collectors will find the uniqueness of each piece a valued addition to their gallery or exhibit.

PRICING: Averaging between $100 and $10,000

Carter Smith
Wall Art / Fiber, page 375

I started out tie dyeing in 1965 while attending workshops in Santa Cruz that my mother, Eloise Smit, was teaching. I very quickly picked up the basics and started immediately exploring new techniques. Since deciding to earn my way through graduate school dyeing in 1969, textile dyeing has been my sole means of support. Over the years it has evolved into a very sophisticated art, encompassing varied techniques to form multilayered patterns and images. I have fused color and technique together to weave intricate detail into large-scale *shibori* landscapes. For the first twenty years I focused on textile art for the walls, and the next twenty years were about wearables. In the past five years, I have again returned to creating textiles for larger-scale environments. I have shown these pieces in museums and galleries throughout the U.S., Japan, and Korea. I am very much an innovator and completely self taught. After forty-four years the passion for dyeing is still growing and the inspiration is stronger than ever. I have been fortunate over the last twenty years to work in collaboration with my son Noah.

Yvette Kaiser Smith
Wall Art / Mixed & Other Media, pages 423, 431

I create my own fiberglass cloth by crocheting continuous strands of fiberglass into flat geometric shapes. These are formed and hardened with the application of polyester resin and the use of gravity. Using traditional methods, I create artwork that has been contemporized by the use of industrial materials, mathematics, and the language of art and architecture. This work engages math as a structural foundation by utilizing the grid and significant number sequences. The sculptures refer to dialogues dealing with the nature of being human, of individual and collective identity. These abstract forms are indoor, wall-based, large, translucent, durable, UV-protected, and reside naturally in public and private spaces.

COLLECTIONS: Philadelphia Ritz Carlton Residences; Englewood Senior Center, Chicago, IL; Old Orchard Towers, Skokie, IL; Deloitte, Chicago, IL; U.S. Embassy, Abuja, Nigeria; Elmhurst Art Museum, Elmhurst IL; City of Port Royal, SC; UIC Hospital, Nutrition and Wellness Clinic, Chicago, IL

Jeff Soderbergh
Furniture & Floor Coverings, page 107

So much today is temporary, disposable, throwaway. Since 1990 I have been creating original works using reclaimed antique architectural materials. I would like my work to have a thoughtful impact on our environment, a nostalgic connection to our past, and be beautiful. It's very important to me that we recognize the elegant and simplistic beauty that our history has to offer. The different materials that I use, dating between 1500 and 1950, come from all over the world from many walks of life, and may include wood, glass, stone, metal, and paper. I design and build furniture and sculpture because I would like to help preserve the history of our unique surroundings in a tangible way that can be passed down through the generations. Simply stated, I want to take materials from an era where we were surrounded by craftsmanship and detail, and force us to re-examine their beauty out of context. Re-claim a piece of history.

Artist Statements

Daniel Sroka
Fine Art Photography, pages 90, 190

I create dream-like abstract photographs from flowers, leaves, sticks, and seeds. My art is about reigniting our awareness and appreciation of the natural world that we live in every day. We tend to see nature as a safe and controlled environment, since the closest relationship most of us have with it is through our backyards and gardens. But what appears as a domesticated landscape is actually an uneasy truce with a thriving and chaotic ecosystem. My photographs examine the small, familiar icons of our backyards and gardens, and reacquaints us with their wild and unpredictable beauty. My photographs make a dramatic visual statement as large prints, or create a contemplative environment when combined into collections of smaller prints.

EXHIBITIONS: *Elemental/Environmental: Space,* 2008, New Orleans Photo Alliance, New Orleans, LA; *Arcadia: Artists Celebrate Trees,* 2007, California Modern Gallery, San Francisco, CA

AWARDS: Nature Category, 2008, Prix de la Photographie Paris

GUILD SOURCEBOOKS: *Residential Art 5, 6*

PRICING Pricing for prints ranging from 11x15 to 40x60 can be found at www. danielsroka.com.

Stanton Glass Studio, LLC
Architectural Glass, pages 60, 61

For over twenty-eight years, Stanton Glass Studio has collaborated with America's finest designers and architects, designing, crafting, and installing beautiful custom stained and leaded glass windows, entryways, domes, cabinetry, and light fixtures for residences, churches, and corporate settings. Working in a centuries-old craft, our talented staff produces masterpieces in glass, ranging from large, hand-painted church windows to decorative elements at the landmark Driskill Hotel in Austin, Texas. Our craftsmen also specialize in the preservation, restoration, and repair of historic stained glass windows, practicing the latest in conservation techniques. Recent restoration projects include the Tiffany windows at Sunset Ridge Church of Christ in San Antonio, Texas. Working from our facility in Waco, Texas, we collaborate with highly skilled blacksmiths and other craftsmen to produce hand-forged ironwork to frame our windows and suspend our domes. Contact Stanton Glass Studio for pricing and more information at 800-619-4882, or visit www. StantonGlass.com.

Todd Starks
Paintings & Prints, pages 222, 223

I create paintings about emotional space, shape, color, and pattern. With a painterly style, I carefully build up impasto layers using wet into wet oil paint, and allowing shards of underpainting to show through. Formally, the pieces are about composition, color harmonies, shape, and texture, yet each piece reveals a sensory connection to the landscape around me, and a dynamic interplay between conscious and subconscious thought. My paintings have been exhibited in group and solo exhibitions in galleries, museums, and institutions across the United States.

COLLECTIONS: University of Wisconsin Hospital and Clinics, Madison, WI; American Family Children's Hospital, Madison, WI

EXHIBITIONS: The Center for the Visual Arts, 2008, Wausau, WI; University of Wisconsin Hospital, Skylight Gallery, 2007, Madison, WI; Ebling Library, University of Wisconsin, 2006, Madison, WI; Wright Museum of Art, 2006, Beloit, WI; Limner Gallery, 2003, New York, NY

GUILD SOURCEBOOKS: *Residential Art 2, 5*

Stephen T. Anderson, Ltd.
Furniture & Floor Coverings, page 108

I offer the finest heirloom-quality hand-hooked rugs made in America today. Since 1985 I have taken hand-hooked rug making—one of America's only indigenous folk arts—and moved it into the forefront of modern design. Offering the highest level of customization, I prepare each rug from wool fabrics hand-hooked into a linen base in my New York City studio. Each rug possesses the nuances of coloration and textual subtleties usually found only in antiques. Leading designers, architects, and collectors from around the world have commissioned my work. In addition to being featured in some of the world's finest homes, my work has appeared in the pages of *Architectural Digest, House Beautiful, House and Garden, Town and Country, Forbes FYI, The New York Times,* and on CNN.

John C. Sterling
Furniture & Floor Coverings, page 109

I am privileged to live and work amidst the beautiful state forests of central Pennsylvania; this provides tremendous inspiration for my work. By carefully hand selecting the wood, my objective is to capture the simple elegance that nature provides through the unique figure and color of wood. My work is influenced by a wide range of traditional twentieth-century American movements, and while I am experienced at building reproduction pieces, I love the challenge of creating my own unique designs. Most recently, I have created a *shibui* line that uses the natural form of the tree to guide the design of the piece. (*Shibui* is a Japanese term for unadorned elegance.) I have found that people really connect to these pieces because they connect them intimately to nature, and fit in a number of different design settings. I most enjoy working closely with clients to design and build furniture that is loved for generations.

David Stine
Furniture & Floor Coverings, pages 22, 110

I design and craft furniture working only with wood that I have harvested and sawn myself from sustainable forests. I hand craft every piece and use only natural, environmentally friendly finishes. I am inspired by the natural beauty of the trees, and the design of each piece is driven by the inner beauty of the wood. As I saw each log, I see what I will build. As no two trees and no two boards are alike, no two pieces of furniture are alike. Each is one of a kind and is a testament to the grace and majesty of the tree, which lives on in a beautiful and functional way.

COMMISSIONS: Washington, DC; New York, NY; Chicago, IL; Harrisburg, PA; Chevy Chase, MD; Baltimore, MD; St. Louis, MO; San Francisco, CA, Aspen, CO; Boston, MA

PUBLICATIONS: *designspace,* Summer/Fall 2008; *Forbes Life,* June 2008; *St. Louis Magazine,* January 2007; *Mary Englebreit's Home Companion,* October/November 2006; *Architecture DC,* Summer 2003

PRICING: As all work is custom, pricing varies. Call 618.954.8636 or visit www. stinewoodworking.com for more information and a portfolio of work.

Artist Statements

Martin Sturman
Wall Art / Metal, page 401

My contemporary sculptures and functional art are created either in carbon steel or stainless steel and are suitable for indoor or outdoor placement. Stainless steel surfaces are hand burnished to create an incredible vibrancy when viewed from different angles. Carbon steel surfaces are acrylic painted with a polyurethane overlay to preserve color vitality. I encourage site-specific and collaborative efforts to achieve maximum client and artistic satisfaction.

COMMISSIONS: City of Alhambra, CA; Bascom Palmer Eye Institute, Palm Beach Gardens, FL; Hyatt Westlake Plaza Hotel, Westlake Village, CA; Kaiser-Permanente Clinic Facility, Santa Clarita, CA; Manhattan Beach Car Wash, Manhattan Beach, CA; McDonald's Corporation, Oakbrook, IL; McGraw-Hill Publishing Company, Columbus, OH; New West Symphony, Thousand Oaks, CA; Royal Caribbean Cruise Lines, Eugene, OR; Thousand Oaks Civic Art Plaza, Thousand Oaks, CA; University of Kansas Hospital Cancer Center, Kansas City, KS

GUILD SOURCEBOOKS: *Architect's 12, 14; Designer's 7, 8, 9, 10, 11, 12, 13, 14, 15; Architectural & Interior Art 16, 17, 18, 19, 20, 21, 22, 23; Residential Art 2*

Suna
Wall Art / Glass, pages 385, 387

I have been a glass artist for more than two decades, with a focus over the last several years in glass carving. In this medium I am able to create a sculptural object within a sheet of glass that is organic and free-flowing. My freehand carvings create shadows that enhance the interplay between shape and light, giving the work a contemporary presence. It is truly unique. I collaborate with professional designers and architects, creating custom representational sculpture or abstract tailored solutions. My glass carvings have ranged in size from tabletop gallery works to large-scale architectural commissions. These include a medical research facility, a chapel, corporate offices, clubs, and residential locations. For images and information, please visit my website, www.designsbysuna.com.

Michael Szabo
Public Art, page 268

Working predominantly in metal, I approach my process as a collaboration between myself, the natural tendencies of my materials, and the setting of the work. In past years I have completed dozens of large-scale public and private commissions—many in conjunction with architects, public art committees, and designers. These types of projects require me to work closely with the client, from initial concept to installation. In public art I search for a deeper contextual root, interweaving the physical place, the individuals and families who spend time there, and the community in which they participate. I look for specific aspects of a site, as well as general themes that can be integrated with the work. My process for creating site-specific commissions is based on the idea that a work of art needs to both complement the setting that it inhabits and stand out as an attractive piece of sculpture.

COMMISSSIONS: City of Palo Alto, CA; Superior Court of California, San Francisco; numerous private commissions nationwide

484

T. S. Post
Murals, Tiles & Wall Reliefs, page 161

Ceramic collage allows me to play with lines and edges, cropping and extending marks and images, abstracting linear elements of organic and architectural forms. Painting and etching directly on glaze creates a uniquely beautiful surface, combining depth of color with soft light—an exciting expression of painting and printmaking techniques in a ceramic medium. Hand-cut sections are painted, etched, and fired separately. Each piece is adhered to a Baltic birch panel and finished with thin grouted lines. Wall works hang securely with a French cleat hanging system. Large-scale works are made and hung in sections. Ceramic collage is impervious to light and humidity and requires no framing, making it suitable for commercial as well as residential applications. Please see www.tspost.com for additional images and installation views.

COMMISSIONS: Northwestern Mutual; Alta Bates Medical Center; Kaiser Permanente; Marriott Hotels; Eisenhower Medical Center

PRICING: Contact tspostart@gmail.com

Tesserae Mosaic Studio, Inc.
Murals, Tiles & Wall Reliefs, page 138

Our studio creates stunning custom mosaics for residential, commercial, healthcare, and education applications. We collaborate with designers and architects to create a design that will be realized in glass, marble, or porcelain. Encompassing many styles—representational, painterly, patterns, and abstract designs—our work ranges in size from 8" x 8" fine art mosaics to a 6' x 76' exterior glass mural. Members of SAMA (Society of American Mosaic Artists).

COMMISSIONS: Hampton Inn Tropicana, Las Vegas, NV; Covenant Lakeside Women's Hospital, Lubbock, TX; Crowne Plaza La Concha Hotel, Key West, FL; Texas Tech University, Lubbock, TX; Gaylord Texan Resort, Grapevine, TX

EXHIBITIONS: Mosaic Arts International, 2008, Miami, FL; *Global Perspectives*, 2008, Miami, FL; *Sum of All Parts: Contemporary Mosaic Art in North America*, 2008, Hillsboro, OR; Mosaic Arts International, 2007, Mesa, AZ

AWARDS: Best Large-Scale Exterior, 2007, SAMA

PUBLICATIONS: *Mosaic Art Now*, 2008; *The French Connection*, 2005; *Mosaic Techniques and Traditions*, 2004

P.T. Tiersky
Wall Art / Mixed & Other Media, page 424

Since my years growing up on an Illinois farm, I have been immersed in the elements of nature. After graduating from college in Iowa, a move to Minneapolis is where a love for artistic endeavors first emerged. As a hobby I started mixing artistic papers with acrylic paints and found objects. Through a job promotion, I migrated to Southern California in 1985. After a successful business career, I decided to retire early and devote all of my attention to my first love of creating mixed-media art on a variety of surfaces. Through this process I was able to experiment with the use of three-dimensional wood panels to create large-scale abstract puzzle pieces. I'm currently expanding on that theme with large installation pieces for public and residential settings.

COLLECTIONS: American Bankers Association (ABA); Toyota Motor Sales USA; Ernst & Young; Anthem Blue Cross Blue Shield; Von Lehman & Company; Town Properties; Cincinnati Eye Institute; Comair Greater Cincinnati/Northern Kentucky Airport; Carson's Restaurant, Fort Myers, FL; MD Business Solutions; Marriot Kingsgate; Town Properties; MRSI; Contech Construction Products

PRICING: Retail pricing ranges from $175-$200 per square foot. Call or email for an exact quote and wholesale pricing.

Artist Statements

Tile Surface Impressions
Murals, Tiles & Wall Reliefs, page 162

We offer a wide selection of original artwork on glass, porcelain, ceramic, or tumbled stone. We represent the work of such fine artists as Sharon Carr, John Ebner, Collin Bogle, Lee Bogle, John Peterson, and others. Our artists work from a variety of art mediums, including watercolor, oil, acrylic, photography, and digital art. Founded by Randy Hopfer, Tile Surface Impressions is committed to the highest quality and individual needs of its customers. We custom build each mural to our clients' specifications, meeting their exact design needs. We work with designers to ensure that the finished work is perfectly integrated into the environment or as part of a larger design. We offer alternative mounting solutions to allow our tile art to be used as movable wall art for residential, commercial, corporate, or public spaces. We are proud to offer our artists' work in eco-friendly porcelain tiles.

Luis Torruella
Public Art, page 269

I design in a contemporary, abstract context. My Caribbean heritage is reflected in my work's color, rhythm, and movement. I collaborate with architects, designers, and developers on public and private commissions.

COLLECTIONS: Museo de Arte de Puerto Rico, San Juan; Mead Art Museum, Amherst, MA; Centro de Bellas Artes Luis A. Ferre, San Juan, PR; Skokie Northshore Sculpture Park, IL

EXHIBITIONS: Palma de Mallorca, 2001, Spain; Galeria Botello, 2002, 1997, 1994, 1992, San Juan, PR; State Institute of Theatrical Art, 1992, Moscow; World Exposition 1992, Seville, Spain; numerous private collections

GUILD SOURCEBOOKS: *Architect's 14, 15; Architectural & Interior Art 16, 17, 18, 19, 20; Residential Art 1*

Milon Townsend
Sculpture / Representational, pages 17, 347

My sculptural glass forms reflect the natural light of their surroundings, and they also provide a window into my own compulsion to explore the transcendent human figure. I continue to find glass a material that provides color, light, form, and depth to the internal imagery that makes up my waking and dreaming mind. Casting glass is a technically demanding process that fully occupies and satisfies my own desire to innovate, while allowing me to work with the ideas and images of a lifetime working in the field of art. I am specifically interested in finding a happy marriage between my own interests, iconography, and style, and the creative vision of those working in interior or exterior spaces in which illumination and imagery are of paramount importance. My work is aggressively priced, creating both affordability and the economic context within which great work may be created.

485

Joel E. Traylor III
Paintings & Prints, page 224

My work has always been defined by rich color, bold composition, and unusual technique. Several years ago I took a radical departure from my previous Cubist explorations; I began slicing paintings into strips and reassembling them by weaving two paintings together. These sliced works have a soothing, hypnotic power, while simultaneously vibrating with hidden energy. I welcome the challenge of commissioned site-specific work in a variety of sizes and modular configurations. Mockups are designed and approved in collaboration with my clients/collectors. From initial concept to completion, I engage my clients/collectors in the process, guaranteeing successful custom artworks. To see more of my work, including woven or reassembled pieces, please visit www.JETgallery.com.

PRICING: Prices range from $175-$350/square foot. Please contact me for a printed catalog.

Rachel Tribble
Paintings & Prints, page 225

My work is a reflection of nature. To explore the dimensions humans cannot see or experience regularly and make them visual to us. Color also reaches through the dimensions; the human experience of color is individual on many levels. We experience color in our daily lives in a routine, but in dreams colors are often expressed in ways that do not exist in waking life. My expression of color is an attempt to reach into nature, explore the hidden realms, and share the beauty and serenity of the unseen natural world.

Ellen Tykeson
Public Art, page 270

It seems that as we travel along in life, our most permanent dwelling is the body we inhabit. The figure in art fascinates me because of the timeless comfort of this knowledge. Each posture or expression can describe a piece of this shared connection for us. It weaves through our human history of myth and storytelling and is seen in the role that the mysterious plays in these traditions. As part of this, I find the challenges and possibilities offered by figurative sculpture to be continually intriguing. For me, the best art quietly insists on a moment of reflection from those who pass by. Fostering this possibility for each piece requires balanced consideration of concept, execution, audience, site, and scale. Designing a sculpture that thoughtfully considers the perimeters of these questions is a great game of problem solving, and a privilege that I enjoy very much.

Artist Statements

Mia Tyson
Objects, page 173

My work is hand-built sculptural clay, both functional and non-functional. I am intrigued by what I feel when viewing my completed work for my forms and lines emerge as a whole and cohesive piece with no intent of my own. Some refer to my work as similar to Matisse, Picasso, and of Greek influence, but I have no real intention when I begin a piece—it is only an extension of who I am, expressed in form and line through time. My greatest challenge and excitement is derived by working directly with the client. It is sort of a journey in which I must find the ultimate answer. I have recently completed two installations: The Hotel Palomar in Atlanta, Georgia, commissioned by the interior design firm of Faulkner + Locke of Atlanta, and a retirement resort development in Plano, Texas, commissioned by Skyline Art Services of Houston, Texas.

Luann Udell
Wall Art / Fiber, page 376

I make wall hangings, small sculptures, and art jewelry inspired by prehistoric and tribal art from around the world. My fiber collage wall hangings range in size from small, intimate pieces to large-scale works. I anchor layers of vintage and recycled fabric with intricate and colorful quilting, then embellish them with my own handmade artifacts—totem animals (horses, fish, bear, otter, bull, bison, birds), masks, shells, stones, beads, and buttons, all made one at a time by me. My award-winning works have appeared in national exhibits. They've been featured in national publications and hang in private collections across the country. I welcome corporate and residential commissions. Ten thousand years from now, who will hold the makings of our hands? And who will know the mysteries of our hearts?.

Karen Urbanek
Wall Art / Fiber, page 377

I build painterly images and sculptural forms, both abstract and representational, in luminous layers of complex color and texture. My extensive palette comes from natural sources and environmentally responsible working methodologies developed over the past thirty years. Ongoing research leads to new approaches: recycling water and solar or no heat dyeing. Constructed primarily of compacted tussah silk, flax, and bamboo fiber, surfaces range from smooth and translucent to dense, high relief. A penetrating coating adds crispness and strength, yet is eco friendly. Works may be double sided and hang freely, or may be composed of separate layers and elements. Various construction techniques are used, including stand-alone three-dimensional sculpture. Light in weight, easy to ship, mount, maintain, and clean. Framing is optional. Commissions accepted. Visuals/pricing available upon request.

COLLECTIONS: Lockheed Martin Corp.; Aspect Communications; Kaiser Hospitals; McGraw Hill Publishing Co.; Grace Cathedral, San Francisco

GUILD SOURCEBOOKS: *Designer's 13, 14, 15; Architectural & Interior Art 16, 17, 18, 19, 20, 21, 22, 23*

486

Aaron P. Van de Kerckhove
Public Art, page 271

I create large-scale metal sculptures that are often kinetic and interact with the viewer and the environment, either by moving in the wind or by human touch. With a strong sense of spatial relationships, I enjoy sculpting steel forms that compliment both the urban landscape and the natural environment. I have made sculpture for architects, designers, galleries, city councils, and private collectors. Created from powder-coated steel, stainless steel, Corten, or bronze, my work is meant to withstand the test of time; as a certified welder, I pay much attention to quality and technique. My studio in Watsonville, CA, is able to produce work from a few feet high to monumental public sculpture. Prices for small to mid-sized work begins around $10,000. Commissions include a public sculpture for Mission Gateway Housing, Union City, CA; a kinetic sculpture for Saks Fifth Avenue, Santa Barbara, CA; and private commissions all over the U.S.

Dierk Van Keppel
Atrium Sculpture, page 75

I create blown, fused, and cast glass objects and combine them with various materials to produce custom lighting, sculpture, and art glass vessels. My projects include public, residential, and corporate environments. Collaborating with architects and designers I am involved in all aspects of design—from concept to fabrication.

COMMISSIONS: H & R Block World Headquarters, Kansas City, MO; Shawnee Mission Medical Center, Merriam, KS; Nelson-Adkins Museum of Art, Kansas City, MO; Milano Restaurant, Hyatt Regency, Kansas City, MO; 1022 On The Lake, Milwaukee, WI; Overland Park Convention Center, Overland Park, KS; Sprint World Headquarters, Overland Park, KS; St. Alexian Medical Center, Hoffman Estates, IL

GUILD SOURCEBOOKS: *Architectural & Interior Art 17, 18, 21; Residential Art 1, 5*

Alice Van Leunen
Wall Art / Mixed & Other Media, page 425

My artworks explore pattern, texture, and reflection. My approach is light-hearted. Many of the works make musical or literary allusions and feature calligraphic marks and symbols. Recent works include poetic text in collaboration with poet Kelly Gill Holland. Works range in size from small, intimate pieces up to major architectural installations. Commissions are welcome.

COMMISSIONS: Mulia Bank Complex, Djakarta, Indonesia; National High Magnetic Field Laboratory, Tallahassee, FL (with Walter Gordinier); Fairview Auditorium, OK; Kaiser Permanente, San Diego, CA; Kodiak Auditorium, Kodiak Island, AK; Playboy Towers, Chicago, IL

COLLECTIONS: Atlantic County Office Building, Atlantic City, NJ; General Motors, New York, NY; Seattle City Light, WA; Calvin Klein Cosmetics, Wayne, NJ

AWARDS: Oregon Individual Artist Fellowship, 1993

GUILD SOURCEBOOKS: *THE GUILD 1, 4, 5; Architect's 6, 7, 12, 13; Designer's 6, 9, 10, 11; Architectural & Interior Art 16, 17, 20, 21; Artful Home 1, 2, 4, 5, 6*

Artist Statements

Helen Vaughn
Paintings & Prints, page 226

I specialize in oil and pastel paintings of landscapes, figures, and still lifes. The works feature rich, velvety textures and vivid colors wrapped in carefully arranged compositions. As a painter I am continually fascinated by the properties of color, light, and shadow as they affect both the image and my own sense of time, place, and inner harmony. While this fascination influences both the visual elements of the work and my needs as an artist, the paintings stand or fall on their own. My work is included in museum, corporate, and private collections, and has been widely exhibited. My aim as a painter is to bring to life a slice of the world as I experience it. Light, color, and form are my vocabulary. Trade professionals should contact me for commission and pricing information.

PUBLICATIONS: *Pastel Artist International,* 2002; *American Artist,* November, 1998

GUILD SOURCEBOOKS: *Residential Art 1, 2, 3, 4*

Susan Venable
Wall Art / Mixed & Other Media, page 426

My work is an exploration of structure, surface, and the relationship between the two. The constructions are bas-reliefs of stacked steel grids woven with copper wire and juxtaposed with encaustic paintings. I want to maximize the physicality of the materials, seeking an energy field through structure and surface. My exploration, on a perceptual and tactile level, is to create a transcendent reality, not to recall a specific place or object. Archaeology, rituals, repetition, ruins, magic, and the art of indigenous societies all strongly influence my creative process. My work can be seen in public spaces, homes, and museums. The commissions/installations have involved collaboration with collectors, architects, and designers throughout the world. The materials are durable, low maintenance, and suitable for installation in public areas.

GUILD SOURCEBOOKS: *Designer's 10, 11, 12, 13, 14, 15; Architectural & Interior Art 16, 17, 18, 19, 20, 21, 22, 23*

Kerry Vesper
Wall Art / Mixed & Other Media, page 427

I am inspired by flowing water, desert canyons, and the mountains of the Southwest where I have lived all my life. I equate my method of layering and shaping wood to the way nature builds up layers of earth and then shapes it with wind and water. Made of domestic and exotic hardwoods, the wood appears to be bent but it is not. I shape every piece by hand with carving, grinding, and sanding tools into flowing forms. My wall sculptures mount simply on screws in the wall and can be hung in any position. They are available in a variety of different kinds of wood and sizes. They are finished with a very durable clear oil/urethane finish. I exhibit and sell my work in fine craft and fine art shows. I especially enjoy working with designers and collectors to create commission pieces for unique spaces.

James Vilona
Public Art, page 272

My bronze and stainless steel sculptures celebrate life, interpret underlying joy in the world, and convey these emotions to the observer. My artistic goal is to create work the viewer will never tire of enjoying, work that creates a permanent sculptural landscape. Owning my foundry has given me limitless opportunities both with my own sculpture and the ability to create custom and site-specific work for clients throughout the U.S. I work with art consultants, landscape architects, galleries, and create many original sculptures for private collectors, universities, and corporate campuses.

COMMISSIONS: The Westin Book Cadillac, Detroit, MI; The St. Regis New York, NY

COLLECTIONS: Civic Center, Cerritos, CA; University of Virginia's College at Wice, VA; Mount Holyoke College, South Hadley, MA; Denver Children's Hospital, CO

AWARDS: Best Artist, Metal, Western Design Conference, 2008; Best New Artist, Lincoln Arts Festival, 2008

PUBLICATIONS: *Southwest Art* magazine, September 2008, *LUXE Magazine,* Winter 2007.

Evgeni Vodenitcharov
Sculpture / Representational, page 348

Our studio specializes in custom sculpture, design, consulting, and manufacturing from large scale to small detail maquettes using clay, foam, fiberglass, concrete, bronze, and polyurethane coating. With over twenty years of experience, we provide concept development, mold making, casting, and fabrication of unique artwork for hotels, casinos, churches, trade shows, museums, theme parks, high-end residential/private homes, and cruise ships. Working on commissions and fine art at the same time can only enrich the experience I have as an artist and everyone involved in the process.

COMMISSIONS: St. Viator Church; The Venetian; Stallion Golf Course; Caesar's Palace; Sirens, Treasure Island; Rio; MGM Mirage Group, Las Vegas, NV; Universal Studios, Japan; Zoological Park, Albuquerque, NM; Wild Life Museum, St. George, Utah; Bob Drake Productions, Oregon; YESCO Las Vegas; Royal Caribbean International

Bilhenry Walker
Furniture & Floor Coverings, page 111

My sculptural furniture was shown in New York City at this spring's Architectural Digest Home Show and International Contemporary Furniture Fair (ICFF). I have expanded my line to include a *Diamond Spine Armchair,* a round *Tornado Table,* a seven-foot-long sculptural *Dining Table,* and a *Starship Sofa Chair.* The ergonomically designed arms of the armchair were carved out of aluminum blocks for cool comfort. The dining table base is a sculpture made with a specially designed aluminum extrusion with ¾" thick glass atop. The sofa chair is the first prototype in a new series that includes loveseats, couches, and sectionals. These seating pieces give the impression of being hard as steel, but they will surprise with comfort due to the eight-way tie spring system and ample cushioning. The matching ottoman has a lid that opens to reveal a polished maple interior, perfect for storing a caftan throw.

Artist Statements

Wanner Sculpture Studio
Sculpture / Representational, pages 315, 349

We have created figurative sculpture for hundreds of architectural settings throughout the United States. Our sculpture spans secular and religious themes, and ranges from small to over life-size in scale. We have worked successfully with architects, art consultants, designers, and contractors for almost forty years on projects for public parks, hospitals, cathedrals, churches, government buildings, corporations, and more. Our in-house foundry has enabled us to maintain a strong, competitive advantage. Please visit www.wannersculpturestudio.com for more information about us and our work.

Libby Ware
Wall Art / Mixed & Other Media, page 428

In using five sides of a cube as the basic statement of the picture plane, I hope to synthesize painting and sculpture, even though my cubes are characteristically attached to the wall. This confounding of two- and three-dimensional space is meant to present a visual puzzle. In addition, I intend for the depth and space of the cubes to engage the viewer in the work. As the viewer moves past the work, the image/illusion changes. Therefore, movement is a key characteristic of the multilevel installations. Another aspect of each piece is the owner's choice of involvement in the work. To help facilitate this involvement, each cube is individually mounted with hidden hardware. A person can choose to arrange the cubes to suit an aesthetic or space. Lusters, which radiate iridescent luminescence, help create the mystery of the material. Clay is an ancient material, which is soft and then hard, capturing both the organic nature and the handmade process. The cubes, separate and apart from each other, have subtle elements of difference from one another. The choice of clay celebrates the use of non-industrial material in our electronic age.

GUILD SOURCEBOOKS: *Architectural & Interior Art 20, 21, 22, 23; Residential Art 3, 4, 5, 6*

Graceann Warn
Wall Art / Mixed & Other Media, page 429

The art I make combines elements of beauty and classical form with an underlying sense of mystery that compels the viewer to look at it over and over again. While the pieces reflect an obsession with logic and numerical rationales, they are infused with a lyricism within the multiple layers of paint and paper that comprise them. My work has always been about the process, as well as the finished product. My labor in the studio is reflected in the surfaces of my paintings so that the human element is revealed and apparent.

COLLECTIONS: U.S. Embassy, Nairobi; U.S. Embassy, Sarajevo; Pew Charitable Trust; Bell-Atlantic; University of Michigan; Delta Airlines; U.S. Comptroller of the Currency; Sprint; and General Motors, among numerous others, private and public

PRICING: The retail prices for my work range from $2,450 to $8,400.

Tim Washburn
Sculpture / Representational, page 355

For over twenty-five years, I have enjoyed sculpting and still counting. Being a Native American Indian, I work with the theme of our traditional American Indian history and its Western scenarios. Through the use of shadow and details, I convey movements in my sculptures and instill remembrance on our history to the viewers in a manner that touches their hearts. I create one-of-a-kind sculpture in marble, limestone, steatite, granite, alabaster, and sandstone; any of these can be cast in bronze. I also work in a variety of clay textures for maquettes, and bronze for original work. My sculptures range from tabletop pieces to monumental work. My largest piece is over 15' high and weighs over 20 tons. I have experience with galleries, corporations, private collectors, public art programs, architects, and national art shows.

Leslie Webb
Furniture & Floor Coverings, page 115

I love the challenge of balancing the aesthetic and utilitarian aspects of each piece I design and build. Many argue that form follows function; however, I believe that form and function are equally important, that they must act together to create a whole. My designs celebrate natural materials and form. As a maker I value craftsmanship and purpose. For me it is paramount to have confidence in the piece after it has left my hands. There are countless ways to leave a legacy in this world; it seems natural for me to craft furniture that will be here long after I am gone.

Jamie and Jeremy Wells
Public Art, page 273

Collaboration is at the essence of our work. We believe that creativity is most beneficial when collaboration between artists, individuals, and communities is delicately sought. In approaching our public work, we seek to define a space and thus create an environment. Our interest lies in pursuing work that evokes a sense of reverence in a space and enables collective and individual subconscious self-reflection. In both our public and personal work, we explore various themes of light, land, texture, social justice, and the spiritual relationship to them. Our life and marriage has been strengthened through art and the experiences it has brought us. Our media typically include acrylic or oil on canvas, photography, and digital. With our public work, we enjoy the opportunity to use unorthodox materials to create whatever the vision requires. We respectfully approach each commission with the utmost professionalism. In-house giclées and custom commissions available. www.JamieJeremyWells.com.

COMMISSIONS: Chevron Art Collection, 2007, TX; Dr. Nikko Cosmetic Surgery Center, 2006, TX; Breast and Bone Hospital, 2006, TX; Brentwood Cafe, 2009, Las Vegas, NV.

PUBLICATIONS: *Houston Design Resource, 2006–09, LUXE 2007–09, The Artful Home, 2007*

GUILD SOURCEBOOKS: *Architectural & Interior Art 22, 23; Residential Art 5*

Artist Statements

Debra White
Sculpture / Representational, page 355

My work involves developing sculptural pieces that incorporate texture and organic forms. We are all surrounded by powerful shapes and forms in our everyday travels, and some may have an element of visual and emotional comfort. Living in a high-tech world such as ours, it is sometimes difficult for us as a people to maintain a spiritual connection with our surroundings. Ancient cultures have contributed so much visually and spiritually; we must continue that journey. My work consists of bronze, stone, and paper-mâché. Most pieces could be cast in a metal for any interior or exterior setting, corporate or private. I look forward to working with architects, art consultants, and private parties to design that special piece for a particular setting. Examples of my work can be seen at www.debrawhite.us.

PUBLICATIONS: *Best of America: Sculpture Artists & Artisans, Volume 1, 2007*

Timothy White
Furniture & Floor Coverings, page 112

I am a contemporary studio furniture maker who works primarily with wood, adding occasional accents of steel, bronze, concrete, or glass. My evolution as a craftsman and artist over the past twenty-four years has given me some unique opportunities, including work at a pipe organ company and an eight-year tenure with Richard Scott Newman. I opened my own studio in 1997 in Crested Butte, Colorado, where I am constantly inspired by the awesome beauty that surrounds me. My work, while often commissioned for private collections, is shown in several galleries and occasional exhibitions around the country. It has won best of show and design awards on numerous occasions, and has been featured in publications including *American Art Collector, Woodworker West,* and *Woodwork.*

GUILD SOURCEBOOKS: *Residential Art 6*

Dana Wigdor
Paintings & Prints, page 227

Paint is a perfect medium for capturing the invisible forces that surround us. Inspired by the dramatic, beautiful Vermont landscape, my paintings portray a world with its own laws of gravity, light, and motion—where a layer of geometry covers the landscape, interrupting the lines of the mountains and sky. I am fascinated with the relationship between nature and culture, between science and spirituality. Each canvas is a stage where light and color bridge the seen world to the elusive place "beyond."

EXHIBITIONS: *Liminal Places,* 2006, The Vermont Arts Council, Montpelier, VT; *Spirited Women,* 2003, Brattleboro Museum, Brattleboro, VT; *Ten Vermont Women,* 2003, Fleming Museum, Burlington, VT

AWARDS: Creation Grant, 2004, Vermont Arts Council, National Endowment of the Arts; Finalist, From the States Program, 2003, National Museum of Women in the Arts

GUILD SOURCEBOOKS: *Residential Art 2, 3*

John Wilbar
Sculpture / Non-Representational, page 313

Education and training in architectural design have influenced the style and spirit of my artwork. My sculpture investigates shape, shade, shadow, and the effects of sunlight on an object. Each sculpture is a continuous form that features geometric abstractions, bold colors, deep shadows, and a depth of field one can visually step into. My sculpture is comprised of a plywood substructure, solid wood blocking, and exterior acrylic stucco embedded with fiberglass mesh. I apply a coat of waterproofing over the completed stucco form and finish with three coats of exterior acrylic paint. The finished sculpture is strong but light for its size and weight (approxmately 200 pounds). If these forms are of interest and a solid steel structure is required, that request may be accommodated. Contact me via email for pricing information at jfwilbar@yahoo.com.

William Wells Studio
Furniture & Floor Coverings, pages 113, 121

My furniture making has been influenced by two remarkable artists who come from completely opposite ends of the design spectrum. I apprenticed thirty years ago with Alfonse Heinlein, a German craftsman who designed and constructed many church interiors in the Detroit area. I learned from him the traditional techniques that he learned from his father and grandfather when he was a child in his homeland. Twenty years later, I was lucky to do an extended internship at the Michael C. Fortune Studio in Ontario, Canada. Michael is widely known for his contemporary designs, which are a stark contrast to what I had experienced twenty years earlier. Consequently, my designs range from Arts and Crafts to Art Deco. My designs incorporate curves, hand shaping, and inlay details, such as fine silver and various shell materials. This adds visual interest and compels people to take a closer look. See more of my work at williamwellsfurniture.com.

Cheryl Williams
Sculpture / Non-Representational, page 309

The energy that comes through my heart and into my hands stirs great passion in me. The light that is within in all of us is reflected in my work. Bringing essence into form, I make the ordinary appear extraordinary. My work is simple and elegant. It gives me great pleasure to share this with you.

GUILD SOURCEBOOKS: *Residential Art 6*

Artist Statements

Laurie Wohl
Wall Art / Mixed & Other Media, page 430

Laurie Wohl's Unweavings® fiber art evokes in a modern idiom the spirit of mystery and celebration found in the oldest traditions of narrative textiles. The gentle radiance of these pieces complements residential, liturgical, and commercial settings. Narratives are conveyed by form, color, and texture, with unwoven spaces forming shapes suggestive of ritual garments. The narrative is enhanced by Wohl's own iconographic language, as well as Hebrew, English, and Chinese calligraphy.

COMMISSIONS: Her liturgical commissions include 12 major pieces for the sanctuary of Fourth Presbyterian Church (Chicago) and four pulpit pieces for Madison Avenue Presbyterian Church (NYC), as well as several synagogue commissions.

COLLECTIONS: Wohl's Unweavings® are held in numerous private and public collections, including the Museum of Arts and Design (NYC), the American Bible Society, The Constitutional Court of South Africa, and Catholic Theological Union (Chicago). Her works have been on extended loan to the United States Embassies in Tunis, Vienna, Cape Town, and Pretoria.

GUILD SOURCEBOOKS: *Architectural & Interior Art 18*

William Wright
Paintings & Prints, page 229

My career as a microsurgeon sensitized me to the interior rhythms of organic form. My second loves of mathematics and computer programming gave me the tools to express these harmonies for others to see. Most art depicts an image of an object, albeit associated with a mood or feeling. My images, which I call *Light Threads,* instead show the energies within, the emotion without physical form, the kinetics without a vehicle. Most people who view my art feel a visceral response that they may find difficult to put into words. It's understandable. My art isn't about the physical world. It's about the energies that drive, unite, and nourish that world. Pure motion. Pure energy. Pure light. PRICING: Retail pricing ranges from $175-$200 per square foot. Call or email for an exact quote and wholesale pricing.

Donna Wojcik
Paintings & Prints, page 228

My paintings are created using bursts of color with the intent to embolden content and meaning. Each of my compositions is unique, its essence will exist alone or co-exist beautifully with my other paintings. My goal is to provide the viewer with the energy and enthusiasm that I put into each piece. I enjoy working with acrylics, however I do incorporate other mediums to achieve varied effects. My artwork develops intuitively, intense color serves as a very moving and inspirational component. Direct yet subtle lighting will enhance the vibrancy of whatever piece you choose and will become the heartbeat of any residential or commercial space. Original works are available along with signed and numbered limited-edition giclée prints. Pricing is available upon request.

COMMISSIONS: Buffalo, NY; Ellicottville, NY; Niagara Falls, NY; Toronto, Ontario; Hermosa Beach, CA

Marlene Sanaye Yamada
Paintings & Prints, page 230

My work celebrates freedom of spirit through the purity of color and flow, spontaneous brush strokes, light, and movement. Each uplifting piece is a glimpse into a boundless environment. A quick glance sets a mood or conveys an emotion. More contemplation reveals intriguing details and surprises. I find it exciting to see the unique and unexpected effects that emerge with each new creation. The gentle shade variations are peaceful and soothing. The bold, bright colors are rejuvenating. I hope that my artwork stirs your emotions, lifts your spirits, and inspires you to reach new heights. My work has been featured in gallery exhibits, private, corporate, and healthcare collections, and has appeared on the television show *CSI: Miami*. Please visit www.artworkbysanaye.com for additional samples. I invite you to collaborate with me on new commissions.

COMMISSIONS: DLA Piper, 2008, Tampa, FL; multiple private collections

GUILD SOURCEBOOKS: *Architectural & Interior Art 22, 23*

Bruce Wolfe
Sculpture / Representational, pages 350, 351

Most of the subjects of my sculptures are imposing, dynamic personalities, and I wish to portray their energy and presence in the bronze. The natural beauty of the human form inspires me. Working from a live model gives my pieces life and movement. I like the truth of concentrated observation and the specifics of each personality I am trying to capture. I wish to express nature and humanity from both exterior and interior levels. All my sculptures, from half life to heroic sized, are in bronze. I have worked as an artist all my life and have experience working with architects, public works departments, heads of churches, developmental departments of universities, and private collectors. I am a Fsellow in the National Sculpture Society and the California Art Club.

COMMISSIONS: Hillsdale University; University of Michigan; University of Texas at Austin; Stanford University and Stanford School of Medicine; St. Mary's College, CA; Youngstown University; Schermerhorn Symphony Center, Nashville; San Francisco War Memorial Opera House; Kansas City, Missouri, Civic Center Park; Austin-Bergstrom International Airport; Foster City Hall; Jacksonville Times Performing Arts Center; San Francisco Asian Art Museum;

GUILD SOURCEBOOKS: *Architect's 9, 11, 13, 14, 15; Architectural & Interior Art 16, 17, 18, 19, 20, 21, 22, 23*

Richard Yaski
Sculpture / Non-Representational, pages 277, 310

I studied art at the prestigious Chouinard Art Institute in Los Angeles. For the past forty years, I have been creating metal sculptures at my studio and residence in Little River, CA, near Mendocino. Much of my work is displayed here, interspersed among the redwood trees, fern gardens, and waterfalls in the Shibui Sculpture Garden, a five-acre landscaped sculpture garden sitting adjacent to a 400-acre nature conservancy. My work, although grand in scale, reflects the spirit and philosophy of the Japanese Shibui: simple, subtle, unobtrusive, and beautifying with age, timeless in design and feeling. In addition to creating metal sculptures, I work in stone, creating water fountains and sacred spaces. My sculptures range in size from monumental outdoor pieces to tabletop and wall pieces. My work can be found in the Kremlin, Moscow; Istanbul, Turkey; the Detroit International Airport, as well as in synagogues, and private and corporate collections throughout the U.S. I have worked extensively with architects, engineers, and design teams, and welcome collaboration for site-specific commissions for residential, commercial, and ecumenical sites. Please visit www.yaski.com for more information.

GUILD SOURCEBOOKS: *Architect's 10, Architectural & Interior Art 22*

490

Artist Statements

Stephen Yates
Paintings & Prints, page 231

I am interested in creating paintings for both public and private spaces. I often work on large-scale individual artworks or in related series shown together. I work with designers, architects, and corporate art representatives to develop site-specific artworks that help to make their spaces visually remarkable, integrated, and dynamic. Paintings shown in this sourcebook are from the *Botanicals* series and the *Waters* series. See my website: www.stephenyatesart.com.

COMMISSIONS: Hyatt Hotels, 2009, Bellevue, WA; La Costa Resort, 2009, San Diego, CA; Overlake Hospital Lobby, 2007, Bellevue, WA; Kitsap Government Building Lobby, 2006, Port Orchard, WA; Hilton Hotels, 2005, Kansas City, MO, Vancouver, WA; Marriott Hotels, 2007, Orlando, San Francisco, Louisville 2005; University of Washington—Cascadia College, 2002, Bothell, WA

COLLECTIONS: Microsoft; City of Seattle; City of Portland, OR; Evergreen College, Olympia, WA

AWARDS: Expressions NW, 2008, 2001, Port Townsend, WA; 18th NW International, Whatcom Museum, 1998; NEA-WESTAF, Collectors Project, 1990. Fellowships: Art Matters Inc., 1989, NY; Artist Trust, 1988, Seattle

GUILD SOURCEBOOKS: *Architectural & Interior Art 20, 23; Residential Art 2*

Jeannine Young
Public Art, page 274

Poise, posture, and profile have always intrigued me. Planes, angles, and textures are utilized in my sculptures to elicit different reactions from the viewer. I weld my stylized men, women, and animals with steel rods and sheet metal, and then have limited editions cast in bronze. This year I was commissioned for a large sculpture by Benson Sculpture Gardens in Loveland, Colorado. It was a lot of fun, and I look forward to new opportunities to work on a large scale. My work is in private collections throughout the United States and Europe.

COMMISSIONS: Benson Sculpture Garden, 2008, Loveland, CO

PUBLICATIONS: *Southwest Art,* August 2007; *Southwest Art,* July 2002; *Utah Painting and Sculpture,* 1999; *Artists of Utah,* 1997

GUILD SOURCEBOOKS: *Residential Art 4, 5, 6*

PRICING: From $600–$60,000

Chin Yuen
Paintings & Prints, pages 14, 232

My acrylic paintings are an exploration and expression of beauty through abstraction. My approach is bold, intuitive, and playful, embracing my love for color and the physicality of painting. I enjoy juxtaposing different textures and color to create dynamic compositions that offer a sense of luxury and creativity.

COLLECTIONS: Dansko Shoes Inc., West Grove, PA, USA; Cumberbirch Insurance Agency Ltd., Victoria, BC, Canada; Hotel Grand Pacific Athletic Club, Victoria, BC, Canada; ISW Wassermesstechnik, Petersdorf, Germany; People Logic Ltd., Sydney, Australia; Taka Dance Fashion and Music Production Company, Ltd., Osaka, Japan

AWARDS: 2005 Herbert Siebner Practicing Artist Award (Canada), 2004 International Expo XXIII Award (USA)

PUBLICATIONS: Book cover for *Understanding Human Communication,* 10th edition, 2008

GUIILD SOURCEBOOKS: *Residential Art 4, 5, 6*

491

Location Index

Location Index

494

Location Index

495

Location Index

496

Index of Artists
& Companies

Artists & Companies

498

Artists & Companies

499

Artists & Companies

500

Artists & Companies

501